Religions for Human Dignity
and World Peace

Religions for Human Dignity and World Peace

Unabridged Proceedings of the Fourth World Conference
on Religion and Peace (WCRP IV)
Nairobi, Kenya, 23-31 August, 1984

Edited by
DR. JOHN. B. TAYLOR
and **MR. GÜNTHER GEBHARDT**

in honour of
DR. DANA McLEAN GREELEY

World Conference on Religion and Peace, Geneva, 1986

MIS
3

ISBN: 2-88235-000-7

132999

TABLE OF CONTENTS

I. REPORTS OF WORKING GROUPS

J. REPORTS

Preface

The Nairobi Declaration of WCRP IV*

In Nairobi in 1984, we of the World Conference on Religion and Peace have met in our Fourth World Assembly. We have come, nearly 600 of us, from 60 countries and from most of the world's religious traditions—Buddhist, Christian, Confucian, Hindu, Jain, Jewish, Muslim, Shinto, Sikh, Zoroastrian, the traditional cultures of Africa and North America, and others. From our diversity of cultures and traditions, we have come to address a theme of urgent common concern: Religions for Human Dignity and World Peace. We address these goals of human dignity and world peace together, for they are inextricably linked and must be pursued together.

Our previous Assemblies in Kyoto in 1970, Louvain in 1974, and Princeton in 1979 have been milestones in the growth and work of WCRP as we strive for peace, united by a spirit of co-operation. In Nairobi, in 1984, we find ourselves at a major turning point.

In the five years since we last met, the world has seen little progress in either the cherishing of human dignity or the movement toward world peace. While the nuclear arms race has continued to escalate in its staggering expenditures, in its rhetoric, and its incalculable danger, the massive human needs of poverty, hunger, unemployment, and lack of education have been grossly neglected. Militarization of societies, trade in arms, recourse to violence, religious and ideological intolerance, and assaults on human rights continue. The structures of economic and political oppression which perpetuate the privilege of a few at the expense of the masses are still firmly in place.

We are encouraged, however, by the widening awareness and public consciousness of the dangers and costs of our present world situation, and by the world-wide growth of grass-roots movements expressing the

---

* Adopted by general agreement and without dissent at the closing session.

i

determination of people everywhere for change. It is time for new strategies and priorities for peacemaking, and for renewed commitment to our work.

We have met in Nairobi as men and women rooted in our religious traditions, and linked to one another in vision and action. We acknowledge the painful fact that religion too often has been misused in areas of strife and conflict to intensify division and polarization. Religious people have too often failed to take the lead in speaking to the most important ethical and moral issues of our day and, more importantly, in taking steps toward change. In meeting together, we have not turned from self-criticism or from very difficult discussions of sensitive issues. And yet our affirmation is one of hope.

The Nairobi Assembly has changed us. The new participation of over one hundred youth delegates has given us the vitality and vision of a new generation, eager to join hands in concrete interreligious projects for peace. The strong and energetic contribution of over 150 women has made clear the necessity of women's equal partnership, not only in family life, but in the leadership of religious communities and social and political institutions. Over half of us here are participants from Asia, Africa, and Latin America, who have called WCRP to a deeper understanding of our global interrelatedness in working for peace.

Through our struggle, we have been able to build trust. We have shared in worship and meditation. We have discovered once again that our differences of culture and religion, far from being a threat to one another, are a treasure. Our multiplicity is a source of strength. We bear the testimony of experience that world community is possible. From our diversity of traditions, we are united in faith and hope, and in our common pursuit of human dignity and world peace.

I. The Context of Africa

Africa has not only been the place of this Assembly; Africa and the concerns of its peoples have shaped the very context and perspective of our discussions. The African traditional cultures have a strong spirit of community and family, and a vibrant sense of the wholeness of life. Many religious traditions now live together in the continent of Africa—the traditional religions, along with Christianity, Islam, Hinduism, Jainism, Sikhism and Judaism. The many religious communities of Nairobi have welcomed us and given us a sense of the riches and challenges of living together in the pluralistic society of Kenya.

The peoples of Africa have also experienced sharply the very issues we have addressed in our Assembly and have helped us all to see these issues more clearly. The affront to human dignity of the apartheid regime in South Africa calls us to repudiate separation and division and to seek the community of all races. The cry of human needs in drought and famine, the growing militarism of African governments, the increasing arms trade in Africa, the instances of political intolerance, the penetration of East-West rivalry into African political affairs—all call us to a wide understanding of the dynamics of global insecurity and the effect of global, political and economic structures on the emerging African States. The new WCRP/Africa is beginning to articulate the common values religious people bring to the creation of a just society. It stresses the need for active engagement in struggles for change and is committed to the realization of a new Africa.

II. Reconciliation in Regional Conflict

We are convinced that a major new priority of WCRP must be to address ourselves to areas of chronic regional tension and conflict—in Southern Africa, the Middle East, South and Southeast Asia, Central America and Europe. Since World War II, over 150 wars, most of them in the Third World, have claimed at least ten million lives. Regional conflicts become swiftly polarized by East and West, and raise the level of instability and insecurity in the entire world.

The roots of these conflicts vary and are complex. But wherever such conflict takes on the language and symbolism of our religious traditions, pitting one against the other, it must be the business of WCRP to be involved, both regionally and with WCRP/International support.

We commit ourselves, as religious men and women, to undertaking the work of reconciliation and peacemaking. We must deal with the issues of religious discord where they arise. We must deal with the economic and political struggles which take on religious rhetoric for narrow or chauvinistic purposes. We must take action, as a multi-religious body committed to peace, in the very areas where religion and peace seem to be in opposition.

III. Disarmament

Disarmament has long been a priority for the work of WCRP, and the urgent necessity of working for disarmament today is undiminished. With one voice, from our various traditions of faith, we insist that nuclear weapons and all weapons of mass and indiscriminate destruction are immoral and criminal, and that the stockpiling of such weapons, with intent or threat to use them erodes the very foundation of moral civilization.

We join the scientists, physicians, educators, and statesmen who have taken an active role in opposing the arms race. We pledge our determined commitment to disarmament as we continue to work as a non-government organization at the United Nations, and as we work to influence our religious communities and our nations.

Specifically, we call for an immediate freeze on all further nuclear weapons research, production, and deployment; the strengthening of the Nuclear Non-Proliferation Treaty; a Comprehensive Test-Ban Treaty; and a No First Use commitment on the part of nuclear nations as essential initial steps toward the dismantling of all nuclear arsenals.

Conventional weapons are also instruments of death and oppression. Halting the spread of militarization and the commercial exploitation of developing countries by trade in arms leading to military and political dependency is a crucial part of our commitment to disarmament.

It is a sign of hope for the future that the youth of this Assembly have called for the establishment of ministries and departments of peace to work for the global security that ministries and departments of defence have been unable to realize.

IV. Development

Delegates from Asia, Africa, and Latin America have given us all a new perspective on the arms race, as seen through the eyes of the poor. For the poor, survival is not primarily a question of the future in a nuclear world, but an urgent question of the present in a world beset with hunger, drought, and disease. Our common commitment to peace is based upon the clear interrelatedness between disarmament and development.

Disarmament means liberation, not only from arsenals of weapons ready for use, but from the perpetual fear and insecurity which have accompanied our obsession with the instruments of death. Development means liberation from hunger and poverty; it means a just sharing of the natural and economic resources of the world, and the investment of our energies in life, and in the future.

As men and women of religion, we cannot tolerate the priorities of a world in which there are at least three tons of explosives, but not enough food, for every man, woman and child on earth. We pledge ourselves, through our religious communities and our governments, and through continued WCRP cooperation with the UN, radically to reverse these priorities.

We have a vision of a world in which the economic and political structures which perpetuate injustice and poverty are completely changed, and in which the armaments necessary to maintain these structures of injustice and oppression may be turned to ploughshares for the work of peace.

V. Human Rights

Along with disarmament and development, human rights are an essential part of the total and holistic peace we seek. We mean not only civil and political rights, but the right to live with all the basic economic, social, and cultural rights of life of fullness and freedom, including religious freedom. We reaffirm our commitment to the UN Universal Declaration on Human Rights, and we insist that these rights are the very basis and foundation of a just and humane society and can never be postponed or suspended in the name of national security.

Our support for human rights must be consistent. Wherever human rights are trampled upon, we must speak out and act. We must resist and unmask the selective and tactical use of human rights issues by nations, especially the USA and the USSR, which raise their voices in one instance and ignore violations in another, as suits their political ends.

Our South African delegates—Hindu, Muslim, and Christian—have all made us sharply aware of the suffering and incalculable violence done to individuals, families, and whole peoples by the racist ideology and "theology" of apartheid. We commit ourselves to work toward changing the international political and economic structures which support the South African regime.

In our concern for human rights, we must also work regionally and internationally on many other affronts to human dignity. Despite efforts being made by political leaders and religious people, there is deep-seated prejudice resulting in many forms of discrimination against scheduled castes and economically oppressed and socially stigmatized classes in South Asia, against the Burakumin of Japan, and against the indigenous peoples of the Americas, Australia, the Philippines, and elsewhere. The world has many millions of refugees, with no right to the roots of home, four million of them in Africa alone. And there are countless human beings stripped of their human rights behind closed doors. They have disappeared; they have been imprisoned without trial; they have been victims of torture. Wherever, and in whatever way, human rights violations occur, it is our concern, internationally and interreligiously.

We support with conviction and hope the 1981 UN Declaration on the Elimination of All Forms of Intolerance and of Discrimination Based on Religion or Belief, and we pledge to support its implementation.

VI. Peace Education

Education for peace is more urgent than ever before. As religious men and women, we pledge ourselves to stressing and raising to public consciousness the foundations of peacemaking within our own religious traditions, through education in temples, churches, mosques, synagogues, and homes. This will require our commitment to planning, training, and funding for peace education programmes. As religious people of action, we must deliberately link our personal lives and daily choices to our wider work as peace-makers.

In our religious institutions, and in schools, colleges and universities, we will encourage new initiatives for peace education. Our public and community life must include knowledge and discussion of the realities of the arms race, the conflicts that lead to war, the means and strategies for non-violent resolution of conflict, and the work of the UN and UNESCO.

Essential to peace education is learning about and coming to understand those of different religion, ideologies, and cultures with whom we share our communities, our nations, and our world. In many cases, the opposite of conflict and violence is knowledge, and so educational efforts must be made that fear may begin to give way to trust. We must strengthen and deepen mutual understanding by sustained dialogue, and by undertaking common work together. We need to understand one another. We need one another in order to see and understand ourselves more clearly. And we need one another in order to undertake together work that will require the resources and energies of people throughout the world.

The spiritual resources of our religious traditions give us strength to dedicate ourselves to the task ahead. We are compelled to turn the faith and hope that sustain us into dynamic action for human dignity and world peace.

Introduction

By Dr. John B. Taylor*

1. Foreword

The Fourth Assembly of the World Conference on Religion and Peace/International brought together some 600 people from all over the world and from all the main religions of the world. Meeting in Africa, participants addressed the theme, "Religions for Human Dignity and World Peace," in a context where there were many examples of conflict and injustice in recent and present history. The agenda tackled not only the issues of disarmament and conflict resolution, but also the major factors which create or complicate conflict, such as political or economic injustice, racism and religious intolerance.

These unabridged proceedings contain not only the reports of the conference, both in its plenary sessions and in its smaller meetings of commissions and working groups, but an important place is also given to the material used for worship and meditation. Since the World Conference on Religion and Peace is essentially an inter-religious organization dedicated to promoting peace and justice in a self-critical and constructive spirit, it was important that much time should be given to sharing the spiritual resources in our respective traditions. Generally speaking worship was conducted in a particular religious tradition by the adherents of that tradition and other persons were welcome if they wished to be reverent observers. At the last session, however, each religious tradition was responsible in turn for a particular part of the closing event of dedication.

As well as these unabridged proceedings, other materials are available which catch something of the spirit of WCRP IV. The preparatory handbook which contains material drawn from many of the major religious traditions of the world and also from various peace and human rights organizations reminds one of the many contributors to the Assem-

---

* Dr. John B. Taylor is Secretary-General of WCRP/International.

bly, some of whom could not be present themselves. An illustrated pamphlet is also available. Many of the local branches of WCRP have circulated translations of parts of the recommendations in other languages, such as French, German, Indonesian, Italian, Japanese, etc.

2. Acknowledgements

Particular thanks must be expressed to various people who worked with me in preparing the Fourth World Assembly. My predecessor, Dr. Homer A. Jack, and his colleague, Dr. Norbert Klaes, arranged the preparatory meeting for WCRP IV in September 1983 at which time I was appointed Secretary-General to the assembly. The members of the Preparatory Committee came from all over the world and brought many creative suggestions for the assembly. It was the Nairobi Planning Committee which bore much of the brunt of preparations, and particular thanks must be expressed to their Chairman, Bishop J. Henry Okullu, their Secretary-General, Mr. Wilfred Maciel, and their Treasurer, Mr. Tarlok S. Nandhra, who worked untiringly with many others. At the assembly itself, I was particularly assisted by Sister Marjorie Keenan and Dr. Norbert Klaes, but the whole spirit of the assembly was such that a tremendous number of volunteers made possible the implementation of many ambitious plans.

It is also important to record the generous giving from WCRP constituencies in many parts of the world, and also from foundations and organizations, including UNESCO, whereby additional funds were raised to enable a substantial participation by young people and women whose presence and contribution greatly enhanced the assembly and gave great promise for the future of the organization.

A last word of thanks must be given to those who helped in the preparation of these unabridged proceedings: the newly-appointed research associate for WCRP/Europe and assistant secretary-general of WCRP/International, Mr. Günther Gebhardt, has worked closely with Miss Renate Belck, Mlle Brigitte Dupraz and Mrs. Jean Spechter in preparing the manuscript. Their work on this project is typical of the dedicated work which they gave and are giving throughout the whole period of preparing and implementing WCRP IV.

3. Looking Back on the Assembly

When the preparatory meeting of people of many different faiths and continents met in September 1983, they drew up an agenda under the theme, Religions for Human Dignity and World Peace. It was an ambitious agenda; it led the assembly into the areas of arms build-up, which may be seen as the symptom of the many conflicts which divide the world East from West and North from South. At the same time it led participants to tackle the causes of such tensions in the unjust economic developments and widening income gaps of today's world; it also led the assembly to self-critical awareness in that religion is too often a part of the problem, especially where it is misused to justify conflict and fails thereby to bring reconciliation between peoples.

The Preparatory Committee had laid down various criteria for participation in the assembly. Not only should many subjects be raised, but they should be raised from many different angles. The speakers, group leaders, and all those who discussed these matters came from a very wide range of countries and religions. Meeting in Africa, there were more participants from that continent than in any previous world assembly of WCRP. Unfortunately, certain countries were not represented because the Kenyan authorities would not issue visas to their citizens; this was true, notably in the case of the Soviet Union and East Germany. Nevertheless, other Eastern European countries took part, together with delegates and participants from some 60 countries, as far apart as China and Chile, Senegal and Australia, or South Korea and South Africa. One important feature of the participation was that there were as many as 150 young people, including many volunteers from Kenya itself. There was a similar number of women, many of whom were full delegates, thereby ensuring that most national delegations included both men and women. The range of participating organizations was also impressive, and it was particularly encouraging that many authoritative religious bodies chose to send fraternal delegates or observers. This marked the way in which WCRP/International is moving beyond a level of participation among enthusiastic individuals to a level of participation by people who are responsible representatives of their communities.

As one looks back on the assembly, one recalls both the satisfactions of the broadly based participation and the disappointments of some who were prevented from coming; these last included some who were denied permission to travel by their own countries, as was the case with the grand-daughter of Mahatma Gandhi who was not allowed to leave South Africa to attend the assembly. The fact that we were meeting in the African continent brought to the fore many of the perceptions of our African hosts as their political, social and cultural achievements and tribulations were brought into the discussion. There was also the opportunity to move beyond the conference centre and to experience, through the hospitality of our Kenyan friends, the many evidences of vital nation-building in Kenya, including the good co-operation between the religious communities which was particularly exemplified in the preparation of the assembly; however, we were not allowed to forget the unsolved problems ranging from the agricultural crisis that accompanies the continued failure of rainfall in many parts of Kenya to the economic and social difficulties visible in the shanty-towns around Nairobi.

A final reflection, looking back on the assembly, must be to record a sense of gratitude that so many difficult subjects could be raised in a spirit of understanding. A striking example would be the way in which the difficult issues of the Middle East were introduced by three women, a Palestinian Christian, an Israeli Jew, and a Lebanese Muslim. Their honest and realistic ability to address painful matters together was an inspiration to others, and led to constructive suggestions from the conference. There were other issues of no less difficulty where it was not possible to formulate final reports which satisfied all the interested parties. It should be noted that the report of Commission II which dealt with human rights left more questions unsolved than answered. This was not in itself a bad thing, so long as it indicated a willingness by all the participants to continue to explore these matters. Some people regretted an element of defensiveness by some national delegations, when a matter of concern was expressed, concerning violations of human rights in their nation. It is a sign that international and inter-religious discussion is still in a relatively early phase; it is to be hoped that no one will be deterred by such setbacks, but rather determined to tackle matters with greater sensitivity and realism in the future. It is a particular challenge for an organization like WCRP/International to refer such matters to national chapters so that issues can be better prepared in local settings before they are brought back to an international forum.

4. *Looking Forward from the Assembly*

Not only did the assembly leave the international staff and the national chapters with a range of important unfinished agenda, whether in the area of disarmament, human rights or inter-religious cooperation and understanding, but it also left many challenges in terms of the very structure and priorities of WCRP. We were made to see very clearly how timely has been the emergence of an organization which links people from the whole range of religious traditions around the world. Nevertheless we saw that some religious traditions are better represented than others, and some are not yet represented at an official or international level. If WCRP/International is to have credibility as an inter-religious organization dedicated to building peace and justice, it must prove both that it is properly inter-religious and also that it has full commitment to those issues of peace and justice. It will be necessary to cooperate more closely with religious organizations, with inter-religious organizations, with peace movements and with political bodies. WCRP has no ambition to go it alone in pursuit of contributions towards solving these vast problems or rising to these great opportunities. The cooperation which we experienced within the assembly must be the style for all our work in the future as it has been in the past.

In the concerns for disarmament, it is clear that we shall continue to see nuclear disarmament as an urgent moral and political concern. Especially since the Strategic Defense Initiative proposed by the United States Government may involve a level of expenditure moving into trillions of dollars, it is clear that the price will be paid all around the world in terms of alternative and reduced priorities for other issues, such as development, education or health care. In the interests of saving lives in some future world conflict, politicians seem ready to sacrifice lives in our present generation where millions die of hunger or disease. The distorted priorities of the super-powers are paralleled by the distorted priorities of many smaller nation states. Moral questions are raised not only by nuclear armament, but also by conventional armament and the loss of lives in countless conventional wars that rage today. In particular WCRP must discuss disarmament issues in the context of religions being used as a justification for defence policies or aggressive policies; in too many instances, politicians claim to be defending religious or cultural values as a way to justify their pursuit of national or personal power. WCRP must have a particular sense of urgency in addressing those local conflicts which separate members of different religions, and where the people who are drawn into the conflict too often perceive their loyalties in terms of defending the rights of one religious community against another.

In looking forward from the assembly to the unfinished agenda of a world thirsty for peace and justice, WCRP must face some of its limitations. While the desired co-operation with many organizations may go some way to mitigating those limitations, there is a great need for WCRP to improve its own potential as a partner in the enterprise for promoting peace, development and understanding among all peoples. It is to be hoped that the activities of local, national and regional chapters will be developed and the international programmes will be further strengthened, not least by bringing into being an international and inter-religious staff team. Already in the months after Nairobi it is reassuring to find that these are not simply dreams, but that various religious organizations have been ready to allow their staff to work for given periods with WCRP/International. The same pattern may be repeated at regional or national levels. Since WCRP has very limited financial possibilities, it must often depend on human power and facilities being volunteered or donated; this can add to the strength of the organization as it learns to elicit many such commitments from many religious communities.

One particular development which arose from the Nairobi Assembly was the commitment to find some ways to work together in the interests of peace and justice. Just as previous assemblies had been followed by projects, such as the response to Vietnamese Boat People or Cambodian refugees, so the Nairobi Assembly saw the pledging of some $400,000 for the victims of drought and refugees in Africa. This amount is very small compared with the amounts which are being given by many other religious organizations, especially as publicity for the problems of Ethiopia and Sudan has greatly increased in the months since the Nairobi Assembly. In some ways that publicity has overtaken the publicity given by WCRP, but the basic principles proposed from WCRP that religious communities should respond co-operatively and should avoid any sense of competition or self-aggrandizement in their aid operations remain truer than ever. It is also a matter of principle that WCRP should not be seen to be empire-building in terms of trying to centralize or organize activity in its own name. Accordingly, the generous gifts of individual members of WCRP and of the organizations which they represent are being channelled through existing projects where inter-religious spirit and practice are evident.

A further evidence that the principles of the assembly are being put into practice has been the way in which a number of national chapters, notably in North and South India, England, Thailand, Australia, and Kenya, have launched inter-religious youth camps and activities during 1985, the International Year of Youth. Not only do these youth camps demonstrate that inter-religious cooperation must be through working together, as well as through talking together, but they also illustrate the way in which WCRP must extend its constituency beyond religious leaders to religious laity and in particular to young people. Deeply as one continues to appreciate the vision and dedication of religious leaders in all our traditions, one also covets the contribution and vision of young people. The youth camps may not lend themselves to impressive publicity, such as commemorative stamps or television programmes, but they may make a lasting and important impact on people's imagination and inspire continuing inter-religious co-operation in areas of tension and even conflict. The readiness of young people of different religious traditions to work together can be a sign of hope, especially in places where it has been assumed that religion divides community from community.

A final area where WCRP/International must work in following-up the challenges of the Fourth Assembly is the whole network of international organizations, especially those connected with the United Nations. While the New York Office of WCRP/International will continue to give priority to disarmament concerns, which are the focus of so many United Nations agendas, at Headquarters in New York, the Geneva office must try to respond to the agenda of the special agencies, some of which are based in Geneva, as in the case of work with refugees, concerns for human rights and many development issues; there will be the further challenge to relate to UNESCO in Paris in its concerns for education for peace and for human rights. The fact that WCRP is a multi-religious and inter-religious organization gives it a particular responsibility in the context of the fact that most religious non-governmental organizations affiliated with the United Nations represent single, particular religious traditions. Yet many of the issues which have to be faced are themselves inter-religious issues. Increasing co-operation will also be necessary with other inter-religious organizations; these may still be relatively few in number and, like WCRP itself, relatively weak in present organizational strength. However, the preparations already being undertaken for the centenary of the 1893 Parliament of World Religions are providing a further incentive for increasing co-operation between inter-religious organizations. Not only in the world of the United Nations activities, but in many other spheres, people are beginning to look for a form of guidance and even moral leadership which could come from religious people, speaking and working together, rather than separately.

5. *An Invitation*

As well as inviting the reader to venture beyond this introduction into the much more interesting materials which follow, I must suggest that each reader will want to select certain matters for further exploration. The purpose of publishing these proceedings is not simply to provide a record of an international assembly which was deeply appreciated by most of the participants, but it is to stimulate further such discussions at many other levels. Not only were the presentations at Nairobi and the recommendations which issued from them equally provisional, but in some instances they may even provoke disagreement or dissatisfaction. The reader will also be conscious that some issues were not tackled or were not tackled from particular perspectives; this should encourage new agendas and call for new constituencies for our work.

It is hoped that a small guidebook will be published shortly to encourage the establishment of local WCRP chapters and to share experiences among chapters that already exist. However, WCRP has not come into being with a very strictly conceived or regulated blue-print for how inter-religious discussion should promote the concerns of peace and justice. This is in many ways an experimental enterprise and we invite as many new partners as are willing to join us. The only qualification or criterion for joining in this movement is a willingness to respect the differences which divide us and a readiness to overcome those differences as common solutions are found. This is a movement which must thrive not only on honest discussion and vigorous cooperative venture, but also on a dedication to pray for each other and even with each other in the enterprise. It is no accident that the materials for the 1985 Week of Prayer for World Peace are drawn from the experiences of the Nairobi Assembly. That invitation to prayer for the whole range of concerns which arose at the Fourth World Assembly of WCRP/International may stand as a fitting conclusion to this introduction.

A.

Opening Session Addresses

1

How Religions for Human Dignity and World Peace," The Theme of the Fourth Assembly of WCRP, Relates to Kenya and to the Nyayo Philosophy

By the Hon. P.C.J.O. Nyakiamo*

I wish, first of all, on behalf of the Government and people of Kenya, to welcome you to Nairobi. Kenya is greatly honoured by your presence here and for choosing Nairobi as the venue for this conference.

The theme of this Assembly, "Religion for Human Dignity and World Peace," is closely related to the basic philosophy of the people of Kenya, the Nyayo philosophy of peace, love and unity. It is thus fitting that the words peace, love and unity should be depicted on the commemorative stamps which the Kenya Posts and Telecommunications Corporation has taken the initiative to issue for this Fourth World Assembly meeting.

The Nyayo philosophy is not simply a political slogan. It is a set of fundamental spiritual values that call upon the rich resources of religion and culture to sustain such ideas. Under the distinguished leadership of His Excellency President Daniel Arap Moi, who is himself a practising Christian, all religious people of this country are encouraged to develop their moral and spiritual potential in order to serve the needs of building up the nation not only materially, but also in moral qualities.

The three themes of the WCRP Assembly are all of great importance to Kenya and relevant to our needs. Just as we hope to give much

* The Hon. P.C.J.O. Nyakiamo is Minister of State in the Office of the President of the Republic of Kenya.

1

to this conference, through participation, so we hope to gain something from the insights of the six hundred participants who have come to us from some sixty countries across the world and from all the world's religions. The first theme of the conference which is "People of Faith Working Together for Peace" reflects the experience and intention of our own country of Kenya where no distinction is made between people of many religions and where all are given respect and equal opportunities to contribute the riches of their own religions and cultures. We are only too aware how religion has often been misused as a cause for division and conflict in the world. Religion can be a force for good but it can also be misused by fanaticism as cause for separation and conflict.

One of the most fundamental areas where religious people must stand on their guard against such misuse of religion is in the area of education. In a country like Kenya where nearly half of the population is aged under sixteen years, education is of fundamental importance and occupies the main claim on our national expenditure. But we must not only educate young people in facts and figures, we must also educate them in attitudes, not least in attitudes of understanding towards the various neighbours within their own country and across the world. People of each religion and culture need to understand and respect people of differing cultures if the world is to avoid divisions and conflicts.

Kenya has a good record for people of different religions and cultures studying together and growing up together and this is one of the fundamental bases for the national unity and cooperation which we enjoy and which we still pray for and always will pray for. But we must never take this for granted and we must work carefully to plan for inter-cultural and inter-religious understanding both at home and abroad. The experience and suggestions of this Assembly as well as of world organizations such as UNESCO are of deep importance in the whole area of education for peace.

The second major theme of your organization makes the fundamental connection between peace and justice. It is impossible to speak of peace unless there is justice at every level of society. This must not only include political and constitutional rights which are equally available for all citizens, but it must also include scrupulous care for the rights of minorities, including those millions of refugees who are scattered across the face of every continent today. Many of these refugees understand themselves as victims of religious or ideological persecution or discrimination and it is the responsibility of every community to try to redress the sufferings which they have received.

There is also the growing phenomenon of refugees from economic issues and causes. Those who are fleeing from drought stricken zones are moving from one country to another or from one part of a particular country to another and their experience is too often similar to that of political refugees. Their social rights should also be safeguarded.

We cannot build human justice when resources are withheld from the very poor for their most basic needs. It is not that the problems have not been identified. For example, ten years ago the United Nations' Year for Women urged the need of making water available to the women of developing countries who must still spend half their lives carrying water, sometimes infected water, from distant supplies in order to provide for their families or their livestock. Yet women and children struggle with these shortages and difficulties. Countless excellent decisions have also been taken through the United Nations environment programme concerning the need for planting forests without which nothing can be done to correct the trend for desertification in so many parts of Africa and elsewhere in the world, but once again resources from the rich countries have been lacking.

The second theme of the connection between peace and justice must also include the whole area of human rights. Since we shall be hearing speakers from South Africa in this meeting, I will not attempt to develop the well-known policy of the Kenya Government to refuse all dealings with the apartheid regime of South Africa.

The South African Government has called for "dialogue" with independent African countries. If South Africa wishes to have normal relations with independent Africa, she should:

1. respect the integrity, independence and security of her neighbours;
2. totally remove her troops from Namibia and recognize Namibia's right to independence without preconditions;
3. abolish apartheid.

May I summarize those points by saying: if only we could accept that we are all daughters and sons of One Creator it may be easier to act on those three.

It should be added that the sort of "dialogue" that is proposed by the South African Government at this juncture is a far cry from the real dialogue of mutual respect and co-operation between the world's religions which this conference will undertake. Kenya rejects the recent elections which purported to establish separate legislation chambers for the Asian and coloured communities of South Africa, in total disregard of the majority African population of that country. It is a cause for relief that "people of faith working together in peace" have refused complicity in such schemes, not least because all their religions teach them that apartheid is wrong.

The last theme of this conference is on peace and disarmament. Kenya stands for general and complete disarmament under effective international control. Yet we have observed with concern the distorted scale of priorities in many of our countries where vast percentages of national income are spent on military build-up. Kenya strongly believes that resources that are being used for military purposes can better be utilized towards social and economic development.

Kenya is also concerned about the dangers of militarism on a wide scale. Not only do we wish to preserve human lives from nuclear holocaust, but we also know that the very sea which harbours so much of our food supply, and the very air from which the rains falls to provide all our water resources, are in danger of irreversible pollution from indiscriminate nuclear testing or usage. However, Kenya believes that nuclear technology for peaceful purposes can be an added asset in the development process.

Kenya has voted with many other third world countries for comprehensive nuclear test-ban treaties, and Kenya cannot stand aloof from the enormous danger which threatens the whole of humanity with the apparently escalating danger of nuclear warfare. The work of the United Nations in disarmament must be supported at every level, from super-power negotiations to education for peace in all our communities. The United Nations has always been conceived as an organization of the peoples of the world as well as of the governments of the world. The Kenyan Government warmly supports the work of those non-governmental organizations which work within the United Nations' family, and if I may say so, your organization, Mr. President, for which we commend you.

On behalf of the Government and the people of Kenya I wish your conference success and declare your deliberations open. Thank you.

2

Religion is for Life

By Archbishop Angelo I. Fernandes*

The African Scene

Exactly a hundred years ago, the major European powers gathered together in the Berlin Conference to divide Africa into colonial extensions of their overseas empires. Today the map of Africa tells a different story. Except for Namibia, over the last thirty years all African territories have acquired political independence. However, the end of the exploitative colonial system did not automatically bring to the region economic and social liberation. What is worse is that the uphill task of development was rendered unduly difficult by two spells of acute drought within a single decade! Hunger currently stalks the entire continent. A food crisis exists practically in all of sub-Sahara Africa. While the harsh climate, mismanagement and internal conflicts may share part of the blame, one cannot ignore the devastating impact on African economies of the current global recession, the tenfold increase in the price of petroleum products and the "balance of payments" deadlock that has been created. A notably aggravating circumstance has been the extension of the East-West conflict throughout the continent, supplying arms to governments and dissident groups. Today's four million refugees of sick and starving children, of hungry and homeless people are a standing condemnation of the world economic and political systems. They constitute at the same time a mute appeal for massive emergency food assistance and for the infrastructures that could prevent such disaster situations recurring in the future. Hopefully, the one hundred million dollars drought appeal and the joint ecumenical study of the root causes of the drought and of food strategies will have a successful outcome.

---

* Archbishop Angelo I. Fernandes is Roman Catholic Archbishop of New Delhi, India, and has been President of the World Conference on Religion and Peace since 1970.

Either Armaments or Peoples' Development

Even though the amount in question by world standards is only a trifle, every bit of aid or assistance in favour of the poor has today become a question mark. The time has come for the world community to take a conscious decision either to continue to pursue the mad arms race and build ever larger and more deadly weapons or to shift its direction and move consciously and with deliberate speed towards the global socio-economic development of peoples. Both it cannot do. The coffers have run dry. There is an absolutely competitive relationship between the arms industry and the ability to invest in the life and future development of the peoples of the world. Peace has now become the name for development, and disarmament is the first step in the quest and search for peace, harmony, concord with justice.

Silent Genocide

The entire world today is in the throes of a common financial crisis which might well take us back to the earlier depressions of the thirties and forties. The unco-ordinated socio-economic and political policies of the nations are, in the long run, a disaster for all mankind. They pose a threat even to our human environment. The resources of the earth belong to all, but the rich countries, the rich North, continue to exclude the rest of mankind from an equitable share in the common heritage. The wealthy nations seem unwilling to accept anything that hinders them from getting richer—a sort of "economic chauvinism". Efforts to bring into being a new economic international order as a base, a first step, a starting point for a more human world economy continue to be thwarted by the nations which are the most affluent of all.

The cumulative resources of mankind, greater than ever before, instead of being used for a long-range global policy for the common good of mankind, are harnessed for narrow, parochial interests and, worst of all, for mutually-assured destruction and the possible annihilation of the planet. What greater folly than the prospect of a nuclear war, started perhaps by a machine and let loose by calculation or miscalculation, mistake or terrorism! The recent Action Programme—"Food and Disarmament International"—launched in Brussels with the backing of 80 Nobel Prize laureates, is right in assessing the current human behaviour of those concerned as the "silent genocide" of the poor and hungry of the world.

Idolatry and Blasphemy

The creative achievements of modern science and technology are a constant source of wonder and joy: the great strides in agriculture and industry, the advances in research and communications, the flawless journeys into outer space, the exploration of the wonders of the oceans and the riches of the seabed, the growth of computerisation and the use of solar energy and, for that matter, even the releasing of the power enshrined in the atom which, if properly used, could prove such a boon to mankind!

6

What is very disconcerting, however, is the mighty gap between the immense material advances and the slow pace of moral and spiritual unity among the peoples of the world. It is distressing beyond measure to find the people of our generation falling down in worship before the golden calf by their blind pursuit of wealth, power and pleasure. The more men and nations have been driven closer together, the more wars have they fought, the more hatred, violence, racial and other forms of discrimination and oppression have they perpetrated.

This suffering of the poor and oppressed, occasioned by the socio-economic and political forces at work in the world, is being gradually understood as being unjust. Its further significance, says an Irish philosopher, is not injustice but blasphemy, the defacing of the image of God in His people, the restriction of the Maker's liberty to be Himself in His own world. We cannot but be appalled at the quality of life of the marginalized masses both in urban slums and rural settings all over the world. This sub-human existence of the vast majority of mankind, brought about by unjust and oppressive structures, continues to stand out as a silent condemnation—a blot on the rest of mankind! This is nowhere more blatant than in the abhorrent, man-made situations of apartheid and untouchability and in the spiralling arms race and nuclear folly. It is impossible to belong to the oppressors of mankind and worship the one true God. To pretend to do so is indeed blasphemy.

Truly, there is hidden in today's mentality and behaviour a profound impoverishment of the human spirit. This is tragic indeed, especially at this moment when there is a colossal task ahead of us in the abolition of poverty, ignorance and injustice, in pre-empting nuclear war and outlawing the arms race, and in the challenge to build a new order in which human dignity becomes the point of reference, the development of the economy, and more just, fraternal and peaceful relations between people. We may not be able directly to prevent war, but we can all work to make people sensitive and concerned to all the values which go to make a "human life". Increasing this awareness more and more, we can force war to recede inch by inch.

The Living Dialogue of Religions
One might well ask at this stage: what has religion to do with such mundane matters? Hasn't religion itself been a divisive force and is it not still occasionally used for unworthy ends? Religious intolerance has far from disappeared. It continues to raise its ugly head ever so often, setting brothers and sisters of a country against each other, erecting barriers between nations and generating bitterness, resentment and bloodshed, partially at least, in the name of so-called religion.

Be that as it may, it is nevertheless admitted on all hands that the need to put the spirit into human affairs is greater than ever before; moral values on all fronts are in danger of being completely shipwrecked! The struggle today is not between religion and science but between two competing trends: one banking on science and technology

7

to bring about an earthly paradise; the other extolling basic human values and prayerful union with God as being much more important to the destiny of man! Rightly understood and renewed in its presentation for the children of a space age, religion, its spirit and genuine experience still provide the best and strongest motivation for fuller and more wholesome human lives, for a greater sense of morality in private and public life, for a more dedicated service to one's fellow-men, thereby strengthening the efforts of men towards a more just and brotherly world. Alexander Solzhenitsyn traces the major crimes of the century to the lack of the divine dimension of human consciousness. He adds: "Only when we reach with determination for the warm hand of God can the errors of the unfortunate twentieth century be set right".

Today's material progress, with its superficial unification of mankind, is clamouring for a matching solidarity that is personal, social, moral and spiritual. Commending "the holy" to contemporary humankind, therefore, becomes a fresh challenge and presents a splendid entry point for religion's prophetic role in our modern world. It imposes a common task on all religions today, beckoning them to gather together, if not for consensus, at least for conversation and joint endeavour. If the current crisis in civilization is to be healed, the dialogue of religions is imperative. The cultural unity of mankind can only be achieved by the spirit of charity and the fellowship of faiths.

The late Dr. Zakir Hussain from India warned us, however, that "for religions to play their historic rôle in the supreme challenge of the century, the move towards one world community, they will have to look beyond dogmas, rituals and practices which obstruct the flow of life from different religious circles towards a new sense of harmony and collaboration. If the spirit of the Sermon on the Mount, Buddha's philosophy of compassion, the Hindu concept of ahimsa and the passion of Islam for obedience to the will of God can combine, then we shall see generated the most potent influence for world peace".

That, in effect, is what the World Conference on Religion and Peace has been struggling to do from its inception. Writing about our First World Assembly, the then Secretary-General of the United Nations, Dr. Kurt Waldheim, stated: "The 'Kyoto Conference' fulfilled an old and important desire for religious leaders from all over the world to meet together to discuss the central issues facing mankind. The real significance of Kyoto was that the Conference was held at all, and that the topics were not specifically those of religion but were the dominant problems which we confront, and the application of religion to them."

The Action-Oriented Religious Dialogue of WCRP

Given the fact that the countries of the world are becoming more pluralistic, that there is ever greater interest in Eastern Religions, in gurus, in forms of religious experience, it is not surprising that the beginnings of dialogue are appearing in many places. This occurs at the level of sharing of faith and growth in mutual knowledge and appreciation, and the results are quite gratifying. The "contemplative" dimension seems to be getting priority in this activity.

The World Conference on Religion and Peace offers the possibility of another type of dialogue, in a sense, complementary to that described above. WCRP is a voluntary association which aims to promote world peace and is made up of people belonging to world religions. The main elements are all major religions in all sections of the world on all aspects of peace. WCRP is essentially action-oriented in its very concept. It is not concerned primarily with dialogue at the level of contemplation or religious experience or understanding, but with living dialogue, a dialogue in action, within which, often enough, the deepest understanding is born and the closest bond of union are forged. Religious dialogue not only means that two or more persons speak about their religious experience, but also that they speak as religiously committed persons with their ultimate commitments and religious outlook on subjects of common interest.

From Kyoto onwards, the search has been on to enlist "the forms of inner truthfulness of the spirit as having greater power than hate, enmity and self-interest", "a realization that might is not right" and "a profound hope that goodwill finally prevails". The main tasks are to share among the people of the world a deeper knowledge of the sanctions and traditions which each religion has for world peace and justice; to discover in the approaches and backgrounds to the different religions some common religious principles conducive to the peace of the human community and to promote a unity and universality of conscience through them; to apply them in a spirit of social responsibility to the obstacles to peace in the areas of human rights, development, environment, disarmament; to create public opinion in favour of using peaceful methods for solving problems and, fostering community, to seek to bring these methods to bear on local, national, regional and international levels.

The specific focus of WCRP is a living dialogue of religiously committed persons to the issue of peace through the application of spiritual motivation. Religion's integrating force may, not least, be enlisted through silent reflection/meditation/contemplation; so that spiritual resources and energies are associated with the efforts of social scientists, statesmen and peacemakers in their search to give a new direction to society.

The Fellowship of Service

WCRP has naturally been involved in issues of justice that arise on the international scene. It has tried to make the voice of religion heard where it is mostly ignored, in the fields of politics and at the meetings of nations. This has been done notably in the fields of human rights and disarmament at UN Headquarters in New York and Geneva, and elsewhere through other available channels. I would like to highlight one significant achievement. WCRP has been at least partially responsible for the UN Declaration for Religious Freedom. This is a major contri-

9

bution to the struggle for human rights, for religious freedom is the most fundamental of all human rights, concerning as it does the burning centre of liberty, the conscience of each person. It holds the key to the future. "Declaration for 1981" goes to the heart of freedom of thought and conscience; it includes every person on the planet, it concerns the source of human dignity, the core of what it is to be human; it glorifies the greatest power on earth, the conscience of each individual person, man, woman and child, and repudiates religious intolerance as one of the greatest tragedies of our times. If seen in proper perspective, publicised and acted upon, the Declaration and its implications could help to restore the true vision of man in society, of a person who has individual and collective rights; one who is equal in dignity to all others and has to fulfil his destiny in solidarity with them. It would be a significant contribution to the welfare of human society if this WCRP Assembly put its full weight behind getting this Declaration to be more widely known and followed.

The Fellowship of Silence

A religious movement like WCRP can ill afford to neglect or softpedal the dimension of prayer and conscious religious motivation. At times, these tend to get lost in the problems of organizational functioning. The source of peace and war is the interior life of each individual human spirit. The application is a corollary and embraces wholeness of life as an enterprise of justice and love. What seems to bring together and unite, in a particular way, believers of all religions is an acknowledgement of the need for prayer as an expression of man's spirituality directed towards the Absolute. Gandhi often spoke and wrote about prayer as the greatest binding force making for the solidarity and oneness of the human family.

Prayer and Action

There will be a conflict within the believer between his dependence on God and his responsibility as a free human being. The dialectic between calling upon the Lord in prayer and behaving as neighbour will always exist. For the comfortable of the rich world to salve their conscience by substituting prayer for action and calling "Lord, Lord" in ritual reassurance at church, temple or mosque, is a facile seduction; whereas for the oppressed of the third world the temptation is to reject God as the totem of the oppressors, to take the world into their own hands, to denounce prayer as futile and to concentrate only on action to change their condition. If the dialectic between prayer and action collapses, the emptiness and frustration of oppressor and oppressed will be further increased. What is needed is a spirituality of liberation for all the enslaved, the powerful and the powerless; freedom for rich and poor alike through a partnership between peoples which becomes a mutually enriching experience: liberation—co-operation (sarvodaya shramadhana). Such a stewardship in the use of the world's resources becomes in effect an act of worship.

In prayer, whether individual or collective, believers act on behalf of the human community and of creation in enabling them to respond and receive the Lord who is both source and destiny. The most remarkable feature of prayer, says the Irish philosopher I referred to above, is not what it does for man but what it does for God. It allows him to enter his own world most intimately by entering the minds and hearts of human beings. The prayer permits God to be Himself in the intimacy of human hearts. Letting the Lord be Himself in His own world is the critical achievement of all prayers. By conferring on God the freedom of the whole city of humanity, all believers at prayer fulfil their primary mission to God and to mankind.

But God's coming in prayer into hearts and minds must be extended to community relationships and structures if He is to enjoy full and proper freedom in His own world. In other words, prayer must be accompanied by appropriate liberating activity, the rallying of all the forces available—national, cultural, moral, spiritual—for the full human development and enrichment of all human beings wherever they may be. There could be no greater or more satisfying human adventure than this quest together for international social justice and cultural exchange in brotherhood and peace! Faith as prayer and faith as social commitment provide the human context for God's rule over man and the universe and the way to peace in freedom, justice and fellowship.

It is with this in mind and in this spirit that on the 10th June I launched the massive "Prayer Campaign" for "Forestalling Nuclear War". Prayer and action are intertwined. Hopefully, the Assembly will endorse the Appeal and pledge itself in solidarity to the recitation of the Prayer for Peace till 24th October and to working with a single-mindedness of purpose to halt, reduce and phase out nuclear weapons. In particular, the Assembly should demand and commission follow-up work for a United Nations Treaty outlawing all use of nuclear weapons as a crime against humanity.

A Call to Faith

Herein lies a challenge for each and all of us and for all religious faiths purporting to make some contribution to the restoration of ethical, moral and social responsibility vis-à-vis today's troubled world. The greatest need today is the need for faith in man and faith in God. The grave injustices in the world have a close connection with the weakness of faith. Where faith is feeble, injustice grows and institutionalizes much more rapidly. On the contrary, a passion for God will of necessity move us towards compassion and struggling together for justice for all God's children, especially the weak and lowly. That is the first step in the path to recovery and health for humankind.

In effect, this is a call to all religions not only to shun religious intolerance as one of the greatest tragedies of our times, but to engage seriously in a constant process of self-renewal. This must be reflected in the lives of all religious persons, and the signs of its presence will be striking integrity, godliness, commitment, fellowship and service. This is an urgent prerequisite, particularly if WCRP seeks to engage in reconciliation within countries, peace-keeping between nations, and to address itself to peace with justice at the world level.

A specific task calling for pointed attention would be, through public opinion, to create a unity of conscience that would blacklist, in the name of all religions, the kind of behaviour that has led to the near total breakdown of accepted standards of public and private morality in the world, and especially in respect of mute acceptance of, indifference to and, in fact, injustice to the poor and hungry. The nuclear menace must be highlighted for the devilry that it is. Even that will not suffice. Stating principles is not enough. To point out injustice is not enough. Prophetic cries are not enough. Words lack weight unless we all become responsible and act effectively. To pass on to others the blame for injustice is all too easy. Each of us has a share in it. The first thing we need is a personal change of heart. Only docility to the divine Spirit within us can really enable us to discern between good and evil and always courageously to embrace what is right and good as distinct from what is merely pleasurable and appealing to our animal nature. Authentic faith unfetters the heart and readies it for joint efforts to change undesirable structures that enslave men and women anywhere in the world. Our moral duty today is, at all costs, to prevent nuclear war from ever occurring and to protect and preserve those key values of justice, freedom and independence which are necessary for personal dignity and national integrity. It is only in and through the power of the Spirit that true human solidarity can become a reality. As John Kennedy reminded us: "We must recognize that human collaboration is not enough; that in times such as these we must reach beyond ourselves if we are to seek ultimate courage and infinite wisdom." This is the secret force at work in the world through which it can be done, the wonder can be wrought, the power of the Spirit, available to one and all who believe and call upon the name of the Lord in faith, humility and openness of heart.

The Yoking of Religion and Science

In the face of the deepening social and spiritual crisis of modern civilisation we need to blaze a new trail. Spirituality will have to be at the core of the answer but its energies will have to permeate the life-size social challenges that confront us. It will have to give meaning and purpose to secular science, whether of the capitalist or socialist brand. Without a moral and spiritual foundation, technology on its own can only lead the world to disaster. The hunger for spiritual meaning must somehow be satisfied. Science and religion must get together and work together. If we divide them, they will divide us. If we bring them together in a harmonious relationship with each other, there is hope for the future. Fortunately for us, we do not have to start from scratch. Thirty-six National Academies of Science from around the world, twenty-three of them through their Presidents, have recently signed a strong declaration on the prevention of nuclear war and will be willing to make common cause with us against the nuclear threat to humanity. The Parliamentarians for World Order brought together by Senator Douglas Roche of Canada, one of our alumni, is another set group that has mounted several actions. They were instrumental in sparking the recent call by the six political world leaders of four continents on mankind's survival in jeopardy. You know, my dear friends, that WCRP sent a multi-religious mission on this topic to Beijing, China, in 1982. Would it be too much to expect that WCRP IV would consider taking the initiative in bringing together suitable representatives from the three groups I mentioned: the Religious, the Scientists and the Parliamentarians, not only to speak with one voice but perhaps to go on a mission to the nuclear states in an effort to reverse present trends, in favour of peace with justice?

My dear friends, the entire enterprise must grow out of an ongoing conviction of a faith-inspired "community of friends" who recognize that some Power larger than themselves is integral to their endeavour to dialogue with each other and to address the larger issues on a nation's programme or on the world's agenda.

Conclusion
"The earth belongs to us all—let us cherish it in peace and true brotherhood based on the dignity and equality of man." More "universal brothers and sisters" are called for to give effect to this clarion call which sums up the hopes and aspirations of the people of our age.

In the heart of every person there is a peace movement, a search for harmony as the only real task of life; there is a will to live in brotherhood; there is a thirst we must mutually intensify for justice and peace, for living and growing together as brothers and sisters in the one family of man. And, as the African proverb puts it: "When spiders' webs unite, they can tie up a lion".

3

World Religions for Human Dignity and World Peace

By Bishop Desmond Tutu*

Preamble

As you know I, together with my fellow South Africans, come from one of the most beautiful lands in this continent. It is a country richly endowed by God with all kinds of resources, human and natural. The scenery is breath-taking and there are wonderful open expanses of land—there is nearly enough of everything to ensure that all the nearly 30 million people of our beloved country should live fulfilled and contented lives. But our beautiful land is one that is desperately short of justice and respect for basic human rights. You might recall that story about Zambia: A Zambian was boasting to a South African about the Zambian Cabinet, going on to declare proudly that "we in Zambia even have a Minister of the Navy." The South African laughed scornfully and said, "But you are a landlocked country. You don't have a navy. How can you have a Minister of the Navy?" Quite undaunted, the Zambian replied, "Ah well, you in South Africa have a Minister of Justice, don't you?"

That commodity, basic justice, ensures fundamental human rights such as security of tenure, freedom from arbitrary arrest and subjection to inhumane forms of punishment and torture; it ensures freedom of movement, freedom of belief and association. That commodity in our beautiful land is in desperately short supply. And we in this Assembly have in fact been robbed of the presence of several persons who should have been here, had it not been for the exercise of this arbitrary form of control: Mrs. Ela Ramgobin should have been here with us today, but the South African Government saw fit not to issue her with a passport;

---

*Bishop Desmond Tutu, Bishop of Johannesburg, was formerly General Secretary of the South African Council of Churches and was awarded the Nobel Peace Prize in 1984.

14

her husband is among the several people who have been detained since Monday in preparation for the so-called elections, and I would hope that this gathering may see fit to issue a statement relating to the current situation in our country.

I come from a country which asserts categorically that what gives value to a human being is a biological attribute, the colour of one's skin. Most even moderately intelligent people know that such an assertion is unbelievably nonsensical. I have often used the example of another physical characteristic, e.g., the size of one's nose, to demonstrate how utterly ridiculous this central tenet of apartheid is. What in the name of everything that is good does the size of my nose tell you about my worth as a person? Can you judge from it whether I am intelligent, humorous or warm-hearted, or any worth-while factor about me except perhaps whether I am handsome or otherwise? Just imagine arriving in South Africa to go to a toilet and discovering signs reading "large noses only," so that if you have a small nose, nature might take its course somewhat embarrassingly because you could not find a toilet reserved for small noses. Or if you were told that the university is reserved for large noses only, the first entrance qualification being not an academic one but a biological one. And if you are saddled with a small nose, having to apply to the "Minister of Small Nose Affairs" for permission to attend the university reserved for large noses only. I just have to describe such situations for you here to see how utterly preposterous such an arrangement of society is.

Christianity and Judaism claim that what invests human beings, all human beings, with value, with an intrinsic and infinite value, is not some biological irrelevance or other, but the fact that each human person is created in the image of God, their maker. Consequently, each person is a viceroy, a representative of their deity. That is what makes human beings so priceless. I know of no major world religion that teaches that human beings are of other than this infinite worth.

For a start, whilst they may not necessarily use the same category of the *imago dei* as Judaism and Christianity, many faiths refer to the fact that of all creatures in the universe, human beings (apart from supernatural beings such as spirits and angels) alone appear to have the capacity to engage in a dialogue with the Divine, whether conceived as a monad or a plurality of Gods. That surely must make an important statement about the partners in this human-Divine discourse. It is to assert that however subordinate the human partner, he/she has been exalted to the level where the Divine considers it important to be involved with him/her in a conversation. This divine condescension serves to exalt the human interlocutor. I do not normally in any significant way engage in conversation with my dog except in the most figurative kind of way and, even when I do, I do not really expect my dog to discourse with me in any profound manner.

In some of the non-Judeo-Christian major religions the value of humans is demonstrated further by the fact that the Divine will assume human form—a kind of incarnation as in the avatars of Hinduism. The reason for this divine descent into the world of creatures is normally for soteriological purposes. I would say that in, the phenomenon, we have incontrovertible evidence attesting to the supreme value of human persons.

The God does not normally, being all holy and transcendent, associate with what would be entirely alien to Divinity and impervious to it. Light does not assume darkness because there is no affinity between these two: they are totally at variance. Humanity and Divinity belong to distinct orders of being quite qualitatively different from each other. Yet in the major religions, humanity and Divinity are not seen as utterly alien from one another nor is human nature utterly recalcitrant and impervious to the Divine. The value of human beings and their history is considerably enhanced through the fact that Divinity has designed to be so intimately connected with both. This has happened as well in Christianity and to some extent in Judaism.

Another index of the value attaching to human beings is surely the divine soteriological interest in them demonstrated in all the major religions. The Gods are concerned in different ways in these religions in the ultimate destiny of human persons. We are destined in most of the religions for a post mortem existence in heaven where we will be vouchsafed the beatific vision, of being privileged to inhabit nirvana or paradise and to exist in a life of union or absorption and complete identification with the deity, however this deity may be conceived, either as personal or suprapersonal. This hoped-for eternal life is a high destiny and can mean inter alia only that human persons are of more than just passing interest to the Divine. The religious *summum bonum* is communion with the Divine. One could go on to point out that in all the major religions, human beings are conceived as having the capacity to receive a divine revelation.

This may be subsumed under the discussion of the human partner in the Divine-human encounter and dialogue referred to earlier. It is significant that so far as we can tell no other creature, except perhaps angels and other superior spirits, is so conceived as participating in the revelatory intercourse. In no known major religion are evil, suffering and the wanton destruction of the individual regarded as desired ends rather than what they are, aberrations that somehow must be overcome or circumvented.

For all these and other reasons that I need not rehearse here, we can assert unequivocally that all major religions have a high doctrine of man and woman. To quote a famous African speaking about the Divine-human relationship, "Thou hast made us for Thyself and our hearts are restless until they find their rest in Thee." Our final destiny, communion with the Divine, speaks eloquently of our high dignity as human persons.

Religious Imperatives
If the premises I have outlined above are true, and I do not know

16

that anyone can seriously gainsay them, then the adherents of all major religions are under obligation to promote the well-being of all human beings and to work assiduously to establish the dignity of the human person unimpaired. Any effort to undermine that dignity, be it undertaken by a repressive government or some extremist group, must be opposed strenuously as a matter of religious duty. St Irenaeus, a well-known Christian thinker, declared: "The glory of God is a living man; the life of man is the vision of God." To treat a man, woman or child as if they were less than a child of the Divine destined for a life of unimpeded unity with the Deity is to commit not just a crime against humanity. It is veritably to be guilty of blasphemy, for it is nothing short of dishonouring God Himself.

You all know just how frequently religious persons are accused of the heinous crime of mixing religion with politics, the moment they declare that a particular socio-political dispensation is unjust, oppressive and evil. It never ceases to amuse me that this is invariably the case. And yet were I to stand up here in Nairobi and say I do not think that apartheid is so bad after all, I can bet you my bottom dollar that my erstwhile critics would hardly accuse me of dabbling in politics.

I want to stress that all religions' adherents are constrained by the tenets of their faith to be concerned about the quality of life or the treatment meted out to the inhabitants of their land and other lands, for all religions are in principle universal in their ambit. It is not that they are motivated by an ideology, political or otherwise, that they are to be so concerned. No, it is that they are under a solemn obligation to subject each human institution, be it political, economic, or social, to the litmus test of whether it is one that makes for life-enhancement or for life-diminishment. Is it the sort of environment that is hostile to a fulfilled life or one that promotes life, helping human persons to become more fully human?

In the case of Christians, they need a humanity that is measured by nothing less than the humanity of Christ Himself who for the Christian is the exemplar *par excellence* of what a human being is intended to be—compassionate, gentle, humble, a spend-thrift for the sake of others, concerned for their well-being, and sensitive to what might undermine their sense of worth and security. Christians need to be aware of that worth in themselves as having been accepted and loved unconditionally by their God and creator. Their love for God, so they have been taught, carries as an inescapable corollary their love for their neighbour; otherwise their worship of God is condemned out of hand and rejected as an abomination and idolatry. Their love for God is to be expressed and authenticated by their love for and service to their neighbour. "He who says he loves God and hates his brother is a liar;" so the New Testament asserts categorically. "For how can you say you love God whom you have not seen when you hate your brother whom you have seen?"

And so in Islam almsgiving is one of the five pillars of that faith. It underscores the fact that somehow we are to be the human partners of the Divine in the eternal transcendent reality's enterprise to establish what in Judeo-Christian terms is referred to as the kingdom of God. The eternal enlists our support to incarnate the divine compassion and love, and to help bring into being the divine intention of fullness of life for all its creatures. And so we behold with awe and pride a Mother Theresa and her nuns together with Hindu and Muslim ladies serving so gently and lovingly the derelicts picked off the streets of Calcutta so that they may die with some dignity. They pour oil on the sick-making sores. This is something which speaks of the divine balm of love and compassion. Many have been inspired to behold the Satyagraha (the soul force) of a Mahatma Gandhi as with his passive resistance he has overcome the recalcitrance of the British Raj, and identified himself with those whom he called the Harijan—God's children, though most Hindus had stamped them as untouchable. We are constrained to work for more just societies in the lands where it has pleased the Divine to place us, to be concerned about poverty, oppression, injustice and exploitation wherever these may occur, striving with all our might and ingenuity to eradicate them, and to speak up on behalf of the divine reality we worship against all that makes us less than what God intends us to be.

To be so involved, to be so appalled by evil and injustice, to be compassionate to the powerless and the voiceless ones, to align ourselves with them against the powerful and the mighty ones, to wax indignant at man's inhumanity to his fellow, is not to be a political animal. It is to have taken seriously the demands of our faiths. It is to be serious about our worship and adoration of the eternal and transcendent one; for although He/It inhabits the very heaven of heavens, yet He deigns to look upon the insignificant thing exalted to be the friend of the Divine. Jesus Christ must have scandalized the prim and proper ones, the supercilious religious leaders of his day, when he told the parable of the Last Judgement. He was telling them what would be the criteria for admission to heaven and consignment to the other place. Amazingly, he did not speak of religious exercises as narrowly conceived, such as for instance praying and attending worship services. What would serve to separate the sheep from the goats (destined for perdition) was whether they had or had not performed thoroughly mundane and secular things—feeding the hungry, clothing the naked, visiting the sick and those who had been imprisoned. And more startlingly, he declared that in doing these things to the least of the brethren, they were doing it as to Himself: the Divine identifying so completely with its human creature. Staggering!—but that is where we get our marching orders from when we declare apartheid to be a heresy, to be wholly evil and immoral, as evil and immoral as Nazism and Communism.

It treats God's children as of little account, rubbing their dignity in the dust, destroying stable black communities for ideological reasons, stripping Blacks of their South African citizenship and turning them into aliens in the land of their birth, and fobbing them off with the citizenship of Bantustan homelands with a spurious independence recognized only by South Africa and her satellites. To accomplish the grand designs of apartheid, human beings, over three million, have been uprooted and dumped as if they were rubbish in poverty-stricken Bantustan homeland resettlement camps. Blacks have to carry passes, instruments of a rigid influx control system, to lock them out of the urban areas where they have some chance of making a living, and imprisoning them in depressed rural areas where black children starve. This is not because there is no food, since South Africa is a net exporter of food (when we have had no droughts); they starve because of deliberate government policy. Black family life is being undermined, undermined not accidentally but by deliberate government policy. Blacks receive an inferior education designed for perpetual serfdom. It was to protest against this travesty of an education that black students demonstrated in 1976 and are doing so again.

Blacks have no meaningful participation in political decision-making in the land of their birth. They have been locked out of the present constitutional dispensation in which Coloureds and Indians are being co-opted to entrench racism and help to perpetuate white minority rule as the junior partners of apartheid. The adherents of all faiths in South Africa, as in other parts of the world, can never remain silent in the face of injustice and oppression and suffering and poverty. If they remain silent, then they are disobedient to the imperatives of their faith and compromise the ideals that have helped to form them.

My call is to all men and women of goodwill, wherever they may be, to stand up to be counted. Many countries in the so-called Third World are ruled by repressive military dictatorships. It is galling for me as a black person to have to admit this to be so, but often there is far less personal freedom and justice in many parts of independent Africa than during the much-maligned colonial days. A small elite in these countries enjoys an unacceptably high standard of living whilst the bulk of the populace often suffers from grinding poverty. There is often corruption and vice in high places and the poor, the powerless, and the exploited find themselves in much the same plight as before their countries gained independence: the only difference perhaps is that whereas the exploiter and the oppressor in former days was an expatriate colonial power, today it is their own brothers and sisters. The only way that seems left to the people to change an unjust and oppressive dispensation is by the all-too-prevalent coup, the epidemic scourge of the Third World.

My sisters and brothers, evil is evil by whomsoever it is perpetrated. If people of faith are to uphold the integrity of their religious profession, then we must consistently condemn injustice, exploitation and oppression, arbitrary arrest and the execution of innocents who happen to be the ones who are pushed to the periphery of society outside the corridors of power. They have no one to champion their cause except the adherents of the different religions, who must stand up and speak out on behalf of the hungry, the homeless, the poor, the oppressed and down-trodden, and the voiceless ones. If they fail to do so, then their faiths

19

deserve to be consigned to the limbo of the utterly irrelevant and useless. To champion the cause of the weak may bring the wrath of the powerful on those who do, but we should not let that deter us. And what of peace? All major faiths teach that the transcendent reality wills that all should live in harmony and peace. Very few religions teach as an article of faith the desirability of war. War is a hostile environment for the enhancement of life. Consequently, all men and women of faith should be active promoters of peace and justice. There is war or the threat of war because there is injustice. There is poverty in many parts of the world because governments spend staggering amounts on weapons of destruction and death. We learn that every minute 30 children die for want of food and cheap vaccines. Yet every minute the world's military budget absorbs US$ 1.3 million of public funds. The cost of a new nuclear submarine equals the annual education budgets of 23 developing countries with 160 million school-age children.

It is a madness that countries can be counted great because of the highly developed technology of destruction and death and yet be short on compassion and caring for the weak. It is possible for the world to feed itself adequately if there is but the political will to do so. In 1983, the USA farmers were paid to take 100 million acres of cropland out of production. In the meantime, 450 million in the world are starving. The USSR spent US$ 1.3 trillion between 1960 and 1981 for military purposes, but ranks 25th among 142 countries in socio-economic performance. To be concerned for justice and human dignity as well as for peace are not optional extras which we may take up or abandon as the whim strikes us. It is integral to being a religious person; for the consummation to which most of our faiths look is a condition of unalloyed bliss, fellowship, unity and true joy.

Peace is not the absence of war; peace in Biblical terms means wholeness, fullness of life, it means righteousness and justice. It means life-enhancement and not life-diminishment. It means all that makes for a fully developed humanity of persons whose dignity is respected and who know that they count and that they are not to be exposed to want and poverty and disease and ignorance, who will have security of tenure, who will participate in the decision-making processes that matter, who will enjoy freedom of worship, of movement, of association, and who will be protected from arbitrary arrest and other arbitrary excesses of power. In short, they will be free human beings, enjoying what the Bible calls the glorious liberty of the children of God. That is the enterprise in which God wants to enlist our support. Is it not exhilarating?

4

Dr. Maria A. Lücker
Memorial Lecture

By Dr. Erika Wolf*

All those who took part in the previous world assemblies of WCRP will remember Maria Alberta Lücker. She was the spirit of all that is best in preparing and conducting these assemblies, and her profound faith and readiness to reach out to others, to create a feeling of community and to involve outsiders with patience and tolerance were an example to all.

Nine months ago she departed from us leaving behind her the work which had accompanied her until death, namely, the preparation of the assembly beginning today.

I thank you for the opportunity of honouring the memory of Maria Lücker whom so many of us miss so much on this occasion.

I would therefore like to begin by providing some biographical details. She was born in Bonn, then a small but important university town, in 1907. To us this seems an eternity ago, but at that time people in Europe believed that they were witnessing the beginning of a good century in a safe and peaceful world. Maria Lücker was still a child when the First World War brought the initial wave of destruction upon Europe and this world of harmony. Her youth, which coincided with rapid changes in society, was spent in a deep belief in God. She went on to study Romance languages and philosophy in Bonn and Paris, and she once said to me how impressed she had been by the philosopher Jacques Maritain who had found a balance between reason and faith and saw philosophy as the servant of theology. Even at such a young age, Maria Lücker succeeded in crossing the barriers which the tide of nationalism set for many of her contemporaries in many countries. She joined the

---

*Dr. Mrs. Erika Wolf is a former Member of Parliament (Federal Republic of Germany).

International Grail Movement, a Catholic women's organization, and took on executive functions. In this way she was able to spend the twelve darkest years of German history far away from home working for the aims of this organization and travelling to other continents.

Later, from 1955 to 1965, she headed the Foreign Relations Office of the Central Committee of German Catholics and was one of the latter's representatives at the Second Vatican Council where she helped formulate "Gaudium et Spes." This period also marked her honest encounter with Christians of the Protestant Church. She was one of the first to acknowledge that relations between people from different continents and different cultures must be cultivated systematically. To this end she helped found Catholic organizations such as the Association for Development (AGEH) which sends young Germans out into the world to help in economic development, and the Catholic Foreign Students Service (KAAD) which offers help to foreign students and trainees in the Federal Republic of Germany.

During these years of acquiring and imparting knowledge, Maria Lücker developed the qualities which we came to appreciate so much. Her devoutness, charity, frankness, intelligence, tolerance, patience and serenity find repeated mention in the letters written by her friends after her death. All those who visited her at home in Bonn (and many people came from all parts of the world) experienced her hospitality and readiness to help.

During her life Maria Lücker followed developments and changes in Europe and the world with interest and anxiety, and many were accompanied by her intercession. She was aware of the growing unrest in Western society, of the undesirable developments in individualism, and in materialism as the measure of success. The break-up of our most natural community, the family, and the insecurity of young people in their search for a meaning and a goal for their lives in an industrial society, gave her cause for concern.

Against this background it is not in the least surprising that after the First World Conference on Religion and Peace in Kyoto, Maria Lücker should resolve to establish a fellowship with members of other religions. It was her intention—on the firm foundation of her faith—to work with them for peace.

Peace meant so much to her. Peace as wholeness, peace not merely as the absence of armed conflicts; it derives from the recognition of the equality and dignity of all human beings. Peace must be rooted in the minds and hearts of individuals and it means liberation and development for all. Lasting peace is only possible among people who know and trust one another.

I first met Maria Lücker at the second World Assembly in Leuven. From then on I followed her work in Germany and Europe, and learned from her experiences.

Coming as I did from the world of politics, it was only natural that we should reflect together upon the tasks ahead and the many other attempts of our time to improve the situation of mankind and to establish peace.

We observed the world conferences of the United Nations and the work of UNESCO, paying attention also to the many international non-governmental organizations (NGOs), the importance of which has increased in recent years. The discussion within the UN on a new economic order in the world which was followed by an appeal by the Director General of UNESCO for a new world order, appeared to us to be a sign of hope. But it is clear that the national governments are not yet in a position to achieve their goal, namely to guarantee each individual a life in human dignity.

We all are familiar with the barriers and, I would say, misunderstandings created by diverging ideologies, for example the East-West conflict in Europe which ties up money needed for development in other continents; the various economic systems which lead to passivity and not to the betterment of the individual; discrimination on grounds of race or sex; and many more.

It is certainly characteristic that those taking part in international negotiations of this kind never consider binding and committing people through their faith, through religion. The members of UNESCO, for instance, even seem frightened to use the insights of faith and religion in their work.

I am convinced that these observations induced Maria Lücker to formulate the three tenets of WCRP which she never ceased to reiterate.

Firstly, the call for more spirituality. She saw a renewal of spirituality and religious forces as the only means to counteract the dangers created by excessive individualism and materialism. She had experienced the great power of meditation and never tired of recommending its use, which she exemplified through her own life, even, and especially, in the industrialized and highly technical world of today.

Her second appeal concentrated upon deepening intercultural co-operation. The experience that she gained in many countries gave her the knowledge that a full understanding of other religions is only possible through familiarization with other cultures, convinced as she was that religion is the heart of all cultures. It was a source of satisfaction for her to see these thoughts gaining ground within her own church under the influence of local churches overseas. She often pointed out that we in Europe should learn from Africa, for instance from the African saying, "I am because we are, and because we are am I."

Her third appeal was directed towards young people, training for peace and imparting hope. Her call led to the foundation of the "Initiative of Hope". She wished to show that not only evil deeds such as assassinations change the world, but that every good deed also bears fruit.

I would like to conclude this Memorial Lecture with the image which Maria Lücker proposed as a symbol of this Assembly—the rainbow which is a sign of God's covenant with man.

There are certainly many ways of interpreting the colours of the rainbow.

Each colour may represent a quality common to all religions such as frankness, sincerity, justice, trust, non-violence, sympathy, hope.

But these colours may also symbolize the religions themselves, the paths to God. The rainbow represents our experience of the Divine, which in its most profound expression is the white light that breaks and shines on in many colours. May this symbolize Maria Alberta Lücker's presence among us.

5

A Call to a Universal Soulha

By Dr. André Chouraqui*

At the opening of the Fourth World Conference on Religion and Peace, let us salute with one heart and soul the advancement of the universal mobilization of the spiritual forces of the world for the service of peace. After Kyoto in Asia, Louvain in Europe, Princeton in America, Nairobi convenes in Africa a growing number of participants and fraternal delegates: the simple fact of our meeting calls the attention of the whole universe to the relentless cry of humanity, threatened with death by its own progress, and to its will to overcome it.

In the commissions, we shall hear of the constant aggravation of the world political situation: let us keep in mind three numbers. Let us be reminded that 40,000 atomic bombs exist in government arsenals, representing two million times the power which destroyed Hiroshima, and 20 times the power to erase the 50 million square kilometres in which are located the vital centres of world civilization; and as if it was not enough, governments are investing every year the dizzy sum of approximately one thousand billion (yes, 1,000 billion) dollars to increase the forces of atomic death, conventional or biological, on Earth and in the atmosphere.

They are deceiving themselves, those who pretend that this arsenal of apocalyptical dimensions will never explode due to its own horror. All the experts with whom I have consulted unanimously admit that a total war can break out any day, due to a fatal chain of events, or an accident, or by the act of a madman, a species which is not absent from the honourable company of chiefs of states.

In addition, the tension existing between the two blocs aggravates the local conflicts which cause bloodshed or threaten many areas of the globe. A simple spark in these centres can release a universal disaster

---

*Dr. André Chouraqui is a Biblical scholar, writer, and chairman of the Israel Inter-Faith Association.

which will surpass in horror the apocalyptic stories. It is necessary to wake the universal conscience to these undeniable realities which we tend to dismiss from our mind. In fact, we live as if all the dangers I just mentioned do not exist. We say that the greatest power of the devil is to convince people that he does not exist. In some respects, it seems to be the same thing with the bomb. The less we are conscious of the dangers of a general war, the more certain and imminent they could be. A constantly clear, aroused conscience nourished by prayer must inspire a universal reconciliation which can only delay or maybe prevent the cataclysm which threatens us. In this respect, the World Conference on Religion and Peace can play a rôle of vital importance in arousing consciences in the areas caught by bloody wars and especially in the Middle East, torn by two "civil" wars, the Iraqi-Iranian conflict and the one between Israel and her Arab neighbours.

It is not our task here to analyse the political realities on which the conflicts are based nor the solutions which can resolve them. Our single desire is to encourage the belligerent countries and the blocs to which they belong to renounce war and to find diplomatic and negotiated solutions to their conflicts, and no more military ones. In this respect the conference convened at the initiative of His Majesty King Hassan II on May 13-15 last was exemplary. A representation of world Judaism, including 40 Israeli political figures and academicians, accompanied by the authorized representatives of the Jewish Diaspora were·invited, for the first time, by the king of an Arab country, who is also the Commander of Muslim believers, by its government and its people. The most moving moment of this historical congress was when His Excellency Moulay Ahmed Alaoui, Minister of State, proposed that we consciously take a solemn oath to reconcile Arabs and Israelis, Jews and Christians, within an Alliance of the Sons of Abraham, Ibrahim El Khalil.

This oath of Rabat I would like to extend here in Nairobi to all humanity and let all of us here, today, take a solemn oath to reconcile man with man, his brother.

There is no true reconciliation without real forgiveness: the Semites have a concept of this, the Arabic Soulha and the Hebrew Seliha. This Soulha, this universal Seliha, we have to offer one another, Jews, Christians, Muslims who, despite our wars, claim to be the Sons of Abraham, the father of every faith in the God of peace and justice, the God of Moses, Jesus, and Muhammad.

But, together, we have also to turn ourselves humbly and clearly to the non-monotheistic world of Africa and Asia and also seek for forgiveness for the misunderstandings, the injustices and sometimes the crimes we have committed against it in the name of our faith in one God. In this regard, let us meditate together on the comment of a Rabbi who was astonished that the God of the Hebrews chose a stammerer, Moses, to be the defender and the propagator of the monotheistic faith. In fact, when God chose him, Moses was neither a "stutterer" nor "tongue tied" (Ex. 4:10), but on the contrary most eloquent. One day, when he was displaying this eloquence in vehement curses against an Egyptian who was praying before the statue of his idol, the one God got angry with his prophet, reproaching him for not understanding that the Egyptian, beyond his statue, also worshipped the ineffable, Adonai, Elohim. And the cost of this lesson was that Moses, the prophet of the Hebrews, became a stammerer. Yes, we have to banish from our hearts intolerance and violence, which are the roots of our religious and national wars. Let us proclaim here in Nairobi, today, the universal Soulha which will allow man to reconcile with his fellow man, which will allow the Palestinian and the Israeli, the Iraqi and the Iranian, believers in any God and the atheist of every sort to recognize each other as brothers: fellow creatures, they are all equal, having the same blood, the same muscles, the same brain, the same limbs, the same eyes, the same voice. To tell the truth, we resemble each other so much sometimes that it is frightening, in our passions and our egotism; we must recognize it frankly.

Similarly, we have to aspire to renew our hearts and spirits, to purify our views of one another and to see in our neighbour more light than darkness, more similarities than differences. Allow me to pose here a poignant question: if a Messiah descended from heaven and took us at our word, us the participants of the Fourth World Conference on Religion and Peace, and transformed all the arms into ploughshares according to the old prophetic promise and thus realized at once our hope for a general disarmament, how soon would men transform these ploughshares into armaments? How soon, can you tell me? And in the meantime, do not we go on fighting, even with ploughshares? It is urgent to work for the birth, in us and others around us, of a new man who will know and want to be a universal brother of man, who renounces the instinct for violence and conquest which inspires all our wars—one who dares to say with the Prophet Micah (4:5): "For let all the peoples walk each one in the name of its gods, but we will walk in the name of Adonai, our God for ever and ever."

In this spirit, the Bible which I translated into French and published in ten volumes, "L'Univers de la Bible," includes not only Jewish, Christian and Muslim commentaries, but is wide open to the polytheistic universe of the Egyptians, Mesopotamians and Greeks. In this same spirit, let us renew here the solemn oath to reconcile the Sons of Abraham who are Jews, Christians and Muslims, so that in their descendants all the nations of the earth can be blessed (Genesis, 22:18, 26:4). I do hope that our conference will accept within it as an integral part of the World Conference on Religion and Peace, the Alliance of the Sons of Abraham, of Jews, Christians and Muslims, fraternally united to save the peace of the world. Their reconciliation, the return of peace in the Middle East, could return to Jerusalem its destiny as the source of peace and a connecting link between the Far East, the Orient and the West, between Asia and Africa, and to make this city one of the world centres of religions and cultures, in our continual, humble and religious search for peace, pax, salam, shalom.

6

Islam Means Peace

By Dr. Inamullah Khan*

I start with my salutations to the continent of Africa, the continent of tomorrow. It is a resurgent continent, it is no longer the dark continent. Its bad old days, when it used to be called the dark continent, are gradually passing, or rather almost finished, except in the land of Bishop Tutu where the struggle is still going on. It is a great continent, a continent of great possibilities, but it is also a continent with lots of problems. On the one side it is rich in agricultural wealth, in its mineral wealth, and its steady people; on the other it is faced with grinding poverty. It is faced with terrible drought, it is faced with one of the world's biggest refugee problems, and these are not only the problems of Africa, but of humanity; as for the problem of our brothers and sisters within Africa, I will plead from this platform that the World Conference on Religion and Peace should take up this problem as our own. We must try to make our little contribution, whatever it be, to alleviate these difficulties and see that this great continent flourishes in the future. Let us all hope and pray that the Organization of African Unity through its continuous efforts gives this continent social security, social justice and economic and political stability.

After these remarks I come to a brief perspective, an Islamic perspective, on religion as such. What is Islam? It is very wrongly called Mohamedanism, which is completely foreign to us. The name of our religion is Islam, that is the word used in our holy book, the holy Qur'an. It is an Arabic word which means peace; peace not only with one's Creator by whatever name you may call Him, but it is also peace with our fellow men. Islam to us is as old as the hills; it is, in the words of the Holy Qur'an, *dīn al-fitra*, which means it is "religio naturalis." It is a religion of human nature; to us it was the religion of Adam, the first man, or the

---

*Dr. Inamullah Khan is Secretary-General of the World Muslim Congress, with headquarters in Karachi, Pakistan.

first Prophet, and it has been the religion of all the Prophets of the world. And we as Muslims are ordered to show deep respect to all the Prophets of the world and wherever we refer to the name, be it Moses, or Jesus, or anyone else, we always say "Peace be upon him." So a good Muslim is a good religionist in the sense that he shows respect to all the religions of the world and to all the leaders of the religions of the world.

Islam stands for peace: peace for all, peace without discrimination; peace on the basis of justice. Islam believes in human dignity, in the dignity of the human person, and we are asked to express our respect for the human person, whatever colour of skin he or she has, whatever be his or her language, whatever be his or her race, whatever be his or her nationality. Islam, as I told you, is a religion which has no discrimination of any sort in various aspects of life. Islam teaches us coexistence. The Qur'an says: "your religion with you, mine with me." We can still live as brothers and sisters of one great human family. The Qur'an is again very clear: "there is no coercion or compulsion in religion." Yes, give your message but give it in soft terms, without criticizing the religion of others. The Holy Prophet said: "How would you like it if they criticized your God and your Prophet?" So why should we hurt other people by criticizing their Gods, their leaders, and their faith as such? Islam wants us to live in harmony and in good fellowship; you must learn to live together and to work together for the good of all concerned.

When a Muslim meets another person, not only a Muslim, he always addresses him or her, *assalamu alaikum wa rahmatullah wa baraka-tuhu*, "may the peace and blessings of God be upon you," and if that person happens to be a Muslim, he or she replies: *waalaikum assalam wa rahmatullah wa barakatuhu*, "may the peace and blessings of God be upon you also." So the sense of Islam is peace, and it is very sad that some people have interpreted Islam in a wrong way and made it appear as if it is essentially a militant religion.

Islam is not content with only the spiritual aspect of life. It treats life as a whole, it treats life as one unit; it does not divide life into water-tight compartments. Islam is as much interested in your material welfare as in your spiritual welfare; in your individual welfare as much as in your social welfare. Islam wants you to be a good person in your own place, to be a good son or daughter, to be a good husband or wife, to be a good father or mother, to be a good neighbour, and not only to be a good neighbour, but to be good not only to the people of your own country, people of the region, but to the people of the world. The Qur'an repeatedly says you all belong to one human family. In another place it says: "You are all children of Adam," but Adam was made of dust. Don't be proud because you're strong, or because you're handsome, or because you're rich. We are all coming from dust and to dust we must return.

Islam wants us to be humble and at the same time to be of service not only to our own self, and to our own family, and to our own neigh-bourhood, but to be in the service of all mankind in all possible aspects of life. The Qur'an has again a very important teaching: "Why do you say things that you don't do?" Islam does not want you to have two standards: you say something, whereas in action you're doing something else. It says there must be uniformity in your thinking and in your actions. And in another place Islam repeatedly speaks of purity of thought, because, according to Islamic teaching, all your actions are based on your thinking, and if your thinking is correct, all else will be correct, concerning your own self or the human society of which you are a member.

"Be a student of life," says the Holy Prophet, "from the time you're in the cradle, till the time you're in the cradle of the grave." You must keep on learning, and learning, and learning until you die. Unfortunately during the colonial days the greatest harm was done to Muslim education and this has brought so much backwardness in various parts of the Muslim world, whereas you all know, and history bears witness to it, that for the first 1000 years of Muslim history they were the leaders in the intellectual field. Look at their achievements in Cordoba in Spain, or in Baghdad in the Middle East! But now the colonial days are over and Muslims are once again coming up on their own and we hope once again they will make real, good contributions in the fields of learning, knowledge and education.

There is lots of confusion. Thus when you speak of an Islamic state immediately people think it is going to be a theocratic state. Islam has nothing to do with theocracy. We do not have a priestly class that way. I, or many others like me, who is not a regular priest, can lead prayers. I can perform a marriage; I can perform the death ceremony. Islam has no room for a theocratic state.

We in WCRP must understand Islam not merely as one of the great religions of the world, but as a religion standing for peace and working for peace, and on the basis of living together, and working together for the common good of all the peoples of the world. Instead of magnifying or multiplying our differences let us pick up the common factors, piece them together wherever possible, and build up bridges of goodwill and understanding between the peoples of different faiths in WCRP. WCRP, let me make it clear, does not want a merger of faiths; let us jointly present a bouquet of different faiths, a bouquet of faith and hope for a better tomorrow.

30

7

The Youth Message

Delivered By Miss Shobna Obhrai of Kenya*

Let me begin by affirming the immense value which participants found in the two-day WCRP Youth Conference, held on 20 and 21 August. It was in fact one of the first recommendations in the Final Document that an extended Youth Conference be held prior to future WCRP conferences. Older delegates who have long cherished and worked for WCRP will be pleased to know that the value of WCRP to young people was evident throughout our meeting. The work of WCRP is work to which young people also feel very ready to make a commitment, and not just a conference commitment, expressed in easy words and resolutions, but one that is expected to be costly in terms of time, money and effort when we return to our homes. But so it should be, and for very obvious reasons. We all know of the bruised and battered life of the human family on the planet Earth. To fail to respond at some personal cost would be both heartless as well as trivializing of our own lives. So then, in that context, let me share briefly some of the specific concerns of the youth delegates as expressed in our workshops, discussion groups, and Final Document. I shall mention seven concerns, albeit briefly.

Our first concern was to improve our communication, our sense of being together in a common work, even whilst separated across the world. A Youth Section in the regular WCRP newsletter was considered one means of doing this. Again, mindful of the International Year of Youth in 1985, there were other ideas. A WCRP inter-faith camp during the International Youth Year was one suggestion; ideally in an area where there are inter-faith problems. Joint national and regional work on issues of peace education, including prayer meetings for peace, was yet another suggestion. We recognized the need for an inter-faith group to do all it can at every level to put its own house in order, to heal divisions between people of faith, to transform hostile mistrust into the

---

* Miss Shobna Obhrai is an active Youth Member of WCRP/Africa in Nairobi, Kenya.

warm friendship we have found through WCRP. We believe it is possible; we believe even the smallest gesture is worth making. We can but continue to reach out, seeking to mend the painful divisions between people of faith.

Our spirituality is not, however, only exclusively expressed at this level of inter-religious activity. Our spirituality is also expressed in our response to issues like human rights, development and disarmament. It went without question that these issues should also be on our agenda. It was taken for granted that they are fundamentally spiritual and moral issues. Accordingly, our final document included many recommendations regarding these issues: refugees, the victims of international violence, living in a waiting room, dependent on some stranger to give them a home; these refugees must receive tangible, sustained help from WCRP. WCRP youth are ready to work directly with refugees in camps as a multi-faith group. WCRP/Kenya is ready to establish a first office in Nairobi to co-ordinate such efforts. We are very conscious that many of the refugees are also young people like ourselves.

Time does not allow me to detail the many recommendations regarding disarmament and development. Our goals are a Comprehensive Test-Ban Treaty, a Nuclear Freeze, and end to the arms trade, aid which is attuned to expressed needs, not military aid; these goals are in any case familiar to WCRP members. Suffice it to say that we strongly recommend WCRP to maintain and strengthen its permanent office at the United Nations, to try again to send a delegation of religious leaders to the leadership of the nuclear weapon states. All such efforts must be sustained and strengthened with a sense of urgency. The resilience of our faiths through many centuries must be expressed in a persistent campaign for peace through disarmament and also for development. Proper use of all resources to meet the basic needs of the human family can only be achieved by justice.

We look to WCRP IV to join with us on these and other issues to push us further, to illuminate the next steps with us on this critical journey. May the abundant blessings of the Most High be with us in the days of WCRP IV, and as we journey onwards together. The youth of WCRP are honoured to share these days, and the opportunity to be with you all, and in Kenya, a land of love, peace and unity.

8

The Women's Message

Delivered By Mrs. Sugi Yamamoto of Japan*

On Wednesday August 22 at the Kenya Technical Teachers' College we, the women of WCRP, held an all-day preparatory meeting. More than 100 women from some 30 countries around the world, representing many cultures and religious traditions, assembled in plenary sessions and for discussion groups. Prayers, meditations, and a warm welcome from women of the religious communities of Nairobi marked the beginning of an unusual and stimulating day of sisterhood.

The Women's Meeting was in no sense meant to separate women from WCRP IV, but rather to take seriously our growing presence in the work of WCRP and to think through and develop our concerns as women. The meeting was not meant to come to a conclusion, with resolutions and statements, but rather to spark and initiate our thinking on major concerns which will be integrated through our active participation in the commissions and working groups of this Assembly.

We were motivated by three major concerns: a sense of urgency with respect to peace, an awareness that religious people are impelled to turn their principles into action, and a sense that women have a special role to play in raising and speaking to the world's problems. Our discussion groups focused on four topics: Peace Education, Womens' Voices in the Peace Movement, Women in Humanitarian and Development Work, and Women and Violence.

Our discussion was intense and exciting. While time does not permit the sharing of this discussion, we would stress a few highlights. First, education for peace must become a priority for all ages. The understanding of one another's cultures and religions, and the generation of global thinking must become part of the curricula of schools, universities, and adult education programmes. Second, our talk of peace must

---

* Mrs. Sugi Yamamoto is Director of the All Japan Buddhist Women's Association.

always include justice. The starving person and the dying child, whether caught in drought, war, or other disaster, cannot be concerned with peace, but only with the struggle to survive. For them "survival" is not a question of the future in a nuclear world, but an urgent question of the present—today. Third, development is not simply a matter of economics, but requires an integrated holistic approach—economic, social, and spiritual. It requires the active participation of all, women and men, youth and adults. It further requires that the vast expenditures on armaments be redirected toward education, the environment, agriculture, and human needs. Finally, violence is not only a matter of weapons and war, but must be understood to include economic injustice and attacks on human dignity.

To redefine and sharpen our understanding of the terms we use—such as education, peace, development, and violence—is more than an intellectual exercise. It is a prerequisite to developing genuine global understanding.

We closed our day with an inter-religious meditation, with women offering prayers in their own languages, and with a non-verbal prayer offered in the language of gesture. A final word: The plenary offered the Assembly a reminder to be conscious of using non-sexist and inclusive language. Women, who comprise half the world's population, should be included not only in the language of WCRP, but in its rôles of leadership and as active, enthusiastic participants in its work. We look forward to the Fourth Assembly of WCRP and bring all our energies to our work and deliberations together.

9

Report of the Secretary-General of WCRP IV and the Newly Appointed Secretary-General of WCRP/International

By Dr. John B. Taylor*

Mr President, Sisters, and Brothers.

Forgive me for beginning this report without the courtesies of addressing the Venerables, Excellencies, and others who are present amongst us in this extraordinarily varied meeting. I wanted to set the tone immediately in terms of an atmosphere of our coming together as members of the one human family. I hope too that we shall remain deeply conscious of a sense of family within our world, within our organization and within our conference. In this we are certainly being helped by the spirit of welcome and support which our Kenyan hosts are showing to us and have shown to us already for many months in such a remarkable degree.

It is a little embarrassing for me to take the floor at this stage. As a "new boy" I can scarcely give a conventional long term report as has already been distributed for my predecessor. Moreover, for many months I have been writing to distinguished and experienced speakers around the world requesting them to limit their remarks to a relatively few minutes when all of them are men and women who could hold us spellbound for an hour or more. The nature of our assembly means that we must hear a wide range of voices, but the constraints of time leave all of us with too short a space to say what is in our hearts.

---

* Dr. John B. Taylor was appointed Secretary-General of WCRP IV in October, 1983, and Secretary-General of the World Conference on Religion and Peace in February, 1984.

I am presuming, however, to submit to you three personal assessments and associated questions. The first concerns the world context and many local contexts in which our movement for peacemaking and bridge-building is set. The second area of concern is how WCRP itself can become a still more vital organization geared not only to words but to actions. My third concern is how we can fulfil the potential of this very assembly which brings some 600 people from all over the world, including, I believe, more young people and more women than ever before at such a world assembly, but at the same time•including more official representatives of religious movements and religious leadership.

On these three concerns I wish to share my own perspectives and I need to receive your comments and corrections as soon as possible lest I fail in the daunting but challenging duties which are laid upon me as Secretary-General/International. I am daunted partly because I follow such a distinguished predecessor, Dr. Homer Jack, but also because I realise the urgency and importance of this organization in its almost unique development as a fellowship of people from all the world's religions coming together to promote peace and understanding. I am challenged because I already feel the tremendous response and support from every level of our various communities around the world.

I must pay tribute not only to a predecessor like Dr. Jack but also to the distinguished office-holders of WCRP over many years beginning with our President, Archbishop Fernandes, our Honorary Presidents, President Niwano, Sri Diwakar, and Dr. Greeley, and then, without being able to mention all the names, the Vice-Presidents and Board Members who have given me such wise advice and heartening encouragement in my still short period with WCRP. The support which I have also had from everyone, ranging from the office staff in Geneva and New York to the countless voluntary helpers in Nairobi, makes me feel deeply grateful to find myself in the family of WCRP.

I. Is Religion a Force for Peace?

Other speakers will document and develop more eloquently than I the way in which we live today in a time of crisis and tragedy in terms of our hopes for peace. Despite the energetic witness of peace-workers and peace movements for many years, the world is living with greater fears of the danger of nuclear holocaust than ever before; no less significant, in my opinion, is the fact that we are also living not only with those fears but with the actual terrors of countless conventional wars. One immediate and obvious element in many of these conflicts, both potential and actual, is the way in which our respective religions and ideologies, all of them claiming to contribute to peace and justice, have again and again failed to be forces for reconciliation.

At a world-wide level we find massive caricatures of one ideological area over against another; in particular there is a tendency to oppose a so-called irreligious world with a so-called religious world, and yet the most elementary honesty must admit that it is not the dividing line or cri-

36

terion of religiousness which separates East from West or North from South. Religion and irreligion are to be found everywhere and real tensions exist between believers and unbelievers but these are not sufficient to explain away the violent hatreds, exploitation, injustice, and self-righteousness which disfigure our world. People of religion cannot simply blame the politicians or economists for failing to find an answer for world justice; religions must acknowledge that they have not practised what they have preached and that they have often failed to provide an adequate and persuasive and disciplined ethic for their followers.

Today more than ever, religion is being called into question and even ridiculed for its failure to be a force for peace. In a frightening number of situations religion is a potent factor in local or regional conflicts, and I have just alluded to the way in which it can even be brought into play as a factor in global tensions. Whether we think of conflicts within African countries, within the Middle East region, within many nations in Asia, or within industrial conurbations in Europe or the Americas, we see that people are invoking religion to justify conflicts which may be essentially tribal or constitutional or economic or national. Religious leaders and religious laity may eventually be speaking out against such manipulation of religion but often it is too late. People have been brought up in cultural isolation, in ignorance of their neighbours, with an arrogant sense of superiority over anybody who belongs to a different religious community from their own; such people, both young and old, can all too easily be drawn into conflicts.

The very credibility of religion in today's world is at stake in the failure of religious people to be effective peacemakers. Although there may be many evidences of the vitality of religion in the modern world, there are also innumerable signs of people turning away from religion, sometimes from disgust with what they perceive to be the failure of religion, sometimes out of ignorance of what religion really stands for, and sometimes because religious establishments have become so exclusive and restrictive that it is impossible for a seeker to find his or her way into a particular religious family. Religious people need to come together in a spirit of self-criticism and to acknowledge the failures of the leaders and followers of our various religions to live up to the principles of those religions. A fellowship such as the World Conference on Religion and Peace has not come into being simply to allow religions to stand in judgment upon the rest of the world. It has grown in integrity and relevance in so far as religious people have acknowledged their own failures, and then have turned away from past failures towards future co-operation and common commitment for peace.

II. Is WCRP an Instrument for Peace-Making?

The World Conference on Religion and Peace is almost unique among non-governmental organizations related to the United Nations and among all international organizations, for its deliberate policy of bringing together both representatives of varied religious groups and individual religious people from all the major traditions in order to promote peace with justice. The deliberately inter-religious nature of the organisation has appeared controversial to some people who have been afraid that this could be a way of suspending our commitment to truth within our respective traditions and of constructing some form of super-religion. This has never been the intention nor the tendency of WCRP, where each person may remain loyal to his or her own tradition but where each person believes that he or she has much to share with and to learn from neighbours of other faiths. The very fact that so many of today's conflicts are in the context of the failure of people of one religious group to relate to their neighbours of another religious group makes the urgency of inter-religious understanding only too obvious. The very fact of WCRP's existence can be a force for peace in so far as it can be a demonstration that varying religious allegiance should not stand in the way of a sense of common humanity, common citizenship, common membership in a local community.

As an international organization with only 15 years of existence WCRP has always been recognised that it must learn to work together with and through other existing organizations committed to peace and justice. Foremost among these are the various programmes and agencies of the United Nations. WCRP has always tried to co-operate in this area and I believe that this should continue to be a basic principle for our loyalties and engagements. However, WCRP has also had a particular role in challenging people to return from the inter-religious fellowship to within the fold of their particular religious family. Much work has to be done within each of our respective religious groups in order to overcome the prejudices and caricatures which have kept us apart from each other. New energies have to be unleashed from within our respective religious traditions to strengthen our common witness as religious people. Together we must promote world-wide awareness of the dangers constituted by ever-escalating nuclear armaments, the ever-widening gulf between the rich and the poor, and the constantly deteriorating situation of human rights wherein phenomena such as racial discrimination or torture, far from being eliminated, are being reinforced.

WCRP has always insisted that one could not support the cause for peace unless one supported at the same time the cause for justice. The work of the last 15 years and the agenda of this assembly bear ample testimony to that. We cannot simply address the symptoms of war and of war-mongering to be seen in our ever-increasing stockpiling and use of arms. We must also address the root causes for mistrust and conflict; very often these causes lie in the area of economic and political injustice or in the area of cultural and ideological exclusivism and intolerance. Religious people must in the first instance be self-critical where they have been complicit in such injustices but they need also to revive their prophetic traditions to speak out against such injustices and to refuse such complicity.

I believe that WCRP should continue to protest against the extravagant expenditures on nuclear and conventional weaponry which cripple the economies of rich and poor nations alike. Especially when so-called defence expenditures reach levels of "over-kill" potential such as we see in the current arms build-up between the super-powers, but also between many local neighbours, defence capacity becomes provocative and at worst becomes a pretext or a temptation for the short-term gains of pre-emptive aggression. The high percentage of national income expended on military hardware, but also the percentages of emotional and spiritual energy wasted in fomenting suspicion and hatred, have held back our present world from achieving the equitable distribution of food, natural resources, and intellectual potential which could have been within our reach in this generation.

The important survey which was undertaken for the WCRP Commission on the Future over the last year established that attitudes for peace-making are very varied within each religious tradition. Among Christians, as among Muslims, as among Jews, as among Buddhists, Hindus, or other, we find that there is a whole range of opinion ranging from an ability to justify war to a refusal of all recourse to violence. Within each of our religious traditions as well as between our religious traditions there is also, across this whole spectrum of opinion, a refusal to despair. Not least because religious people look beyond their own personal resources to the ultimate truth and justice and peace which their religions uphold, they have a duty both as individuals and as communities to try to implement truth, justice and peace as far as they may.

When people meet together under the auspices of WCRP in order to confer, to study together or to prepare active co-operation together, they share their visions but they also share their particular engagements. The research prepared for the WCRP Commission on the Future has pointed the need for practising an inter-religious sharing of visions and resources in order to develop together common standards of ethics for constructing peace with justice. We cannot seek peace and justice simply for our own community but must be equally scrupulous for the rights of all our neighbours, particularly for those minority groups for whom we may have a particular responsibility.

Over the last 15 years WCRP has reminded our respective religious communities that there are certain things which we could do better together than separately. In making a political witness against the arms race, in making a humanitarian contribution in favour of the victims of war, notably refugees, in preparing projects of reconciliation to heal wounds inflicted in conflicts, in preparing imaginative programmes of education for peace and even in seeking for ways to express in prayer or meditation our separate or common search for spiritual resources to undergird our peace-making efforts—in all of these areas WCRP at inter-national, regional, and local levels has shown the potential of inter-religious co-operation. Very often WCRP has worked with existing religious, inter-religious, or secular groups. We have not had the ambition to be empire-builders for our own institutional glory and yet we have seen the movement grow at many levels and we have seen expectations grow of how far a movement like ours could be a sign of hope, a voice of sanity, and above all a helping hand of reconciliation in many situations of tension and conflict across the world.

Like any organization which refuses to make its own existence its chief justification, WCRP has had to face the possibility that it had served usefully over the last 15 years but that it should be ready to die gracefully if other better organizations were ready to take up the challenge. However, one of the results of the world-wide survey and the Commission on the Future has been to insist that WCRP is at the beginning rather than at the end of its potential usefulness. Accordingly we come to our Fourth Assembly not so much with the intention to take stock of the past or to analyse the present, important though these activities may be, as to prepare for the future.

III. Can this Assembly be a Sign of Hope?

As someone who has been preparing this assembly for nearly one year, I am deeply moved by the level of dedication and sacrifice which has been shown all over the world in order to make possible the participation of so many people coming together at this time. Our organization is called the World Conference on Religion and Peace and the energies required to organise such world assemblies might indeed suggest that the main purpose of WCRP was to realise an international gathering once every four or five years. The previous three assemblies in Kyoto, Leuwen, and Princeton were certainly inspiring occasions not only to those who attended but to those, like me, who heard of them through others who had participated. And yet the real fruits of those assemblies lay not so much in the immediate deliberations or resolutions as in the development of trust and confidence which could then be used in local situations to establish regional, national, or local chapters of WCRP; there was the still greater justification that the assemblies provided stimulus for consistent contribution, for example to disarmament or human rights concerns, in the United Nations networks. The assemblies also stimulated humanitarian co-operation by people of all faiths in some of the great human tragedies of our time, such as refugee crises; the assemblies pointed to new directions in peace-education which should be beyond information about expenditure on military budgets or statistics about destructive capacity of warheads to a more experiential appreciation of how far attitudes to neighbours, to allies, or to enemies can be blinded by prejudices and need to be tested and purified by ethical and spiritual principles.

We come together here to share our convictions and our hopes that our religions can bring such ethical and spiritual powers to bear even in the most difficult situations of our time. We come together not so much to pass judgment upon others or even upon ourselves for these conflicts as to prepare for modes of response and action to these existing conflicts and injustices. It is my personal hope that this will be an assembly not so

40

much of resolutions about what others should be doing as about laying plans for what we ourselves as religious people, young and old, men and women, could better do together in the service of peace and justice. We have a particular responsibility to lay plans for WCRP itself whether at international, regional, national or local levels, but we may also wish to take stock of actions that need to be taken within our own religious communities or within other action groups or study circles of which we are members. I believe that the main justification for the energies and expenses of this Assembly will be seen in the study and in the activity which should follow the Assembly and I would appeal to us in our work in commissions and working groups to be as practical as we can in translating our concerns and visions into realistic programmes for the future.

In any organization as relatively recent as WCRP, there could be a temptation to spend a lot of time in trying to formulate the best constitution or rules of procedure for the organization. We might even be tempted to spend time on choosing a better title for our organization or in establishing better structures to carry out our work. Important though such work may be we should not lose sight of the basic intentions of the organization; those push us to plan in much more concrete terms for appropriate study programmes, humanitarian activities, lobbying procedures, spiritual disciplines, etc. How far can we dare to make of this Assembly a sign of hope not only to our various WCRP organizations around the world, but to those who are watching us with a mixture of enthusiasm and scepticism as to whether we really can achieve the enormously ambitious goals which we have set ourselves?

The very phenomenon of our Assembly is a not inconsiderable achievement. For individuals and representatives from so many of the world's religions to have come together from all the continents of the world is already a sign of hope. For us to be meeting in a multi-cultural and multi-religious society like Kenya is also an important sign of hope, especially when we consider how difficult it is to achieve such inter-cultural and inter-religious harmony in so many other countries near and far. We hope that the Assembly will not only be a meeting-point between varying religions and between the leaders and laity of our respective religions, between the elders and the younger people, between women and men, between those more given to theory or theology and those more given to action or politics. If we can learn to work together despite our many differences within the short period of the week that we spend in Nairobi this could be a great stimulus for us all to return to do better within our local situations but also with our neighbours in our region, or further afield in the world.

I believe that a WCRP World Assembly should be a stimulus to build up close and continuing working relationships between WCRP groups in different parts of the world. I should like to see each national delegation of WCRP choose one, or two, or three other national partners in a different part of their continent, or in a different continent altogether. Could we in this way become more conscious of the world dimension of our organization so that, when we study about efforts for peace or struggles for justice in another part of the world, we can be in touch with and informed by the people living in that very situation? Would it be possible that when we undertake such studies we could quickly discern ways in which our understanding and studying about the situation could lead us to some practical or humanitarian involvement with that situation or perhaps to some form of spiritual solidarity with that situation?

In order to choose such studies and projects wisely we need to be advised by people who are at the heart of the struggling or suffering. I should also like to see a World Assembly establish certain WCRP networks, among for example the youth participants that are here, among the women that are here, among members of particular religious traditions that are here, or perhaps in bilateral or multilateral relationships between particular religious traditions who are involved in situations of regional or local conflict.

Sometimes people meet neighbours of another faith or even members belonging to a different group or sect within their own religion more readily at an international conference than they do in their home situation. We can have no credibility as an international inter-religious organization to promote peace and justice unless we can find appropriate ways in our home situations to work with neighbours who belong to other religious or ideological traditions. An international conference draws a great deal of impetus from what is already happening at many local levels, but an international conference should also recharge the energies and enthusiasms of people as individuals and as communities when they return to their home situation.

IV. Conclusion

Having shared with you some of my convictions that this Assembly can be a sign of hope not only for the future activities of WCRP but for the wider struggles for peace and justice in which we should all be involved, let me turn in conclusion to a few more practical and even domestic concerns about this Assembly itself. Some of you will know the story in the Bible about the Tower of Babel where humanity in its early history became divided into so many different languages that nobody could understand each other. But it was not only the language barrier which was the problem. It was above all human pride and self-sufficiency which led to the breakdown of communication and the eventual conflict of the Tower of Babel. In this Assembly we shall have to overcome with patience and humour the problems of communication across the language barriers and the cultural barriers that exist between us. But above all we must break down the barriers which we have set up in terms of self-pride or self-sufficiency.

Unless there is a sense that we need each other there can be no purpose for our meeting together. We have come not only to tell each other about ourselves but we have come above all to learn from each other. We shall learn that some people are still justifiably suspicious of us because of the past heritage of our community in its relationship with others; we may have to explain that we ourselves have difficulty in understanding or trusting a particular neighbour because of something which we perceive his or her community to have done to us or to our community. We have to be honest with each other but we have to be open with each other and we have to open a new relationship with each other.

We must be careful that when we come to sensitive political issues we do not look at these issues from too self-centred or nationalist a perspective. We should always be self-critical but we may also develop sufficient trust and confidence with each other to share criticisms of each other in a spirit of patience and forbearance. We may come in our proceedings to cast votes either for the adoption of particular resolutions or the approval of programmes or the invitation of people to serve on particular committees or boards. When the delegates amongst us cast their votes we hope that there will be no spirit of rivalry or competition but that we shall always preserve sensitivity for each other and patience with each other.

Many of you have a far greater experience of WCRP than I do. I have shared with you my own hopes and hinted also at some of my fears for this Assembly. I wish to be guided by you all as Secretary-General not only in this Assembly but for the future. I pledge myself to be open to you, as far as I may, for all your suggestions about our activities and our styles of work in WCRP. The very agenda of this Assembly must remain open, within reason, to modification according to the needs which are felt by you as participants and which you may always convey to the officers, or the Steering Committee, or the Drafting Committee.

The ways in which WCRP develops and operates in the months and years to come must be constantly informed and corrected by the advice of the world-wide membership. The international secretariat and the international officers need such regular communication from local and regional situations. Similarly we may sometimes from the international organization raise particular challenges or concerns with local groups. This Assembly is a wonderful opportunity for us to get to know each other, to share our ideas, to plan co-operative projects, but also to seek appropriate ways to share our distinctive spiritualities. It is my hope and prayer that the remarkable spirit of co-operation which has been obvious throughout all the preparation for this Assembly will continue throughout the Assembly itself and beyond. I pledge myself to be at your disposal in every way possible and appeal to you for your continuing advice and support. Thank you.

B.

Addresses on "People of Faith Working Together for Peace"

10

Introduction to the Theme, People of Faith Working Together for Peace: "DOJI"—Helping Others by Putting Oneself in Their Place

By President Nikkyo Niwano*

I am grateful to have the opportunity to speak to you today. The first time WCRP took place, it was in Japan, the second time in Belgium, the third assembly was held in the United States, and now its Fourth Assembly is happening right here in the beautiful city of Nairobi. This is an occasion of infinite happiness to me.

Dr. John Taylor has been appointed as the new Secretary-General following in the steps of Dr. Homer Jack, who served in that capacity for many years. The conference is made possible today thanks to the efforts of Dr. Taylor.

In past history, countless tragedies have occurred in Africa. On the other hand, it is not an exaggeration to say that wonderful latent values lie still uncovered in this great continent. At the same time, for us religionists who have set to work for the salvation of all, Africa can teach us a great deal by calling to us and letting us know what should be accomplished, and also by having us reflect upon our actions.

As a follower of the Buddhist faith, I shall speak to you from such a stance; in Buddhism, we have the word "Doji". "Doji" means "to help

* President Nikkyo Niwano is President of Rissho Kosei-kai, a Buddhist lay organization, with headquarters in Tokyo, Japan. He is one of the founders of WCRP and also one of its Honorary Presidents.

the other by putting oneself in the place of the other". In other words, it is not possible for all-important love and mercy to manifest themselves, if religionists do not understand the situation to which they are applied.

On one occasion, I had the opportunity to meet in India, Charles Duke, the astronaut. He was in command for the lunar landing of his capsule and actually spent three days on the Moon.

Back on Earth, he gained instant fame and wealth. However, he was also faced at the same time with the collapse of his family. Following this experience, he realized that instead of trying to gain from life, it was more important to try to give, and that if people forget the notion of gift, then it is likely that one day the Earth could become a desolate place similar to the Moon.

After having realized the truth, Charles Duke, who had been a believer in the world of high technology, became a fervent believer in the world of religion.

We are assembled here today at the Fourth Assembly of WCRP in order to seek ways that can prevent the globe from becoming a lunar desert. I hope that all of us will carry earnest dialogues during this time, leading to the enrichment of all concerned.

Thank you for your attention.

11

Coming Together in the Cause of Peace: The Role of Religions

By Dr. Soedjatmoko*

I am greatly honoured to have been asked to open this afternoon's discussions on the first theme of the Fourth Assembly of the World Conference on Religion and Peace—a theme which asks us to address the compelling need for peoples of all faiths to come together in the cause of peace. One needs only look at the many suffering corners of our globe today where the fabric of peace is being shredded—with the innocent, as always, among the first victims—to realize the legitimacy and the urgency of our agenda here today.

I think it particularly appropriate that the World Conference on Religion and Peace is assembling this time in Africa. In coming to Nairobi, WCRP IV signals its concerns with the inequities and indignities that so sorely beset the men, women and children of this continent. Most of the problems that humankind now faces are present in Africa: the hunger and poverty that afflict the lives of so many millions; the pressures of population, overcrowded, unworkable cities, unemployment, the millions of refugees of war and natural disaster; the widening disparities between rich and poor; the conflict between dictatorship and democracy; racial and tribal violence and strife—and the conflicts engendered or aggravated by the intervention of outside powers. One could go on and on. Your Nairobi Declaration states the case starkly: Africa has become one of the major seed-beds of all that is dehumanizing and destructive.

We approach this question how best to come together, from our various faiths, in seeking to fit our separate cultural and historical experi-

---

* Dr. Soedjatmoko is Rector of the United Nations University, located in Tokyo, Japan.

ences and aspirations into some sort of common effort at caring and tending to the overarching truth of our oneness[1] on this increasingly limited planet.[2] We do so at a time when confronted with a number of threats to peace in our world:

First, we need to see the world situation in the harsh light of present realities—which is to say a state of near international anarchy. War is part of the fabric of life in many parts of the world. Since the end of World War II, more than 130 wars have been fought in the Third World, and lethally so, with conventional weapons.

We are going to have to learn to live together in conditions of high population density. In the few short years remaining in the 20th century, the world population will swell from its present four billion to about six billion. Only a few years after that, the global population is projected to be about eight billion. In such an increasingly crowded, hungry and competitive world, we will have to learn new ways in order to live together in reasonable harmony at unprecedented levels of population density.

A large part of the future global population will be concentrated in urban areas, particularly in "megacities" of the Third World. Demographers now talk about future cities of 15 to 20 million people and beyond, many of them living at very low income levels. These are bound to be seed-beds of social conflict.

Both the sheer size of the world's population and the unparalleled densities these numbers imply will challenge our ability to put science and technology to better use than we have been able to do so far. In principle, science and technology should have made possible the elimination of poverty—whereas, in reality, it has been expanding. Much too much scientific expertise has been employed in devising better means for warring upon each other in more deadly efficient fashion. Increasingly, reliance on military force is seen as the most expedient solution to our problems, in the process militarizing whole societies. We simply cannot afford the continuance of such trends in which technological expertise sustains and stokes our fears rather than liberating us from them and helping to overcome the tremendous disparities which exist between rich and poor.

Narrow nationalism has in a sense made us all prisoners of our concept of the nation-state. This is in no way to question the importance of the nation-state as a foundation for independence, identity and a place in the global community. At the same time, we must learn to transcend narrowly-conceived nationalism and accept the ultimate importance of ensuring the survival of *all* humanity—and our responsibility for that task. It is no longer possible for any nation, however powerful, to solve many of its most important problems by itself, in isolation from the rest of the world; or to define its security needs unilaterally. It needs to be recognized that freedom from violence, or its threat, is a collective neces-

---

1. Q. XXIII:51-52.
2. II:30, VI:165.

sity of the human race, which implies taking into account the security needs of one's adversaries. The human community will have to devise more just and viable international systems for managing and governing itself—capable of looking beyond narrow, often conflicting, national interests to the security and welfare of humankind as a whole.

Simply put, we are all members of the human race, with common fears, hopes, delights and loves which transcend ideological, cultural or religious differences and conflicting interests. While nationalism is a necessary fact of the modern world, we need to find ways to gentle its darker impulses and accept the reality of pluralism in our condition of mutual dependence and mutual reliance on good will, justice and civility.

Another threat to peace stems from the massive population movements of our time which have frequently outstripped the adjustment capacities of our institutions and societies and have led to social conflict, and, in some cases, to mass killings. Migrations, of course, can enrich and give new vitality to a society. But the immense scale of the present movements, from countryside to city, nation to nation, and continent to continent—as an increasingly assertive poor reject passivity and vote with their feet in search of a better life—taxes the absorptive capacity of countries and cultures and leads to discrimination, exploitation and violence.

In many parts of the world, we see signs that the poor and the marginalized no longer accept their condition of wretchedness, unemployment, insecurity and oppression. Migrants and refugees are a manifestation of this drive, evidence of our inability to resolve poverty and injustice. Much of what fuels these vast movements are man-made, not natural disasters, and as such they are a challenge to our religious conscience.

Linked to this is the increasing strain on the job market—some one billion jobs, it is estimated, would have to be created in the Third World by the year 2000, largely to accommodate the demands of young people entering the labour market. This will strain all political systems, whatever their ideologies, to their limit and, if pushed beyond, could lead to serious domestic implosions and conflict. And interdependence means that small brush fire wars can too easily turn into major international conflagrations.

Job needs on the scale of one billion will require that we rethink our concepts of work, leisure and social and cultural productivity. We will have to devise alternative ways of shaping a meaningful life—based not only on economic success but also on the satisfaction that can come from social and cultural usefulness and creativity.

Civil strife and turmoil, and their frightening implications for larger international hostilities, can also be the unintended and unwelcome accompaniments of misdirected (as well as successful) development, regional hegemonic aspirations, or outside attempts to destabilize societies and governments. In the pluralistic societies that are so often

51

the colonial legacy of many Third World countries, minorities of different tribal, racial or religious castes are frequently those left behind, ignored or persecuted. The successes of other minorities can be the breeding ground for resentment and hostility. Whether neglected, bypassed or envied, minorities remain a seed of conflict unless they are successfully integrated in the national policy

The devastating impact of the economic recession has, of course, only exacerbated these various tensions that threaten world peace. This has been especially severe in the Third World and its effects will continue to be felt there even after the North starts on the road to recovery. Already in several countries, tensions from the recession are beginning to erupt along the fault lines of class, race, religion and ethnic groupings.

Underlying many of these problems also is the rapidity and magnitude of social change which is outstripping the capabilities of our social institutions to adjust to change. Unable to deal with the impact of rapid change in life situations, many people tend to fall back on the traditional and the familiar. The turning anew to religious or spiritual values which we witness everywhere—what Daniel Bell has termed "the return of the sacred"—is in part a response to the pace and scale of social change, in which old established values seem to be crumbling and to have very little relevance to contemporary problems while new value configurations have yet to crystallize.

We would do wrong, however, to explain this increase in religious awareness merely as a harking back to old traditional values, although it has taken that expression in some instances. We need to view this reawakening rather as something intrinsically much more important—as renewed realization that the ultimate meaning of life is of transcendental nature. This heightened religious intensity should lead to higher levels of spirituality. The challenge to people everywhere who live by their religious convictions is how to turn this spiritual reawakening away from narrow reactionary medievalism and channel its energies toward the search for a peaceful and pluralistic global community.

Above all, perhaps, we need to see the many changes occurring, and the tensions they engender, within the whole horrifying context of the power now available to humankind to destroy—deliberately or unintentionally—all human civilization through nuclear holocaust. Taken together with the pace, depth and sweep of change, this constitutes what one could only call a mutation in the human condition.

This mutation fundamentally changes the definition of peace as the absence of war sustained through the threat of mutually-assured destruction. Under the conditions that obtain in the world today, peace of that sort is simply too fragile. We need to learn to deal with change more humanely and adopt peace as a culture and a way of life, not a balance of terror. It must be possible to maintain peace despite the rapid social changes which inevitably breed conflicts. We need to look for new ways to resolve our differences—to delimit and even ritualize conflict. With the weapons of mass destruction which we possess today, in our closely woven condition of inter-dependence, peace is a necessity to the survival of humanity.

Considering the state of human affairs today, religious people need to ponder just how much religious differences have contributed to the problems we currently face in breeding tension and conflict. Like it or not, we have to ask ourselves whether religion has not as often been a part of the problem as it has been part of the solution. The essential message we need to take away from a conference such as this, in my view, is what efforts we should make, together, to help our respective religions, in all their diversity, become a more clearly definable part of the solution to the troubles of this disquieted, competitive and inequitable world. In short, what do we have to offer?

At the core of our efforts, I believe, should be the recognition of religions and religious people that the survival of the human race has now become a very central part of their responsibility, a responsibility requiring loyalties that reach across the boundaries of faiths to the ethic of human solidarity and the brotherhood of man.

All religions speak about peace. But throughout history, religions have often taken us down the road to war. And this is not just a matter of history—there is continuing fresh and bloody evidence of this fact in many parts of the world today. In putative defence of creed, man too often would rather kill than love his brothers of a different faith.

What then should be the responsibility of people of religious conviction in times such as ours—a religiously and culturally pluralistic world, in a process of fundamental and rapid change, where we, for the first time in human history, have the capacity to destroy all human civilization?

Three interlocking sets of concerns assign a new role to the world's religions today: 1) The potential for extinction of humankind with the weapons of mass destruction we now possess; 2) the hunger and poverty which trap hundreds of millions in a life of daily misery and degradation; and, 3) the urgency of managing more wisely and prudently the limited resources of the earth. These define the responsibility of all religions to work for peace and for equitable development of the global security—not just those members of one particular creed. No matter what the validity of any religion's hold on truth, and its charge to bear witness to that truth in conduct and life style, no religion can escape the inevitability of this religiously pluralistic world. All bear responsibility for creating conditions of justice on which peace can rest.

The sorts of concerns that we face today—swelling population pressures on the earth's resources and our limits of existing in conditions of great density, ethical dilemmas raised by advances in biotechnology and microelectronics, and, above all, the threat of nuclear destruction—are of a nature and scale that have begun to escape the religious precepts and ethical norms by which traditionally humankind has lived over the centuries. "Thou shalt not kill" loses much of its meaning in a world where violence has become not only the last, but increasingly the first resort when confronted with seemingly intractable problems. Given the deep-seated and structural nature of problems like poverty and injustice in today's world, charity and compassion—even on an international scale—are simply not enough. From within each of our religions we must devise solutions that are true to the central tenets of each creed but, at the same time, are not incompatible with social arrangements worked out by other religions. This requires that higher levels of religious intensity be matched with higher levels of tolerance in this pluralistic, interdependent world. This is a requirement, it should be noted, that obtains both between and within religions.

While developing higher levels of both spiritual intensity and tolerance might seem paradoxical, this is the challenge we face. It is out of this very tension that we will have to create a more viable, just and peaceful world.

All religions are predicated on the concept of the transcendental significance of human life, although they may differ in their separate meanings of just what this means. For the sake of human survival, religions must learn the utter necessity of learning to live with others who may profess differently.

The responsibility confronting those of us who are religious may be simply put: to seek harmony; harmony within each of our respective religionswhere too often warring cults have diverted our energies; harmony between the various religions of this pluralistic global society; and harmony between those who are religious and those who profess no religion—where the task of the religiously committed person is to seek to demonstrate that religion does, in fact, have the capacity to offer real answers to the many questions that torment the human condition today.

In that light, it is well to remind ourselves that the quest for salvation and redemption is ultimately not a collective, or communal affair, but a profoundly individual and personal one. We should therefore confront squarely the incompatibility between the pursuit of religious values and the pursuit of power. Likewise, the relationship between religion, nationalism and ideology will have to be addressed. The great ideologies of the 19th and 20th centuries appear to have spent their force. New ideologies have emerged in the process of nation-building which followed the post-World War II independence of so many millions from colonialism. But we have yet to define clearly what the relationships of religion to these new ideologies are or should be.

We do know, however, that somehow religions, working together, will have to learn how to shape the world anew. Given our present capacity to destroy all human life, we really have no other choice. We have seen how often religion, with its capacity to bring forth powerful loyalties, has been used by unscrupulous and greedy leaders to serve their own ends. We have also witnessed how easily religion can be used to play on our fears. In today's pluralistic and interdependent world, we need to learn to live, not just down the street from, but among our brothers and sisters of different faiths, in conditions of density where we jostle each other's daily lives intimately. All religions will have to devise new ways to spread the message of "love thy neighbour," however different his belief, to all their adherents.

Particularly with the onset of greater religious intensity, we are challenged to develop, within each of our societies and cultures, the social institutions and arrangements which will make it possible for our religions to live together, in our myriad differences, at higher levels of religious intensity while working towards a single, cohesive, a relatively stable polity. This is a particularly essential element in the process of nation-building and development in the Third World, particularly in those nations with boundaries that are largely legacies of former colonial rulers.

In the face of the convulsions in today's world, our search for better solutions inevitably throws us back on our innermost convictions about the ultimate meaning of life—convictions rooted in our respective religious faiths. It is essential that we differentiate these perceptions of ultimate truth from their cultural and social manifestations over time. The social and cultural differences that have divided us should be seen in historical and not absolute terms.

There is, of course, the inescapable disjunction between faith and history. But the success of the search for new responses to new situations will turn largely on our ability for constant reinterpretation of the basic precepts of our faith without sacrificing their fundamental integrity.

Looking at the troubles of this precious planet we all call home—problems so starkly manifest here in Africa—I believe that one can define four clear contributions that religions have to make to the cause of world peace.

First, they need continually to emphasize that the world is a pluralistic one in which many different ideologies, cultures and beliefs must be allowed to flourish—where, in the view of the Qur'an, the purpose of diversity is to *compete in goodness.*[3]

Second, they must be ready to extend a hand across the boundaries of religion to those, whatever their belief, who are hungry, who are poor, who are victims of injustice. This stresses the importance of empathy, compassion, and the view that all people are equal before God.

Third, religions need to stress the importance of our caring more prudently and widely for this planet and its limited resources. Nature is not only there to be used at the convenience of man—man, rather, is also a part of nature.

Finally, and perhaps most importantly, religions can carry the message that inspires courage and hope: courage, drawn from our faith, to manage our fears and confront the complexity, unpredictability and fulnerability of the modern world; hope, without which the world surely will be lost.

---

3. V:48.

These are not really new causes for most religions. My own faith of Islam, for example, claims no proprietary interest on truth—it casts a special duty upon its adherents to solve the problems the world faces jointly with humankind and not in isolation.[4]

But, let us be honest, most religions have not lived up to these injunctions to practise peace, love and compassion for one's neighbour, and to take care of the earth and its life-support systems. A great deal of soul searching, therefore, is needed within each religion, to rediscover our common spirituality, and recommit ourselves to these timeless commandments, unbounded by the specific particularism of each religion.

It is incumbent on religions to redefine the problems of humanity in their moral, ethical and spiritual dimensions and search for solutions to these problems within that context. This reminds me of a discussion I had with Thomas Merton, the Trappist monk, a few months before he died. As he was on the verge of making a trip to Asia, I asked him why, knowing what he already knew about Asian religions, he wanted to go. He smiled and said: Mankind is in a desperate situation. We need to respond to this challenge. I am doing so, by paraphrasing Karl Marx: Mystics of the World Unite. It should be clear by now that defining humanity's problems merely at the materialistic level, as many present-day political leaders and decision-makers of various ideologies do, is a dead-end street. This, I believe, was what André Malraux meant by his remark that the 21st century would be a religious century—or there would be no 21st century.

There are, to be sure, many deep doubts expressed about the potential of religions as our guide to the new kind of world in which we must co-exist, or perish, in the 21st century. While religions have fashioned deep commitments to their own respective communities of the faith, they have also been a divisive force in the affairs of humankind. In the present state of the human condition, the religions of the world must now be the unifiers of the human race by coming together in the cause of peace and justice for all its members.

At the United Nations University, we are exploring the rôle that the major religions might play in helping shape coherent visions of viable futures in a pluralistic but interdependent world. Thus, we are hoping to contribute to the process of reflection that will help in building more appropriate responses to the major challenges the world faces today—responses grounded in ethical and moral reasoning that are consonant within faiths and across faiths. Our interests are, therefore, very much in common with the aims of this World Conference on Religion and Peace and we will be following the outcome of the discussions here with a great deal of interest. We must approach our deliberations of the rôle religion has to play in bringing us together in the cause of peace with the utmost sincerity and relentless honesty—labouring under no self-delusions.

---

4. III:110, II:143.

Above all we need humility of the mind in submission to God's will. As the Qur'an tells us—in a passage meant specifically to reach out to all known religious communities:

"Say: O People
Of the Book! come
To common terms
As between us and you;
That we worship
None but God;
That we associate
No partners with Him;
That we erect not,
From among ourselves,
Lords and patrons
Other than God."[5]

---

5. V:48.

12

Some Projects for International WCRP Sponsorship

By Archbishop Francis Arinze*

The World Conference on Religion and Peace is one of the precious gifts of God to the world of our time. It is a significant achievement in inter-faith dialogue, in mutual collaboration between believers of various religions to promote peace, and in the promotion of mutual understanding through the process of working together, not through the process of merely intellectual debates.

Religion makes a fundamental and irreplaceable contribution to peace. The working out of true, just and lasting peace cannot be entirely the work of governments, disarmament talks and inter-governmental commissions and committees. These have their importance which is undeniable. But even more important than such initiatives is that contribution which religion makes or should make. Peace must begin with interior conversion of heart, with spiritual and mental attitudes, with ideas on the origin, worth, dignity and destiny of the human person, and with a philosophy of life which gives meaning, synthesis and direction to human existence on earth. Religion does all this. Jesus Christ said to His Apostles: "Peace I bequeath to you, my own peace I give you, a peace the world cannot give, this is my gift to you." (Jn. 14:27) And the prophet Isaiah calls Christ: "Prince of Peace. Wide is his dominion in a peace that has no end." (Is. 9:6-7)

Religion is one of the deepest motive forces of human action. Our religious convictions, attitudes, sensitivities and prejudices do influence to a great extent our approach to questions of the day. Religion underlies many of our attitudes. It is therefore an important contributory factor to decisions.

---

* Archbishop Francis Arinze is President of the Vatican Secretariat for Non-Christians; in 1985 he was appointed Cardinal.

May I therefore mention three particular projects which seem to me to merit the sponsorship of the International World Conference on Religion and Peace. These projects rotate around human dignity and rights, together with their protection.

Interracial Harmony

It is a fact of human existence that there are many races on earth. Time was when people of each race lived all by themselves in splendid isolation from all other races. Those times are now long over.

Today we find people of various races not only in the large cities such as New York, London, Rome, Paris, Cairo, Nairobi, Lagos, Kinshasa, Singapore, Melbourne, Rio de Janeiro, Mexico City, and Montreal, but also in cities of smaller size.

In many technologically more advanced countries of Europe there is a growing inflow of people of other races and cultures who seek better paid work and higher living conditions. The larger cities and industrial centres of the Third World countries attract especially young and middle-aged people of various races who are in quest of work and amenities of modern life and who are running away from agriculture.

Racial conflicts are not unknown. Attracting less attention from the mass media, but not any less significant, are the difficulties of interaction, adjustment, preservation of the best elements in one's own culture, and fashioning of a sense of loyalty to the country. Ethnicism, tribalism, closed group mentality and behaviour, or whatever other name we wish to give to this failure at interracial harmony, does injury to human dignity, rights and solidarity. WCRP should sponsor projects aimed at solving, or at least reducing, this problem.

Untouchability, Caste, Social Rejection

A second wound on human brotherhood is that attitude of avoidance of a group of fellow human beings which sets itself up as an institution, as a whole attitude in life. Some human persons are regarded by some others as being of lower class. Social relations with them such as marriage, clubs, visits, feasts, meals together, and even friendship, are avoided.

Well known forms of this social discrimination are the treatment given to those called Untouchables in India or to those of lower caste. But this prejudice also exists in varying form in other parts of Asia and in Africa. There are parts of Africa where a group of people and all their descendants are avoided by the rest of society especially in marriage relationships. Lesser forms of this human prejudice and injustice can be traced even among seemingly advanced countries.

Religion must come to the rescue. WCRP can help, for example, by appointing a commission to keep it constantly informed of the situation in various countries, by appropriate action to precipitate change of attitudes, by appeal to the interested governments, and by direct help to some victims of this unjust treatment.

Apartheid

In South Africa discrimination against people because of their race and colour assumes the ugly shape of government policy. Apartheid is given the status of a way of life. Effort is made to justify it as separate development. Religion is even sometimes invoked as a justification.

But we cannot avoid the simple truth that all human beings are created by God, that we all are persons and that we have certain God-given dignity and rights. It follows that all human beings must be given the opportunity, freedom and resources to exercise responsibility for their lives and to relate to it their fellow human beings. Discrimination on the basis of race is wrong. Religion is morally and fundamentally opposed to apartheid. As the Second Vatican Council says:

"We cannot in truthfulness call upon that God who is the Father of all, if we refuse to act in a brotherly way towards certain men, created though they be to God's image. A man's relationship with God the Father and his relationship with his brother men are so linked together that, as Scripture says: 'He who does not love does not know God.' (I Jn. 4:8) As a consequence, the Church rejects, as foreign to the mind of Christ, any discrimination against men or harassment of them because of their race, colour, condition of life and religion." (Vatican II: Declaration on the Relationship of the Church to Non-Christian Religions, n. 5)

WCRP can help by encouraging appropriate action within each particular religious community, by promoting or supporting shared action between various religious communities, by encouraging initiatives of religious people and human rights and peace movements, and by helping religious people to help victims of apartheid.

Conclusion

Religion based on belief and worship must lead on to action. Violations of human rights and dignity are offences against love and justice. Peace cannot be built upon foundations of negation of love and justice. The golden rule is extolled by all religions. Jesus Christ tells his followers: "So always treat others as you would like them to treat you: that is the meaning of the Law and the Prophets." (Mt. 7:12) Love is the law of Christ: "This is my commandment: love one another, as I have loved you." (Jn. 15:12) And this love is built on justice, giving each one his due, respecting the dignity and rights of each fellow human being. Violations of human rights and dignity call from religious persons appropriate response. And who of us will refuse to make his contribution?

13

People of Faith
Working Together for Peace:
Which Road to the Future?

By Rabbi Alexander M. Schindler*

(DELIVERED BY DR. JANE EVANS)

Recently there was published in the United States by two historians a book entitled "Which Road to the Past?" One author is a cliometrician, a person dedicated to statistical data as the valid interpreter of all our yesterdays. The other author is a traditionalist who upholds the older school of historical belief that a contemporary statistical approach cannot portray nor understand all the shades and vagaries of humanity's past. For us, as persons of religion from many countries and differing faiths as well as varied ethnic, cultural, economic and political backgrounds, "Which Road to the Future?" may be of far greater concern than "Which Road to the Past?"

Of course this is not meant to deny the significance of our respective and often uniquely separate historical roots. We all know the adage that he or she who denies or ignores the past is doomed to repeat its mistakes. But surely living in the midst of the enormous complexities, paradoxes and, yes, conflicts, of the modern world, we are deeply concerned about shaping the future. We even dare to ask ourselves, in a world threatened with the ultimate mushroom cloud of atomic destruction or with hydrogen bombs or war from or in space, or chemical or biological atrocities, whether there is a future for fragile planet Earth and all of us, its vulnerable inhabitants.

---

* Rabbi Alexander Schindler is President of the Union of American Hebrew Congregations in New York City, USA. (See biographies of delegates for information on Dr. Jane Evans.)

But surely religion, and this is true of my faith of Judaism, inspires and lays upon us the burden or, shall we say, the duty of hope and action. By itself hope is an energizer but it is only deeply meaningful if we use it cemented to realistic effort to change for the better that which we see needs change.

What, then, are the tasks of people of faith working for peace? First and always it is to develop our personal sense of spirituality through study and adherence to the disciplines of our particular religion when dedicated to the welfare of others. Next, to go beyond tolerance of differences to understanding and fully felt respect, to the end of genuine cooperation toward mutual goals. These must be sought with courage and conviction, in a world of pluralism.

In these co-operative endeavours we need not demand an ideological consensus before we proceed to work together. It is sufficient that we agree on a common goal. Thus, for instance, Reform Jews in the United States are members of a variety of coalitions on different issues in none of which we seek one hundred percent ideological purity. Thus, we disagree on the Middle East with the National Council of Churches on its support of the P.L.O. but we work with them on free choice on abortion, strategic arms limitations and a host of other significant issues. We disagree with the Roman Catholic Bishops on abortion and birth control but we unite with them to give voice to a common concern on aid to refugees, world hunger and racial justice. Indeed, at our 1983 great convention of Reform Judaism our highest honour, named for Rabbi Eisendrath—the Maurice N. Eisendrath Bearer of Light Award—was presented to the Catholic Bishops of the United States for their superb effort for nuclear disarmament and peace.

This last subject, nuclear disarmament, is certainly a task in which all the religious groups of the world can join. The unchecked proliferation of these arms is surely the gravest, most imminent threat to human survival. It is a madness which shatters the mind, when the arsenal of overkill weapons is so large that the land and sea-based missiles of the Soviet Union and the United States can destroy 150 cities of these respective continents 50 times each. It is a madness when the combined nuclear arsenal of these powers has the destructive capacity to target three tons of TNT on each and every one of the four billion human beings on earth. It is a madness when we have enough deadly nerve agents to kill 100 billion people, that is to say, to wipe out the world's population not once but 30 times over. It is a madness which we as the leaders of the world's religions should jointly resolve to bring to its end.

But before going further, it is necessary I fear for all of us to face a number of painful facts. No people, no religion, no nation, is untainted in the areas of war, turbulence, conflict and violation of rights. As a rabbi, deeply devoted to and appreciative of the states of Israel, and without tracing too much of history, I am keenly aware that there are Jewish persons, both within and without Israel, who are opposed to many of her policies on the West Bank as well as to her rôle in Lebanon.

This latter is true in the face of involvement of other nations and, tragically, the religious and economic battles between Lebanon's own groups.

But despite much misunderstanding of Israel, let us never forget the splendid contributions she has made to hundreds of persons annually from this very continent of Africa where we are meeting. Black students over the years have been educated in Israel's universities and technical institutes, to return to advance their respective peoples of Africa. To note only one centre, the Mt. Carmel International Center for Community Services has prepared black African students for numbers of diversified tasks in their countries. And Israel has indeed expertise to offer. In her Foreign Ministry there is a Department of Co-operation which upon request freely extends Israel's specialized experience and knowledge to development, in agriculture and food production, in training doctors, nurses and health technicians in Israel's medical centres. On an informal, rather than formal basis, much cooperation does indeed exist between Israel and many African nations.

Here in Nairobi there is in residence a member of the Permanent Mission of Israel to the United Nations working on the UN Environmental Programme.

Which road to the future? Certainly there is one with many branches for religionists and which requires co-operative effort to overcome often great obstacles. Let me partially recapitulate and expand our thought without needlessly trespassing on speakers and subjects to follow:

1. People of faith must work together to deepen their own spirituality and commitment to the highest levels of understanding of their own religious insights in a world of pluralism.

2. Volunteerism and co-operation in many fields of human rights, justice and peace may yet reduce areas which breed conflict that thwart peace.

3. Together, as well as singly, people of faiths must have the courage to speak out when necessary against actions of governments or groups or individuals. Speaking truth to power, even when it seems a lost cause is essential. In the words of the French essayist Montaigne, "There are some defeats more glorious than victories."

4. People of faith, both co-operatively and within their respective religions, must be deeply concerned about the often wide gaps between the positions for peace of their leaders and the differing positions and actions of their followers. Conversely, there are times when the followers or "grass roots," as they are referred to in some countries, are more right than leaders. Then they must educate or oppose their leaders or find by non-violent means new ones.

5. Many, especially Jews, are deeply disappointed and distressed by various diatribes against Israel in the United Nations. Yet there are more non-political successes of the UN, especially through its Specialized Agencies, than are recognized. The world would be the worse if there were not a United Nations. Persons of faith have many opportuni-

ties through Non-Governmental Observers accredited to the world organization to be a bridge between peoples and the UN. Their voices must be raised in defence of their own and other groups and needs. 6. And now I touch on another sensitive point: If we would work together for peace—if we wish to make the Voice of Religion truly significant in a world trembling above an abyss—there can be no holy wars, no denial of human dignity, no breaking down of the too thin veneer of civilization through justifying on grounds of following orders or any other basis, a repetition of genocide or the denial of emigration to any people nor the lack of welcome by others. There must be no refugees and no borders across which citizens may not voluntarily leave a nation.

The Prophets of Israel, whose words are recorded in the Bible, lived in the period which began in the eighth century (750) before the Common Era. Many of the truths they proclaimed are as valid now as then, despite the vast differences of time and surroundings. Their teachings challenge us relentlessly: "Seek peace and pursue it." Or, Jeremiah crying:

"My heart moans within me
I cannot be silent;
For I hear the blare of horns,
Alarms of war."

People of faith must together struggle against the arms race, must turn the vast expenditures on arms from preparations for war to preparation for peace. The child killed by a conventional bullet is as dead as the larger numbers destroyed by atomic weaponry. But lack of war, whether conventional or otherwise, by itself does not spell a true peace. The real task of people of faith is to work and be, simultaneously, on many fronts—developing and advancing the dynamics of peace. In the meetings of this conference, in the Commissions and various sessions, there will be opportunities for all to participate in exploring these dynamics. If we succeed both here and later among our constituents then truly the word or the gun or the bomb shall not come further into the world because of justice delayed or justice denied. Rather, at last, the dream of peace shall not turn to ashes but will be a new reality for the advance of humankind.

14

Religion and Peace

By Ven. Dr. Kàkkàpalliye Anaruddha Thera*

I consider it a great privilege and an honour to have been invited to speak a few words at this august Assembly. This Conference presents a unique opportunity for people professing diverse faiths to meet on a common platform and discuss topics of mutual interest. The theme of this discussion being Religion and Peace, it is essential that we should first have a clear idea of what these terms signify. Religion does not confine itself to the mere observance of rites and rituals guided by a set of beliefs. It means much more because it refers to a way of life that stimulates and guides a person to a good life. The practice of a good life consists of "Samacariyà," which means harmonious, peaceful living with one's fellow beings. The word peace means not the mere absence of strife but a positive state of harmony among people. It is therefore clear that both religion and peace are inseparably connected with the welfare of human beings.

The Buddha has always shown equal compassion and kindness towards all living beings whatever species they belong to. Yet he has acknowledged that human beings occupy the most important place among all living beings. He has declared that being born a human is one of the most difficult achievements (*Kicchomanussa-patilàbho—Dhammapada*) and that birth as a human being is one of the rarest events (*Dullabham manussattam*). The human life is of tremendous worth as it is only man who has the capacity and the possibility of gaining the highest state of perfection. This is why human life is considered the highest in the teachings of the Buddha.

I wish to cite here a Buddhist story which illustrates the inestimable value of human life. The two clans, the Sakyas and the Koliyas, who were both relatives of the Buddha, had their kingdoms on either side of

---

* Ven. Anaruddha Thera is Vice-Chancellor of the Buddhist and Pali University in Colombo, Sri Lanka.

river Rohini in India. The normal practice of the two clans was to divide the water in the river amicably for agricultural purposes. During a particular year a severe drought brought down the level of water in the river and each clan decided to use the available water without allowing the other's normal share. This resulted in a confrontation between the two clans. The Buddha, seeing the warriors of the two clans assembled on each side of the river, came there and enquired what they were preparing for. Each party said that they were compelled to wage war as no compromise was possible. The Buddha asked the leaders of each clan how much they wished to gain by getting the water for themselves, and each of them gave an estimate of what they would gain. When the Buddha asked them what they considered to be the value of a human being, killed in war, the leaders of both clans said that the worth of a human being is inestimable. The Buddha then asked them what they considered to be of greater worth, water or human life. When they answered in unison that the human life is of greater worth the Buddha made them realise how foolish it is to destroy a thing of inestimable value for the sake of something that is of estimable value.

Buddhism does not speak of man's supremacy over any other species of living beings. Yet it stresses man's superiority over all others. Therefore it devolves on him to live in harmony not only with his own species, but also with all other living things.

Buddhism also recognizes the oneness of the human species. Buddha says that, unlike the case of different species of plants and different species of animals, there are no biological differences of genus among human beings. (*"lingam jàtimayam tesam, aññamaññahi jàtiyo"*—Sutta Nipàta). From the biological point of view all men belong to one species. Whether they live in the West or in the East, whether they live in the Arctic or in the Antarctic, the differences are only in colour, hair form, the shape of the head or the shape of the nose. Buddhism thus emphasizes the oneness of mankind and urges all men to be treated as members of one family irrespective of caste, creed or colour.

War begins in the minds of men. According to Buddhism lust (*lobha*), hatred (*dosa*), and ignorance (*moha*) are the primary causes of all evil actions including war. The only achievement of war, if it can be called an achievement, is the destruction of life and property. Those who survive in war will rise up again to destroy and to be destroyed. This shows that man can never be subjugated. Buddha says that the aggressor begets aggression (*"hantam labhati hantàram"*—Samyutta Nikàya). Every man has his own dignity which should be recognised and respected.

The necessary environment for the realisation of this ideal could be created through a re-orientation of the content and method of education. It is of course true that general and technical education has taken vast strides towards secular progress. But we notice with regret that the same is not true of religious and moral education.

Whatever doctrinal differences there may be among the various forms of religion they all attempt to lead men away from evil and direct them in the path of righteousness. May I suggest, therefore, that we use this Assembly as a forum for making a concerted effort at evolving a common programme of action to ensure peace and happiness among all men.

While thanking you for the patient hearing given me, I should also sincerely thank the organisers for affording me this opportunity of speaking a few words today. Let me conclude my speech with a saying of the Buddha: "Victory breeds hatred; the vanquished live in sorrow. The peaceful live in harmony giving up both victory and defeat." Thank you.

15

Accepting the Truth of Suffering and Avoiding its Danger

By the Most Ven. Phra Bimaladhamma*

It is a great honour and privilege to have been invited to participate in this Fourth World Conference on Religion and Peace. I must praise the organizers of this conference in bringing together religious leaders from all parts of the globe to meet in this beautiful city of Nairobi in an atmosphere of friendship and peaceful co-operation. I am pleased to be among you and congratulate you on your righteous action in the arrangement of such an important World Conference. The success of this conference will help to create a feeling of loving-kindness among the peoples of different faith and ideology and attempt to achieve World Peace.

Once again I wish to thank the Secretary-General, Dr. John B. Taylor, who has arranged for my participation in this conference to contribute in a small way towards its success.

It is the nature of things that all human beings who are born on this earth, though they may be of different nationalities and be of different faiths and religions, their bodies and minds are similar. They are the products of the same God who creates all creatures. We have to live together on the same planet. There should not be any reason for us to think that we differ from each other. This ideal is the basis of different religions to understand and love each other sincerely. We are all the same.

My dear brethren, we, the delegates from Thailand, believe that all human beings, though we may be of different religions, believe in different creeds and vary in the colour of our skins, yet we have the same objectives; that is not to be the evil-doer, to perform only good and to

---

* Ven. Phra Bimaladhamma is President of Mahachulangkorn University in Bangkok, Thailand.

purify our minds from all defilements. This is the same basic truth for all religions. It cannot be changed and no one can escape from this natural course of events; each being on earth will live his life-span, some may have long lives, some may have very short lives, some may have happy lives and some miserable. All these differences are due to their deeds and all will die in the end. Those who have done good will prosper, those who have done evil will suffer. This law of truth is justifiable. The prophets of all religions have found this law of truth and teach their followers in accordance with their ability and surroundings. We, therefore, wear different garments for different religions. If I were to take off my robes and you to take off your clothes, then the appearance of our bodies would be the same. I, therefore, can say that we are all brothers and sisters who have to co-operate and work together harmoniously and strive to convince our brothers and sisters who are quarrelling, fighting and even making war in many corners of the world to stop these silly deeds and come to their good senses and live in harmony.

Quarrelling, fighting, making war and disharmony are the causes of suffering. Loving kindness and harmony result in prosperity and happiness.

We have assembled here to discuss ways and means toward accomplishing a durable peace in the world. It is not the objective of any religion to divide people into religions, nationality or political groups or parties and quarrel among themselves. Quarrelling, fighting and making war are due to ignorance. We must have sincere co-operation and strive towards the destruction of ignorance and thus bring forth the true meaning of religion. We must try to lead them on to the right path of thinking, which cannot be done by force, but only through the realization of truth.

The religious goal is to teach people to accept the truth of suffering and to avoid its danger. We practise meditation to reduce suffering and to escape from it in the end. We should not quarrel or kill one another. This is not the aim of any religion nor does it present the possibility of a pleasant future.

My dear brethren, we must try to bring peace to the world by destroying ignorance, trying to practise the true meaning of religious teaching and then all humanity will understand loving-kindness and harmony and live in peaceful co-existence.

May all be well and happy.

C.

Addresses on "Human Dignity, Social Justice and Development of the Whole Person"

16

Introduction to the Theme, Human Dignity, Social Justice and Development of the Whole Person

By Sri R. R. Diwakar*

You might remember that Gandhi's first fight began in South Africa, in this very continent, on the matter of human dignity. Why should a human being here, coming from India and working here, not be looked upon as any other human being? This is not a question of mere status or anything of that kind, but a dignity which is due to human beings. I may here refer to the principle of the Chinese. The Chinese, centuries before Buddha, thought that the whole universe, and everything in the universe, even an atom, were all marching towards perfection; and therefore if we cannot help them, let us at least not come in their way. This is how the principle of non-violence was first recognized by Ashoka, and for the next 40 years he saw to it that there was absolutely no war in the whole continent of India.

It is not enough if a man simply lives. There is a human rights convention and life has to be dignified. The second thing is social justice. Social justice includes, naturally, social, economic and political justice. We must cry out against all kinds of exploitation by privileged classes. The third thing, development, is the most important; but not only economic development. When a human child is born, it is not merely for the sake of economics. It might be a great poet, it might be a great administrator, it might be an inventor, it might be a benefactor of the whole of humanity. Development includes all these different aspects of a

---

* Sri R. R. Diwakar is Chairman of the Gandhi Peace Foundation, with its headquarters in New Delhi, India.

human being. So human development must include all these potentialities and equal opportunity ought to be given to all these people. Today we have advanced in science and technology, but science and technology are not taking into consideration what I call the moral considerations, the good of all, that is the concern about the good of all people, and today mere humanism is not enough; we have to look into what is called ecological humanism. Unless the ecology of the whole of humanity, and the whole of the earth is healthy, it is not possible for many to live any longer. Mere humanism was once the religion, so to say, of all people who thought rationally about humanity and its future, but today, it is ecological humanism. It is everything round about man: earth, water, forest, and air have to be healthy so that they may promote humanity. Everything has to be healthy in order that human beings also may be healthy.

I am not at all despairing about what is called this potential holocaust. No doubt the fear is there, but I should say that it was the great warlords who fought for six years who, with their hands still covered with blood, sat together and drew up the Charter of the United Nations. It was not Gandhi who wrote the Charter, it was not Tolstoi who wrote the Charter, it was not the pacifists who wrote the Charter, it was these warlords who thought that now we should see that a world without war comes into existence. I think there was the spark of God, there was a light which shone in the hearts of all these people; they thought that there should be an organization here which would be called the United Nations Organization.

If you look at the whole sociology of humanity, from the cavemen of millions of years ago, through cannibalism, through village life, through city life, we are today four and a half billion human beings living in over 150 nations and with the United Nations Organization to give us some direction. The times may be dark, but the eclipse will go away, the sun will shine as bright as ever, because the sunshine of God is in the heart of every one of us ...

74

17

Human Dignity, Social Justice and Development of the Whole Person

By Dr. Adamou Ndam Njoya*

The Fundamental Problem of Ethics of Values

Any action in favour of world peace, especially if such action is undertaken by religious bodies, leads to the heart of the question of ethics and values as the underlying and dynamics of human undertakings, at the concrete level of ideas as well as the level of concrete actions. The whole problem of human dignity and world peace lies in ethics and values: how can these be attained? Such is the fundamental question for an institution in favour of peace such as the World Conference on Religions which is founded on the uplifting of the humane and striving for the triumph of the humane side of man and society.

These issues of ethics and values as the driving forces underlying human endeavours involve other equally essential questions; they are relating those to the ways and methods of actions of making human dignity, social justice and the advancement of the whole human being a profound reality in our world today. The basic problem facing our institution and ourselves as individuals and participants directly involved in the field is, therefore, to carry out the role of conception and implementation; in other words, to come up with principles and standards which will correspond to realities and given situations, and then to determine the mechanisms by which such principles and standards can be expressed in action. Therein lies, clearly laid out, the direction of our search, if we intend to come up with positive and concrete results at the end of our Fourth Assembly.

---

* Dr. Adamou Ndam Njoya, former Minister of Education, Foreign Affairs and Administration Reform, is Plenipotentiary Minister of Cameroun.

Awareness of Man's Dual Nature: Generosity and Selfishness
    As we settle down to work, there is a good reason to bear in mind that human actions, which require an ethical basis, are strongly marked by man's dual nature: generosity and selfishness. Selfishness, which comes easier, outweighs Generosity which requires an effort and demands that we put ourselves in the place of the other person and submit to self-sacrifice. This overriding selfishness leads to what we would term the phenomenon of the "situated" state which, in turn, creates the situated Man, and the situated society, that is, closed in itself and concerned, first of all, with the ascendancy of its own interests first. And very often, it is to defend this situated man and situated society that barriers are raised and acts contrary to human dignity, social and the advancement of the whole human being are committed.

The Content and Method of our Investigations
    The preceding section gives us an idea of the content of our reflections on this sub-theme and on how to achieve results which would generate direct or indirect action to create situations in which human dignity, social justice and the advancement of the whole human being shall triumph in a world where aggressiveness in man and society is continuously on the rise.
    What is important to our investigations, to achieve this, is to outline the evil as it manifests itself in real situations, so as better to fight it. To this end, and within the framework of an organization such as ours, what is more fundamental than to determine, on the one hand, the most appropriate strategies, ideas and actions and, on the other hand, the mechanisms by which they can be put into concrete form within our Conference, in its regional and national branches, and amongst ourselves as members of this Conference?
    This is precisely what we shall attempt through the following three points:

A) HOW CAN WE ACHIEVE RELIGIOUS AND IDEOLOGICAL TOLER-ANCE AS A VITAL CONTRIBUTION TOWARD A HUMANE SOCIETY AND RESPECT FOR HUMAN RIGHTS?

B) WHAT CAN BE DONE AGAINST THE CONTINUOUS VIOLATION OF ECONOMIC AND POLITICAL RIGHTS AND THE INCREASING NUMBER OF REFUGEES AROUND THE WORLD?

C) HOW CAN TECHNOLOGY AND DEVELOPMENT BE HUMANIZED, NOT ONLY IN ECONOMIC TERMS BUT ALSO IN CULTURAL AND SPIRITUAL TERMS?

Here lies what we shall try to do:

1) *Understand the difference between religion and ideology and, first of all, recognize the finality which is the humane*

    Such is the first goal we must endeavour to buckle down to. The problem of tolerance is fundamental and, together with its solution, constitutes the starting point for dialogue and understanding. Therefore, there is a good reason to find out from amongst men and people, whether the development of ideologies, with their often violent and revolutionary manifestations, has not been due to the breakdown of values, especially religious values that encourage solidarity amongst men. There is no doubt that such has been, and still is, the case, in so far as some religious leaders have often had to transform their religions into real ideologies in favour of certain selfish interests. This has only served to strengthen the phenomena of the situated man and the situated society, which generate often open aggressiveness, tension and conflicts, whereas religions appeal to the humane aspect and the essence of man, and basically allow no room for constraint. This is what, for example, the Muslim religion, which we practise, teaches us. Furthermore, to encourage acts of constraint in religion is like trying to be God's substitute. When He tells us in the Bible that He created man in His own image, or when He says in the Qur'an that He has made His lieutenant on earth, God is actually inviting us to exercise tolerance and solidarity.

He is referring to Man, the whole human being. He also says in the Qur'an that, had He so wished, He could have made us all one people; this is implicitly understood in all religions when we become aware of the Divine Almighty.

Religion thus stands out as an essential asset in bringing people together. And to proceed by any other means than explaining, teaching and setting the example is to go against divine prescriptions, an attempt to take the place of God. This view differs fundamentally from ideologies which develop as a reaction to certain situations and are basically characterized by constraint. The idea of force is always present behind ideologies, but since they strive for the well-being of man and the blossoming of society (though primarily within a situated framework), we find here starting elements for dialogue, understanding and tolerance. In other words, when dealing with religious and ideological tolerance, and working toward achieving it, our ideas and actions must bear essentially on the objective to be attained. This objective, all things considered, is one and the same, in so far as man and his happiness are the target of all religious and ideological concerns, although religion reaches beyond earthly realities.

In our reflections, we should first all realize that the men who act on behalf of both religion and ideology are deeply marked by prejudices, have specific concerns, and have achieved some results. From this we can establish a lasting basis for tolerance and dialogue, and set up conditions for working together and toward an understanding of the human being who is the ultimate goal for all of us.

2) *To outline the elements for an education which forges values in the face of the aggressiveness of the situated society*

How can this be done? This brings us to the very question of what formulae are to be developed to contribute to the genesis and continued existence of the state of mind that is tolerance—that would do away with confrontations and violent conflict and thus give room for dialogue amongst ideological entities on one hand, and between ideological and religious entities on the other hand. Since man's being and his mental environment must undergo a profound change, and the humane aspect of many be recognized and made to stand out, the only way to proceed is through education. In fact, it is through education that man and society acquire and transform values; our perception of the human being and our approach to his development is a view of the triumph of humaneness in man and society and should, therefore, pass through education.

The Humane Beyond National Boundaries

In the first place, everything leads to the humane. All rulers proclaim themselves in favour of the human being, but generally, in the reality the human being in question is actually the one enclosed within the exclusive framework of the state; preference is given to nationals within boundaries, and this is not fully in keeping with the meaning of human dignity. First of all, through the phenomenon of the situated man, it creates a source of aggressiveness against all that does not obey the principles and rules of the situated environment. Secondly; it leads to the internal regimentation of men, everything being related to man as seen through the phenomenon of the situated state. You either play along or are eliminated. All this is fertile ground for seeds of internal tensions which assume other proportions when it comes to dealings with other states that do not share the same aspirations or ideologies. And, on the whole, aggressiveness tends to be a mechanism of self-defence. This phenomenon must be well understood for us to strive for human dignity, social justice and the development of the whole human being, all of which require that the human be viewed without national or State boundaries. It is most fundamental, especially as boundary issues have often been raised through the actions of religious officials who, as history shows us and as we witness today in various regions of the world, thus contribute to increasing tensions and conflicts, even in areas where elements of civilization rooted in the past are such as could enable certain conflicts to be overcome.

Since this can occur within a given religion, amongst various religions and in the relations between countries, and leads to blind power struggles and a whole series of constraints which reduce man to the rank of animals, our objective should be to break away from such boundary issues and arrive at expressing human dignity by striving for an atmosphere of togetherness; this would strengthen the awareness of humaneness in man and society. This is the fundamental issue: to engineer the victory and predominance of the awareness of humaneness in man. Thus can the triumph of human dignity, social justice and the advancement of the whole human being be achieved.

Methods and Formulae for Action

For speeches and the actions to be applied to attain this goal, we require a set of methods and formulae to be released by believers—by men—and applied by them in their lives and their dealings with other men. To draw up these methods and new formulae, it would be necessary, within each spiritual family and in the relations between spiritual families, to examine the past and the present to see what makes human dignity, social justice, and the development of the whole human being such a serious problem. So proceeding to such a study is, in itself, already a formula and a method—two highly positive factors; highly positive because they urge us toward our goal, which is to break away from the overriding phenomenon of the situated man and the situated society. In fact, changes in mentality can be generated by critically analysing ourselves, each spiritual family or the ties binding spiritual families. And as long as the goal—human dignity, social justice, and the advancement of the whole human being—is accepted and proves to be a priority, the likelihood is that such changes will be irreversible. This is all the more important in that the changes shall take place at different levels: in individuals and institutions where the analysis is done.

Such analysis shall provide concrete elements and the basis of information and education which are the primary and basic formula for attaining our goals. Fresh ideas, new lines of thought and solid grounds for action shall spring from these analyses, questions and reflections. They can be applied by those who do the analysing, then transmitted to others in a much wider circle.

Investigations will also generate greater awareness of the predominance of the phenomenon of the situated man and the situated society. This phenomenon of the situated man and the situated society is detrimental; it leads to violations of rights, because perversity and selfishness in man are mor active and stronger than generosity.

The weak points in the establishment and recognition of man's humane duties shall also become more obvious. This cannot but facilitate our task of emphasizing and making it possible to highlight humaneness and generosity, for a positive and progressive dynamism in favour of a breakaway from the enclosure of the situated environment; we would then be able to view human rights from an angle which obliterates any idea of enclosure within a specific system. That is how, through a series of concrete actions which will be a consequence, or even through intellectual, cultural, and spiritual activities that shall be developed, we can create ideal conditions for humanization. This is indispensable, more so as our world today has fitted itself with mechanisms for violating rights, in varying degrees and subtleties that can be easily seen on the human rights' violations chart.

After outlining the means to attain tolerance for the advent of a more humane society in which human rights shall come first, it is necessary, in the perspective of the goal of our Conference, to see how we can analyse and understand these violations so as better to determine what should be done to correct current practices. In this light, our immediate and essential task, as mentioned above, is to come up with strategies and ideas for action and the mechanism for implementing such action in the field. This is what we shall attempt to do in the next section.

B) WHAT CAN BE DONE AGAINST THE CONTINUOUS VIOLATION OF ECONOMIC AND POLITICAL RIGHTS AND THE INCREASING NUMBER OF REFUGEES AROUND THE WORLD?

Within the present scope of our discussions, the question is not to proceed to an analysis of the various political and economic rights violations and the refugee situation in the world; we should, however, bear in mind that this will have to be done because it will have to be included in the programme of future action of our institution, notwithstanding the clear fact that other institutions that are concerned with the same problem would be working on it. We will thus avoid duplication of effort and concentrate on an original and longer-lasting achievement laying emphasis on the basics in the values that characterize religions. This could even lead to the drawing up of a geographical map indicating human rights violations and the refugee situation in the world; this we can and must objectively do, in accordance with the religious dictates of our conscience. God is truth; He wants us to act with truth, clarity and openness, and not hypocrisy, for only then can we best detect and face up to wrongdoing, and correct it. But for now, we have to outline the origins and roots of this evil in order to know where to act within our Conference as a universal, regional, and national institution, and also amongst us individuals, active members or supporters. The essential thing therefore is to determine the means and directives for such action, so as to go one step further than what has been achieved so far and to do what should be done.

Ways of Action in the Face of Violations Which are Phenomena of the Humane and of the Society

It is a fundamental matter to recognize first of all the fact that violations of political and economic rights and the increase in the number of refugees around the world are basically the direct result of selfishness and, consequently, of the accompanying phenomenon of the situated man and situated society. Indeed, selfishness in man becomes that of society through the actions of men, who may be rulers or who, as citizens, are able to determine and direct the actions of rulers. Violations of political and economic rights and the reasons for the refugee situation must therefore be examined in man and within social structures so as to determine the actions and remedies we are concerned with. Internal problems arising from the management and administration of society often generate tension, and even open conflicts, which result in violations of rights and all types of confrontation. Such situations arise in varying degrees and are most serious where there are no signs of democracy requiring a responsible individual to take part in running matters of public interest through free choice and not to be harassed because of the consequences of his choice.

This brings us to the matter we are concerned with: to determine lines of action aimed at putting an end to these evils. Convinced, as all of us here must be, of the need to take such action, and given the commitment of our Conference to that end, we can lay down directives and concrete lines of action which would affect both man and society. For this, there is one requirement: to undertake objective studies of the phenomenon, using the stimulating religious values in us. We should try and understand what leads to these violations of rights and the increase in the number of refugees in various regions of the world. In this approach, we should avoid blunt verbal condemnations and controversies. Instead, in the light of sustained actions to be carried out, we should identify those factors that are responsible for the perpetration of the evil we are dealing with, always bearing in mind that a human phenomenon linked to the personality of man is involved, and that any remedial action in that direction should bear on men and their personalities. Of course, we should also note the negative effect of this evil on man and society, and the permanent threat it represents for peace.

The fact that all regions of the world are represented within our Conference allows for optimism in the results and the quality of such studies which would make it possible to draw up an accurate geographical map. As believers, we must delve deeper into the issue; we should not seek to find the phenomenon in our neighbour and forget what happens inside us and in oneself.

Remedies by education, information, and promotion of the sense of responsibility

As we carry out objective studies on the violations of rights, we should also think of means of concrete action to correct this state of affairs. Thus, because the evils in question are related to man and to his personality, which rebounds on society, we can say that two ways of action are called for: education and making man more responsible. These ways of action actually place us in line with the principles shared by all religions, and are thus the right ground for action which shall depend on the characteristics of the environment and the sensitivities of the existing political systems or on rulers; formulae have to be devised, depending on the situation. In our discussions, we can only outline the factors that favour such an enterprise, and determine the basic orientations involved.

Without dwelling on education, we shall simply point out that it is through education that the phenomenon of egoism—and therefore that of the situated man and situated society—becomes crystallized within a given framework; it is through the same way that we can break down the phenomenon and create new humanizing openings through which man can become more responsible in society. To reduce or even do away with violent tensions and situations which lead to violations of political and economic rights and an increase in the number of refugees, it would be best to create more responsibility whereby everyone would be conscious of their rights and duties on the one hand, and wherein society and its

81

structures will find no reason to trample on man. We must be aware of this fact, since the task of sharing responsibility is that of both the governors and the governed. We can thus work better towards achieving solid formulae and traditions, or even institutionalizing a real formula of education towards promoting responsibility for the distribution of tasks to the various actors within a given community. The goal is to bring everyone to identify with public life without constraint, and by common agreement, and to realize that those who uplift us outlive individuals of any time. Therefore, in order to assert themselves and grow, individuals must strive to maintain and improve all that contributes to the continuity of public life. Such actions, which would lead to awareness of a situation by the very fact that they exist, are in themselves direct formulae for cating the governors and the governed. By simply being implemented, they can lead to a reduction in some violent tensions in certain societies where man and humanity often suffer the most serious extortions.

Shared responsibility and consciousness of duty will enable us not only to become aware of the means at our disposal and to use such means with restraint, but also to organize the structures and mechanisms of management in such a way as would facilitate savings. Thus, we shall avoid poverty-related excuses that are often put forward to justify evil practices that destroy human dignity, especially as man has the capacity of making do with poverty. Of course, tensions, and even conflicts, will not disappear completely. They will instead become marginal issues, since, through education and sharing of responsibilities, society will be organized to deal with them. They will no longer be as important and as radical as we see today in certain areas where real traditions of human rights violations have taken root.

As we strive to bring about profound changes in mentalities—and therefore to humanize the governors and the governed—we also create the right conditions for changes in the mentalities of future generations. This should be our goal as we look for ways and means of educating people and getting them to become more responsible. With this in mind, we can determine the content of this education and the manner in which responsibilities can be shared in view to destroying the negative animal nature of man and creating a mental environment in which man and society would be more open and clear-minded to master and use their sensitivity for positive ends. This cannot but lead to a better knowledge of certain rights and duties, their popularization, and the dissemination of the notion of human dignity itself. Therein lie pathways for reflection and research on the actions to be undertaken. One of such actions is the humanization of technology and development, not only in the economic sense, but also in cultural and spiritual terms.

C) HOW CAN TECHNOLOGY AND DEVELOPMENT BE HUMANIZED, NOT ONLY IN ECONOMIC TERMS, BUT ALSO CULTURALLY AND SPIRITUALLY?

This point places us right in the very heart of the dynamics which must be released in the framework of our reflections; consequently, that means in other words, our reflections must have a dynamic characteristic. Thus it is first of all a question of working method which would outline what can, must, or should be done.

1) Man and the humane in man and in society as finalities

First of all, it is important to agree on the fact that man is, or should be, the finality in all human undertakings and that the humaneness in man and society must be the finality. This most fundamental fact in the humanization of technology and development is often forgotten. The urgency of such humanization is increased by the fact that one of the basic characteristics of man—communication with one another, with men—is becoming increasingly marginal. The machine is replacing man and chasing away human warmth; the result is that man's spiritual and humanistic appraisal of things has become limited.

In fact, man was made to communicate, to exchange ideas. And underlying this ability to communicate are cultural and spiritual factors generally present in man, which he transmits, reviving and enabling them to grow and become richer. Technology has brought along other realities; in fact, machines are increasingly speaking and acting for man, replacing him. In the absence of protective formulae, it is difficult to undertake actions which would lead to the humanization of technology and development, not only at the economic level, but also at the cultural and spiritual levels.

In this regard, we should try to recognize, first of all, the importance or the great need for technology which would free man from certain difficult, and even servile tasks. Such is the case today with robotization, data processing, and computers which free man from tedious tasks, and perform others which would take man years to perform. However, it so happens that through the desire for quick material results, the humane aspect of technology and development has never been fully pursued; technological feats have been achieved, forgetting the finality of man and humaneness in society. Our problem concerns the relations between man and technology, how to fit humaneness into the technological process, bearing in mind that man is the finality. The problem, therefore, is basically the cultural and spiritual dimensions of all human undertakings. Humanization will be achieved through the solutions to this problem.

For the sake of realism in our search for answers, we should find out and take note of what is going on. Actually, there are concern for and trends in favour of humanizing technology, but matters are viewed essentially from the angle of the situated man and the situated state. Any attempts at humanization have had a selfish character in that the main concern has always been with people within a given state or territory; and within this framework itself, a certain category of people is concerned: the rulers.

If ever we could talk of humanizing certain technological projects and attainments which are basically against man and out to destroy humaneness, we could also roughly verify that phenomenon. In fact, it all comes with formulae for protection against atomic and chemical warfare; it is as if, having built nuclear and chemical weapons, man awakens from a dream and remembers that man and humaneness exist and should be saved. But then, torn between a dual finality—the man to be destroyed and the man to be saved—he arrives at the conclusion that the ones to be destroyed are the others, those on the periphery. Every nation in the world builds weapons with the aim of destroying the others and creating structures for its own protection and that of its people. Thus the world is increasingly being transformed into an entrenched camp with atomic shelters, to meet the aspirations of all the rulers and the wealthy citizens of the most powerful and technologically advanced countries. So, in principle, it would be logical for events to lead us through a conflict at the end of which there will be rulers without subjects, the latter being left out in the cold. And, on the whole, the greater majority of those left out is made up of people in underdeveloped countries who have not mastered advanced technology. Human dignity and social justice have not taken root in these countries; they are absent from the system of values. This situation is worsened by the fact that, in almost all countries, the greatest development effort is centred on and devoted to defence issues; weapons and mechanisms for destroying the other party are to be found at the base of technological and development undertakings.

Through the above example, we can grasp the basic concerns of rulers. In fact, man—the human being—as a finality, and humaneness within a boundless society as a finality are not considered as the essential finalities which should and must predominate and for which we must struggle. Selfish interests are overriding and leave their mark on technological achievements and development.

In order to break off from this state of affairs as we intend to, we have to arrive at a profound change in mentalities. This requires a delicate, meticulous, and sustained effort from committed men of faith, working at all levels to keep the evolutionary and positive aspects of cultural and spiritual factors constantly present in man's undertakings. This effort is necessary, more at the lower levels of society than at those concerned with the atomic weapons mentioned above. In fact, because of concern for profit, technical mechanisms and technological achievements have not often taken account of man and humaneness as finalities. And this becomes more obvious with the introduction of technology in developing regions in the world. Here the spirit of the people is often sacrificed and the pre-existing cultural and spiritual values which guarantee the everlasting nature of humaneness are overlooked. What is worse, the technology these people receive tends to destroy them; they contribute to the development of negative and destructive animal characteristics in men, sources of actions contrary to human dignity.

2) *Elements and programmes of concrete actions*

We can thus outline the directives of action in the effort to humanize technology and development: to develop cultural and spiritual values and get the people to accept and live them fully; to expand the cultural and spiritual dimensions of co-operation between states and peoples who are most often more concerned with economic and technological exchanges with no human or humanizing foundation. To implement this programme of action, which the World Conference on Religion and Peace should strive to break down into programmes for other institutions and men, we must study the present phenomenon of humanization of technology and development. Out of concern for the realism we must exhibit, we should carry out this research according to the various countries and regions. We do not have a standard formula to propose, except that we should, right from the start, remember the objectives to be attained. These are, on the one hand, to understand that man is a finality, and humaneness is also a finality, and, on the other hand, to outline what must be done to ensure the predominance of these finalities. As a starting point, the concrete results the participants in this Fourth Assembly will come up with once they return to their respective countries or regions could be compiled and published, after undergoing a synthesis which would enable us to grasp the extent of the problem in the world and to see how individual and collective action can lead to remedies. Such remedies shall consist of actions at the local level, within the framework of factories and workshops. There, attempts can be made to expand cultural and spiritual factors liable to spur the participants in question. Depending on the cases and situations involved, we shall see what can be done in the light of present efforts and their shortcomings. This can be done by undergoing the experience of man within a situated framework and viewing him and humaneness beyond this framework, then making a critical study of the situation. This could lead to a whole series of books, pamphlets and teachings on humaneness and the humanization of technology and development. All this should, in the long run, make it possible to establish a tradition of informing, educating and performing basically—humanizing cultural activities that would be open to man, irrespective of state boundaries.

FINAL REMARKS

Having said all the above, there is a good reason to remember that the basic issue concerning human dignity, social justice, and the development of the whole human being is really that of the incitement of the spiritual evolution of man. It happens to be a time-consuming job having to be done through education, so that present-day man can emerge as a new man, devoted to human values without consideration for national boundaries.

History provides us with points of reference and the stages undergone by human endeavours and achievements in this direction. After witnessing divisions and struggles amongst Christians, we are presently in the era of dialogue among Christians—the era of ecumenism; after years of fierce fighting between Muslims and Christians, we have now come into the era of dialogue; after showing total indifference toward each other, and sometimes maintaining relations of unconcealed hostility, men of faith and believers from every camp have gathered within the Conference on Religion and Peace. But the results obtained so far remain accessible to a small circle of actors—us, the élite. The issue now is to break this restricted circle and allow the masses—the people—to absorb and adopt this knowledge, and then take the step from ideas and principles into concrete facts and realities.

We will be closer to our goal which is thus clear when we realize that, in fact, we are here to draw up a strategy, or strategies, to this end. Such strategies would enable all concerned (the given individual and the given society) to discover that they have something better in them, and that other individuals and societies can also have something better; consequently, all must work toward the flourishing of this better factor which will thus constitute a meeting point for men and cultures. This will be conducive to the respect for and the triumph of human dignity for a guarantee of peace in our world. How can we reach this stage? Such is the fundamental question for any institution for peace such as the World Conference on Religion and Peace based, as it is, on the exaltation of the humane and labouring for the triumph of the humane in man and in society.

18

Human Dignity, Social Justice, and Development of the Whole Person

By Mrs. Ela Ramgobin*
(Delivered by Mrs. Dorothy Ramodibe)

On June 26, 1945, when the Charter of Human Rights was signed, President Truman commented that the Charter is dedicated to the achievement and observance of human rights and fundamental freedom. Unless we can attain these objectives of all men and women everywhere, without regard to race, language or religion, we cannot have permanent peace and security. Today in 1984 we see a world where hunger and starvation, disease and death, violence and deprivation continue. We need to address ourselves to the problems of poverty and starvation, race, class, caste and religious prejudices, and the growth of militarization.

We also need to address ourselves to the unjust and vicious systems such as the "apartheid" régime in South Africa, and look at ways and means to help bring about fundamental changes. For us in South Africa, the attainment of human dignity and social justice means the attainment of certain basic conditions. These conditions were set out at a historic congress by the peoples of South Africa, held on 26 June 1955. The conditions were: the people shall govern; all national groups shall have equal rights; the people shall share in the country's wealth; the land shall be shared among all; all shall be equal before the law; all shall enjoy equal human rights, liberty to speak, to organize, to meet, to publish, to preach, to worship and to educate their children; there shall be wealth and security for all; the doors of learning and culture shall be open;

---

* Mrs. Ela Ramgobin, the grand-daughter of Mahatma Gandhi, was prevented by the South African authorities from travelling. Her speech was delivered by Mrs. Dorothy M. Ramodibe. (See biographies of delegates for information on Mrs. Ramodibe.)

there shall be houses and security and comfort; there shall be peace and friendship.

We in the Progressive Democratic Movement in South Africa continue to uphold these ideals and are committed to their attainment; we have pledged that these are freedoms we will fight for side by side throughout our lives until we have won our liberty. But, as usual, the apartheid régime in our country found this document to be undesirable and banned it in terms of the Suppression of Communism Act until a few months ago. Having thus identified a model for attainment of peace, justice and human dignity, I should have liked to look further at poverty and deprivation, prejudices and militarization. Unfortunately, due to the pressure of time, I can only list these topics here as ones deserving further examination.

I shall turn, instead, to explaining the actual South African experience. The early history of South Africa reveals the victory of the armed forces over the indigenous people ending in the massive land grabs which have led to 82% of the total population of South Africa being forced into approximately 20% of South Africa's total land mass. The remaining 80% of the land is shared disproportionately among the "Whites," "Coloureds" and "Indians," as they are referred to in South Africa, with a very large portion of the land in the hands of the "Whites." Mahatma Gandhi once said: "No man should have more land than he needs for dignified sustenance. Who can dispute that the grinding poverty of the masses is due to their having no land that they can call their own?" However, we see even from the early days of white occupation of South Africa that, apart from a racist political policy, there also developed an economic system of exploitation. The taxes imposed on a community which had for ages survived on an agrarian economy and which did not rely on currency as a means of trade can be seen as a systematic attempt to force the people to leave their land and seek employment or sell their lives in order to pay taxes. On the other hand too, the impoverishment of the over-populated land caused people to look for survival to the big cities, thereby providing a reservoir of cheap labour.

Towards the latter part of the 1940s, the South African government, under National Party rule, brought in the policy of group areas. In terms of this policy, people of different races were separated and forced to live and trade in separate group areas. This heralded the beginning of forced removals. The group areas policy was developed into "separate development," "apartheid," "homelands" or the "Bantustan" policy; and more recently it has been set up in a more sophisticated way and presented in the form of the new "constitution" of the Republic of South Africa.

Some of the striking features of this policy are that some six million Africans have been moved from their homes and, in most instances, dumped in some bare remote area where livelihood is difficult and basic amenities are not available. This is done to consolidate the so-called "homelands". The "homelands" which are economically independent on South Africa are given so-called "independence." A particular leadership is imposed on the people and it is seen that this leadership has over the years helped in further repression and exploitation of the people. The over-crowding and over-utilization of the soil has made the population of the so-called "homelands" impoverished and dependent. It is believed that over 85% of the people of Transkei and Siskei, for instance, are living below the recognized bread line.

Ill health and disease arrive and in some areas of these "homelands" the child mortality is believed to have risen to 50%. These poverty-stricken "homelands" then are sources of cheap labour and dumping grounds for the exhausted labour force of the cities. It has been seen that the unpopular leaders and officials of these "homelands" are propped up by the South African army and security forces. The harsh, repressive laws and the harsh realities of detentions without trial, solitary confinement and torture are difficult to believe, until one is actually confronted with the experience.

The vicious pass laws will now be replaced by passports, but this will make it even more difficult for people to move out of the "homelands" to seek more employment. Moreover, people can always be easily deported back into the "homelands" if they pose just any threat in the cities. Workers and old people would have to look to the "homelands" for their pensions and security, if ever such luxuries are available.

Having thus dealt with 82% of the population, the South African government has now sought to deal with the "Coloureds" and "Indian" communities. Accordingly, it has amended or rather scrapped its old constitution and introduced a new constitution. On 22 August the so-called "Coloured" people will be called upon to elect 90 members into their own "parliament" and on 28 August the so-called "Indians" will be called upon the elect their 45 members into their own "parliament;" the "White" "parliament" of course will remain. This "constitution" has been rejected by the vast majority of the peoples from South Africa and we are confident that a large and significant majority of the "Indian" and "Coloured" people will instead boycott the elections. State-supported propaganda and coercion by the candidates have been very evident in the election campaign.

We see that apartheid is entrenched in this "constitution" which enforces the setting-up of three mutually-exclusive racially-determined parliaments. Africans, who constitute 82% of the population, do not even feature in the "constitution." The "constitution" is designed to divide the people along ethnic lines, weaken the popular struggle and unity of the people, entrench the economic, social and political supremacy of the White and enforce apartheid policy.

To contest this "constitution" and the "homeland" policy 600 organizations joined together to form the United Democratic Front. The popular struggle of the people has been dealt with harshly by the recent detentions without trial. Repressive legislation is making peaceful protests and demonstrations by the people illegal. Police harassment has been common. Tear gas, police dogs and early morning raids are common features of our society. Harassment of the so-called "squatters" and the insecurity and tension under which they live are unbelievable and cannot be adequately described unless once actually experiences life in a "squatter" tent. Each morning they leave their homes wondering whether they will find their homes and family still there when they return. People live in tents for years until one day it happens, and the bulldozer strikes.

It is seen that the "apartheid" system breaks up families through the migrant labour system, separates the urban from the rural Africans, the student from the worker, and so on. In every way it is a system which thrives on divide-and-rule tactics. In summary, we see a society where there is poverty and deprivation in spite of the vast natural resources and wealth that exist in the country. There is the blatant race prejudice entrenched by law. There are ethnic divisions imposed by the state. There is the practice of enforced removals on a large scale. There is the policy of migrant labour. There are harsh repressive laws and army involvement within and outside the country.

The question, however, is—what can the outside world do? There are several ways in which you can help to create a climate for restoration of human dignity, peace and justice in South Africa. You can ensure that "apartheid" continues to be isolated, treated with the contempt it deserves and you can ensure that in no way do countries actually help to prop up "apartheid." You can also isolate and refuse to co-operate with or entertain those who are helping to prop up the "apartheid" regime. You can inform people of what is in fact happening in South Africa so that people do not fall prey to the deceptive propaganda of the state. You can support the popular struggles in the country in whatever creative ways you can think of. You can protest against and help to publicize the violent and vicious repression practised in South Africa, e.g., the death of 60 people in detention. You can help to build up outside support for the authentic and popular organization and leadership of the people. You can join the many millions of people who have declared "apartheid" a heresy and condemn it as a violent attack on humanity.

In the end, however, the struggle will depend on how much we ourselves are prepared to sacrifice and what commitment we are prepared to make. I want to apologize if I sound ferocious in my approach to this very important subject of human dignity and social justice, but while we see our commitment here in global terms, it is imperative that we see our own involvement in localized terms. In conclusion, I would like to quote Mahatma Gandhi who said: "A spirit filled with truth needs to direct all actions to the final goal."

19

A Testimony of Suffering and Hope

By Fr. Christian Precht*

A few days ago a stream of people converged on the Catholic Cathedral in Santiago, Chile. They brought flowers and candles in their hands and sang "gracias a la vida" ("we are grateful to life"). As they passed next to the main entrance of the Cathedral they deposited their flowers, as an oath of peace, and lit their candles to continue giving witness to peace and non-violence in the streets of Santiago.

This endless pilgrimage (more than 100,000 in Santiago Cathedral alone) also took place in other Cathedrals of my country, and in many temples throughout the villages, the suburbs and slums of our cities. This was the response of the people to an urgent appeal issued by the Catholic Bishops to respect life in Chile. A plea issued as a reaction to the more than 100 who had died, victims of violence, during 1984.

Yes, my dear friends, I come from *a continent of suffering and hope*—and from a country that has undergone strong violations against human rights but whose youth is still grateful to life and hopeful of a non-violent future.

In this context I would like to share with you some of what we have learnt trying to promote social justice and human dignity, rather than listing an endless litany of sorrow and distress.

Human Rights

Through my five-year experience as Executive Secretary of the Ecumenical Committee for Peace in Chile and later as Episcopal Vicar of the Vicaria de la Solidaridad, I retain at least two convictions that I would like to share with you:

1. A Holistic Approach to Human Rights

There is deep solidarity and mutual complementarity of all the

---

* Father Christian Precht is Vicar General for the Archbishop of Santiago, Chile.

human rights listed in the UN Declaration. If one of them is violated the rest are immediately weakened or menaced. If you work for one of them you need to include the others.

Moreover, we have learnt that there is an evil logic in the violation of human rights. It normally starts with arbitrary arrests and torture, and it ends up depriving people of their social, economic and cultural rights. After all, those who are arrested are singled out precisely because of their leadership or social influence . . .

What should, then, be our response to this evil logic? I believe that the response of the Churches has to be the defence and promotion of all human rights. We are not entitled to privilege civil rights rather than social rights, or social rights rather than civil or cultural rights. Our Utopia is to foster a living person forming part of a living people, until the fulfilment of the Kingdom of God.

2.   *Human Rights, a Matter of Spirit*

The challenge of social justice and human dignity is much more than a problem of proper legislation. It even goes beyond the Universal Declaration which we all quote. It is a matter of Spirit, and it is our task and mission—as believers or religious people—to provide the Universal Declaration with the energy of the Spirit if we want it to bear proper fruit. Without the Spirit the Charter of Human Rights risks becoming a dead covenant, a statement to be quoted but not a proposition of humaneness and justice.

Furthermore, we should always keep in mind that the UN Declaration is *a limit and not a horizon*: the least we can do for humankind and not the summit of humanity. Far be it from me not to acknowledge its priceless contribution and its intrinsic value as an expression of the human conscience of most nations. Yet, its text is provisional, or better yet, incompleted. The best homage we can pay to those who conceived it and made it possible, is to enrich it, spelling out more human rights of the Spirit and the progress of humanity, and, of course, to do our best to promote and defend the rights which are actually stated in the Charter.

Preferential Option for the Poor

1.   *A Preference of God*

As an expression of its contribution to human dignity and social justice the Catholic Church in Latin America has made and reaffirmed a *preferential option in favour of the poor*.

In very simple terms this means that we want to practise what we have learnt from God in history. His revelation has led us to understand that He prefers David to Goliath, the poor and the weak to those who are rich and powerful. That is why St Paul states that Jesus was born poor to enrich us with His poverty.

This is not an exclusive option. The pastoral option the Church has made simply means that we want to favour the poor and try to announce the Gospel to the rest of society through powerlessness and weakness, just as God has done it through the person of Jesus Christ.

2. *Complementary Aspects of this Option*

This pastoral option has three complementary aspects:

a) SERVE THE POOR: This is a traditional aspect common to all religions. In Christian terms it means that we want to act as the Good Samaritan. In other traditions it means giving alms to the poor. In all humanity it is a sign of immediate fraternal solidarity.

b) SUPPORT THE CAUSE OF THE POOR: This aspect of the option demands a promotional mentality, that is, an effort to look for the causes of injustice and not only help to alleviate its effects. It also means that we consider the great value and feel it our duty to support what the poor themselves do to liberate themselves from injustice and oppression.

Yet, this is not only a tactical attitude. It is enrooted in a profound conviction which leads us to *conceive or consider life and history from the perspective of the poor.* It is this conception of life that urges us to support, promote and defend the "cause" or the causes of the poor.

An example may be useful to explain what we mean to say by this "perspective of the poor." I shall refer to it as a hospital. As you all know, there are different ways of getting to know a hospital. You can require information from its Director, from nurses and doctors, from the staff, etc. and you can also talk to the patients. Normally we tend to consider the opinion of those who are in charge and we seldom ask for the opinion of the patients, who know a lot about the practical activity and functioning of the hospital. The patients have a "perspective" that nurses and doctors don't always have.

In this huge hospital of humanity, in which many patients are even left outside its walls, we usually have big ears to hear the opinion of presidents, generals, bankers, scientists, technicians. Undoubtedly they have a very important point of view which we ought to consider. The only problem is that after hearing so much we seldom have room or interest enough to hear what the "patients"—and sometimes infinitely patient—of humanity have to say. And they know a lot more about how they want to lead their lives than those who take decisions on their behalf.

We have learnt that the poor and the suffering, the weak and the marginalized brothers and sisters of our society, conceive a much more human, just and dignifying world than those in power. They think in terms of *inclusion and not of exclusion* and through their daily lives they have given proof of being masters in the art of human solidarity.

Can you imagine what would happen to humanity if we made a world-wide option for the poor? If we could only hear the voice of the minorities (which added up are the majorities) of the world. If telex and teletypes, television and newspapers, forums and assemblies would give priority to the poor or to the marginalized, or even to children and young people. I can assure you that the result would be a much more reasonable world and a better humanity. Permit me if I insist: they know how to build up a world of inclusion and of communion. They have learnt it as they shared shacks and small houses with large families and even with their relatives. They have taught it to us sharing the scarce loaf of bread that sometimes feeds a whole family.

c) TO LIVE IN THE STYLE OF JESUS: A third complementary aspect of this option commits us to try and live in the style of Jesus. In other words to try to be disciples of the Sermon on the Mount. We feel a strong appeal which invites us to be poor, non-violent, searchers of justice, peacemakers, clean of heart, merciful to one another. We all know that if we are able to live even a part of the spirit of the Beatitudes we shall endure persecution, ill-treatment and misunderstanding. We hope to rejoice when this happens since that was the fate of all the prophets who have preceded us.

A Contribution to Hope

I started my testimony stating that I come from a continent of great suffering and deep hope. I now dare say that there is true hope partly because we know what it means to suffer.

Permit me to express this certitude with an image of Christ that is very dear and inspiring to me. It is the image of the risen Christ marked with the wounds which we inflicted upon Him and that became His glorious wounds. He is a living testimony that the best way to overcome the pains and sufferings of humanity is to recognize, assume and offer all that really hurts our lives. If we hide our wounds or use a blindfold that stops our eyes from seeing the plagues of our fellow brothers and sisters, we shall never heal or be healed. Whereas if we are able to acknowledge them we shall have enough energy to struggle for life, for human dignity and social justice.

The experience of Jesus teaches us not to fear the tombs that hold life and freedom in captivity. He teaches us to enter into these tombs and assumes our plagues and wounds giving the hopeful certitude that there is true life and true joy awaiting us beyond the path of suffering and even death.

D.

Addresses on "World Peace and Disarmament"

20

Introduction to the Theme, World Peace and Disarmament

By Dr. Dana McLean Greeley*

It is wonderful for us and for the world for us to be together here and to learn truly to understand each other and to know that questions of war and peace are the priority in our thinking and in our lives. Disarmament has been one of three or four major concerns of WCRP from the beginning 15 years ago. Our total preoccupation and dedication are to peace and must continue to be to peace. But most of us believe that disarmament is an absolutely necessary prerequisite to peace. On the third page of our Workbook there is reference to the spiritual role of religion. Religion should also be wedded to moral principles and purposes. And peace at this point in history is both a moral and a survival necessity.

I am sorry to have to say that I think that my own nation, the United States of America, is a major offender and on the wrong track; it seems to believe that it has the responsibility of preserving the peace of the world through strength and military superiority. And it also makes the tragic mistake of thinking that what is good for one nation is good for the rest of the world. The so-called national interest is its demi-God though it is not the first nation in history to manifest such a spirit.

To achieve disarmament and peace we have to change the whole psychology of governments and people or of many governments and people. Do we believe in peace or don't we? If we really believe in peace, we must trust negotiations and diplomacy or arbitration to the nth degree. There can be no more war, not even as a last resort. So we cannot go to war or prepare for war, but must bear out swords into ploughshares, and diffuse our bombs for hunger's and humanity's sake;

---

* Dr. Dana McLean Greeley, a former President of the Unitarian Universalist Association of North America, is a founder and Honorary President of WCRP.

that is applicable to the Middle East, and to Central America, and to many other places. In the nuclear age we must really make war psychology unthinkable: truly outlaw it as the Kellogg-Briand pact did a long time ago.

Two statements of Jesus in the New Testament were: "Satan cannot cast out Satan." War will not end war; and "You cannot serve both God and Mammon." Can we in every case, learn to put the human family ahead of national sovereignty and even national pride? Right now we need to approve for the nuclear powers a nuclear freeze but not let the politicians pretend to favour a nuclear freeze and actually create more and worse weapons of destruction. The religions of the world have the grave responsibility of leading the way, not lagging behind. They, not least, should put an end to religious strife—we cannot say it too often—under whatever guise; they should pioneer for unity even amid diversity. Archbishop Fernandes has said also in our Workbook that silence is sometimes not silence but acquiescence; we should speak with one voice, as with the sound of the trumpet in behalf of peace, not peace under one power, not peace by fear, but a positive peace, peace with justice and peace with love. May we think hard and pray hard together this week, and then bear our witness. Amen.

21

World Peace and Disarmament

By Ambassador Olu Adeniji*

The Fourth World Assembly of the World Conference on Religion and Peace is being held at a very crucial time. The twin pillars on which the hope for maintaining peace rests—disarmament and development—are at this time suffering severe reverses. Ten years ago the New International Economic Order was launched at the Fifth Special Session of the United Nations General Assembly. A Programme of Action was adopted the following year at the Sixth Special Session designed to liberate the wretched of the earth (almost two-thirds of humanity) from the cycle of desperate economic and social conditions which engulfed them. Today the economic conditions of most of the developing countries have become more desperate; hunger, poverty and a crushing debt burden are everywhere in evidence, most especially in this continent, which has been chosen as the venue for the Fourth World Assembly. It is the continent that has 27 of the 36 Least Developed Countries, where the ravages of nature have combined with the ill effects of the world economic recession and the inhuman policies of a mindless racist régime to increase the suffering of the people. But side by side with this desperate economic condition is the ever accruing world expenditure on armament which is runing close to $700 billion annually. While solutions to urgent human problems are neglected, more than a quarter of scientific resources and expertise are diverted to military purposes. Thus the continuation of the arms race is totally incompatible with the realization of world economic potentialities. All this is a great impediment to the New International Economic Order.

Six years ago, the First Special Session of the UN General Assembly devoted to disarmament adopted with great fanfare the Final Document

---

* H.E. Mr. Olu Adeniji, Officer for Economic Affairs and International Organizations of the Nigerian Ministry of External Affairs, represents Nigeria at the United Nations.

99

which contained a blueprint for world peace and security through disarmament. By consensus, the international community agreed that "enduring international peace and security cannot be built on the accumulation of weaponry by military alliances nor sustained by a precarious balance of deterrence or doctrines of strategic superiority. Genuine and lasting peace can only be created through the effective implementation of the security system provided for in the Charter of the United Nations and the speedy and substantial reduction of arms and armed forces by international agreement and mutual example leading ultimately to general and complete disarmament under effective international control." As in the case of development, the situation in the area of disarmament is fast deteriorating.

The conditions which led to the initiative of the Non-Aligned countries in proposing the convening of a First Special Session of the General Assembly devoted to disarmament are very well known. The vast destruction caused by World War II had inspired the creation of the United Nations "to save succeeding generations from the scourge of war." However, instead of pursuing the collective security concept in the Charter, the world became polarized into two alliances, each seeking its own security by massive arms build-up. The development and use of the atomic bomb at the tail-end of the war a few months after the Charter of the United Nations was adopted, signalled a new twist in the arms race. True, the destruction caused in Hiroshima and Nagasaki initially introduced an urgency in the United Nations determination to prevent the proliferation of the new weapon and to eliminate from national armouries atomic weapons and all other weapons of mass destruction. However, the Cold War that ensued led to the rapid development, refinement and massive deployment of nuclear weapons by the two rival alliances.

Equally significant are the doctrines which were developed to make possession of nuclear weapons by the two alliances acceptable to the rest of the world. Deterrence has been the great justification for the retention of these weapons. Europe has not been engulfed in another war since World War II, according to this doctrine, because of the deterrent effect of nuclear weapons, the fear of Mutual Assured Destruction. Meanwhile the arsenals to assure deterrence have grown to immense proportions. Far from the crude bombs that killed over 300,000 people in Hiroshima and Nagasaki, the arsenals of the two super-powers today contain more than 50,000 nuclear warheads varying in explosive power from 100 tons to 20 million tons of TNT. The total strength of the arsenals is estimated to be about 13,000 million tons of TNT, or three tons of TNT for every man, woman or child on earth. Yet deterrence has obviously not achieved its limit. Being based on the subjective perception of the capability of one super-power by the other, the limit to ensure deterrence is constantly adjusted upwards. Hence, as long as research and development continue, so will deployment proceed in the name of enhancement of deterrence, and therefore of security. However, periodic deployment of new systems of nuclear weapons by one super-power only serves to provoke a feeling of vulnerability in the other, thanks to what Frank Blackaby of the Stockholm International Peace Research Institute (SIPRI) refers to as the central fallacy that there is some military need for parity in nuclear weapons development. A response deployment by the other super-power which is caused more by political rather than military decisions does not end the game, nor does it make either side more amenable to negotiations. There is another side to the fallacy of tying security to nuclear weapons. If political influence as well as security is generally presumed to emanate from the possession of nuclear weapons, how can anyone prevent every ambitious country from acquiring nuclear weapons?

The danger posed by the existence of the enormous arsenals of nuclear weapons far outweighs any strategic or doctrinal justification. Any nuclear exchange, intentional or accidental, is bound to lead to calamity. It is clear that there can be no limited nuclear war; it is also not unthinkable that a nuclear war can begin by accident. Whatever its cause, the consequences of such a war are unimaginable and can no longer be said to emanate from the exaggerated imagination of alarmists.

In the consensus Final Document on the First Special Session devoted to disarmament the international community affirmed: "nuclear weapons pose the greatest danger to mankind and to the survival of civilization." The document warned "removing the threat of a world war, a nuclear war, is the most acute and urgent task of the present day. Mankind is faced with a choice: we must halt the arms race and proceed to disarmament or face annihilation." The same thought is graphically expressed by Dr. Homer Jack in the title of his book on the Second Special Session on Disarmament, *Disarm—or Die*.

In an article (in the periodical, *Foreign Policy*) entitled "Nuclear War and Climatic Catastrophe," Carl Segan wrote: "Recent estimates of the immediate deaths from blast, prompt radiation and fires in a major (nuclear) exchange in which cities were targeted, range from several hundred million to 1.1 billion people . . . Serious injuries requiring immediate medical attention (which would be largely unavailable) would be suffered by a comparably large number of people, perhaps an additional 1.1 billion. Thus it is possible that something approaching half the human population on the planet would be killed or seriously injured by the direct effects of a nuclear war."

This estimate of the initial victims however is just the tip of the iceberg. For the long-term effect will be more devastating. Social disruption and infrastructural destruction leading to unavailability of food, fuel, medical services, etc. will surely claim more lives. The effect of such an exchange on the atmosphere is likely to produce a nuclear winter both in the Northern and Southern hemispheres. The result:

"Species extinction could be expected for most tropical plants and animals, and for most terrestrial vertebrates of northern temperate regions, a large number of plants and numerous freshwater and some marine organisms . . . It is clear that the ecosystem effects alone resulting from a large-scale thermonuclear war could be enough to destroy the current civilization in at least the Northern Hemisphere. Coupled with the direct casualties of perhaps 2 billion people, the combined immediate and long-term effects of nuclear war suggest that eventually there might be no human survivors in the Northern Hemisphere."

In their Call for an End to the Nuclear Arms Race, the International Physicians for the Prevention of Nuclear War stated: "If even a single nuclear weapon is exploded over one of our major cities, hundreds of thousands will be killed. If many nuclear weapons are exploded, radioactive fall-out and disturbance of the biosphere will cause suffering and death—particularly from starvation, radiation illness, infectious disease and cancer without regard to national boundaries . . . An all-out nuclear war would end our present civilization . . . As physicians and health care professionals we believe a nuclear war would be the final epidemic."

These are very frightening conclusions but are by no means alarmist. The lesson should be that security based on nuclear weapons is at best an illusion, at worst an inexorable march to mass suicide or worse still to mass genocide. For suicide implies some degree of deliberateness, some degree of voluntariness to end one's existence. Most countries will not be party to a decision to launch a nuclear war. Yet adversaries as well as innocent by-standers will suffer directly from its effect. It is no longer only the secondary economic effects of the arms race on developing countries that is worrisome, important as these are, it is the threat to the very existence of these countries resulting from a nuclear war in which they have no part. "Countries as far apart from the centre of a likely nuclear conflict as India, Brazil, Nigeria or Saudi Arabia could collapse in a nuclear war without a single bomb being dropped on their territories."

The concept of world security based on the deterrent effect of nuclear weapons is the greatest fallacy of all. So concluded a group of experts that undertook a study on all aspects of nuclear weapons. If the greater refinement of nuclear weapons has not enhanced the security of the nuclear weapon states, neither has it guaranteed peace to the world. It is true that so far there has been no direct war between the super-powers since the end of World War II. However, the simultaneous development and ready availability of cash for ever more sophisticated conventional weapons has encouraged several proxy wars. Since 1945 there have been more than 150 armed conflicts around the world, with the loss of over ten million lives, not to mention the inestimable destruction. In many cases conflict has been provoked by the competitiveness engendered by rival accumulation of weapons. As in the case of the nuclear weapon states, the illusion of greater security with greater armaments gathers its own momentum and accumulation becomes a way of life. Whatever it does, it is clear that it does not enhance security, since it has not deterred attacks on each other. Rather, accumulation of weapons has encouraged wars of aggression, has contributed to the suppression of the rights to self-determination of peoples and has enhanced the perpetuation of fascist and racist doctrines such as apartheid.

This Assembly is being held in a region which has not known peace since the end of World War II. Revolts against oppressive colonial and racial systems have taken their toll. Lately the apartheid régime of South Africa which has constituted itself into an international outcast has, by sheer brute force, embarked on a persistent policy of destabilization through armed attacks on neighbouring states. It rests its legitimacy not on acceptance by the people it purports to rule but by the force of arms. It defies the entire world not by the moral strength derived from its ideology but through its belief in force as an instrument of state policy.

The destabilizing effect of the accumulation of weapons can be seen throughout the regions of conflict, whether in the Middle East, in South East Asia or in Central America. World peace cannot be maintained until there is a change from the present race in armaments to a return to a saner world order. Common security on which lasting peace should be based requires a general feeling of security by all countries. With increasing knowledge of the danger constituted to humanity by the arms race, with greater awareness of its economic and social consequences, efforts at disarmament are no longer confined to diplomats and professionals. Massive demonstrations, interest of non-governmental groups like yours, persistent efforts by the Non-Aligned Movement have all combined to keep in focus the need for disarmament.

Though the United Nations General Assembly pronounced general and complete disarmament under effective international control as the goal of disarmament efforts as far back as 1959, the world has moved further from, rather than nearer to that goal since then. After initial efforts to negotiate a Treaty on General and Complete Disarmament failed in the early sixties, attention was turned to the negotiation of collateral measures. Meanwhile, the arms race in nuclear weapons proceeded by leaps and bounds demonstrating a singular lack of will by the nuclear weapon states to control it. The 1963 Partial Nuclear Test-Ban Treaty and the 1968 Non-Proliferation Treaty which were then considered as real achievements have since been vitiated by advances in weaponry tests and by the unwillingness of the nuclear weapon powers to undertake meaningful measures of nuclear disarmament. In the decade of the 70s which was proclaimed by the United Nations as a Disarmament Decade, no effective disarmament measures were adopted. SALT I whose significance lay in its laying the basis for reduction in strategic weapons was not followed up when the United States refused to ratify SALT II. The multilateral negotiating body, the Conference of the Committee on Disarmament, concentrated on collateral measures.

With the collapse of détente and the heightening of confrontation between the super-powers, the world is again alive to the urgent necessity for effective measures of disarmament. the First Special Session of the General Assembly Devoted to Disarmament established a programme of action aimed at ensuring progress along the road to general and complete disarmament which remains the ultimate goal. Measures of nuclear disarmament occupy the priority place. The achievement of nuclear disarmament will require urgent negotiation of agreements at appropriate stages and with an adequate measure of verification satisfactory to the states concerned for:

—Cessation of the qualitative improvement and development of nuclear weapons systems;
—Cessation of production of all types of nuclear weapons and their means of delivery and of the production of fissionable material for weapons purposes:
—Comprehensive phased programme with agreed time-frames for progressive and balanced reduction of stockpiles of nuclear weapons and their means of delivery.

If nuclear weapons pose the greatest danger to mankind and the survival of civilization, measures of nuclear disarmament should be expedited. Yet the speed of research and development has made the lack of progress in negotiations all the more worrisome. Even when active negotiations were proceeding, the pace of weapons development was far quicker. It is with this in mind that the call for a Nuclear Freeze assumes great importance. Such a freeze will prevent the continuing escalation of nuclear stockpiles and pre-empt the development of new systems. With the standstill of a Freeze, agreements on reduction will be meaningful. As long as improvements continue to be made, so long will escalation continue. The fresh round of deployment of INF in Europe is a case in point. Under the guise of modernization, one super-power deploys a new system. Under the pretext of catching up, the other super-power seeks to match with the deployment of its own system. So the vicious cycle continues. Given the over-kill capacity of the arsenals of the two super-powers, the argument that a Freeze will favour either side seems irrelevant. There is rough parity which should sustain both sides even in the unlikely event of either side taking advantage of a Freeze agreement. Indeed a Freeze agreement is practicable and verifiable.

Over the years one of the most basic steps toward nuclear disarmament has been identified as a Comprehensive Test Ban Treaty. Its importance lies in its effectiveness in preventing the vertical as well as horizontal proliferation of nuclear weapons. It is already 21 years since the conclusion of the Partial Test Ban Treaty in which parties expressed the objective of "seeking to achieve the discontinuance of all test explosions of nuclear weapons for all time." The General Assembly has since set the achievement of a CTBT as one of its topmost priority items. However, the lack of political will on the part of some nuclear weapon states has frustrated all efforts. All the technical studies, even on verification, that need to be carried out have been undertaken. Yet despite its importance and urgency the trilateral—UK, USA, USSR—negotiations on a CTBT were cut off in 1980 while the multilateral negotiating forum (the Conference on Disarmament) is yet to be enabled to commence real negotiations. Failure to conclude a CTBT is a clear indication that the nuclear weapons states, party to the Non-Proliferation Treaty, are unwilling to honour their commitment in Article VI whereby they understood "to pursue negotiations in good faith on effective measures relating to cessation of the nuclear arms race at an early date and to nuclear disarmament." Considering the importance of that article for the maintenance of the viability of the Non-Proliferation Treaty, it will be a great disservice to the non-proliferation régime if obstacles continue to be placed in the path to a CTBT. In a situation where countries with substantial nuclear energy programmes stay out of the régime of NPT because of their objection to its unequal and discriminatory nature, horizontal non-proliferation can only be assured if the nuclear weapon states were to be seen to be prepared to arrest vertical proliferation. In the light of the state of the art, it would seem that unilateral measures of cessation of nuclear tests by one super-power (even if for a temporary period) should be encouraged in the hope that it will evoke a positive response from the other super-power.

Other elements in the nuclear disarmament agenda which require urgent attention concern strategic weapons and intermediate range nuclear weapons. The First Special Session of the General Assembly Devoted to Disarmament was held amidst hope that the bilateral SALT negotiations between the United States and the Soviet Union would result in significant agreement. The fate of SALT II is common knowledge. The successor to the SALT Talks, START, has since been suspended, the victim of the controversy that resulted from the deployment of Cruise and Pershing missiles in Europe. In effect no negotiations are now being undertaken at all on nuclear weapons.

Based on what is now known of the possible effects of the use of nuclear weapons, it is clear that the only effective defence is that they never be used. Any use will constitute the greatest crime against humanity. To this end commitment by nuclear weapon states through unilateral undertakings is helpful. The Soviet Union gave an undertaking at the Second Special Session not to be the first to use nuclear weapons. China gave a similar undertaking years earlier. The remaining three nuclear weapon states have not reciprocated. Notwithstanding, there is the need to go beyond unilateral declarations. A Convention on the Prohibition of the Use of Nuclear Weapons has become an urgent necessity. The General Assembly has adopted a resolution with an overwhelming majority on such a convention.

The uncertainties are meanwhile being compounded by the intensification of the extension of the arms race into outer space. The race to develop anti-satellite weapons systems will introduce new destabilizing elements. Both the USA and the USSR have conducted tests of anti-satellite devices. Though it seems that the present devices are capable only of attacking low-orbit satellites, research and development are proceeding fast. Unless agreement is reached early, the capability of the anti-satellite systems will improve to attack on satellites in high orbit. This will affect the entire concept of verification of disarmament agreements which rely extensively on the use of surveillance by satellites. Development of anti-satellite and anti-missile systems will also increase the risk of war in that it will encourage the possibility of a first strike based on the confidence of being able to ward off any retaliatory response. Thus the idea of waging a winnable nuclear war will once more gain credibility with all the attendant consequences.

The General Assembly of the United Nations has called on the Conference on Disarmament to undertake urgent negotiations of agreement or agreements on the prevention of an arms race in outer space. Disagreement on the mandate of a Working Group has prevented such negotiations. While some members of the Conference wanted such a Working Group to undertake negotiations for the conclusion of an agreement or agreements, others wanted a mandate restricted to identifying issues relevant to the prevention of an arms race in outer space. The need for a moratorium followed by urgent negotiations is most urgent. It is easier to pre-empt these systems before they are perfected than to expect dismantlement once built.

On the whole, the outlook for world peace is very grim. Disarmament negotiations have come to a standstill. Even the efforts to develop a Comprehensive Programme of Disarmament are at an impasse. It should be recalled that a CPD was considered to be the centre-piece of the Second Special Session on Disarmament held in 1982. Its significance had been recognized as far back as 1969 when, in declaring the 1970s as a Disarmament Decade, the United Nations General Assembly requested the Conference of the Committee on Disarmament to elaborate such a programme. In its Final Document, the First Special Session of the General Assembly Devoted to Disarmament called for the elaboration of a comprehensive programme of disarmament "encompassing all measures thought to be advisable in order to ensure that the goal of general and complete disarmament under effective international control becomes a reality in a world in which international peace and security prevail and in which the new international economic order is strengthened and consolidated . . ."

In the years between the First and Second Special Sessions, interest was rife in a CPD. Not only did the Disarmament Commission agree upon Elements of a Comprehensive Programme, non-governmental organizations made very concrete proposals for such an effective programme. Unfortunately, failure to reach agreement on the Comprehensive Programme constitutes the biggest disappointment of the Second Special Session. But what is even more disheartening, of course, is that interest seems to be waning even within the non-governmental organizations themselves on such a programme. Yet the break-up of the negotiations between the super-powers seems to me to be a clear indication of the necessity for a universally agreed disarmament programme which will commit them to a definite course of negotiations that will ensure continued progress towards the goal.

One of the difficulties of the present situation is that the nuclear weapon states unilaterally decide what they wish to negotiate on, and equally decide when to break up negotiations for whatever reason. They do not feel that they are accountable to any other country but themselves; they do not sense the same urgency in proceeding to disarmament negotiations as to complete the process within a definite future. This reluctance is reflected in their insistence on a Comprehensive Programme without a time-frame, without definite schedules of implementation, without a detailed elaboration of the measures; it seems to me to have a non-binding character which carries hardly any commitment for implementation.

In conclusion, may I put on record that in trying to salvage the Second Special Session from total collapse, I assumed personal responsibility, as Chairman of the Ad Hoc Committee, for drawing up the Concluding Document. In that document the General Assembly regretted that it had been unable to adopt a document on the Comprehensive Programme and on a number of other items on its agenda. "However, the General Assembly felt encouraged by the unanimous and categorical reaffirmation by all member States of the validity of the Final Document of the Tenth Special Session as well as their solemn commitment to it and their pledge to respect the priorities in disarmament negotiations as agreed to in its Programme of Action." Taking into account the aggravation of the international situation and being gravely concerned about the continuing arms race, particularly in its nuclear aspect, the General Assembly expressed its profound preoccupation over the danger of war, in particular nuclear war, the prevention of which remains the most acute and urgent task of the present day.

The great disappointment today is that even this minimum commitment has not been honoured. Peace and Security have been further jeopardized by the reciprocal deployment of nuclear weapons, by the aggravation of tension in the relations of the super-powers, by the continuation of localized wars and armed conflicts and by the continued diversion of scarce world resources into the unproductive arms race at a time of grave economic crisis.

The one ray of hope is the opportunity for peoples generally to become involved in the campaign to bring pressure on their rulers to show greater commitment to disarmament. The World Disarmament Campaign which was solemnly launched on the opening day of the Special Session provides an opportunity for the continuous pursuit and follow-up of that unprecedented March for Peace on June 12, 1984.

Non-Governmental Organizations have always played a significant role in the field of peace and disarmament. The challenge for them to intensify their efforts is immense. The Fourth World Conference on Religion and Peace should pronounce itself clearly on world disarmament as the means to world peace.

22

Peace Means Life

By Dr. Anezka Ebertova *

We come together for the Fourth World Assembly of the WCRP in this beautiful country and this nice city. But we have come together in a very complex and dangerous time in which we have a very important and, I hope, common aim: to raise our voice for peace, built on justice. We came to raise our voice against the escalation of armaments, and this means for disarmament. We came to demonstrate the possibility of human understanding and co-existence across our differences and existing obstacles.

Until yesterday afternoon I did not know that I should be asked to speak to this Assembly, but I received this invitation as an honour and in the hope you will hear in my voice, which could not be prepared as I would like to do it, but which comes from my heart, the very serious peace voice of all our churches and Christians in Eastern European countries.

Not merely formal activities are done by our people but there are very serious decisions to bring a contribution to the world peace. This work is done through our possibilities, structures and instruments, which may be different from the ones used by people living in other parts of the world but which are motivated by the same goal and by the same human need—the need for peace, and this means for disarmament.

We are all united in this need for peace, because peace means life, and life means peace; in the present conditions, weapons and war mean death.

Peace is an essential need for human beings of all races, of all nations, of all religions. Peace is the main right of human beings. We are called to preserve the sacred gift of life in very dangerous times. We are living, as it were, on a big pile of weapons, nuclear, chemical, biologi-

---

* Dr. Anezka Ebertova works at the Women's Desk of the Ecumenical Council of Churches in the CSSR in Prague.

cal, as well as conventional, which are all able to destroy the whole earth and all living beings.

I believe that in all our faiths life is precious to us. Not only our own life but that of all people, of future generations and of all other creatures of nature. The present biological threat to the very essence of life poses a serious spiritual and moral question.

Confronted with the present widespread disorientation of values we have to confess that our religious, spiritual and moral attitude towards life implies a recognition of its value, its dignity, and the fact that it cannot become the instrument of a greed for power and profit.

Life is a gift that must be developed and lived. It cannot be merely spent in consumption. It should be shared with one's fellow-men and fellow-women. It can be defended only in co-operation with nature, through a responsible management of the gifts of the Earth and of human work in relations of justice and love and in sharing with one's neighbours.

I belong to a generation and I come from a country which experienced the catastrophe of the Second World War with its own body and soul. It is quite different to speak about peace and war without such personal experiences. It is something different to speak about the hunger and death of others and to suffer hunger and to be in war. It is necessary to stress too that women are the ones who are suffering twice and they, with their children, have always been the biggest victims of war.

Therefore our people, and especially our women, are engaged in the struggle for peace. I would like to share with you a small testimony and experience from two meetings which we had last spring. The first one was a meeting of Christian women from socialist countries with West European and American women in peace activity. We experienced not only linguistic difficulties but all types of barriers in human communication: prejudices, the influence of disinformation and propaganda, as well as different concepts of peace-work and the diversity of socio-political pre-conditions. But where there are good will, faith and hope and a true decision for peace, understanding and co-operation can finally and easily be discovered.

Similar experiences were gained in a meeting of the co-ordinating committee of the European Women's Forum connected with a seminar conducted with church women in Czechoslovakia. We learned from them, as well as from the other activities, and especially in common prayers for peace, that one thing is necessary: to be open to others, prepared to listen and hear what they are really talking and thinking about. It is necessary to love others even if they are different and if they have different opinions from ours.

A most difficult but most necessary thing is to search for change in our own thinking, our hearts, our attitudes and relations. Changes of our methods of writing are also important and difficult. It is especially necessary to change unjust social structures. All of that means change in the

110

whole of our present life.

The inability to change and lack of hope are the main obstacles to peace work. We all have a common enemy: the sin of greed, the lust for power and riches. This sin originates in the human heart, and it penetrates social and political structures and then further personal sins are possible. We are here to struggle against this sin.

I came here in order to receive and to share the spirit of mutual solidarity and, at the same time, to contribute to our common hope, to the encouragement of all those whose hearts tremble in these days of anxiety about the future, and whose hands and mouths are almost giving up the struggle for peace in the face of increased danger of a nuclear catastrophe.

Therefore our voices must reach those who are conspiring against the lives of all of us. There is still time to beat the weapons into instruments which would produce bread and satisfy many other human needs. If thousands of technical engineers and economists in all parts of the earth are involved in exhaustive studies of the world's resources of coal, oil and uranium why should not we—religious people and WCRP members—be among those who watch over humankind's desire for life, take its temperature, promote it, look after it and expand its value and dignity?

I am glad that I can participate in the struggle here, and I pray that the Fourth Assembly of WCRP can become a significant contribution to the search of humanity for peace, justice, happy life and life in fullness.

23

The Connection of Religion and Peace

By Msgr. Bruce Kent*

I think we are not sufficiently aware of the perspective of the world in which we live. Our theme speaks of religion and peace. There are millions of people who would say "What has religion to do with peace? What is the evidence of religion being connected with peace?" We can look back through history and we see centuries upon centuries where blood has been shed in the name of religion by one creed or another. We ought to be embarrassed by that; we can look around the world of today; in Ireland, in the Lebanon, in Palestine/Israel, in the Philippines, in India, there are conflicts going on where religion is playing a major part or at least a part in the conflict.

In the nuclear world let us be reminded that the crew that flew the plane to destroy Hiroshima was crewed by practising Christians and practising Jews, and many of them justify today what they then did. In my country neither of the two major religious Christian churches has condemned the deployment of yet more first-use and first-strike nuclear weapons in Europe. We even have a bishop who actually supports the possible use of nuclear weapons. In countries of the East and, I would say, countries of the West, there has been an unholy alliance between established religious bodies and governments in the persecution of conscientious objectors. I say these things not to be unpleasant, but simply to be realistic about the world in which we live. Religious people are seen on the whole as being the uncritical servants of the nation-state; that is how we are seen in history, and we should know it, if we are going to create a change. How do we become as St Francis called us to be, "instruments of Thy peace"?

---

* Msgr. Bruce Kent is General Secretary of the Campaign for Nuclear Disarmament (U.K.), based in London.

What does this mean in terms of practical action? Information perhaps first of all. It was the historian Toynbee who is supposed to have said (I cannot find the reference) that 90% of the real religion of 90% of the people is nationalism. I think that in my country we saw not a few signs of that in the public reaction to the conflict in the Falklands in 1982—a time when the quiet voice of peace, dialogue, patience, negotiation and non-violent settlement of conflict was almost drowned by the cries of those who wanted at once military reparation for national injury. Yet we are once again learning that war solves no problems.

We have to struggle against our nationalisms and look at the injuries of our human family with a compassionate, international eye which does not vary its judgment according to the acceptability or unacceptability of the régime in question. The world cannot be divided into good and evil empires. Honest information is an essential part of that process. In my country every household is now spending nearly £16 a week on "defence". The funding for research into new methods of killing is now sixteen times greater than that awarded to medical research, and our arms export trade, largely directed at the poorer countries of the world, is now approaching a value of nearly a billion pounds a year. But my country is not alone. It is typical. Indeed the figures would actually be proportionally worse for countries with a lower Gross National Product. I commend to you for an international perspective on the social damage effected by this sickness of militarism the annual statements of Mrs. Ruth Sivard, whose annual report "World Military and Social Expenditures" provides regular and dismal reading. The arms race is killing millions *now*.

But ignorance goes beyond the facts and figures. The ignorance about this particular world disease extends to the effectiveness of the whole process. It is supposed to make us safer. People will pay a lot of money and make many sacrifices if they believe that they are buying security. Otherwise insurance companies would not prosper. But they are not getting security. With stockpiles of 50,000 or more nuclear weapons in the world, with the ever-present possibility of accident, with the time for rational reaction being regularly reduced, with the deployment of first-use and first-strike weapons of high accuracy and great speed, security has another meaning. We have moved into a new age and we do not—or too many religious people do not—realize that no country can now increase its security by increasing the insecurity of another. That excellent international report called "Common Security" said just that two years ago, yet its authoritative judgment, endorsed by experts from East and West headed by the Swedish Prime Minister, has fallen into some forgotten hole. So also has the report of the first United Nations Special Session on Disarmament of 1978. Yet both are critical documents. The latter made clear, with the full support of all the 149 participating governments, that we have entered a new world of danger. *"The increase in weapons, far from helping to strengthen international security, on the contrary weakens it. The vast stockpiles . . . of weapons of all kinds . . . pose incalculable threats to peace"* (paragraph 11). Yet on we go and political leaders as well as the mass media do suggest that, somehow, if we have more we shall, somehow, be safer. Exactly the opposite in this nuclear age is true.

The religious bodies of the world have a massive responsibility, in schools, colleges, seminaries, monasteries, convents, temples, synagogues, mosques and churches, for public education. My first call to religious leaders is that they look at their present priorities and think again about Toynbee's words. Times have changed I know, and I have no wish to make judgment on those who saw things in other ways 40 plus years ago. But I know that my education, full of faith and religion as it was, nevertheless was set in a national rather than an international context and in one that was military rather than peace-based-on-justice. Our school heroes were those who had won military decorations. Of the heroes of non-violence we knew almost nothing.

Let us therefore, if we claim to be members of one family under God, make it our business in every part of education—and that goes on for life—to be sure that we concentrate on initiatives for peace, on internationalism and justice, and especially on the work of the United Nations. That body is often enough derided and mocked. It remains a fragile hope in a dangerous world and needs our practical positive support, not our indifference, or worse, our scorn.

Once aware of the situation, as education can make us aware, then we have to move to a series of practical steps. In England we owe a great deal to a very small band of Japanese Buddhist monks and nuns who have for years faithfully witnessed for peace in practical ways unmatched, I would suggest, by any Christian community. We can all learn from them. I want our religious denominations and families to make it possible for their own full-time clergy and religious to devote themselves wholly to work with the movements for peace.

There are no great problems in releasing clergy and others to work full-time as military chaplains. That pastoral need is there and I do not begrudge it for a moment, through I would prefer that such chaplains were *not* paid by governments and the military. But I think that if we, who say we are working for peace, intend to be taken seriously then we will have to reconsider our priorities when it comes to the deployment of our full-time personnel as well.

It must be the same with our financial resources. Property is not sinful of itself, most of us would agree, though obsession with it certainly is. Churches have property and financial resources. I want us to move to a new way of thinking in which it is as normal to fund a peace worker or to make generous grants to peace movements as it is to find the funds to build a church or a temple or to set up a Commission to study church art or Canon law. I once saw a good American cartoon. It showed a sad-looking general baking a cake. The text said that we shall only have made progress for peace when it is the military that have to run cake sales and the peace movements who get their millions from public taxes.

Education and proper use of our resources are therefore items for any religious peace agenda. I can think of many other areas where we might have effective things to do as well as to say. A major industry has grown up around war-toys for children. I wonder what we do to their minds as we let them play with flame-throwers, tanks and now even mini-nuclear explosives. We trivialise war and even make it attractive. Should not religious communities, especially in the rich West where the luxury of such toys is possible, agree not to support such industries?

But we can go beyond toys. The military export business is a major one in the world today. It is operated by both the major powers and by a host of lesser countries. Those who are not pacifists can make some justification for such a supply. No one can justify the ruthless creation of a demand which has nothing to do with any perceived or possible threat. Many of our churches own shares in the major companies of the capitalist world—companies responsible for 'our' side of this export business. Yet the idea of shareholder responsibility remains a strange one to many of those in church life. This is a pity. The use of shareholders' rights can be a very constructive means of non-violent social change as we move towards a world where killing is no longer an acceptable way of settling conflicts.

Perhaps I have already given you enough examples and I am sure that I am on the edge of exceeding my time. I end by repeating my conviction that those of us organised in different religious families with a belief in the unity of all humankind and our trusteeship of the world in which we live have great responsibilities today. Let us have a freeze on all nuclear weapons. But let us also have a freeze on all further church documents, reports and memoranda. Let us get on now with what we can *do* for peace, and as we do it remember the striking words of the Dutch Bishops in 1968:

"Looking for peace means giving peace work a real place, not only as a pious wish in our hearts and on our lips, but in our thoughts, in our interests, in our educational work, in our political convictions, in our faith, in our prayer and in our budget."

Please let us lead and not follow in the business of peace!

24

Nuclear Disarmament: The Universal Imperative

A Farewell Address by Dr. Homer A. Jack*

In an address to the Third Assembly of the World Conference on Religion and Peace—WCRP III—, I asked that it "launch a great new movement: to begin to build a world-wide moral and religious crusade which will say 'no' to nuclear war and 'no' to the nuclear arms race as the Old Abolitionism launched a crusade to say 'no' to slavery". I added that "the new Abolitionism is based on this single proposition: the development, production, stockpiling, threat to use, and use of nuclear weapons by any nation or any group of individuals or nations is a crime against humanity".

That plea was made five years ago. At the end of April this year, in Tokyo, I renewed this plea: "There is only one priority for humanity today. That is the abolition of nuclear weapons through nuclear disarmament. Such universal goals as 'freedom' or 'justice', or such ideological hopes as 'democracy' or 'socialism', these are quite secondary. The prime goal must be to stop turning every city everywhere into another 1945 Hiroshima or Nagasaki."

Today I can only reinforce, on the continent of Africa, the plea for nuclear sanity which I made in North America and in Asia. I further suggested at WCRP III that "we human beings have been extremely lucky that a nuclear device has not been detonated since Nagasaki by accident or terrorism, by calculation or miscalculation". Our luck has now lasted five more dangerous years. In the meantime, 50 nuclear weapons tests have been made annually—one sure index of the nuclear arms race—and world military budgets have been substantially

---

*Dr. Homer A. Jack was Secretary-General of WCRP from 1970 through 1983. He is now Secretary-General Emeritus of WCRP and Minister of the Lake Shore Unitarian Universalist Society in Winnetka, Illinois, USA.

increased. Will any rational person declare that, during these past five years, deterrence has increased our national security? Will anybody assert that our personal safety has been greater because of larger nuclear stockpiles? We have indeed been lucky, but the wise person, as the prudent nation, tries to substitute policy for luck. We must do so by adopting a sane nuclear policy for each nation and for the whole world.

In order to achieve nuclear disarmament quickly, I suggested at WCRP III in Princeton that we must proceed along two tracks simultaneously, one diplomatic, the other normal. Let me discuss the diplomatic or political route first. At Princeton I proposed a seven-point nuclear programme. At Tokyo I suggested a simplified, four-point programme which I will reiterate today.

Reversing the Arms Race

The first step to reverse the nuclear arms race is that the testing and deployment of all nuclear weapons be immediately frozen by all countries, initially by the USA and the USSR. This means that no additional nuclear weapons and their delivery systems should be tested or installed anywhere. This is the popular, world-wide campaign called "the nuclear freeze". A freeze on the testing and deployment of nuclear weapons can be verified by so-called "national" means of inspection to prevent cheating. Also any State may announce that it is embarking on a six- or twelve-month moratorium or halt of testing and deployment of nuclear weapons in the hope that its adversary might reciprocate. The acceptance of this first step to disarmament is shown by a vote of 124 to 13 for a nuclear freeze resolution of the UN General Assembly in December 1983, with only eight abstentions.

The second step back from the nuclear abyss is that nuclear weapons tests in all environments be quickly prohibited by treaty. The partial test-ban treaty of 1983 has still not been signed by all States—some have refused, such as China, France and India—and, in any case, the treaty does not prohibit underground tests. A comprehensive test-ban treaty prohibiting nuclear tests in all environments (including underground) has been under negotiation since 1983 and could be made final in a few weeks. Any of the five acknowledged nuclear weapon States might immediately announce that it was stopping underground tests until a comprehensive treaty were signed and ratified. Indeed, the Democratic candidate for the presidency of the USA has pledged, if elected, to initiate a six-months moratorium or halt on underground tests in order to challenge the Soviet Union to respond in kind—and create a favourable climate to sign and ratify a comprehensive treaty.

The third step to prevent nuclear holocaust is that the use—and not just the first use—of nuclear weapons be prohibited by treaty, and that any use be made a crime against humanity. The Non-Aligned group at the UN, led by India, has persisted towards this goal. Indeed, 126 States voted in favour of taking this initiative at the UN General Assembly last December, but 17 States opposed (mostly the major NATO partners)

117

and six States—including Japan—could not make up their minds. It is almost a crime against humanity to equivocate about whether the use of nuclear weapons is a crime against humanity!

The fourth and final step, on my short list, to prevent nuclear disaster is to phase out the nuclear arsenals of all nuclear weapons States—those five acknowledged States and perhaps as many as half a dozen additional States. This dismantling should commence at once and be finished as soon as possible, certainly by the end of this decade. The whole world must become a nuclear-free zone. This is nuclear disarmament down to zero nuclear weapons—to be accomplished in this decade, quickly. This is not a dream; the continuation of the nuclear status quo is the nightmare.

These four steps for nuclear disarmament can be negotiated bilaterally between the two super-powers, or multilaterally by the 40-nation Conference on Disarmament at Geneva. Yet there has been almost no progress in all the nuclear negotiations for many years. The present bleak international climate suggests little hope for progress in the immediate future. In order to break the deadlock, unilateral steps may have to be taken by one or more countries. The nuclear and conventional arms races have been fuelled by unilateral initiatives, often by the USA. The huge, world-wide stockpile of 50,000 nuclear weapons can also be lessened by initiatives independent of negotiated treaties. A nuclear weapons freeze could be unilaterally begun, as a 1983 UN General Assembly resolution recommended. Indeed, each of these four steps to comprehensive nuclear disarmament could be started unilaterally. Which country, nuclear or non-nuclear, is courageous enough to begin the process, to break the nuclear deadlock? Which country in our time will begin to travel the road to nuclear disarmament, regardless of how much company it initially has?

A "Northern" Issue?

At this point I want to discuss priorities, for the world, for all countries, and for all individuals. Speaking today south of the equator, I want to suggest that the avoidance of nuclear holocaust is not the exclusive concern of the peoples and nations in the Northern Hemisphere. Nuclear disarmament is not exclusively an East/West or "Northern" issue, despite some who insist that it is.

Dr Allan Boesak, a theologian in South Africa, recalled a debate held during meetings of the World Alliance of Reformed Churches in August 1983. In the midst of putting together a statement on peace, an African delegate poignantly said, "In this document, the word, 'nuclear', is used a number of times, but I don't even see the word, 'hunger'. In my village, the people will not understand the word, 'nuclear', but they know everything about hunger and poverty."

Is nuclear disarmament a "Northern" concern, an East/West issue—or indeed is it universal? My answer is: don't believe those who feel that the developing world can sit this issue out, can watch the super-

118

powers decimate each other through atomic war, and then can rule whatever remains of the world from the South! For one thing, much of the developing world is in the Northern Hemisphere: Central America, all of the Middle East, two-thirds of Africa, and all of Asia except Indonesia. For another, the Non-Aligned group—comprising almost 100 developing countries of Asia, Africa, and Latin America—has repeatedly put nuclear disarmament at the top of its priorities since its first Summit of Heads of State in 1961. Finally, the new research on so-called "nuclear winter" clearly indicates that, even if the immediate biological effects of nuclear war can be somewhat limited to the "North" geographically, the ultimate climate effects are world-wide.

"Nuclear Winter"

Let me reflect in a few sentences on the new research on "nuclear winter". Carl Sagan, an American astronomer, has recently publicized this research, based initially on a major study of which he was one of the authors. He recalls the recent report of the World Health Organization that 1.1 billion people would be killed outright in a major nuclear war, mainly in the USA, the USSR, Europe, China and Japan. The report revealed that an additional 1.1 billion people would suffer serious injuries and radiation sickness for which medical help would not be available. The Northern Hemisphere would indeed be reduced to a "state of prolonged agony and barbarism".

Here is where the new research begins, initially based on data received from the US Mariner 9 spacecraft which arrived at the planet Mars in 1971 as a global dust storm engulfed it. Researchers on earth then began constructing scenarios on the climatic implications of nuclear war—a nuclear-weapon-induced dust storm. They concluded that, in a 5,000 megaton war, because of the fine dust and soot in the earth's atmosphere, "a deadly gloom would persist for months". Temperatures would drop below freezing and virtually all crops and farm animals, at least in the Northern Hemisphere, would be destroyed. As in the Martian dust storms, the fine dust particles would cross the equator and the Southern Hemisphere would experience effects which, while less severe, would be "extremely ominous". If the clouds carrying dust thinned out, "every time it got better in the Northern Hemisphere, it would get worse in the Southern".

More than 100 scientists in the USA and the USSR have studied this new research. They confirm the result: "sub-freezing temperatures in a twilit radioactive gloom lasting for months or longer". Those human beings who survived the nuclear blasts might starve to death. The human population through nuclear war might be "reduced to prehistoric levels".

This new research should make all of us realize that nuclear war, if only because of the "nuclear winter" effect, is of concern to all human beings, whether North or South, East or West, poor or rich. Nuclear disarmament is the universal imperative.

Before leaving the diplomatic or political dimension to nuclear disarmament, I want to discuss nuclear-free zones and how religious institutions and leaders may help create them. The diplomatic effort to establish nuclear-free zones has been long and difficult. So far only three areas are nuclear-free zones. Two are uninhabited—Antarctica and outer space—and the third is Latin America, although Argentina, Brazil, and Chile are dragging their nuclear heels. However, a number of municipalities on several continents have declared themselves—symbolically—nuclear-free and are urging their country to qualify as a nuclear-free zone. Even some institutions, such as churches and synagogues, have posed signs—"Nuclear Weapon Free Zone"—in their windows or on their lawn. All can play this symbolic game. Indeed, I hope that WCRP IV might encourage all religious institutions everywhere symbolically to become nuclear-free zones as a prod to their countries and the whole world quickly to go in this inevitable direction.

Moral Approaches

We must go beyond diplomatic action to educational and moral approaches in stopping the nuclear arms race. One superb educational example is the work of the US Catholic bishops. They launched a careful study of nuclear weapons and war which became a historic statement and is now an educational crusade for nuclear disarmament. They have given leaders of all religions everywhere an enviable model which more should emulate.

Beyond study and statement is direct action and moral witness. Here we might adapt the methods of Mohandas Gandhi and Martin Luther King for nuclear justice. Religious institutions have scarcely begun to demand, using direct action, that their nations take the road to nuclear disarmament, unilaterally if necessary. Small groups, worldwide, have resorted to civil disobedience for nuclear peace since the mid-1950s, but the effort has so far not coalesced and certainly has not become universally visible. Nuclear safety is too important to leave to the traditional methods of influence and policy formulation, at least in societies which call themselves democratic. World religious leaders could become initiators and supporters of these new, non-violent efforts to prevent nuclear suicide.

I have not time to discuss efforts for non-nuclear disarmament. Yet there is a real threat to earth if the arms race is not curbed quickly in outer space through the control of anti-satellite weapons. The threat to the developing world by its own "conventional" arms races is severe. Blame Moscow and Washington if you wish for fuelling the arms races in parts of the developing world. Both account for two-thirds of total arms exports. But one-third comes from other countries, increasingly from Third World arms suppliers. The total volume of the world trade in major conventional weapons was 80 per cent greater in the 1978-82 period approximately since WCRP III than it was in the previous five-year period, after WCRP II.

I conclude this first section of my address, dealing with disarmament, with a quotation from Father Theodore Hesburgh, President of the University of Notre-Dame in the USA and a relatively new recruit to disarmament. He recently stated that "if we don't solve this problem (of nuclear war), if we can't achieve peace, there won't be any other problem, because there won't be any people."

Human Rights

Since this address constitutes my swan-song—although I prefer to call it here in Africa an elephant-dance—I have much on my mind. However, I will confine my comments to one additional substantive issue—human rights—and then give a few suggestions about the future of WCRP. I will conclude with some acknowledgements and then some one-sentence experiences from my time as your Secretary-General. My four-and-a-half year report, beginning with the end of WCRP III to the end of the calendar year 1983 (when I resigned as Secretary-General of WCRP), is independent of this address and is being distributed to this Assembly separately.

I want to make several observations about human rights, partly based on our WCRP representation to UN human rights organs. First, we must all acknowledge that human rights include economic, social, and cultural rights on the one hand and civil and political rights on the other. The socialist world sometimes emphasizes economic, social, and cultural rights—and they should—while the Western world frequently emphasizes civil and political rights. The UN is correct in asserting that both are necessary for a humane society and we of WCRP must never forget this wholeness. It is never either/or, but always both/and.

Second, I want to acknowledge at this time the elaboration of the UN Declaration on the Elimination of All Forms of Intolerance and of Discrimination Based on Religion and Belief. This was a 20-year battle, which WCRP has joined ever since our first Assembly (WCRP I) at Kyoto in 1970. We helped advocate this instrument in UN circles, along with representatives of other non-governmental organizations—NGOs—and finally in 1981 the Declaration was adopted. In the past two years preciously little discrimination based on religion has been reduced because of the adoption of that Declaration. Yet the international standard can be increasingly useful over the years to reduce religious discrimination. What is still needed is a treaty against religious discrimination and it is hoped that the UN community will soon begin to elaborate such a convention.

One of the real disappointments of my administration of WCRP was our inability to deal directly with regional problems of religious conflict. A religious organization ought first to help religions make peace with one another—even before it deals with so-called secular conflict. Religions should first heal themselves. We have had difficulty in becoming constructively involved in conflict with at least a religious dimension—whether in Northern Ireland or West Asia. As Secretary-General, I felt that we should become involved only if we could play a useful, needed role. There is little point just "to become involved". In some of these conflicts, there are organizations galore and traffic policemen are needed—more than healers—to keep organizations from clashing with each other. The fact is that we of WCRP have made no impact on some of the chronic religious wars of our time. We must surely try in the near future to do so.

A third aspect of human rights which has especially concerned me is human massacre. The 20th century has seen such human massacre: the Armenians; the Jews; Christians, and liberals in Nazi Germany; the Hindus, Muslims, and Sikhs at the partition of the sub-continent; and several places in Africa and Asia since the 1940s. In this electronic era can we watch on television human beings being massacred—and do nothing? Or can we somehow rescue victims in the midst of massacre?

It has been my privilege, working with WCRP, to learn about massacre in Bangladesh and Cambodia/Kampuchea and to speak out against it in UN forums. At the UN and before the US Congress, I have suggested that if scientists today can rescue wildlife on the verge of extinction—and they do repeatedly—humanists ought to find means to rescue human beings on the threshold of extinction. The legal hurdles are formidable, the perils are great, but the gains would be magnificent. Cannot some group take some innovative steps to help the about-to-be massacred? Indeed, does the world do nothing as the leadership of the Baha'i religion is being systematically massacred in Iran?

Speaking on the continent of Africa, I must express once more the hope that apartheid will soon disappear. Meeting here, WCRP must oppose apartheid strongly, as it did in Kyoto, Louvain, and Princeton. The world has isolated South Africa, and this is a correct strategy, one in which religious groups are widely co-operating. One day soon apartheid will be dead, gone, eradicated—and all the peoples of South Africa will be free, including the whites.

South Africa is not the only country which separates and divides. It seems that many nations have their special victims. Few religious leaders, even in WCRP, appear able to put universal religious values above parochial nationalistic ones. Few feel comfortable in condemning repression of minorities in their own countries. For many, even of religion, nationalism runs deeper than religion.

On the Indian sub-continent, untouchability has only partly lessened, and new world attention must be paid to this continuing evil, principally in India. We mentioned the plight of the Baha'is in Iran, but also there are other disadvantaged minorities: the Copts in Egypt, the Ahmadis in Pakistan, the Muslims in the Philippines, the Koreans and Untouchables in Japan, and the Blacks in the USA. Racial and religious discrimination still appear almost endemic to humankind in this penultimate decade of the 20th century, including the bad treatment of indigenous people everywhere.

WCRP Policies

In this portion of this address, I want to give some parting advice as the former Secretary-General of this organization. I was privileged to participate in the meetings of the Commission on the Future and its report deserves careful study and implementation. Let me make some additional comments.

First, WCRP should keep close to the UN. I concur with the recommendation that the international office of WCRP be removed to Geneva. But the international headquarters of the UN are in New York and WCRP/International must have a professional presence there—a representative with experience. With all of its faults, the UN is the best institutional hope for world peace. Its headquarters are the best single venue for WCRP to implement its array of positions on international questions; Geneva is a distant second best. The virtue of being close to the UN is that a consultative organization, such as WCRP, comes close to reality, to next political steps. Too often international, non-governmental organizations are politically irrelevant and cannot relate to what is politically possible but not inevitable. Keeping a professional observer, but not always the Secretary-General, at UN Headquarters helps the organization become and stay relevant and keeps it away from constantly tilting at windmills. Also the Secretary-General of WCRP must do more than keep books and deal with correspondence; he or she must make substantive contribution to peace and that may be through frequent contact with the UN.

Second, WCRP should keep close to traditional religion, and even to the mainstreams. The task of WCRP is big enough in dealing with the existing, major religious groups. Some organization other than WCRP can deal with the newcomers, be they the Unification Church, Scientology, Anand Marg—you name them. All "old" religions were new once and one should not penalize a sect because it is new. Yet WCRP need not become involved with, or include, all religious groups everywhere. WCRP can arbitrarily decide—and, in effect, it has already decided—not to get involved with the so-called new religions. Also, WCRP should not deal with ideological conflict. The latter is an important field—socialism, capitalism, other "isms"—but WCRP has a big enough task working with traditional religion, from Buddhism to Zoroastrianism. Again, to exclude ideological conflict may be an arbitrary decision, but it appears to me to be the right decision.

Third, WCRP should keep close to the fields of peace: disarmament, development, human rights, and conflict resolution. These are the major categories on the UN agenda. This spectrum is sufficiently wide, perhaps too wide, but this reflects the holistic approach to peace with justice. There are, I know, temptations for WCRP even on the international level to delve into the field of comparative religion. WCRP in the past has made a decision not to turn itself into an international seminar on world religions. I think that this is also a wise decision. Other organizations can fill this obvious educational need, if not vacuum, in an increasingly multi-religious planet.

Fourth, WCRP should keep its unofficial nature. We started as a handful of individuals, prominent in their religious groups. In the process, we have had some success relating officially to religious groups, to denominations. Yet this has been mostly for financial reasons. There is a tendency to want WCRP to become a formal, official world council of world religious bodies. There would be some advantages, not only financial. But there would be disadvantages also. The great virtue of WCRP so far is that it has been intentionally balanced: it is not dominated by any one religion from any one part of the world. This delicate and necessary balance might well be placed in jeopardy if religious groups were asked officially to join WCRP, since some might do so much faster than others.

Acknowledgements

Now let me shift gears quickly for a round of thanks. Sincere, heart-felt acknowledgements could fill an entire address, but bear with me for a few moments to cover more than 13 years.

I want, first, to thank—and you also should thank—the four founders of WCRP/USA. They first dreamt the dream of WCRP/International. Two are still alive, Bishop John Wesley Lord and Dr. Dana McLean Greeley. Indeed, Dr. Greeley especially deserves our praise for his continuing and wise leadership and involvement from the beginning to this minute. Also we cannot forget John Cardinal Wright and Rabbi Maurice Eisendrath.

The second group to be commended are those present leaders of WCRP/International who joined with the US leaders in New Delhi and in Kyoto in January 1968—before WCRP was officially born. Those who are still active today include Archbishop Angelo Fernandes, Sri R.R. Diwakar, Rev. Toshio Miyake, and President Nikkyo Niwano. Each one of these four persons has continued intense activity with WCRP since 1968—16 long years—and each deserves my personal tribute and yours. Archbishop Fernandes has been our only President, since 1970, and has served with great distinction, giving careful attention to substantive issues. He has served us longer than the tenure of most recent popes! Sri Diwakar, our junior citizen, continues to give us valuable counsel, with as alert a mind as ever. Rev. Miyake is in an enviable class by himself, with his sustained religious leadership for peace. President Niwano has contributed much, including the facilities and resources of Rissho Kosei-Kai. Also I am indebted to the Niwano Peace Foundation for awarding me the 1984 Niwano Peace Prize.

Since 1968 many people from many parts of the world, and many religious groups, have become active in WCRP. I do not have time to give their names. I cannot name here all those who left us, strong leaders whose time to depart had come. Their names are in my report. I must, however, name two. One is the Ven. Riri Nakayama, a Buddhist of

124

Japan who was a persistent link between religious leaders in Japan and the USA in the formation of WCRP. Another is Dr. Maria A. Lücker, a Christian from the Federal Republic of Germany, whose death in the past year was a blow not only to WCRP/Europe but to religious workers for peace everywhere.

Also I must thank national WCRP officers and members in many countries on all continents. My wife and I, on various occasions, had the opportunity to visit many of them. We never did get to the Soviet Union, South Africa, and Latin America. Yet I fondly recall visiting groups in Fiji, New Zealand, and Australia, all across Asia, several times in Africa, much in Europe, and so often in the USA and Canada. Whether in Tokyo, Dhaka, or London, visits to WCRP groups have been challenging and, I hope, our presence brought them closer to our international body.

Outside our WCRP family, we must thank the sister organizations— religious or secular—with whom we have worked. We must especially thank the UN community—secretariat, diplomats, press, and non-governmental organization representatives.

I must thank members of our small WCRP staff, where the national or regional committees had staff, such as in Tokyo and Bonn, but also in New York City. Renate Belck was my hardworking associate for six years—and I appreciate her hard, dedicated work. Also I thank my wife for bearing with me these years, again in various parts of the world, but especially her help in the Boat People Project off Malaysia, and in the Khmer People Project in Thailand. Lastly, I thank my successor, Dr. John B. Taylor, for filling my role so quickly, and also Sister Marjorie Keenan and Dr. Norbert Klaes for their staff work with us.

No doubt I have left out more persons than I have mentioned, but I have tried to remember a few without whose help WCRP would not be what it is today—and hopefully what it will be to tomorrow.

Emotional Experiences

Finally, I must recall, if only in check-list fashion, some of my most emotional experiences as your Secretary-General for more than 13 years:

My most thrilling moments were both the opening session of WCRP I at Kyoto—when we finally but initially came together—and the march through the streets of ancient Louvain at the end of WCRP II.

My greatest joy was the arrival at WCRP III in Princeton of representatives from religions of the People's Republic of China.

My greatest regret was the series of blunders, and worse, of the Boat People Project in Southeast Asia.

My most dangerous moments were visiting the guerilla village inside Kampuchea maintained by the Khmer People's National Liberation Front.

My most exhilarating moments were to see co-workers attain high political positions: Justice Abu Choudhury becoming President of Bangladesh and Son Sann elected Prime Minister of Democratic Kampuchea.

My most unreal moment was when President Jimmy Carter in the White House before the WCRP reception turned to me and asked, "Homer, what happens next?"

My most tense moment occurred during denunciations from diplomats of eight nations after I gave testimony before the UN Commission on Human Rights in Geneva.

My most hard-earned moment was the adoption by the UN General Assembly in New York of the Declaration against Religious Discrimination.

My greatest WCRP trip was the visit to emerging religious groups in China.

My most legal moment was suing US Secretary of State Alexander Haig for refusing visas to certain non-governmental observers to attend the Second UN Special Session on Disarmament.

My most illegal moment was getting arrested for civil disobedience against one of the five nuclear weapon States at the UN for their refusing to disarm.

My most humorous remembrance was at the inter-religious consultation in Honolulu when Dr. Greeley appeared on the first morning in a business suit while President Niwano wore a Hawaiian shirt; at the next meeting Dr. Greeley arrived in a Hawaiian shirt and President Niwano in a business suit!

My most tearful moment was receiving word that I won the 1984 Niwano Peace Prize.

My most fulfilling moment here so far at WCRP IV was to hear the report of the two-day youth meeting. I can now retire, knowing that the future of WCRP is in good hands, even in terms of substance.

As many of you know, I have always believed on being on time and staying on time; thus my most delayed moment is now in Nairobi, finishing this address.

Goodbye.

E.

Presentations in
Commission I
"People of Faith Working
Together for Peace"

25

By Sri Shrivatsa Goswami*

The hymns from the Vedas, the earliest religious documents of humanity, inform us that: "The hearth-fire was in heaven, the Sun was in this world; these two worlds were then disturbed. God said, 'Let us transpose these two'. . . Then indeed, these two worlds became free from disturbances."

Human existence is a situation oscillating between "is" and "ought," reality and ideal. We all desire prosperity, well-being, and peace, yet are mostly stuck with poverty, suffering, and war. This strife-torn dark picture is sufficient to put us in a gloomy mood. But, we, being conscious of our real nature, and having faith in the higher values of human existence, strive to put brighter, happier colours in the picture.

Despite the tremendous odds against world peace and human survival in the forms of selfish economic interests and fierce competition among nations for military supremacy, under the threat of nuclear holocaust, the hopeful note exists. This Fourth Assembly of WCRP has brought together people from all over the world—East and West, North and South—all concerned with a single issue, i.e., peace.

Today, this peace gathering is in the best Vedic tradition, where we should direct our deliberations towards giving a proper diagnosis of the present distressing situation. We shall have to find out what is wrong with our understanding and with our doings. We have not only to desire peace, but also to strive for those things which make peace possible. Taking the cue from my personal experience of my own larger religious tradition, i.e., Hinduism, I share with you all the conviction that the real crisis lies in a loss of faith in the Ultimate Reality, the ground of our existence and hope; we may call it God. Our turning away from God is the sole misery; remembering it shows us the way back to happiness and to insight into the means of meeting the crisis.

What is this God? Our Scriptures answer: God (*Rāmā*) is the embodiment of *dharma*, our essential nature, our rights and responsibili-

*Sri Shrivatsa Goswami is Director of Sri Caitanya Prema Sansthana in Vrindaban, India.

129

ties. (The same lessons which Krishna teaches us in the Bhagavad-Gita.) *Dharma* is one word which defines and covers the totality of human experience. *Dharma*, derived from the root, *dhr*, meaning to uphold, to support, to nourish, to integrate, etc., is the sum total of essential values and ideas on which the political, economic, cultural, and religious expressions of life are based. These values, to be universally acceptable, must also be recommended by collective human wisdom born out of experience.

To explain and understand the social reality, one aspect of *dharma*, there is *varna dharma*. It delineated the duties of individuals in the social context. It put them into four classes. The myth of these classes springing out of the four parts of the creative spirit emphasizes the organic character of society. Dr Radhakrishnan succinctly stated that the individual is in solidarity with all human beings. Society and individual are bound together in a common destiny. The social units of family, tribe, clan, nation, are successive stages toward universal humanity. The individual has to be mindful of the needs of society before declaring his own rights and ends. At the same time, society should not forfeit the individual's freedom and rights.

This relation does not operate in a vacuum. A social group is formed, regulated by character, behaviour, and function of its member-individuals. Not only for Hindus, but for the whole human race, we can generalize that spiritual wisdom, executive power, skilled production, and devoted service are the indispensable elements of any social order.

The intellectual class pursues knowledge and gives moral guidance, which it can do only if it pursues the truth without any compulsions, material cares, or competition. In our time, when human good is confused with racial and national chauvinism, we need free Brahmans to ensure that we do not stray away from the truth.

Such objective truths and values are to be enforced, executed, and actualized by persons of power and action, who are daring, fearless, noble, and who resist injustice and oppression. The irony is that precisely these persons are most liable to corruption and often turn into degenerate, power-hungry, brute tyrants. This may happen if we commit the mistake of meekly accepting the principle that reasons of state justify any crime. The function of the ruler is to protect the law and defend the values that make for personal freedom and true happiness. Some may argue that the use of force is the last alternative, and that, too, to be adopted only in an ethical way, with the highest good in view. Any coercive action causes resentment in its victim and tempts the user into further violence. And, when no code governs the conduct of war and the tools of destruction are totally devastating, as is the case today, the total rejection of the use of force is the ideal. We must desire and strive to attain it. There is no middle way; nothing short of it will do.

Craftsmen, farmers, and traders sustain the material well-being of a society. It will be a perversion of the true economic order if some earn wealth and power at the expense of others. However, this has become the chief mode of our social behaviour, resulting in ruthless exploitation of the poor by the rich.

Last, but not the least, is the service class, which significantly is represented in the myth mentioned above as the feet of God, which symbolize work and labour, which provide the basis on which the entire social fabric rests.

It will be wrong to conclude that the characteristic qualities of a particular class are exclusive. They are in all classes, but some special qualities, dormant in one class, are dominant in another. This is a natural hierarchy, emerging from the process of social development everywhere. It has nothing to do with the rigid caste system as it took a distorted shape in Hindu social history during the period of slavery under foreign powers and cultures for over ten centuries. The *skt* word for caste system is *varṇa*, literally meaning colour. It is most unfortunate that this ugliest form of caste system, based on the colour of human skin, is still practised in highly civilized parts of our planet. The true *varṇa* scheme, as mentioned earlier, has a spiritual basis; it is functional and open-ended as far as movement of individuals from one class to another is concerned. Initially, this spiritual value system of class or *varṇa* is intended to guarantee personal freedom to the individual, provide status and dignity equally to members of every class, and a chance for spiritual fulfilment unrestricted in any way.

Dharma has another dimension which relates to the individual persons who constitute society. The social order attains its fullest realization of peace and prosperity when the individuals comprising it themselves go through a number of essential steps in their own lives. The earlier part of life is the formative period when one sees, encounters, and learns about oneself and one's surroundings, values, and situations. In this learning process one is equipped to meet the challenges and demands of one's vocation in social life. Then, as a member of society, an individual contributes most by actively producing in his own social/vocational realm. In his relationship to other human beings are defined his rôles in family and society, his responsibilities and obligations. Fulfilment of these is the social order.

One's advancement in age brings about a retirement from active participation which is prompted by the maturity gained through the formative and productive periods. What one receives in early life from society is paid back as a householder and worker. With those obligations discharged, one advances into the life of reflection and meditation, related to society only through detachment. This state of detachment helps us in understanding the basic and essential nature of human beings—our own reality.

The social, political, religious nature and dimensions of human reality vary according to their own cultural, national, historical factors. Each different ethos divides our human family. Our process of learning and understanding only adds to the refinement of these distinctions of nationalities, languages, ideologies, etc. This turns human history into a document of hatred, disbelief, and violence.

Even our membership in the highest club of the faithful has not helped us establish friendship. Past as well as present is the striking reminder of the most sad fact, that in the name of God, faith, and a particular religious tradition, we have betrayed each other, shamelessly. A faith in oneself without understanding the other is devastatingly cruel. It may well prompt us to deny religion. We have experimented on these lines, but humanity still suffers.

The clue to the situation lies not in denial of natural human tendencies, but in understanding and properly defining our own essential being. Hindu wisdom acknowledges that "non-violence, truth, unselfishness, compassion, purity of mind and action, self-control, contentment, mercy, charity," etc., are essential attributes of human beings, cutting across all racial, sectarian, linguistic, national, and cultural boundaries. Human interaction based on these values will sustain any society at any time. The eternal truth and universality of these human values is the common ground on which we can all relate. These values, which include and transcend all cultural shades, we all share.

Someone who realizes this inner self (*sva-dharma*) with the help of a proper spiritual, moral, and social discipline (*varna-asrama-dharma*), is able to transcend all limitations. This deeper awareness makes one responsible towards others as they also share in this essential nature. One's freedom and compassion allow one to work for the welfare of all beings. Such a person is a true ascetic (*sannayasi*) who renounces his ego and selfishness and thus belongs to everyone equally, without any motive or compulsion except compassion. By dissociating from the self-serving interest of his family, society, nation, sect, etc., he enjoys and expresses his freedom as a critic, watchman, guide, and teacher.

The realization of these highest human values (*paramadharma*) alone makes the religious experience—man realizing God—significant. Hinduism has the courage to reduce God and the Ultimate Reality to these principles of truth, consciousness, and blissfulness. Cosmologically, the emphasis is on human activities in relation to other human beings, nature, and "the divine". The most important act of God is to endow us with consciousness "to know" the truth and also with free will to shape our own reality.

But, in our over-confidence, born out of ignorance, we spoil the kingdom of God, this, our own world. The harmony of nature, human and divine, is disturbed; the order (*dharma*) is upset. Instead of respecting and sharing our life with life-giving nature we only intend to exploit and do away with it. The consequences we all know. In the social realm—our relationship with other humans—the same selfishness spoils the game. We have shown the consequences above; in our own context, we all face them. Similarly, in our spirit of arrogant adventurism in the realm of the unknown, we have depended too much on unguided technology and created a deadly power which is sufficient to wipe us all out of existence thousands of times. We were given divine powers, but we have created a realm of death.

Due to ignorance, we may be arrogant and behave irresponsibly, not realizing our spiritual nature and potential; God, however, is not cruel. Whenever God "sees" human beings suffer, He comes to us Himself or sends His messengers to correct our path, time and again, in all human settings. In my own larger Hindu tradition I remind you of three such events.

God Himself appeared as Krishna, to participate in and guide the conflict between good and evil forces. He did not fight for the good ones, but revealed what was truth. His message was of peace and non-violence but to save and restore them he did not run away from the war of righteousness. In the socio-religious realm, he established a harmony based on the relation of love. He was a pioneer in raising ecological concerns and dedicated towards cleaning the biosphere.

The second example of divine grace is the appearance of Sri Caitanya Mahaprabhu five centuries back. It is a unique and complete manifestation of divinity in an ordinary human form. His message, his method of love and service, affirmed the doctrine of the humanization of divinity. He met the challenge of evil oppression with only the weapon of loving persuasion and non-violent disobedience in the face of oppression.

The third such story of divine intervention begins on this African continent at the start of the present century. Mohandas Karamchand Gandhi actualizing Krishna and Caitanya in our time experimented with truth and was successful in demonstrating the process of divinization of the human. He reached *Rām*, i.e., God. through truth and completely melded them: truth was *Rām* and *Rām* was truth. He lived the example of an ascetic involved in worldly problems; developing and practising non-violence as the only tool, he showed that any true human virtue (*dharma*) is sufficient for the highest realization. He never distinguished between religious and secular modes of life. His own words state:

"My motive has been purely religious. I could not be leading a religious life unless I identified myself with the whole of mankind; and this I could not do unless I took part in politics. The whole gamut of man's activities to-day constitutes an indivisible whole, you cannot divide social, political, and purely religious work into watertight compartments. I do not know any religion apart from human activity. My devotion to truth has drawn me into the field of politics; and I can say without the slightest hesitation, and yet with all humility, that those who say that religion has nothing to do with politics do not know what religion means."

And that is the problem of modern man. We are not discerning enough to distinguish religious dogmas and creed from true spirituality (*sanatana manava dharma*) the basis of all human religiosity. This task is gigantic. The present era of our creation is described by Hindus as a decadent age, where the *dharma* (values) will lie low, due to the dominance of technology (*kala yuga*). But, at the same time, it is accepted as a blessing in disguise. The technology has shrunk our planet and brought all of us to interface. Now, we can't ignore each other. Instead of fighting with each other, we had better find our commonality of humanness (*manava dharma*) to start a sincere dialogue which could lead to peaceful co-existence. Actually speaking at this critical moment of history, we people of different religious traditions have gone beyond the luxury of dialoguing and, in that guise, fighting among ourselves. Now the dialogue is really between all religions on one hand, and the forces of death, i.e., the forces of war and total annihilation, on the other.

By coming here, to Nairobi, we have agreed to accept peace as our "ultimate concern". WCRP is our religious sect, including and transcending all our religious individualities. This meeting reminds me of the ancient Vedic worship for peace (*santi ya jna*) which is for the restoration of order in our world. In this ritual (*ya jna*) of peace, all the participants have to make their offering by declaring that what each offers does not belong to him or her. We give it away for divine satisfaction. For optimum results, something precious is to be offered. And, what can be more dear to us than our own selfishness and ego? If we have courage and willingness to sacrifice our false and limiting identities of all kinds, even including religious and spiritual egos, then, I assure you, the outcome will be peace. "Peace is not the mere absence of war; it is the development of a strong fellow-being, an honest appreciation of other peoples' ideas and values," declares a modern Indian saint.

In conclusion, I invite you to read with me the resolution of our peace-worship from the Vedas:

> "Let there be peace in heaven, in space,
> on earth, in the waters,
> in herbs, in plants,
> for all the gods, for Brahma, the Ultimate Reality;
> let all be peace—nothing but peace.
> Let our peace ever increase."

26

By Ven. Visuddhananda Mahathero*

On this auspicious occasion we have gathered here at Nairobi, the capital of Kenya, Africa. On the one hand we see economic, political, cultural and social structures which seem to be lagging behind in comparison with the rest of the globe. On the other hand, this is a country which represents revolutionary upheaval of human aspirations after centuries of colonial exploitation, racial discrimination, and backward systems of life and livelihood. We have gathered at a time when a renaissance of emancipation is visible throughout the continent.

It is quite befitting that WCRP IV is being held at this present phase of human history and on a particular continent which needs the materialization of the declared principles of WCRP. These stand for safeguarding human dignity and are warning against large-scale massacre of the human race. In this mammoth gathering of international significance, I shall give voice to my views as a Buddhist monk belonging to a country where Buddhism flourished as an original creed of nourishing the best spirit of rational achievements. My country, Bangladesh, having a tradition of compassion, tolerance, co-operation and dedication, still holds the principle of "Live and let live" and advocates the ideology of co-existence in the international forum and committee of nations.

My religion, Buddhism, stands for uniting all people in the realization of essential principles of thought and reflexion. It is through unity of mind that people can understand one another and serve one another. In the present day world crisis, all peace-loving people, no matter what their political or religious identity may be, should strive to create an atmosphere of peace and an environment of co-existence.

All the world's thinkers, past and present, contributed towards peaceful and good neighbourly relations. The best canons and doctrines of mankind are described in religious texts. So it is admitted on all

---

*Ven. Visuddhananda Manathero is Supreme Patriarch of the Bangladesh Bhikkhu Sangha Council and founder of a Buddhist monastery and orphanage in Dhaka, Bangladesh.

hands that religion is the only panacea for the diseases of the world today and for advancing civilization. It is high time for all religious faiths to work together on a common platform to attain common ends. Otherwise this very world may be damaged on a global scale by nuclear weapons. All leaders of religious bodies should understand this momentous question, how to survive, how to save civilization, built up through centuries of human endeavour. WCRP works in that line and pursues a policy of universalism. Its object is to keep the world fit as a human abode. The task may appear gigantic. But unity and integrity or purpose can make it easy.

In Pali literature there are several instances which prove the strength of unity. Buddha emphasized unity: "*Samagganam tapo Sukha*," "Unity is the root of happiness." In one sermon in the Mahavagga, he pointed out that when floods occur portions of land are inundated. Ants find no way out. In that case they come closer, make a lump of themselves and the lump floats on the water. Thus not a single ant dies. We should take this moral instance from tiny insects like ants. Hence, the leaders of the world religions should make their followers aware of the fact that each and every individual has the responsibility for his own survival and for humanity as a whole. The selfish mind prepares for war; the compassionate and understanding mind unites for peace. And being so close to a total calamity, we should prevent it by unity, concord and moral force.

Let me cite another brilliant example of unity. The Bodhisatta, the future Buddha, was once born as a parrot. He was the leader of a flock. A hunter used to set a net and caught four or five every day. The Bodhisatta, the leader of these parrots, was worried and hit upon a plan. He called all the parrots of the flock and explained his plan. The next day they flew to the cornfield all in a body. The hunter had already put his trap to catch parrots. He thought that he would score a lot that day. The trap was a net. When the hunter was coming to wind up his net, the leader of the parrots ordered all to fly up at a time. So they did and flew to a distance. Then they placed the net on a tree and all of them escaped downwards. The hunter took the net from the tree and went back home in despair. Thus all the parrots escaped death through unity, devised by the Bodhisatta, the future Buddha. Whatever our denomination, being Buddhists, Christians, Hindus, Jews, Muslims, Sikhs, etc., first and foremost we are human beings, having to live together in this world. So in order to cope with the threat humanity is facing, let us unite, being conscious of the noble principles of human behaviour we have in common. Let us fly like parrots throwing the nets of racial discrimination, apartheid, aggression, etc., into the ocean for the establishment of permanent peace in the world.

From the two world wars, witnessed by the world's population, we have learned how to save ourselves. The Charters of the League of Nations and of the United Nations Organization are not sufficient for the safety of the world and for stopping world wars for ever. The Charters must be enforced, must be translated into reality. Otherwise they will remain as high sounding phrases, nicely printed on the nice pages of world history.

It is obvious that the declared mottoes or proclaimed missions have no real value if they are not applied to yield fruits. WCRP can fulfil this historical task. Every individual is a member of a particular religion. So the total enrolment of religions is absolutely the largest. With this biggest number of followers the religious leaders may mould our future history, provided good will and sincerity prevail through unity. If religion is used for the profit of vested interest, it will be a tremendous loss for mankind. Though religions have brought their blessings in the world's history, sometimes they have been utilized as instruments for malpractice and exploitation by the priests, churches, and temples. So there is no denial of the fact that religion has lost its original fervour, universal appeal and humanitarian approach, at least to some extent. All the same, religion stands as champion of universal blessings and an organ of moral force. Man seeks relief from despair and dismay through religion. Now religion should have no scope for going astray. In religious institutions decisions should be taken democratically, consciously, and judiciously. The modern concept of religion is not bigotry or prejudice. So religion and religion alone can save this world from total collapse and disaster.

To deal with any subject or topic prescribed by the initiators of this conference of WCRP, the common points must be dealt with. The religions of today may be called the cradle of human civilization of tomorrow. Religion is for the good of the whole. But some enjoy the entire product of science and technology, allowing others to live and die in utter poverty, helplessness and ill fate, defying the teaching of religion.

Peace within the race, within the family, within the nation is a prelude to peace in the world. Some big nations are wasting millions of dollars manufacturing war materials, money that might be used to feed the hungry multitudes of the Third World. Every minute, millions of dollars are being spent for killing man. Every day tons of food are thrown into the sea, leaving millions of people in starvation. This is not a means of peace, but a menace to peace.

I believe that this conference of WCRP will indicate a path of peace, progress and dignity of the human race.

Sabbe Satta Sukhita Bhavantu
(May all beings be well and happy)

27

By Dr. Victor C. Goldbloom *

This is a large assembly; yet in relation to the size of the world's population, we are a very tiny gathering indeed. We must therefore approach our task with humility, so as not to exaggerate our own importance; but we must also be bold enough to see clearly the magnitude of the challenge we have chosen to face, and to take up that challenge in the name of, and for the sake of, all humankind.

Our common task is complicated by the many differences that exist between us, differences not only of religion and race and language, but also differences of life experience, of economic and social situation, of political context, of short-term objectives. We share, however, at least one long-term objective, that of peace, and therefore our differences must not be obstacles to our friendship, our mutual respect and our cooperation.

Also, we have at least one quality in common: we are people of goodwill. We are people of hope and purpose, and we cannot allow ourselves to leave the world the way it is. We cannot passively wait for peace by luck or miracle. We do not find it enough to say, with the prophet Jeremiah, "Peace, peace, but there *is* no peace." We have come together here so that we can go forth from this assembly and *act*, wake the world's conscience, change the course of history. In the scope of the world's present danger, our objective can be nothing less.

So let us not be dismayed, discouraged or depressed by the smallness of our numbers and the magnitude of our challenge. I turn to the words of a man whom I had the privilege of meeting some 40 years ago, whom I heard speak on more than one occasion, and whose book, *Recovery of Faith*, from which these words are taken, occupies a place of honour on so many shelves, Sarvepalli Radhakrishnan:

> "In every religion today we have small minorities who see beyond the horizons of their particular faith, who believe that religious fellowship is possible, not through the imposition of any one way on the whole world but

---

* Dr. Victor Goldbloom is President of the International Council of Christians and Jews, and lives in Toronto, Canada.

through an all-inclusive recognition that we are all searchers for the truth, pilgrims on the road, that we all aim at the same ethical and spiritual standards... The widespread existence of this state of mind is the hope of the future."

We here, then, are the hope of the future. I say that humbly, not arrogantly; with awe, not with pretentiousness. We have the obligation to ensure that at the end of this conference *we*, at least, shall be one small step closer to peace. Then, we shall have to go forth and be examples.

Four and a half years ago, only a few weeks after taking up my present responsibilities, I was in Vancouver, where many of you were last summer, for an inter-religious and inter-cultural gathering co-sponsored by the Canadian Council of Christians and Jews. The opening invocation was offered by the Roman Catholic Archbishop of Vancouver, Msgr. James Carney, and I have treasured it ever since: he prayed that we be blessed with the ability, in our dialogue, to rise above simplifications and platitudes.

Peace is not simple, and it is certainly not a platitude; but it is terribly easy to talk about it simplistically and platitudinously. If we talk together in this assembly, agree that we are all in favour of peace, and then go our separate ways in the afterglow of that agreement without having devised specific, effective action, our service to peace will have been lip-service and our travel costs and efforts will have been wasted. No, it is particularly when we talk of peace that we must rise above simplifications and platitudes.

Five words, to me, are watchwords: patience, persistence, realism, restraint and trust.

We need patience, because peace may not come quickly. We have even to consider the possibility that peace may not become pervasive and permanent in our lifetime. Indeed, one of our most important tasks is to teach it indelibly to our children and so leave it to them as heritage. They, at least, must do better than we.

We need persistence, because patience alone is too passive. Peace is elusive, and the road to it is winding. If we do not find it at the next bend of the road, or the next, or the next, we must have the courage and the fortitude to persist. We, of all people, must not become discouraged.

We need realism, because if we set unrealistic objectives for ourselves, we shall become discouraged. We must find realistic solutions to the escalation of armaments: the escalation of quantity, the escalation of deployment, the escalation of sophistication. Unable to turn back the clock of research, we must turn the results to the benefit of humankind and make them safe from madmen. Our proposals must have credibility and workability, and they must attract consensus.

We need restraint, because peace will probably not come dramatically. It is unlikely that world leaders will suddenly fall on their knees in a burst of sunshine, and then there will be universal peace. No, peace is much more likely to be a slow process, beginning with some small measure of restraint which will then be matched by a small measure of restraint on the other side, so that step-wise the tension will de-escalate. Let me add: we need restraint not only in deeds but in words as well. Rhetoric may give emotional satisfaction; but the rhetoric of denunciation is likely to breed only counter-rhetoric, not peace. Let us strive also, therefore, to de-escalate the world's use of words. Let us really talk of peace.

We need trust, because it is the only possible foundation upon which peace can be built. Trust is the fundamental objective of dialogue; we tend to mistrust the person whom we do not know and whom we consider to be different from ourselves. Trust requires patience, persistence, realism and restraint. Peace is trust; trust is peace. In order to achieve both, we must talk to each other in respect and love across the dividing-lines of our differences. That is why we are here.

The American historian, Thomas Sowell, in a book published last year and entitled, *The Economics and Politics of Race*, wrote these words:

> "History is irrevocable... We must never imagine that we can either recreate, or atone for, yesterday. What we can do is to make its experience the basis for a better today and a better tomorrow."

I close with a prayer from my own worship:

> "So teach us to number our days,
> that we get us a heart of wisdom."

May we of this conference receive the gift of wisdom; may we rise above simplifications and platitudes; and may we together make one small step—and then another, and another—on the road to peace.

28

Presentation By Ven. Jing Hui*

Homage to Buddha
Homage to Dharma
Homage to Sangha

At this auspicious time of the World Conference on Religion and Peace, we heartily pray that the Triple Gem, with its compassionate light, guide and help WCRP that it be able to preserve its noble wisdom for world peace and human righteousness, and develop its true function, and achieve greater results.

Heartily we pray for WCRP's mission of world peace and that its right cause will continue fruitfully.

Heartily we pray that humanity's good consciousness and righteousness will be fulfilled through this principle:

Not to do bad
To do good
Purify the mind . . .
. . . so that humanity will find harmony,
security and a happy life.

Especially, we heartily pray that all the women in the world enjoy their dignities and all the equalities; that all the young people will grow up and live successfully in the world without war.

Heartily we pray that the leaders of all the nations in the world will be prosperous, and that their people will have security and happiness.

Heartily we pray that all the members of WCRP will enjoy good health and happiness.

May the merit we have found be adhered to by all people.

May we and all living beings obtain enlightenment and liberation.

---

*Ven. Jing Hui represented the Buddhist Association of China, based in Beijing, in the People's Republic of China.

F.

PRESENTATIONS IN COMMISSION II
Human Dignity, Social Justice, And Development of the Whole Person

29

By Dr. S. K. Chaturvedi*

Economic and social injustice are the darkest shadows of our society. They are the root-causes of hunger, misery and oppression. They lead individuals, families and countries to jealousy, selfishness, conflict and war. They generate and nurse disregard to other's rights in common wealth and even survival.

Differences in per capita income of countries are awe-inspiring. The Lao People's Democratic Republic and Bhutan try to survive with only $80.00 per capita as compared with $26,850.00 in the United Arab Emirates.[a]** Besides high-income oil exporters, industrial market economies provide interesting material. Switzerland has a per capita income of $16,440.00 followed by the Federal Republic of Germany ($13,590.00), Sweden ($13,520.00) and Denmark ($12,950.00).

Income disparity in a society and a country is equally striking. The lowest 20% of households share only 1.9% of the GNP in Peru, 2% in Brazil and Panama and 2.6% in Kenya against 42.9%, 50.6%, 44.2% and 45.8% respectively of the highest 10%. Nearly 31,000 households in Bangladesh receive less than $80.00 income per year and 186,000 between $80.00 and $120.00. Per capita income figures for these families will tell you a different tale. Simultaneously, 263,000 families in the same country claim over $2,000.00 per year.

According to some estimates, nearly one billion people are living in absolute poverty in the world. The majority of the absolute poor—about 80%—live in rural areas working on farms and other farm-related work. In the low-income market economies of Bangladesh, India, Pakistan, Nepal, Indonesia, etc., the unfortunate poor strive with the minimum necessities of life. Nearly 82% of the population in Bangladesh, more than one-third in Pakistan and 41.5% in India is still below the poverty line. A large number of poor go to bed half-fed, walk bare-footed and

---

*Dr. Chaturvedi, an employee of the Indian Government, has represented India at several international conferences. He was also Associate Secretary of WCRP in 1981.
a. World Development Report 1982, pp. 111, 158.

half naked and die medically unattended. They are least vocal and simple and easily fall into the everlasting clutches of exploiters.

Gaps in income are bound to widen at the present rate by 2,000 A.D. A UNICEF report estimates that the per capita GNP in most of Latin America will be about $2,000.00 by the end of the century. On the other hand, the poorest countries of South Asia and Sub-Saharan Africa will achieve a per capita GNP of less than $300.00 a year. The message of these estimates is clear. The poorest nations stand to be by-passed by the next 20 years of development just as surely as they have been in the past. It means that the dimensions of economic injustice will grow and clouds of poverty will get denser. With the current inflationary trend, $300.00 may fail to purchase what $80.00 can buy now.

Effects of economic injustice are shocking. Approximately 40,000 infants and children die every day in developing countries on account of malnutrition and infection. According to a recent World Health Organization report, in most African and Southeast Asian countries over 100 babies out of every 1,000 die before their first birthday. The figure for most developed countries in below 13 per 1,000. The death rate among Third World children under 15 is ten times the number in developed countries. Out of the present world population of 4.5 billion, 100 million are now disabled through malnutrition. Every year, 250,000 children lose their eyesight through lack of Vitamin A alone.

There have been some efforts at the international level to narrow the economic gap between the rich and the poor nations. However, such efforts have failed to pay any dividend so far. Growth rates in the developing countries are disappointing. Third World economies have been shrinking. Even the modest rate of growth has become totally negative in the last few years. The economic policies of the industrialized countries including the United States, Japan and Western Europe, instead of contributing to the development of the poor countries, have caused their growth rate to alter. Recent events in Latin America are a pointer in this direction. In a joint statement on May 19, 1984, the Presidents of Argentina, Brazil, Columbia and Mexico said that the debtor nations were in an impossible situation. They warned that rising interest rates in the United States—to which their loans are linked—are creating unbearable costs for their countries. They also warned that a growing tide of protectionism in the industrialized nations is making it impossible for them to earn enough to pay their debts. The situation has become so hopeless that Ecuador announced on June 4, 1984, the suspension of payments of its debts to foreign governments. Bolivia went a step further and decided to postpone repayment of debt to foreign commercial banks.

Despite progressive taxation and various social security measures, most of the capitalist countries have not succeeded in narrowing the rich and poor gap. Socialist countries claim to have succeeded in providing basic necessities including food, shelter, clothing and education to all. However, the number of poor and needy remains large.

As renunciation is the keynote of Hindu philosophy, it denounces

146

accumulation of wealth. According to Hindu Dharmashastra, *Dharma* is a mode of life or a code of conduct which regulates a man's work and activities as a member of society and as an individual, and is intended to bring about the gradual development of a man to enable him to reach what is deemed to be the goal of human existence. "It was conception of obligations, of the discharge of one's duties to oneself and to others. This *Dharma* itself was part of " 'Rita,' " the fundamental moral law governing the functioning of the universe and all it contained."[b] In the Hindu religion, God realization is not possible without a moral code of conduct and an ethical character which among other things includes loving service of all beings and setting aside of selfish considerations of greed. Welfare of not only human beings but of all the creatures (*"Sarva Bhootha Hita"*) is the essence of the Hindu religion. It lays great stress on the sharing of wealth with the poor. Realizing that force can be partly effective in narrowing the rich-poor gap, it lays emphasis on voluntary sharing of wealth. Charity, or *'Dan'*, is considered one of the greatest virtues. According to the Hindu religion, a man who supports many others to live, lives in the real sense and should live for a longer time. Others who feed only themselves are no better than a crow who strives throughout its life only to fill its belly.[c] Persons who do not perform any good to others are like worms living inside a wild fig tree (*"Gular"*) whose wings have no use.[d] The Gita says: "The people eating the remnants of Yagya are freed from all sins; but those who cook food only for themselves, those sinful ones eat sin." The Brihandaranyaka Upanishad inculcates in all the great need of three cardinal virtues, viz., *Daman* (self-restraint), *Daya* (compassion or love), and *Dana* (charity). Sharing one's wealth with others is one of the nine duties of all Hindus.[e] The great Hindu sage Adi Shankara strikes the key-note of the Hindu conduct in a couplet "Sing the Lord's thousand names, read the Gita, meditate over the form of God, direct the mind to the company of holy men and give wealth to the poor and needy." The couplet contains in simple and short language what a Hindu should do.

Various verses in Sanskrit literature sing in praise of charity. "Hands are decorated by giving alms, not by wearing bracelets."[f] The great king Harsha of Kanauj used to donate all his wealth every year at the confluence of the rivers—the Ganges and the Jamuna—at Prayag, and when nothing was left, he used to request his sister Rajyashree to give him a piece of cloth to cover his body. The Hindu religion lays great emphasis one simplicity and condemns ostentatious living. It becomes, therefore, on of the basic duties of a Hindu to share his wealth. Even the

---

b. Discovery by Jawaharlal Nehru, the first Prime Minister of India.

c. Hitopadesh, Second Park Shloka 37.

d. Vairagya Shatakam Shloka 121 by Bhartihari. Mahabharat, the great Hindu epic.

e. Mahabharat, the great Hindu epic.

f. Chanakya Neeti, Shloka 297.

147

poor Hindus give something to charity. A Hindu without charity is considered a living dead.

The second important question is with whom to share one's wealth. It prescribes that the receiver of charity must be *Supatra*, a deserving person, and this includes the poor, needy and hungry. The object is to achieve maximum economic justice by reducing economic disparity. The Mahabharta says: "As rain is beneficial in the desert and food to the hungry, similarly charity is beneficial, if it is to the poor." Hindu religion prohibits the sharing of wealth with the well-to-do who are considered non-deserving. Anything given to such persons in charity does not bring any merit and should be considered a waste. It has been laid down in Hindu scriptures: "As a healthy man does not require any medicine, so a rich man is not entitled to charity." The Rigveda lays down: "Bounteous is he who gives to the beggar who comes to him in want of food and feeble." It is still customary with a large number of Hindu families to feed the hungry first. The digging of wells for providing water to thirsty travellers, construction of *Dharmashalas* for shelters and planting of trees by the roadside are considered acts of *Paropkara* (doing good to others). Kautilya in his Arthashastra prescribes that the State should provide support to the poor, pregnant women and their offspring, orphans, the aged, infirm, the afflicted and helpless.[g]

The third important question is how much to give. Hindu religion commands every well-to-do Hindu to share at least one-tenth of his wealth with the poor. It also advocates progressive sharing of wealth. Those who donate more in charity are considered materially better persons and spiritually racing towards immortality. It is probable that if these commands were to be observed by the well-to-do in society, it would go a long way in bridging the gulf between rich and poor. It could disperse the clouds of poverty on the economic horizon of society to a large extent and bring a smile to many tearful faces.

g. Kautilya wrote his Arthashastra in the beginning of the 4th century B.C.

30

By Mr. Ian Fry*

We meet in an atmosphere of continuing world crisis. The world is a maze of trouble-spots. Between us we have the capacity to feed, clothe, educate and provide medical care for every man, woman and child on this wonderful planet. And yet we live with poverty, famine, ignorance and disease all around us. We also live in constant fear that someone will do something that will trigger a war which will commit us to Armageddon.

I can only speak as I am. A White Western Christian from one of the most privileged countries on earth. But I pray that my limited grasp of the Gospel, coupled with the influence of my African and Asian friends, has given me enough understanding so that I can contribute to whatever partial solutions we can generate through this assembly.

I cannot deny that many of our national leaders mouth platitudes about aid for under-privileged countries from the comfort of high office but show little understanding of the enormity of the tragedy which is called twentieth century civilization. They show no shame for their part in it, very little sense of responsibility for either the causes of it or to find solutions to it. And they show equally little will to persuade their nations to do anything about it as they struggle to balance their budgets and keep gross national product rising at a rate acceptable to international investors—draining even domestic welfare programmes to pay for bombs and bayonets in an effort to preserve their positions of national privilege.

There is a critical preoccupation in the West with the confrontation between the Capitalist and Communist power blocks. This leads to a distracting emphasis on consumer spending and capital investment in an effort to avoid domestic socio-economic crisis which might encourage people to look again for a new economic system. As a result our leaders cannot focus on fundamental issues for long enough to recognize the state of crisis which is the world around us.

However, let there be no misunderstanding. We are indeed in a crit-

---

*Mr. Ian Fry, former Communications Officer of the Presbyterian Board of Local Mission in Australia, is a journalist.

ical situation. We are at a pivotal point in humanity's history and evolution. But it is not a stage which is concerned with biological evolution, with the development of physical characteristics or even with the development of human capacity. The present phase of humanity's evolution is concerned with the development of community. It is concerned with relations within the human family and it is concerned with humanity's understanding of God. Only when we recognize that can we also recognize that the global problems which engulf us must be tackled on two levels.

At the first level we must analyse our theology and identify misconceptions, decisions and actions which have allowed us to blunder along to this critical point in human relations. We must use all of our capacity and goodwill as, together, we re-assess our most deeply held convictions and religious doctrines. Many of us will find it an agonizing experience.

At the second level we must work together to re-assess the physical problems and economic concepts which, in simple terms, account for the practical aspects of our crisis.

We are in a position to tackle our problems at both levels concurrently and we have no other options. Unless we want to take the short-cut to Armageddon we must move ahead prayerfully, steadily, but with confidence and determination—together.

I want to outline briefly my understanding of the first level of the problem and then propose a plan to tackle one aspect of the second—production and distribution of basic resources.

There are a number of trouble-spots around the world where relationships damaged by exploitation and oppression may fester, erupt and trigger a war leading to a catastrophe of unthinkable proportions, but the key one is the Middle East.

The crisis in the Middle East is a microcosm of mankind's problems. It is the one on which we must focus our attention and to which we must devote a paramount effort in order to find a solution. It revolves around the city of Jerusalem and the establishment of the State of Israel. But it involves the West's most crucial resource need—oil for synthetic chemicals and solvents as well as energy—and it also involves critical inter-faith relationships across a range of resource-producing counties. We must briefly review how it came about.

The establishment of the State of Israel resulted from the efforts of people of Judaic faith to free their community from oppression in Europe through a movement which became known as Zionism.

That oppression was imposed by powers associated with Christianity as a consequence of the Christian Church's self-understanding which was intimately linked with, and sustained by, doctrines which the church had developed over a very long period. Those doctrines were developed in an effort to ensure consistency in the church's teaching about the life, the person and the rôle of Jesus of Nazareth and its perception of its own role.

It was around the questions of life, the person and the rôle of Jesus of Nazareth and conflicting expectations of the Messiah of earlier Jewish prophecy that the Yahwist community had split into two streams of Christianity and Judaism.

Subsequently those questions, and the personal and corporate conduct of communities linked to those two competing streams of Yahwism, were central to the prophetic mission of Muhammad and the development of Islam as the third stream of Yahwism—or the third side of the triangle of Semitic Messianic faiths.

But the key people and the powers to whom Muhammad addressed his message, with its challenge to their theology and to their self-understanding, rejected it and went their own way. Mankind also went its way, with its population expanding, quite naturally and progressively, until all of the available productive land was occupied. Its empires were often oppressive and exploitative and certainly they were competitive as they vigorously pursued their own interests within the framework of their particular self-understanding. In the case of the European powers, that self-understanding was shaped by the aggressive self-understanding of the Christian Church. In intimate collaboration with the Church they set out to subjugate and to reconstruct the rest of the world in the image of Christian Europe. Then for the next four or five hundred years the bulk of the world's people suffered under the rule of, or from the conflict with, European colonial powers as they were reduced to units of labour with stockpiles of resources to enable Christian Europe to grow wealthy and more dominant, and their social and communal structures were undermined.

That period of Christian reconstruction of the non-European world left its people without a vision of salvation and crying for relief. But, in the early years of this century, Britain, the greatest of the Christian powers, sought to exploit the growing Zionist movement in a competitive grab for more resources and to bolster its imperial power. In doing so it unwittingly tripped a safety valve so that, instead of strengthening its position, it triggered the progressive dismantling of the structures of the European colonial era. It also forced the Jewish community into the position in which it confirmed the Qur'anic prophecy of a third transgression and a third scourging.

At the same time it brought powers linked to each of the Semitic Messianic faiths into conflict over the one city which is central to the historical self-understanding and theology of all three—Jerusalem—and it provided another in a long series of challenges to the self-understanding and theology of the Christian Church. However, the Church, overall, again failed to understand the challenge. After World War I, the Vatican took steps to bolster its temporal authority and to resist challenges to its theology from both Zionism and the Christian ecumenical movement by means of concordats and other instruments, notably those with Spain, Poland, Italy and Germany. In doing so it contributed to the slide into the second world war. Christian self-understanding then ensured that Hitler's plan to eliminate the Jewish community would be put into operation. Consequent European guilt complexes then ensured that the State of Israel would be established and that Zionism would continue to provide a source of conflict in the Middle East and a potential focal point for the ultimate catastrophe for mankind.

We have therefore reached the point at which steps must be taken so that political Zionism ceases to be a point of conflict. However, Zionism is, as already noted, a consequence of actions taken by European Christians which were, in turn, a consequence of the Church's self-understanding based on doctrines developed over a very long period. Therefore Zionism cannot cease to be a point of conflict until and unless those fundamental Christian doctrines are reassessed and re-stated so that they can no longer provide a basis for confrontation.

However, the Church is incapable of carrying out such a reassessment in isolation. It has only ever reformed in a situation of crisis and in any case there is no isolation. All three partners in the triangle are intimately involved in the crisis in the Middle East and therefore all three must be involved in the reassessment—in the harsh glare of international scrutiny by people of all faiths who will be just as much affected by a breakdown in international relationships as will be the people of the triangle of faiths. Theological perspectives change progressively with changing circumstances and as new insights become apparent. Consequently fragmentation occurs around particular aspects of belief and practice from time to time, and religious groups have a frightening propensity for self-indoctrination in order to consolidate their particular perspectives. Once adopted, those perspectives tend to be written into either guidelines, regulations or doctrinal statements of one kind or another and to be represented as the complete and absolute truth. Naturally, all three of the Semitic Messianic faiths have been through this process so that all three are fragmented and no fragment has a monopoly on religious perception.

The process of dialogue is slow and tedious but because we are at a pivotal point in mankind's evolution there is no time to lose. In the three of these Messianic religions it cannot stop at the level of achieving more inter-faith tolerance in a pluralistic society.

Within the three Semitic Messianic faiths there are those who are content to believe that the Messianic Age is already with us. There are others who anticipate a total breakdown in international relations and a forced march to Armageddon as a prelude to the Messianic Age, but there are also those who believe that through the conscious effort of mankind at large it can be prevented, remaining as a threat or a guide to the consequences of mankind's failure to act on the Will of God and a constant encouragement to do so. Many would agree with the view of Maimonides that the reign of the Messiah will be marked by a high intellectual and moral level, without domination by any "master race" and with the abrogation of all dictatorship—with neither famine nor war, nor jealousy or competition, but with widespread prosperity, comfort for all and with the whole world preoccupied with the knowledge of God.

Mankind now stands at the point of decision. We can take the path towards the view of a new world community perceived by Maimonides, a Jewish writer of Spanish birth, through sharing resources, mutual support and through love and trust. Or, we can continue along the course of short-term self-interest towards a breakdown in key international relationships and nuclear devastation which would degrade mankind. In the manner of a game of dice our leaders can throw us straight to Armageddon or they can lead us along the path to the Messianic Age. They have the resources at their disposal to do either but unfortunately the balance of indications is that they will not change course.

In the Western World the assumption of technical and moral superiority still runs deep. There is confidence that it can prevent any change in world trading or military patterns which will undermine its position of privilege and force it to share the world's resources. There is also a belief, encouraged by political and business leaders in the interests of domestic stability, that recent economic difficulties are a temporary "blip" on the graph of economic growth.

In other words, the West has yet to understand the significance of the events of 1973. Its leaders fail to see that the crisis in the Middle East ia a turning point in history and they cling to the belief that it is simply another regional conflict to determine who shall occupy various portions of Palestine. They also resist the notions that the political and economic relationships between the three partners in the triangle of faiths are changing. They appear either to cling to the well-established Christian self-understanding or to have no concern for religious belief except in the sense that it has an influence on the ballot box. They must be persuaded otherwise.

This means that while the first-level dialogue is going on the leaders of the Western World must be persuaded to a new world-view at the second level, and they must be persuaded quickly. They must be persuaded that the way to meaningful and lasting peace is through sharing resources and not through military might. And sharing resources does not mean hand-out aid or the rescheduling of bank loans. It means a fundamentally new economic order.

However, as a consequence of their own decisions and actions in recent years the Western group of countries has become dependent on key resources of developing countries over which they no longer have absolute control. This has led to increasing political and economic manipulation which has become so much an accepted part of efforts by Western countries to maintain their positions of privilege that the majority of their people are not even conscious that it is taking place. If they were, they would most likely still accept it as quite justified—not on the grounds of their religious self-understanding but out of simple self-interest.

However the community of mankind and that community's needs have become so complex that the supply of foodstuffs and the exploitation and use of strategic and exhaustible resources can no longer be left

153

to the whim of people and enterprises motivated solely by profit. This is true irrespective of whether they can claim to be acting in the immediate interests of the community in which they happen to be operating at a particular time.

Many competing and contradictory proposals for international trading and monetary reforms have been floated in international fora in recent years. However it is probable that the emphasis in proposals from Western authorities will continue to be on private control of resources, with direct negotiation between operators and governments on an industry basis, and on development programmes financed by international loan funds made available by institutions in countries which happen to be the current home-base for capital in excess of their market requirements because of either political or economic considerations such as the level of interest rates.

A few adjustments can be expected to the formulae used to allocate international loan funds as a means of dampening down pressure for significant change, together with the re-negotiation of existing loans when current terms are not being met by borrowing governments, as a means of avoiding the collapse of Western currencies. But in the absence of either a major international upheaval or a co-ordinated and sustained push from non-Western governments, any really significant changes are unlikely.

All indications are that if the West continues to insist on economic management which is heavily in its favour it could help to trigger a confrontation involving resource embargoes and economic and political reactions. These could then bring relations between national and religious groups to a breaking-point. Such a confrontation could be linked to the worsening of any of a number of crises around the world, but it is most likely in connection with events in the Middle East.

It is not in the interest of any group in the world community for a new economic order to be devised in an atmosphere of world crisis after such a confrontation. It is better that co-ordinated pressure should be brought to bear from the widest cross-section of the world community now, to force the introduction of a radical new economic order.

Any scheme to reorganize international resource-trading should have, at least, these aims:

* To ensure that the governments of developing countries receive funds which are consistent with their contribution to the economies of the world community, which are more consistent with their development requirements and which are also more consistent with what their people aspire to.

* To increase world food production, to ensure adequate food supplies for all mankind, to ensure more realistic distribution of available food supplies and to provide for an international famine and emergency relief scheme.

* To minimize competition for resources, to reduce tension

between nations and to reduce the likelihood of armed conflict.

An essential aspect of any economic plan which is intended to promote development is that the funds being used for development must come as much as possible from local activity and then must be under the direct control of national governments. Contrary to the old arguments which we hear from both extremes of the political and economic arena, this does not require the nationalization of all of industry and commerce. But it does require two things: a clear understanding of the role of government, and acceptance by the private sector of strict technical, economic and social guidelines within which to operate.

One scheme which would meet those minimal aims which would stimulate development where it is most needed would be the setting up of an international agency, responsible to the United Nations, to plan and supervise international trade in essential commodities on a more orderly basis.

It is better that such an agency be set up at the earliest possible stage through the existing machinery of the United Nations—rather than as a last resort when every country and every industry has had a go at whip-hand negotiations out of self-interest after a serious confrontation has erupted between those countries which now dominate world trade and those from which raw materials are obtained.

In the meantime, until a genuine new economic order is achieved, every encouragement should be given for trade on a government-to-government basis in essential commodities. This can be through bilateral trade or barter agreements covering either one or several commodities; multilateral agreements covering a single commodity; marketing boards or agencies; or through other forms of government-to-government negotiation.

The scheme now proposed resembles a giant barter system. All international trade in critical commodities would be under the control of each sovereign government, through a central international agency. Supplies would be obtained and managed so that funds would flow preferably from highly developed countries to developing countries and developed countries would be encouraged to produce food for export to balance their international trade. The scheme would not reduce the domestic sovereignty of any government nor presuppose any particular political or economic system. However, it does anticipate greater government control over the private sector. It would operate as a programme of the United Nations with an international "central agency" established by, and responsible to, the UN General Assembly.

Commodities to be traded through the agency would be determined by the UN from time to time, but it is envisaged that the scheme would cover unprocessed foodstuffs, other unprocessed primary products such as rubber and fibres, exhaustible resources including energy and base metals, and other economically strategic materials.

Each country's requirements for each commodity would be determined according to its "basic requirements" and "additional requirements". Both factors would be carefully defined but, in general terms, a country's basic requirements for foodstuffs would be sufficient to ensure an adequate diet for the entire population. In the case of other materials it would be sufficient to satisfy achievable development programmes and to ensure stability in the country's economy, but not to provide for the luxury consumer market or for re-export of goods.

Additional requirements would include supplies for luxury market, processing for re-export and stockpiling.

All basic requirements would be supplied and obtained through the agency. Additional requirements could be obtained or supplied either through the agency or by direct negotiation with another country, except that no country could obtain or supply additional requirements of a commodity until it had honoured its obligations in respect of basic supplies.

The proportion of supplies which would be obtained from each supplying country would be determined by the agency according to criteria such as each country's need for funds, its ability and willingness to supply, and its relative dependence on either one or a series of exports.

The relative level of prices at which the agency would buy from and sell to each country would be determined by factors established by the UN. They would be weighted in favour of developing countries. A mean price would be determined for each commodity and each country would be charged or paid at the price determined for it within the range of mean price minus one quarter to mean price plus one quarter. The price levels or a classification for each country would be determined each year according to an agreed set of criteria which would reflect the real needs of each country. They would be based on:

(1) its current level of economic activity, assessed from its national import/export ratio, energy consumption and personal income levels;

(2) its current level of community advancement, assessed by the availability of education, the level of employment and the population growth rate;

(3) the current level of personal fulfilment, assessed by protein consumption, community health and housing and/or mobility.

All trading through the agency would be on the account of the national governments and not on the account of either individual suppliers or marketing authorities. Movements in national accounts would be adjusted quarterly and not against individual shipments of individual commodities.

The distribution of the funds paid to each government by the agency would be at their discretion. Payments by a government to its producers need not be based on the same unit-value as the payments by the agency to it. A government could, therefore, within the limits acceptable to its electorate, encourage one industry in relation to another according to world needs for particular commodities, such as food-grains, or according to its own national planning.

World commodity supplies and their availability would be kept under constant review, but allocations would be made annually at least a full year in advance when the scheme became fully operational. Discipline within the scheme would be relatively easily maintained because of the ease of supervision and because of the ease with which economic embargoes could be applied by the majority against a country which set out to bypass the scheme.

An amount would be debited to the trading account of each national government to provide for the operation of the scheme and for the establishment of a food stockpile for famine relief and other emergencies. It is envisaged that this amount would be determined as a percentage of the total trade transacted through the agency by each country, say one half of one percent to establish the food stockpile, plus the actual costs of operating the scheme, but a range of alternatives is available.

Foodstuffs for the stockpile would be purchased at the basic exports price. They would be stored in facilities established on the seaboard of the exporting countries, or elsewhere as appropriate in the case of land-locked countries. They would be rotated with annual export-supplies in line with good practice for each commodity and they would be distributed by the agency at the direction of the UN.

We can be satisfied with nothing less than a radical restructuring of the world economy. Any scheme which forces the people of any community to accept poverty, hunger, inadequate shelter or clothing and the prospect of disease and human degradation is simply not acceptable. If such conditions persist because of any other community's wish to maintain a position of privilege then that community deserves absolute condemnation.

It will do us well to remember that if the Western World either permits or precipitates a nuclear war it will come out of it in no position to determine the patterns of world trade and, following the success of barter agreements between Warsaw Pact countries and certain oil-producers between 1961 and 1973, a central distribution system is most likely to be set up by the non-Western countries which will have a dominant rôle in world affairs.

I believe it is both competent and appropriate for WCRP to take steps to bring together scholars from all three of the Messianic faiths in order to begin a thorough reassessment of Messianic theology and at the same time to press for a radically new economic order.

31

By Mr. Harold Belmont*

It is in the power of the True Hopi People to unify minds and spirits of all true peace-seeking people of the earth . . .

"Hopi" means "peaceful people" . . . and the truest and greatest power is the strength of peace . . . because peace is the will of The Great Spirit.

But do not think that just because the True Hopi People have been told by the Great Spirit not to take up arms . . . that the True Hopi People will not fight . . . even die for what we know to be the right way of life.

The True Hopi People know how to fight without killing or hurting . . .

The True Hopi People know how to fight with truth and positive force in the light of The Great Spirit . . .

The True Hopi People know how to educate their thoughts . . . good pictures . . . and by carefully chosen words . . .

The True Hopi People know how to show to all the world's children the True Way of life by setting an example . . . by working and communicating in a way that reaches the minds and hearts of all people who are truly seeking the methods of a simple and spiritual life, which is the only life that will survive . . .

The True Hopi People preserve the sacred knowledge about the way of the earth because the True Hopi People know that the Earth is a living . . . growing person . . . and all things on it are her children . . .

The True Hopi People know how to show the right way of life to all the world's people who have ears to listen . . . who have eyes to see . . . and who have hearts to understand these things . . .

The True Hopi People know how to generate enough power to link up the forces of the minds and spirits of all the true children of the Earth . . . and to unify them with the positive force of the Great Spirit so

---

*Mr. Harold Belmont, a member of the American Indian Traditional Elders' Circle, is a consultant to American Indians on issues of racism and oppression, especially in the areas of fishing-rights, political prisoners, and religious freedom.

that they may put an end to affliction and persecution in all afflicted places in this world . . .

The True Hopi People declare that Hopi power is a force which will bring about world change.

32

By Chief K.O.K. Onyioha*

The subject on which I was requested to speak ... is, "How to Dismantle Ethnic and Religious Prejudices in Building a Shared Society" – everywhere–I should add–on Earth.

Man in Igbo African cosmology is by nature good. That is why in Igbo African language man is regarded as "Mma Di Na Ndu" which means "the beauty of creation," compressed into one word–Madu–as a name for a human being, in Igbo-African language. As a matter of fact, Igbo African cosmology does not see creation as incorporating any evil. That is why when Igbo Africans meet, they open their address–not with ladies and gentlemen–but with *Nde Ibe Anyi Mma Mma Ni*–which is a reminder to all, that around man on earth is nothing else but goodness– incorporating no evil–to tell them that the prejudices that today molest and rumple harmony among men in every facet of human interactions are not inherent and incurable maladies of the human mind. Godianism upholds this cosmology.

Man in philosophy is a response to the system, to the concept and to the environment to which he is exposed. Expose man to systems, to concepts, and to environments that are conducive to good behaviour, man remains man, and remains basically good. Expose man to a system that is not conducive to good behaviour, man becomes a perversion of himself and a veritable devil on earth. Therein lies the tragedy of man and his society.

To dismantle, therefore, ethnic, religious, racial, ideological and all other prejudices in order to build shared human societies everywhere on earth, we need then to re-examine existing human systems and concepts to be resolved as to the extent to which each of them has contributed to the warping of human minds to create prejudices and chaos–here, there and yonder–on earth.

Let us, to begin, look at the on-going arms race which has thrown human welfare to the winds and you will see it propelled by the false

---

*Chief K.O.K. Onyioha, from Umuahia, Nigeria, who is Head of the Godian Religion, was unable to deliver his address at WCRP IV.

concept which the so-called super-powers hold of what is civilization, which puts premium upon exploitative economic opulence, and fantastic technological know-how of going to the moon, and mass production of nuclear weapons for mass destruction of God's own creations to the utter neglect of the human mind—thereby making human society utterly amoral and no longer responsive to the pleas of religion. This raises a crying need for religions here gathered in Nairobi to re-define civilization and to resolve today for man to be understood not in terms of wealth, but in training the human mind to live in harmony with fellow man despite creed or colour.

Let us make an appeal to the minds of men with this re-definition of what is true civilization; preach it daily from the pulpits of religions throughout the world; teach it to the budding new generations of mankind in all institutions of learning; call on the United Nations—through a five-man-all-race delegation of this Assembly to the United Nations Secretary-General—to adopt it, and institute a trophy of civilization that would be awarded to a nation that has been watched and seen to have guaranteed national peace and security of life and property to its citizens for a period of five years, and contributed largely to international harmony; insist that until a nation wins this United Nations trophy of civilization, it must continue to remain regarded as uncivilized—and you would have greatly embarrassed those nations who today flaunt nuclear weapons as their yard-stick of superior civilization, and re-oriented their muddy hearts from sadism to humanism; drum it over and over again into the heads and ears of all men till the ideal has suffused and possessed all hearts and you will be surprised how soon the world would become a better place with the super-powers pushed to a new race from the arms race to seeking for who would sit on the throne of love among men as the Super-Power of Peace—for under the influence of an idea which possesses the mind of a people, a nation soon confounds the arithmetic of the mathematician, and achieves a success out of all proportion to their means, like the Saracens did in history.

I had dwelt at length on this when I delivered an address entitled—"World Disarmament: A Conceptual Approach—Redefining Civilization"—to the General Assembly of the United Nations Special Session on Disarmament, in 1978, in my capacity as Spiritual Head of the Godian Religion, and Chairman of the Organization of Traditional Religions of Africa. To re-read that United Nations address is to recapture the totality of this insight.

If religions must recapture their control on the behaviour of man and restore morality and peace among men, religions must mobilize and launch this assault on the false concept of what is true civilization which has debauched humanity and made religion irrelevant in this second half of the 20th century. But it would seem to me that even in this despair, religions themselves have continued to behave like the Three Grey Sisters of Kingsley's Heroes in Greek mythology. They sit in the sun weeping—every passer-by pities them—but they don't pity themselves. In their plight, religions still lend themselves as instruments for sustaining decaying national and racial vanities—preaching ideals which they have not the courage to insist their nations should live. May God give us courage from this Nairobi conference to return to our countries and preach and live this new WCRP version of civilization.

Talking about ethnic prejudices, and using Nigeria as our guinea-pig for the study, one can say that the party politics and ballot-box democracy of Western civilization are the major source fountains of ethnic prejudices and other chauvinisms in Africa and in most other parts of the world. Ballot-box democracy is inherent with all manners of evils—bribery, corruption, rigging, gerrymandering, tribalism, religionism, nepotism, favouritism, mutual abuse and disrespect for elders, legalized in electioneering campaigns which more often than not blow up into riots, murders, arson, mass destruction of lives and property, coups and counter-coups. The political instability to which independent African countries are prone can be traced to this germ of the Western world. And, worried about all these social problems concomitant with Western civilization, and determined to end them, the Godian Religion conducted research into Nigeria's traditional political systems, and singled out Africa's traditional age group system of government as the surest means of ending ethnic, tribal, religious and other prejudices in the body-politic, not only of Africa but of all the world, for it names a procedure of selection which does not give room for any appeal to ethnic, tribal, religious and racial prejudices.

Whereas party politics of Western democracy exclude those who do not belong to the political party in power from sharing in the plums of office and in effective participation in the government of their country, the Age-Group system of government is a synthesis from black Africa's political traditions, involving every family in the government of their country, putting none in opposition, making the government of the country every man's business, giving every citizen a sense of belonging—sharing with everyone else the blessing and sorrows of the society. It is in the age-group system of government that democracy fulfils itself, as one finds in it an ultra-democratic one-party system which makes democracy in theory, and practice, a government truly of the people, for the people, by the people. The details are spelt out in a memorandum entitled: "Age-Group System of Government for Nigeria in 1987 With Communalism as Guiding National Philosophy"—which I have recently submitted to the military rulers of Nigeria for study. It would make interesting reading to all the world as its recommendations are of universal application in man's efforts to dismantle ethnic and other prejudices in the politics and lives of nations by way of re-written human systems.

Mention of communalism in the memo to the military rulers of Nigeria calls to mind the fact that in philosophy man is behaviour, and behaviour itself stems from thought, and so ultimately, man in philosophy is thought. *Mma Bu Egwa*, as Igbo African philosophy puts it—Beauty which means "man" is behaviour. I relate with you in harmony

162

not because we come from the same mother and father, nor because the same gene runs through our veins. In our living experiences we have seen parents who would not want to share the same roofs with their sons because of their bad behaviour. We have seen parents who took their sons to the police and asked for their imprisonment. I relate with you in harmony because we behave alike; and we behave alike because we think alike. Thus the real basis for harmonious interactions among men is behaviour which stems from thought. So that to harmonize humanity you have to reduce them to a common thought pattern. While it is true that men can be organs of supernatural powers, it is difficult to channel the minds of all men into a common groove of philosophical thinking, yet their ideological philosophies of capitalism and communism respectively can be compromised in communalism—taking what is best in each of them—in accordance with human nature—and compromising them in communalism as their means for world peace. Ring this truth around the world, and racists would see just how hollow in the head they had been emphsizing race as a basis for man-to-man relationships.

Religion concerns itself with the welfare of the human mind—its morals are food for the souls of man—and given the saying, *Mens sana in corpore sano*, which means a healthy mind must live in a healthy body, religion can no longer shy away from concern about the kind of social system in which souls and minds of men, for which religions are seeking salvation, dwell. For otherwise religions can never, no matter what morals they preach, produce healthy souls that can survive in body-casings badgered by corrupting socio-economic and political systems—thereby making it not an extraneous concern for WCRP to project the age-group system of government and communalism as substitutes for ballot-box democracy, partisan politics and the gun-toting ideologies of capitalism and communism. This would guarantee healthy physical bodies as dwellings for the healthy minds and souls which religions have been struggling to produce with their sermons of love.

For, as an Igbo African proverb puts it, *Idua Osi, gi adua Owu, gi adua Ikpakpa Ugo Agu ma ochachitukwala uzo*, which means that if you want to stop stealing, you have to warn the thief, warn solitude, and warn the owner of things stolen, never again to keep his property care-lessly. To solve a problem, you have to take a panoramic view of it.

Yet there is a higher conceptual approach to ending ethnic and racial prejudices among men. Ethnic, tribal and racial prejudices result from man's ignorance of the rationale of heterogeneity in creation. God, in his infinite wisdom, created all things on the principle of variety as the spice of life, in order to make life worth living. For were everybody on earth white, life could have been a terrible bore, lacking lustre and not worth living. Nor could justice have been kinder for all, given experi-ences such as Northern Ireland where homogeneity in nationality has not guaranteed social harmony and justice for all. Irish Protestant Chris-tians and Irish Catholic Christians have continued irreconcilably to kill one another for many past years, despite the religious, racial, and linguistic homogeneities they share.

The same is true of Lebanon, or of Iran where, despite total homogeneity in race, colour, language, tribe, nationality and creed, Iranian Muslims have continued to kill fellow Iranian Muslims, this time on the excuse of what is orthodox Islamic faith. Nor could the story have been different and better were everyone on earth just black, or just yellow, or just red, speaking one language, sharing the same creed, and packed into one geo-political definition.

To promote this high philosophy, this rationale of heterogeneity in creation, send a civilizing mission from this Nairobi Assembly of WCRP, made up of five persons drawn from the five continents of the world, comprising the black, white, yellow and red races of humanity, to preach this new light to apartheid South Africa and everywhere else on earth where racism and tribalism are still monarchs, and you will in time bring them grovelling on their knees, these canker-worms of social harmony—apartheid, tribalism and racism—which have converted God's wisdom in heterogeneity of creation as excuses for hate. It was in my letter to President Jimmy Carter of the USA, dated June 1980, that I spoke in detail of this new light and recommended it as a useful instrument of persuasion against apartheid, racism, and tribalism everywhere on earth. To that letter I received a reply from President Jimmy Carter, dated July 1980, telling of his peace efforts and citing his success with the Egypt-Israeli peace agreement after 30 years of war, to prove it. I am glad that the Rector of the United Nations University, Dr. Soedjatmoko, is here with us, and we should ask him to introduce the teaching of these new lights to on-coming new generations of mankind in UN Universities. Bishop Desmond Tutu can make this his daily sermon in South Africa.

On religious prejudices, one can say that while religions of the world preach the same absolutes and lofty morals of "thou shalt not kill," and "love your neighbour," the very undoing of religions which has badly shaken their credibility now among men, lies in their morphologies. Built around the persons of men born of women, who can be identified with ethnic, national, racial, language and tribal groups, religions have thereby become inherent with all manner of these prejudices and fertilized excuses for mutual killings among men. To end religious prejudices, therefore, we need to rally religions back to God who is the common denominator for all religions, and offer them Godianism as a co-ordinating and harmonizing philosophy without prejudice to the continued existence of each of them but as liturgical variations preserving the cultures of the communities they permeate, but with their fangs of hate lost in Godianism, since no peace-loving religion can raise any serious objections to the philosophy of Godianism wound around the person of the one universal God in whom all religions believe, particularly as the religion of all the ancestors of all the races of man was the Godian religion, by the fact that before the prophets and the Messiahs were born, they were speaking to God directly without passing through any medium. Adam and Eve, Abraham and Moses were Godians. And

164

when an issue gets murked-up in mid-stream, you return to the beginnings for a solution.

It is high time that religions rewrite and make more flexible those principles, doctrines and dogmas they have preached over the past many centuries, as many of them no longer make sense to the scientific minds of this second half of the 20th century—in this age of reason—particularly as those dogmas created the prejudices which have made the religious front a chaotic asylum of warring religious factions and eroded the credibility of religions as reliable agencies for peace-promotion among men.

"How to Dismantle Ethnic and Religious Prejudices in Building a Shared Society Everywhere on Earth" is so vast a subject that it cannot be done even one-quarter justice in a four-page paper which WCRP asked me to prepare on it. But I think I have given enough of a hint within the short space of a new direction to keep WCRP thinking and working for many, many years to come.

Once upon a time lived a mad man in my Ukwa-Ukwu village of Nkporo, in Imo State of Nigeria. One day he sang and sang throughout the night, and disturbed the sleep of his neighbours. Very early in the morning, he left the compound, went to the village square, sat on a log, and began again to whistle. When those he had disturbed through the night saw him again whistling in the village square, so early in the morning, they asked him: "Dear Friend, you sang throughout the night and would not allow us to sleep. What again are you whistling about this early morning?" And he said to them: "My song during the night, is still my whistle this morning."

My dear brothers and sisters in God, regard me in this presentation to you as that mad man of Ukwa-Ukwu village of Nkporo, standing before you. At all previous meetings of leaders of the world's major religions, which I attended and where I had the opportunity to speak, whether at the Catholic University in Leuven, at the United Nations Church Centre, at the United Nations Special Session on Disarmament, at Princeton, at the NGO annual conferences of the United Nations, at Logan Hall of the University of London, at Eminence Hall of the Kio Plaza Hotel of Tokyo under the auspices of the Japan Buddha Sangha—from 1974 to 1983 when WCRP/Africa was inaugurated—I have sung the same songs, canvassed the same ideas, and made he same pleas. I am today whistling them back to you, here in Nairobi, like the mad man of Ukwa-Ukwu village. . .

33

By Dr. Eric Prokosch*

Torture does not attack the body alone. The torturer aims to break something very precious—the will, the personality, the spirit, the soul.

He does this by seeking what is most vital to the victim, and then attacking it. He inflicts excruciating pain. He tortures, or threatens to torture, the victim's wife, husband, or child. He brings the victim to the point of death, insisting that he has absolute power. He operates in an atmosphere of terror. He insults and humiliates the victim, seeking to destroy his or her sense of human dignity.

By breaking the victim's will, the torturer hopes to make him renounce his faith; to make him give information about others; to deter him from undesirable political activity; to make him sign a "confession," true or not; or simply to punish him.

In confronting torture, we have to deal, not merely with an act of cruelty by an individual, but with the workings of some segment of the apparatus of the state. Somewhere within that segment of officialdom it has been decided to use torture as a means of achieving one or another of the purposes mentioned above. We are speaking here of what is defined in the United Nations General Assembly's 1975 Declaration Against Torture as "any act by which severe pain or suffering, whether physical or mental, is intentionally inflicted by or at the instigation of a public official on a person" for a series of purposes such as those specified in the Declaration as examples.

In confronting torture, we have to deal not merely with an act of cruelty by an individual but with the workings of some segment of the tries not so many centuries ago. The prohibition of torture is enshrined in the Universal Declaration of Human Rights and other international human rights instruments. This means that the community of nations has agreed that torture is illegal—an understanding which is reflected in the laws and constitutions of many countries. But this very illegality poses another problem. If torture is illegal, it must be kept secret—thus

---

*Dr. Eric Prokosch is Campaign Co-ordinator for Amnesty International in London, England.

the difficulty of getting information.

Between January 1980 and mid-1983 Amnesty International made urgent appeals on behalf of 2,687 individuals in danger of torture (excluding mass arrests) in 45 countries. These cases were only a fraction of the tens of thousands of people believed to have been victims of torture and maltreatment during the same period.

Urgent appeals, to be effective, depend on receiving reliable information quickly from those close to a detainee, as torture so often occurs during the first days or weeks of detention. In many cases the information only comes out later, if at all.

Amnesty International has received reports of torture and maltreatment from 98 countries since 1980. While some governments have taken remedial measures, elsewhere governmental inaction indicates a lack of will to stop torture or even a conscious decision to torture. More than a third of the world's governments have used or tolerated torture or maltreatment of prisoners in the 1980s. These figures indicate the magnitude of the problem.

Amnesty International works for the world-wide abolition of torture. This is one of the organization's main concerns, along with working for the release of prisoners of conscience (generally including conscientious objectors), fair trials for political prisoners, and an end to executions, both judicial and extrajudicial.

Indeed the death penalty can be seen as a form of torture: in Amnesty International's view it is the ultimate cruel, inhuman and degrading punishment.

Amnesty International has prepared a 12-Point Programme for the Prevention of Torture. The recommendations in the programme are addressed to governments, but they can also provide goals for action by non-governmental organizations. One of the most important points is number 2, "Limits on incommunicado detention." Here we say that it is vital to break through the wall of secrecy which shields the torturer from the outside world—by ensuring that relatives, lawyers and doctors have prompt and regular access to prisoners, and by ensuring that all prisoners are brought before a judicial authority promptly after being taken into custody. These and related safeguards can be summed up in the phrase: "Access to prisoners."

Other points in the programme are taken from the UN Declaration Against Torture and other international instruments, both existing and evolving. All complaints and reports of torture should be impartially investigated. Those responsible for torture should be brought to justice. There should be regular independent visits of inspection to places of detention to ensure that torture does not take place.

A further point, included in the draft Convention Against Torture now before the UN General Assembly: No one should be forcibly returned to a country where he or she risks being tortured.

Much important work against torture is done by local and national religious organizations and individuals acting on religious grounds.

167

Their activities include:

—Collecting information and exposing individual cases of torture;
—Initiating legal proceedings on behalf of victims;
—Organizing public appeals against torture;
—Providing aid and rehabilitation for victims and their families;
—Engaging in religious forms of action, such as prayer and religious services; and
—Working to persuade public opinion that torture can and must be stopped, in the framework of educational programmes to promote and defend human rights.

34

By Mr. Saichiro Uesugi*

In defining the basic attitude toward the Buraku problem, we wish to say at the beginning that WCRP/Japan has deeply examined itself and sincerely regrets that it showed an incorrect understanding of that problem through discriminatory words used by the participants at the assembly of WCRP I held in Kyoto and at the assembly of WCRP III held in Princeton, and also regrets that at the same time it let a golden opportunity to take up the Buraku problem slip by at those two assemblies.

People of religion, who should proclaim human equality, admitted discrimination on the Buraku problem, and in so doing they renounced the equal footing of all people, which was regarded as the keynote of religion at the WCRP I and III assemblies. The Japanese Committee of WCRP realizes that this was conduct unworthy of people of religion. The Committee was also informed that, taking the opportunity of WCRP III at Princeton, discriminatory elements which had long existed in the field of religion were brought to light. Viewing such discriminatory practices produced by religions, the Committee became aware of the fact that discriminatory words were not spoken accidentally by the participants at the WCRP I and III assemblies, but rather they symbolized discriminatory aspects which have been retained in the field of religion even today. Therefore, remembering this fact, the Committee sets forth its basic attitude toward the Buraku problem by taking up the following points of issue from discriminatory expressions used by participants at these two assemblies. The Committee confirms and reflects on each of them, and moreover states clearly its position in regard to these problems.

That which the Committee must clarify in the first place, is what discriminatory expressions we people of religion have been accused of using. The accusation was based on a participant's false assertion that, "Now there no longer exists discrimination with regard to the Buraku Problem in Japan," and also on his international attitude of suppressing

---

*Mr. Saichiro Uesugi is Chairman of the Buraku Liberation League in Fukuoka, Japan.

discriminatory facts concerning the Buraku Problem. Some must ask themselves from where such an attitude came and what were the circumstances of his background which produced such an attitude.

At the WCRP I and III assemblies, the participants expressed their discrimination through statements such as the following: "Because the Buraku problem is a domestic issue of Japan, it should not be discussed at this world conference (WCRP I);" "At present there is really no discrimination with regard to the Buraku Problem in Japan. Therefore it would be very annoying if that problem were to be discussed at the world conference." (The statement of Rev. Soyu Machida at WCRP III). Those who spoke such discriminatory words aimed to shut out the Buraku Problem from workshops on the problem of human rights at the world conferences, even if that meant swimming against the international current of defending and enhancing human rights.

According to the report submitted to the Japanese Government by a Special Integration Policy Deliberations Committee, the Buraku problem is described as follows: "Through discrimination based on the structure of social position which has been formed through the process of historical development in Japanese society, some groups of Japanese people have been placed in a low position economically, socially, and culturally. Even in modern society, these groups have had their fundamental human rights seriously infringed upon, and especially they have been confronted with the most serious and important problem of not being adequately guaranteed the civil rights and liberties which should be guaranteed to every person as a principle of modern society." The report further makes the following definite statement" "On the other hand some people have regarded the Buraku problem as a thing of the past, and have believed that this kind of discrimination no longer exists in today's Japan, where democratization and modernization are remarkably advanced. Existence of this problem of discrimination, however, is based on objective truth which transcends individual, subjective points of view." Therefore, the discriminatory expressions of the participants who denied the existence of the Buraku Problem at the WCRP I and III assemblies are not only without any basis of argument, but also deviate from the report which suggests that the immediate solution of the Buraku problem is the responsibility of the nation, but at the same time it is an important problem with which the citizens of Japan are confronted.

The statements of the participants who refused to take up the Buraku problem at the assembly of WCRP III, saying it was a domestic issue of Japan, should be viewed only as sophistry used for the purpose of concealing discriminatory attitudes. Why? Because if the Buraku problem should be regarded as only a Japanese domestic issue, people of religion in that country must tackle this problem as their responsibility and appeal to all people concerned with the question of human rights to join with them in this struggle.

Since its establishment in 1970, WCRP has taken up the question of human rights as one of its main themes, and has earnestly and repeatedly discussed this issue up to the present time. The following references are made in the findings of the WCRP assemblies, as published by the Committee:

From the Findings of WCRP I:

"The social convulsions clearly evident in the world today demonstrate the connection between peace and the recognition, promotion, and protection of human rights... Generally speaking, it is at the domestic level that human rights can most effectively be protected. The representatives of religions should actively use their influence in each country to secure the application of the principles of the Universal Declaration in national laws. ... Another cause of disrespect for many governments is their failure to ratify and implement international conventions which they have advocated and voted for. . . This applies particularly to the Convention on the Elimination of all Forms of Racial Discrimination, and the two UN Covenants of Human Rights. . ."

From the Findings of WCRP II:

"Gross violations of human rights have occurred and continue to occur in small and large countries alike. We deplore these violations wherever and whenever they occur. We pledge ourselves, and call upon all religious people and groups, to take the lead in exposing and correcting such violations of human rights. . . The most urgent priority lies in improving the implementation of those basic human rights which have, in principle, received almost universal acceptance. In this task, the part which religious organizations can play is of primary importance. . . We call upon the religious communities of the world to press their governments to ratify the covenants and conventions that alone can make the United Nations standards operational in the life of the nations. . ."

From the Findings of WCRP III:

"We pledge our support to all societies, organizations, and groups sincerely struggling for human rights and opposing their violations. . . We are encouraged by the efforts of many nations throughout the world to eliminate prejudice directed at ethnic, racial, and social minorities. However, prejudice and bias—both overt and covert—continue in many places, causing suffering and great economic and social disability to the victims. We strongly urge all people to root out these prejudices in their own neighbourhoods and wherever else in the world they exist. . . We reaffirm our commitment, made at Kyoto and Louvain, to the UN Declaration on Human Rights, and we deplore the denial of human rights to any individual or community. . ."

Judging from the above-mentioned findings quoted from the three assemblies of WCRP, the participants' discriminatory words on the Buraku Problem spoken at the WCRP I and III assemblies implied "an act of treachery to the purport of WCRP", as the Buraku Liberation League pointed out, and these words ran counter to the spirit of religion and WCRP itself. Such discriminatory statements run counter to the spirit of WCRP, and as such they make the assembly resolutions no more than a scrap of paper and cause WCRP to become a mere shell of a world conference.

One thing we must take into account here is the fact that the discriminatory remarks were not pointed out nor contradicted by the participants at the WCRP and III assemblies. This fact indicates the present attitude which people of religion have held toward the Buraku problem. When we see the actual circumstances in the field of religion, we realize there have been many instances on gravestones or written on death registers; discriminatory books; discriminatory sentences found on tombstones and in scriptures and sutra; discriminatory speeches; and discriminatory inquiry into personal records concerning marriage, etc. At the same time we are clearly aware that such discriminatory features have been deeply rooted in their religious institutions and dogmas. The fact that discriminatory features have been questioned means that they have been rebuked for their mistaken attitude as religious people. Religious groups have forgotten their original principles, having fawned upon the powerful men and persons of high birth, having looked down on the weak, and having plotted simply how to survive. They have furthermore wrongly used the law of cause and effect and the concept of bodily purity and impurity in order to justify their powerful position and establish their discriminatory ideas.

Therefore we people of religion should return to the original foundation of religion based on human respect, which we can find in such Christian expressions as "the image of God" or "love of neighbours", and also in a Buddhist verse meaning "all sentient beings have the Buddha-nature innately". For the sake of practising our religious teachings, we deeply examine ourselves and our discriminatory conduct, carefully investigating each of the discriminatory elements which may be involved in religious institutions (authoritarian structures) and doctrines, and endeavouring, through our religious practices, to eliminate all kinds of discrimination.

In the fourth assembly of WCRP, we should like to tackle as practical subjects the following specific problems:

1)   As a group or as individuals, we who represent religious institutions repeatedly and earnestly endeavour to expose and remove existing discriminatory practices. As the first step toward this goal, we meet together with other concerned persons and hold here a meeting for self-examination. Our purpose is to set a goal for concrete plans for the future and reflect on several problem-points which have been raised by the use of discriminatory statements by certain participants at the WCRP I and III assemblies.

2)   We express both in Japan and abroad our self-examination and apologize for the discriminatory expressions used by the participants at

172

the WCRP I and III assemblies. Before attending WCRP IV—the first world conference to be held after WCRP III where discriminatory words became an issue—we will try to make the participants and others concerned know the true meaning of WCRP IV, and we confirm the following items as issues for full discussion at the assembly:

a) We will promote better mutual understanding among the Japan Buddhist Federation, Rev. Soyu Machida, the Soto Sect, the Buraku Liberation League, and the Japanese Committee of WCRP.

b) At the coming assembly of WCRP IV, we will appeal to the participants to recognize the Buraku problem as a problem of human rights in the world, and to wrestle with this problem at the assembly. To this end the representatives of religious bodies will explain about the discriminatory words used regarding the Buraku problem at the WCRP I and III assemblies, and also explain the progress of the ensuing situation, including our self-examination on this issue, and they will also seek to work on the relationships of the Buraku Liberation League, and will pose the problem of what the Buraku should mean to the participants.

c) The Japanese Committee of WCRP is applying in advance to the International Secretariat of WCRP to ensure that both representatives will have the right to speak on the Buraku problem at the WCRP IV assembly.

3) As a movement to eliminate all kinds of discrimination within Japan, we endeavour to arouse public opinion so that the Japanese Government will ratify the Convention on the Elimination of all Forms of Racial Discrimination. We have strongly urged the ratifying of this Convention at each of the three assemblies of WCRP. Therefore, we regret our delay in tackling this issue, and will make utmost efforts to promote the ratification of the Convention.

4) We promote the movement to eliminate all discrimination. As has been clearly stated, this Committee was born out of the co-operation among religious leaders who belong to various religious denominations and organizations. With such a background in the field of religion we vigourously promote activities to eliminate discrimination on the Buraku problem.

G.

Presentations In Commission III "World Peace and Disarmament"

35

A Holistic Approach to Peace and Disarmament

By Prof. Yoshiaki Iisaka*

I. Peace

In the course of WCRP's strivings for peace in the past almost fifteen years, there has emerged an idea which came to be clearer with the accumulation of common experiences: that is, A Holistic Approach to the Problems of Peace and Disarmament. It is indispensable if they are to be grappled with in an appropriate and effective way. Holism, in this context, refers to the idea that the whole is qualitatively different from a mere sum of the parts, and this difference is made because of the interrelatedness, interconnection, and interdependency of parts, without which, they will make, not a whole, but an aggregate of discrete parts. Applied to the problem of peace and disarmament, a holistic approach emphasizes the interconnection of many problems, which cannot and should not be mutilated into separate parts, and thus be reduced to a simplistic solution that a certain element is exclusively essential to the achievement of peace. Of course, this does not mean that the consideration of priorities should be neglected, when one approaches the problems of peace. We have to distinguish the understanding of the nature of peace as a whole from the strategic consideration of priorities for the attainment and maintenance of peace. The consideration of priorities, however, should be based on the right understanding of the nature of peace. Then, what does a holistic understanding of peace imply? When one talks about a peace movement, one tends easily to identify it with an anti-war or anti-nuclear movement. Disarmament, nuclear or conventional, is necessary for peace, but peace is more than that. Peace needs the achievement not only of disarmament, but also of development and

---

*Dr. Iisaka is Professor of Political Science at Gakashiun University in Tokyo, Japan.

177

human rights. WCRP has constantly been pursuing those three objectives.

Disarmament means liberation from war and violence. Development implies liberation from hunger and poverty, and human rights demand liberation from oppression and discrimination. Peace means liberation from these evils and injustices as a whole. Realization of peace implies achievement of disarmament, development and human rights. Peace has a trinitarian structure. The relationship between disarmament and development has been keenly subjected to scrutinizing review in the documents prepared for the UN Special Sessions on Disarmament. Interrelatedness of development and human rights has crystallized into such important concepts as "basic human needs" or "quality of life". Interconnection between disarmament and human rights is also to be noted, as so often a government's preoccupation with security through armament leads to the negligence of human rights, and in many countries national security is used as an excuse to curtail human rights. In many military governments, human rights problems have been burning issues for which the populace struggles. Thus, it is appropriate for us to have a clearer understanding of the interrelatedness and mutual consequences of disarmament, development and human rights, even though our commission theme is "World Peace and Disarmament".

A holistic idea of peace defines peace, not only as a state of non-war in a negative way, but also positively as life together in harmony, as fullness and completeness of life, as is shown by the word, shalom, in the Judeo-Christian tradition. World peace means realization of world community in its fullness. Peace is not only an objective conditions but also an existential posture on the part of "peace-makers". A holistic understanding demands the synthesis of subjective as well as objective dimensions of peace. It also demands the interrelatedness between peace in one's heart and peace in the world. Peace in each individual has to be related to peace in society. The private and the public dimensions of peace have to be co-ordinated. A holistic view of peace takes peace as a whole but it distinguishes different dimensions of peace which comprise peace as a whole: peace within oneself; peace among persons, groups, societies, and nations; peace between human beings and nature; peace between human beings and their source of being, i.e., God, Buddha, or any other names to denote it.

Religious insight will see peace as the origin and source of humanity and the world. The whole creation was made for peace. Human beings, being created as such, can strive for peace, in spite of and in the midst of war, conflict and violence in the present world. Peace is an unending process. Peace, in some religious traditions, is a promise, an eschatological hope, to be realized as an ultimate *telos* through divine providence. Thus, peace is origin, process, and *telos* (end), and all of them together.

Another important understanding of peace, in this holistic approach, is its inseparableness from freedom and justice. Peace without justice and freedom is a sham and will not last long. The so-called "balance of terror" or "armed peace" does not deserve the name of peace. Peace under a dictator is not a true peace. It is transient and ephemeral, because it is lacking in freedom and justice.

Thus, peace has many facets. It is and should be an integrated, interrelated whole, or a unity in diversity. In this connection, it is very appropriate to refer to the short lines, which were composed by a member of WCRP/Pakistan and placed in our Conference Workbook under the section titled "Meditations for WCRP IV:"

We do not want a piece of peace
But peace as a whole.
We do not want a piece of peace
But all the pieces.

Surely, this is a holistic approach to, and understanding of, peace, put down in poetic form. Such an understanding is very relevant to the actual and concrete works of peace. Needless to say, in actual circumstances, one cannot pursue all and every dimension of peace all at once and at the same time. Which dimensions most urgently are to be tackled depends upon the situations in which we find ourselves. Priorities will be made in the context of the actual needs of the times. Emphasis may be different according to the groups or movements, so that a system of specialization and division of labour will be established among them. If they lack in this holistic understanding of peace, however, it is difficult to build up relationships of co-operation and solidarity which are a *sine qua non* for effective efforts at peace. The holistic approach also envisages the necessity of co-operation among religions as well as that between religionists and non-religionists. WCRP continues as a multi-religious movement for peace based on the dialogue and co-operation among various religions, and must be ready to co-operate and co-ordinate with other secular movements in common tasks for peace. The holistic approach reminds us of the importance of parallelism and co-ordination in our efforts for peace.

II. Disarmament

A holistic approach to the problems of disarmament requires us to work on two levels. One is on the subjective level, aiming at the attitudinal formation of peace. Those who envisage the cause of war originating in the mind of people, as typically formulated in the preamble of the UNESCO Charter, tend to emphasize this subjective approach. They think that the surest way to peace is to change the mind of people through the media of education and propaganda, through mutual understanding and cultural exchange and through the measures of confidence-building. Those who are often critical of this kind of approach base their understanding of the cause of war on the socio-economic contradictions of the present world. They emphasize the importance of structural change in society and the world as the practical way to world peace. Again, holism will enable us to comprehend the interrelatedness of these two levels. The one cannot be replaced by, nor identified with, the other, though each has its own distinct contribution to peace.

What should be WCRP's contribution to attitudinal as well as structural change for peace? It has pledged to co-operate with the World Disarmament Campaign of the UN and to launch an educational programme for peace. In the field of nuclear disarmament, we have to expose the fallacy of "nuclear deterrence" which is held and utilized as an excuse by the government of many nuclear or non-nuclear states. Religion has to grapple most radically with the problems of fear, hate, distrust, pride, envy, arrogance, etc. which often express themselves as spiritual perversion. Our world-wide fellowship and network should be used to the utmost to influence the minds of people, which will facilitate disarmament negotiations and the process of arms-control on the part of governments. Though we give a top priority to nuclear disarmament, to avert the destruction of the earth and annihilation of humanity, we should not think that the task of nuclear disarmament is left solely to the nuclear powers. Non-nuclear states have more reason and a better position to facilitate the process of nuclear disarmament. The Japanese people, as the only nation which experienced atomic bombs, have a special task to be witnesses to the inhumanity of nuclear arms. The Japanese people incorporated "the renunciation of war" clause in their post-war constitution and a definite policy towards nuclear arms was adopted. It is called "three non-nuclear principles," which signifies a ban on the production of nuclear arms, on stockpiling them, and on having them brought into Japan. Japan's commitment to non-nuclear policy will give her a moral strength, on the basis of which she can challenge and persuade, together with other non-nuclear states, nuclear powers to launch upon nuclear arms-control or disarmament. We have to recognize clearly that the states committed to non-nuclear policy have a moral strength which has to be utilized to influence the nuclear, and potentially nuclear, powers.

Disarmament of conventional arms is also an important task on the part of non-nuclear states of the developing area. Parallelism, which a holistic view suggests, demands taking initiatives in arms-control and disarmament, unilateral or multilateral, of those developing states, simultaneously with the efforts for nuclear arms-control and disarmament on the part of nuclear countries. In this connection, we should be reminded of the proposal included in the report of WCRP II on "Disarmament and Security", to the effect that taking an initiative for substantial disarmament, through the renunciation of military power and committing security to the guarantee of the United Nations by concluding treaties between the states concerned and the UN, will be feasible for the militarily smaller nations. Through these measures, the UN's rôle in peace-keeping and collective security will be strengthened, and its authority be reinforced. It may be noted that militarily smaller nations have a freer hand in disarmament when contrasted with heavily armed nations. For that matter, non-governmental organizations will have more flexible thinking and more consistent perspectives about disarmament than most governments. Thus, a closer pattern of co-operation and criticism must be established between the militarily overwhelming and the militarily smaller countries, as well as between non-governmental organizations and governments.

Dr. Homer A. Jack, our former Secretary-General, has placed before us four proposals for nuclear disarmament: a nuclear freeze; a complete ban on nuclear tests; the establishment of a moral and political consensus which makes not only the first use, but also any use of nuclear arms "a crime against humanity"; the expansion of nuclear-weapons-free zones all over the world. We may also add that a statement and adoption by governments of a non-nuclear policy, as exemplified by Japan, is highly desirable. Many cities and towns around the world have declared themselves to be nuclear-free. As suggested by Dr. Jack, our religious organizations, churches and synagogues should play a symbolic and prophetic rôle by declaring themselves to be nuclear-free. This can be a mass campaign on the part of various religious organizations all over the world.

III. Nationalism and Beyond

Nationalism, so long as it is an expression of identity of a people called a nation, shall be respected and maintained. Nationalism, however, tends to become a self-asserting, self-aggrandizing, and other-destroying force, when equipped with sovereignty and military forces. In the same manner, each religious tradition expresses and retains its own identity, but more often than not, it tends to be trapped by "the crusading mentality" through its own arrogance and Messianic perversion.

There is a very close parallel and analogy between religion and nationalism. Inter-religious dialogue, as engaged in here, will give us a clue to the desirable interrelatedness of nationalism and internationalism. With the growing realization of the unity of humanity, political nationalism, which takes the form of sovereign states, will give way to cultural nationalism, liberated from oppressive and military shackles. Inter- and multi-religious co-operation must go hand in hand with inter- and multi-national co-operation. Dialogue between religions is best executed when they engage in common service to the needy, the poor and refugees. In the same manner, the best way to overcome narrow-minded nationalism is to participate in common service for humanity beyond nationality, race, colour and so on. Service unites, though dogma and power divide. Religious insights have always to disclose and overcome human weakness and wickedness which corrupt human beings' best intentions and noblest efforts. Religious faith will serve to cleanse the heart and sinful tendencies and to make people better fit for the tasks of peace.

In 1963, John F. Kennedy addressed Amherst College by saying, "When power leads man toward arrogance, poetry reminds him of his limitations. When power narrows the areas of man's concern, poetry reminds him of the richness and diversity of his existence. When power corrupts, poetry cleanses, for art establishes the basic human truths which must serve as the touchstone of our judgment".

Even though he referred to poetry as a best corrective for the evils of power, we may put the words, "religion" and "faith", instead of "art" and "poetry". Thus we declare:

When power leads man toward arrogance, *faith* reminds him of his limitations. When power narrows the areas of man's concern, *faith* reminds him of the richness and diversity of his existence. When power corrupts, *faith* cleanses, for *religion* establishes the basic human truths which must serve as the touchstone of our judgment.

36

a) By Mrs. Jean Zaru[*]

In the search for peace in the Middle East, some people begin with the Camp David agreements, others with a new status for Jerusalem. Still others see peace primarily in the withdrawal by Israel in whole or in part from lands occupied by Israel in 1967. Many others start by speaking of withdrawal of Israel from Lebanon. Palestinians begin with the loss of their lands and their rights. There are about four million Palestinians, half of them uprooted and forcibly thrown out more than once, and the other half subjected and oppressed and strangers in their own land.

Chaim Weizman, later to become the first president of Israel, once remarked long before the establishment of the Jewish state, that the world would judge Zionism by the way they treated the Arabs and Palestine.

It was a wise utterance, but half a century was to pass before the world gained a clear picture of the relationship between Jews and Arabs in Israeli-occupied Palestine. But the increased awareness of the injustice suffered by us and the results in terms of discrimination and spiritual and material hardship has been one important factor in bringing about a reappraisal of international attitudes towards the Arab-Israeli conflict.

There are several reasons why all of us should be concerned with this conflict and work towards peace in the Middle East:

1. The Arab-Israeli conflict is potentially an explosive situation which could be a threat to world peace. It now affects the lives of millions of people in the Middle East; if it widens, it could affect the lives of tens of millions of people elsewhere.

2. Several governments support Israel militarily, politically and financially. Each individual has the right, if not the duty, to know the facts in order to judge whether the support which his or her government

---

[*] Mrs. Jean Zaru, a social worker and teacher, is involved in the work of the World Council of Churches and the World Young Women's Christian Association in the Middle East, and particularly the Occupied Territories (West Bank).

is extending to Israel is given for a legitimate cause, and whether this support is in the long run in favour of Israeli citizens or in favour of peace.

3. The Palestine Question has been on the agenda of the UN since 1947. Many resolutions have been adopted and nothing has been implemented. Therefore every individual has a responsibility directly or indirectly for the action or inaction of his or her government.

4. The present-day struggle for human rights all over the world for us and for others is a struggle in which all people must engage if we are to be faithful to the demands of our religious values.

5. In Judaism, Christianity and Islam the concept of the divine nature existing in harmonious relationship with human nature and the natural order has been a dominant one. The teachings of these religions helped undergird the belief that human beings have rights. Created in the image of God our value comes from this likeness. God's nature is loving, free and just; God's purpose is to liberate human life from inhuman conditions, which exist because humans of free will have chosen behaviour that disrupts the intended harmony which provides peace, justice and freedom for all.

As a Palestinian Quaker woman, native of the Holy Land, I have been confronted all my life with structures of injustice. These political, cultural, economic and social structures have been at work in a destructive way throughout our community and have caused so much spiritual as well as physical suffering for many including myself. I started to think about this: "If there is that of God in every person, why is there so much evil and darkness in the world? Why is it hard for us to see that of God in others?"

My inward struggle was reflected in my outward action. I became increasingly sensitive and aware of the suffering which reflects the evils which plague the human race. But my struggle also opened me to God's redeeming love and activity.

Involvement in any action takes an effort and there is always a price to pay. Am I ready to pay the price, to share the suffering of others? Suffering for me is bearable, if it is for the cause of liberation to find a new community with each other and with God. I do realize that those who operate the structures of oppression are dependent on the people they oppress and are equally in need of liberation and God's grace. Yet it seems to me that the will and strength to end the oppression comes from those who bear it in their own lives rather than from the privileged persons and nations.

But where do we begin? If life in its fullness, if the children of God, wherever they are, are created in the image of God, then they are our brothers and sisters! What do we do to preserve the dignity of their lives? What do we say to the arms race and nuclear weapons? What do we do when in the name of "national security" our scarce resources are used to buy weapons instead of combating poverty and hunger? What do we say when these arms-sales promoted by industrialized nations are often used for internal repression, violation of human rights and wars within a country and between neighbouring countries? What do we do when our style of life, or our silence, is the cause of the presence of war without arms where the victims are millions of people who are dying from hunger and poverty?

What about social justice? Can there be peace between the starving and the affluent? Between the oppressor and the oppressed, occupier and occupied? Can arms bring security or keep peace? Are we concerned when the Bible is abused in a pagan way to worship all kinds of false gods like money, material wealth, race, and other idols? What do we do when individualistic interests are often justified by quoting Biblical passages out of their historical context? What are we in our particular countries called to do? We are called to conversion, to be converted to the struggle of women and men everywhere who have no way to escape the unending fatigue of their labour and the daily denial of human rights and human worth. We must let our hearts be moved by the anguish and suffering of our sisters and brothers throughout the world. How can we bear the pain and where do we look for hope? Is there anything we can do to solve our present political chaos and the crisis in the world? Is there anything we can do to stop wars of all kinds?

Let us take a look into ourselves, for the outward situation is merely an expression of the inward state. It requires great self-denial and resignation of ourselves to God to be committed to peace and to non-violent action to bring about change. This technique may have no positive effect and it may lead to outward defeat. Whether successful or not it will bring suffering, but, if we believe in non-violence as the true way to peace and love, we must make it a principle not only of individual but of national and universal conduct, but we should try to do so without any feeling of moral superiority, for we know how soon we may stumble when we are put to the test. We may talk about peace but if we are not transformed inwardly, if we still want position, power, if we are motivated by greed, if we are nationalistic, if we are bound by beliefs and dogmas for which we are willing to destroy others, we cannot have peace in the world.

Living under military occupation has made me go through deep self-searching, and I have been confronted with three loyalties. The first loyalty is to Christ who calls us to love our enemy. The second loyalty calls us to aid our fellow-men and women in need or trouble. The third loyalty calls us to love our country, its people and its way of life. This loyalty prevents us from being willing to aid our invader. In our situation, no one can set rules for us to follow, but what we can do is to testify that in our experience the spirit of God leads us into the truth and gives us the needed guidance in every situation.

We have gone through circumstances of great privation, anxiety, and suffering. All these seemed at times to weaken my dependence on God, but what joy and hope I gain when I know, wherever I am, whether in affluent circumstances or in poverty, whether I have personal liberty or not, I am under the guiding hand of God, and God has a service for me to render wherever God has placed me.

I call myself a Quaker or Friend, and Friends throughout history maintained a testimony for peace. War, we say, is contrary to the mind of Christ and it is laid upon us to live in the virtue of that life and power that wins through love and not war. This is not an easy testimony for it has three aspects:

1. To refuse to take part in acts of war ourselves.
2. To strive to remove the causes of war.
3. To use the way of love open to us to promote peace and heal wounds.

But how can I interpret this pacifism to my children and my students when we are all victims of violence? How can I have peace within when I worry so much about life in general and the lives of my family members? How can I have peace within when others label my people as terrorists and justify our oppression by quoting the Bible?

When I have peace within, it is not because I approve of the violence around me, it is not because I sit in silence and accept all the injustices. It is when I am liberated to help my people, it is when I have the strength to endure, and the strength to attempt to love all women and men that I really feel that peace.

I see things differently now. I know the oppressor is not freer than the oppressed. Both live in fear and do not have peace. No government, no army, no country, no leader is going to give us peace. What will bring us peace is inward transformation that will lead to outward action. Our miseries are not going to stop through disapproval; if we see the urgency for immediate action, then only we shall transform ourselves and peace will come when we are peaceful, when we are at peace with our neighbours.

Peace is not only the absence of war or force. There is no peace when I treat others as nothing; when I hate, when I lie or think evil thoughts or when I offend others and harbour uncharitable thoughts, I am being violent.

It is not easy for us to think of the sacredness of life when our dignity is rarely recognized. But maybe through the hurt, the pain, the wounds, we try to realize our power and become agents of change for the better rather than agents of change to transfer power from one group to the other. It might be a dream but it is my human right to dream and to work towards the reality of that dream.

b)   By Ms. Shelley Elkayam*

One should view disarmament as a strategy, just as armament is. The building up of weapons was aimed at defending a society—so is disarmament. The building down of weapons aims at the very preservation and defence of a society in a physical sense—the here and now.

The real importance actually lies in the spiritual guidance of this physical force. People who are giving in to irrational thinking have no straight and direct sense of reality. We should look at reality with both our eyes open, not only with the left one or the right one as we so often do.

Knowing that weapons were and still are only means, only a society made up by a consensus of good-hearted and God-loving people can prevent irrational elements from having a part in the decision-making of the executive arm of governments. This danger became very clear for us in Israel in the last elections, as for the first time in Israeli political history, a racist mind with a fascist architecture of policy, using Judaism for ideological and political interests, entered our democratic scene with one seat in our Knesset.

A narrow nationalism is now endangering our nation-building. We, in the East for Peace, see that as a red light, though we know that the so-called Rabbi Kahana and his close circle are definitely not a pure Israeli product but mainly a kind of evil import planted into our young society which is carrying the Jewish age-old mission. Yet we cannot ignore that it was certain elements within our own society which paved the way for such a phenomenon. The trend in Judaism to allow ideological developments is not new, nor it is in other religions.

Most manipulations are based on confusion and superficial irrational arguments in any essential discussion. The conflict within Israeli society was for years pushed down or ignored. The myth of "we have no conflict" was implied also about the Israeli-Palestinian issue.

Let me say something about our brothers who took the leadership in the state of Israel and still have it. The trauma of the Holocaust is imprinted in the behaviour, architecture and policy of the Israeli establishment. The trauma of pogroms culminating in the Holocaust designed by the Nazis caused fear. Fearful people are not easy to communicate with.

I love the way our Arab brothers used to build houses in the Middle East. I hope we will also manifest love to nature and to the land which is so important for use. The behaviour of the Israeli Jewish establishment towards the oriental elements, the majority of the Israeli population, the Sephardic Jews (traditional Jews)—e.g. the suspicious way in which they

---

*Ms. Elkayam, a poet and author, is a member of the East for Peace in Jerusalem.

have been treated—acts as a boomerang against the presence of Jews in the Middle East. The real issue in Israel is to try to turn suspicion into respect. This is a mental shift and a holistic mental shift. A stranger is a stranger. Yet there are two ways to approach a stranger. One is to suspect; the other is to respect. Shifting the gear is not an easy task. The media and the educational system should support this shift and the political norms should change accordingly.

Let us be aware that the beautiful young Israeli people are like flowers who grew under the Eastern sun with the light of the Hebrew language and with a lot of love and care from each mother and father. Thus the creativity of mind to cultivate their own way in this world, to make it harmonious with the place they live in. But how can we have peace of mind while living in the mouth of the news industry? And if we happen to be such a hectic industry of so-called news (political, economic and military sensations) we must change our concept of real news.

At the moment real news should be that we let ourselves get used to the place which we love and belong to, and have all our relations with the place where we are with ourselves and with our neighbours.

The need for peace is not that we become richer and owners of land and property, but that we be peacefully in contact with the essence of our being, each in our place; only so can we be free and not bothered by wars, free to have time to deal with the Torah and the teachings of wisdom and knowledge.

c) By Ms. Nahla Haidar

Ms. Haidar, a Muslim from Lebanon, is Relief Co-ordinator for the United Nations Development and Relief Organization (UNDRO) in Geneva, Switzerland. Unfortunately, the text of her address was not available by printing-time.

37

By Sr. Dadi Janki*

I start with the words "Om Shanti." Perhaps all of you are aware of the beauty, significance and power of the depths of peace. "Om" means "I am" and "Shanti" means "peace"—"I am Peace." And this is all the Conference is about—peace. In a gathering of such people it is a rare privilege to be sharing with people who have a deep commitment to their faith and are not afraid to share that faith with others in a world so very, very materialistic where it takes courage to stand up and say: "I believe in God." I believe we work towards a positive future and then we find people who have faith and who also have a concern for applying it into the physical world so that faith works and makes things happen in the world. So this is what this Conference is about, I feel, and we are moving towards that goal of peace, the "Om Shanti". The translation of that spiritual exercise into a reality is a translation of that spiritual experience into a physical reality here in this world.

One of the things that I would like to touch upon is to think back to some point not too long distant in the past when we would speak about the world situation, maybe the political, religious or economic situation; then we probably used the term "problem"—that there was a problem in those areas, and now we don't even seem to use the word "problem" so frequently anymore. Whatever the religious, economic or political situation, another word has become very much part of our vocabulary, and that is "crisis." We seem more and more to use this word, rather than any other.

One particular experience in England recently gave us a very grave indication of what the future holds. Setting aside the awareness that one generation always feels that the new generation, the younger generation, has standards that have deteriorated more than its own (it is really true that there has been a decline in the conditions of the world, and we have really reached that state of crisis), the children are a very clear mirror of society. Our Centre was asked to organize a series of classes in the London Comprehensive Schools for 13-year-olds. This is the age at which

---

*Sr. Dadi Janki is a member of the Brahma Kumaris Spiritual Assembly.

they study world religions specifically within their syllabus. Our experience was not one we would have expected: in one particular class, eight series of classes were conducted for a class of approximately 25 students each. Those of you who are familiar with London are aware that any one group within one school will have black, brown and white children from multi-racial, multi-cultural and multi-social backgrounds. When these children were asked: "Do you belong to a religion?" there were only four children who said that they had a religion to which they belonged. When asked: "Do you believe in God?" the answer was one that would have touched even the most stony-hearted of human beings: that they do not know God, that they do not know who he is, and so how is it possible for them to believe in him and to experience him? Is it society, the custodians of religion or parents that have brought about this particular state of crisis? These were quite intelligent children, because when asked: "Where is the mind?", they would come out with answers like "it is that which thinks," "it is that which feels," "it is that which creates". Asking them further: "What is it that the mind thinks about?", again a shock, because this was the pattern throughout different classes. One girl said it was jealousy, a boy said hatred, another one said violence. On being asked: "Is there anything positive that the mind ever thinks about or experiences?" there were very shy and hesitant answers: happiness, love, but certainly not with the same assertiveness that the others answers had come. Perhaps this is a tiny reflection, but not an insignificant reflection, because if this is the state of 13-year-olds today, where shall we be in four years, or in forty years' time?

Here is another example that may interest you. To the question: "How is it possible to experience peace?" a bright boy answered "from a bottle of Disprin". So perhaps peace is something that these children have never experienced, and perhaps it is an area of which these children are totally unaware. Another interesting experience was asking them: "What do you think is the greatest problem that faces the world?" The answer was unanimous: "War". Thus children are aware of the threats to humanity and civilization; they are aware of war and the danger of war, and that peace is something of which they have no consciousness.

It seems that peace is definitely fading from the picture of human life. But the fact that we have gathered here today means that we can change that; we can bring peace back into the picture and restore it to the world. It indicates the attention it requires, the education that is necessary, because peace is really and truly education. One has to learn to be peaceful; one has to learn to maintain peace within the self, so that one can become a unit that can create or be a brick within the building of society that has peace.

It is a strange paradox that perhaps all religions accept the divinity of human beings, that within human beings there is that spark which is eternal, that spark of consciousness which has peace, love and light; and yet on the individual level, peace is something that has got trapped in the stress and tension to which we are exposed, or even the negativity that we generate within our own minds; and on the external scale we come to the point where the world can be destroyed 40 times over, if that were possible. So this is the state of peace and violence in the world at the moment, and this is where the responsibility of religion lies in all of us. We should remember here what happened in the panel this morning: two sisters sitting here, after sharing their experiences with us this morning, so wonderfully kissed each other. Looking at it on a theoretical level, three women from three different religions touched on one of the most severe trouble spots in the world. Sharing such an experience together and sharing their lives together was perhaps something that restored hope and faith in all of us who were present, and I thank them for what happened this morning. It clearly came up at that point that perhaps it was not so much a question of "religion", as of "spirituality".

I think it is important that all those who belong to a religion should come to an awareness of what peace really means. In our Indian texts the word *dharma*—a word that comes from the *Gita*—can in one translation be religion, but in another translation it can be a state of peace, the natural state of the soul, a way of life; and I think this is where religion has to examine what is going on, because there seems to be a discrepancy. One of the speakers at a series of seminars organized by our Centre in London who is present today put forth that religion in essence and the truth of religion are essentially the same within each and every religion, but the problems are "Have we fallen into dogma?" and "Have we fallen into external ritual?" If we claim that this is the foundation of religions, this is where the whole apparatus of missionaries, conversion, conversion by the sword, war and so on takes over. We should turn to the essence of religion, religion as the way of life, religion as the path of truth.

Let me share with you a very beautiful image. Recognizing that every branch of a tree has its own value and is part of the tree, and if the tree has been a little disfigured it would be unhealthy, even in the absence of just one of its branches, so is the beauty of the tree in its totality. There is the reality that the entire tree grew from one seed, and one should thus perhaps recognize the beauty, validity and strength of each one of these branches, just as the different religions to which we belong, and turn our thoughts and hearts to the one seed, to the one Supreme, the Father and Mother of humanity. In this state of "Om Shanti," we are led to believe that "Shanti," peace, is our religion; experience the relationship of a child to the parent, and this experience will bring out the beauty that is inherent within us.

Let us look at another problem that exists today. It is the crisis not just of loss of faith, not just of loss of faith in ourselves, seeing our own defects, not just of loss of faith in God, but perhaps the greater crisis of loss of faith in the future of humanity; and it stems from a question that has come into our minds and that is of our own origin, because there is an interesting debate that goes on. It is: "So many people feel that perhaps the original state of human beings is aggressiveness, for the innate quality of the human being is aggressiveness; and if that is what I believe, then I might as well go to sleep, because if I cannot experience peace for a period of time, I cannot work for peace in the world. But if I come to the realization that originally, in eternity of our own state, there is peace, then there is validity and then there is hope; then we can move forward with courage and faith and bring about the qualities in our own life and into the world once more." And so the term that has come up, which I would like to underline, is the term "psychological disarmament." We have been hearing about disarmament and specifically this is the theme of our workshop. Look at it and see how absolutely true it is in the sense that, even if we did not have atomic bombs, we would have ordinary weapons. Even if we did not have weapons, we would still have sticks and stones; and so my point is that it is not weapons that are in fact the cause of war; the cause of war is the human mind. And when peace is restored to the mind, and anger, ego and fear have been removed from the human mind, then there has been psychological disarmament. Only then can we hope to have stable peace in the world. That is not to deny the efforts that are being made on the other level, that, while we still have materials for destruction and annihilation, fear and distress are increased; and so we have restored some sort of humanity in human minds by removing the stress. Yet we certainly have to continue efforts on that level, but also be aware that the long-term solution and the only effective and ultimate solution is psychological disarmament. For this there are a number of practical measures.

Firstly there should be the possibility to spend some time in silence together. Archbishop Huddleston, one of the leading figures within the inter-faith dialogue movement, once a guest in one of our London Centre's seminars, asked "What is more important, dialogue or silence?" to which we answered that there had to be a balance of both. Dialogue to share, but then silence to contemplate what is being shared, and also a greater depth of realization so that the sharing is more effective; thus from dialogue into silence and from silence, with that added strength, into dialogue.

I know that a lot of those who are gathered here have the experience of drawing strength, peace and inspiration through their own silence, but the Brahma Kumaris' Spiritual University has initiated a programme which has simultaneous meditation taking place at 1,300 centres in 52 countries around the world; this is scheduled for 12:30 GMT on the third Sunday of every month. Vibrations move at a speed which is even faster than the speeds of sound, light or even conscious thought; they are the most subtle form and source of energy. So when we share our vibrations of God's love and remembrance of that communion of the soul with the Supreme, that method of sharing and generating further energy is a method by which peace can be restored to our struggling planet.

Another system which we use, we call traffic control. What we mean by this is that the mind constantly has the traffic of thoughts, but for a few minutes, every few hours, at times convenient to each of us, we stop and focus our attention on the source of eternal energy to recharge our battery and move in the correct direction once again. Traffic control is a very effective system for maintaining peace and generating peace within the atmosphere.

The third system is one which perhaps you may not feel inclined to start off with; it is the one of meditating at a time which is described as the time of nectar, early in the morning, at about 4:00 a.m. This is a good time, for in these very quiet, still, morning hours, the gravitational pull of the earth is actually less; and this is not my imagination. According to research done in San Francisco, the pull of the earth is less, and the vibrations are very pure and peaceful. It is in that communication with the Supreme that you can be instruments to create a canopy of peace within the world.

The last point I would like to make is that you have been part of this Conference and you have seen how living together and coming together bring about a closeness of relationships which is the practical experience of peace in the foundations of our lives and relationships. For two years we have had conferences in Mt. Abu, the headquarters of our Spiritual Assembly, gathering some 3,000 people from 50 countries; and our next one is planned for 9-12 February 1985. It is an opportunity to be in a spiritual atmosphere where there have been 50 years of intense meditation going on; and so we carry the strength of these vibrations into our deliberations. It is an opportunity for people of all religions, all backgrounds and all professions to come together, so that peace can be in our hearts and our lives, and for us to learn how to bring justice into our actions with each other.

38

By Dr. Lubomir Mirejovsky*

I consider it a great honour and unique opportunity to have received the invitation to WCRP IV and to be allowed to witness the joint search of all the participants for an answer to the urgent contemporary human problems. It is both encouraging and inspiring to listen to distinguished representatives and teachers of world religions expressing their understanding and hope that every religious tradition contains the motivation, and moral and spiritual strength that could contribute to the desired goal for a basic change and renewal of history.

I bring you greetings and best wishes for success in your deliberations and expressions of profound solidarity from the leaders, as well as the world-wide constituency of the Christian Peace Council (CPC). The CPC was founded in the fifties, during the agonies of the Cold War period. It was initiated by Christians living in the socialist countries of Eastern Europe who, together with their friends in the western world, felt that the time had come for articulating a religious response to the issues threatening human existence. Several concerns were expressed from the beginning and they continue to be the most important elements of CPC work today:

—to mobilize Christians in an effort to stop the nuclear arms race; this position was taken before the era of missiles and at the time when the first hydrogen bombs were tested;

—to encourage Christians to contribute to a dialogue between east and west, at the time when such a dialogue was difficult and seemed to be impossible;

—to encourage Christians to search for and contribute to international structures which would make co-existence between different social systems possible; and

—to encourage Christians to understand whether and how points of common interest could be discovered between adherents to antagonistic

---

*Dr. Mirejovsky is Secretary-General of the Christian Peace Conference in Prague, Czechoslovakia.

ideologies, i.e., Christianity and Marxism; the idea of a dialogue for peace and justice between Christians and Marxists was developed.

The members of CPC soon discovered that peace could not be achieved unless an understanding of and solution to the problem of basic human rights were found. The rights to shelter, food, medical care, education, independence and personal dignity are the prerequisites for a stable and just world. This understanding was gained by sharing experiences with our brothers and sisters from the Third World. A struggle for peace, disarmament and security is at the same time a struggle for justice, for national, economic and cultural liberation and against racial discrimination.

Where does CPC stand today? We speak about global threats to humanity and about global responsibility for the preservation of the sacred gift of life. By the growing threats, we mean the continuing development of nuclear arms and their delivery vehicles, the plans for the militarization of outer space (ideas to be abhorred by adherents of any world religion to whom the sky is the symbol of light, life, salvation and eternity), uncontrolled pollution of the environment by the industrial process, and accumulation of power in the hands of transnational corporations ruthlessly seeking profits and so introducing chaos into the economic structures of the world community, the structures of racism, exploitation, dependency and under-development in the Third World.

By global responsibility, we mean the search to unite all people of good will who are aware of the evils and dangers and who are willing, in spite of their religious, philosophical and political differences, to join forces in the struggle for peace and understanding among nations, justice, and to contribute by all possible means to preserve life on Earth.

We believe that many positive things were achieved. There is an encouraging growth in peace movements and activities all over the world. Important steps forward were achieved by the United Nations Organization on the issues of disarmament and the relaxation of political and military tensions. It is very encouraging to see people from different world religions come together in a meeting, like this World Assembly of WCRP, with courage and dedication to build the ways and bridges that should bring the divided and alienated people together into one family of co-operating nations. I would like to assure you that we in CPC want to support you in this struggle and share with you our experiences and our hope that the future of humanity is one of peace, justice, security and fullness of life.

39

By Shen De-Rong*

The Chinese delegation, consisting of representatives from Buddhism and Christianity, is very happy to have come to Nairobi to attend the Fourth Assembly of the World Conference on Religion and Peace, and to discuss the important questions of defending world peace with our friends from religious circles the world over. On behalf of Chinese believers of various religions, we would like to offer warm congratulations to the Conference. We pray to the Heavenly God for blessing our Conference with a complete success.

Friends, since the Third Assembly of WCRP, five years have elapsed. During these five years, the outcry for peace by the people and religious believers in different countries has gone higher, and they have taken part in the peace movement on a broader basis; and the actions to defend world peace have become more dynamic. However, due to the intensifying military expansion of the two super-powers in their contention for hegemony, world peace is in grave danger. This tells us that the people and religious believers of the whole world must make still greater efforts to defend world peace.

... The two super-powers have been keeping their military expenditures on an increase by a large margin. Their annual military spending surpasses the total annual national income of China with a population of one billion. They have constantly augmented and renewed their conventional and nuclear weapons. They possess about 60,000 nuclear warheads, 95 per cent of the world's total, with an explosive force equivalent to more than ten billion tons of TNT. Therefore, only when the two super-powers take the lead by drastically reducing their armed forces, especially nuclear weaponry, will it be possible to prevent atomic disaster from falling on the heads of the people of the world.

Friends, China is a developing country. At present, the Chinese people are engaged in large-scale material, spiritual and cultural civilization; therefore, a peaceful international environment is essential to

---

* Mr. Shen De-Rong is a church worker in Shanghai, in the People's Republic of China.

China. Even in the future, when China achieves even greater successes in construction, the Chinese people will also need peace in the world in order to defend the fruits of labour and to ensure the happiness of the generations to come. The small, limited number of nuclear weapons which China has to keep at present is solely aimed at resisting the nuclear blackmail and intimidation by the super-powers. The Chinese government long ago undertook the unilateral commitment never to be the first to use nuclear weapons or to use them against non-nuclear states or nuclear-free zones. In May this year, Chinese Premier Zhao Ziyang stated publicly that China will support any proposal for disarmament which is in keeping with the principle that the two super-powers take the lead by reducing their arsenals of nuclear and conventional weapons.

Friends, in accordance with their respective religious doctrines, all Chinese religious believers will support every just action to defend world peace. We Chinese Protestants take Jesus Christ as the God of peace. Early last month, an important meeting was held, during which the leaders of Chinese Protestants unanimously adopted a resolution: to make the second Sunday of January each year "the Day of Praying for World Peace", and to call upon Protestants throughout the country to pray for world peace in their service on that day and to make concrete actions for world peace.

Friends, we highly appreciate the enormous work done by WCRP in the past five years, in defence of world peace. For the purpose of world peace, religious circles in China are willing to strengthen contact and co-operation with our friends from religious circles in other countries and make joint efforts to realize the complete prohibition and thorough destruction of nuclear weapons and to defend world peace.

H.

Final Reports of Commissions

40

Report of Commission I
People of Faith
*Working Together for Peace**

What is this peace for which we seek?
Our various religious traditions affirm that peace is more than the
absence of war. A modern Indian scholar, Dr. S. Radhakrishnan, has
spoken of peace as "the development of a strong fellow-feeling, an
honest appreciation of other peoples' ideas and values". In most of our
languages the word for peace includes wholeness, well-being and relationships of trust, openness, respect, compassion and love. There is an
inner dimension to this peace involving self-respect and an interior tran-
quility as well as openness to the divine.

There is also a social dimension. To live at peace with our neighbours goes beyond tolerance and goodwill. It also calls us to become
actively engaged in the pursuit of justice. Peace becomes not only an
objective to be sought but a way of life to be embraced; it is therefore
closely bound up with action. When we consider peace among the
nations and peoples of the world we are compelled by the urgency of the
task. As members of religions that teach the importance of peace, our
credibility is threatened if we do not take seriously the imperative to
become involved in the struggle against threats to peace and become
peace-makers.

Working together for peace
Sadly, religion has been a source of conflict in the world; but our
very presence here is a witness that it need not be so. We have become
aware of much that binds us together. Ultimate Reality is infinite, while
our ways of describing and understanding it are necessarily finite, so we
have learned that we must listen with respect and humility while others

---

*This report was adopted by the closing plenary session of the Assembly.

worship or describe their spiritual experience. We have also discovered that all of our religious traditions urge compassion and kindness upon their followers, even though we have often failed to live up to our own high calling. These teachings, which represent the best of our spiritual heritage, we want to share with a broken world, with all people of goodwill, not out of any sense of superiority but as our contribution to the pressing concerns of our time.

There are those in the larger society who would rightly call on us to set our own house in order and heal the divisions not only between our different religious communities but also within each one of them. We acknowledge the need to continue to have dialogue among ourselves, to overcome prejudices and hostility. At the same time we cannot wait until all outstanding differences are settled before turning to such questions as war, poverty, racism, injustice and oppression. There is a two-fold pattern to our relationships which one of our speakers expressed by saying, "Sometimes we talk face to face, sometimes we talk together to others".

Approaches to dialogue

During our discussion four main approaches to dialogue seemed to emerge, although it is not suggested that this is a comprehensive list. Some called on us to rise above our separate traditions and recognize that the ultimate goal of all religions is the same. They propose that we work for a federation of religions and present a common position in the interest of peace.

Others preferred to think of dialogue as a bridge by which we reach out to others, but which must be firmly anchored at each end. We must be deeply rooted in our own tradition and find within it the dynamic toward peace. Only in this way can we maintain our credibility with others of our own persuasion and engage them also in the search for peace. This is also a reminder that religion cannot be simply boiled down to a set of beliefs but is a closely knit fabric of cultural and personal loyalties, involving an integrated approach to life. At the same time, however, we turn with love and humility to others recognizing that they have many treasures to share with us.

There were those who challenged us to concentrate on common projects and the struggle for social justice in the cause of peace, and to discuss theological issues only in so far as they arise within and may in turn support such collaborative effort.

Another set of voices called on us to find our underlying unity in silence. In this spirit monks, nuns and others have come together across religious lines to share in common work and meditation. Indeed, during this Conference some very meaningful moments have occurred when we sat together reflecting quietly.

What can be separated logically on paper cannot be so readily separated in practice. None of these approaches is necessarily exclusive of the other, but it is helpful when engaging in inter-religious dialogue and co-operation to be aware of the sometimes different premises from which we begin.

Challenges before us

Co-operation between people of different faiths is not simple. We experience, even before we start, barriers of race, gender, language and culture. We come from different background and different life-situations as well as from different social, economic and political systems. When we speak to each other about the world's problems we have a tendency to speak out of these perspectives, often unaware of the extent to which our presuppositions are shaped by our background.

Historical relationships between our various religions have not always been happy; they have been marred by oppression, persecution and bloodshed. While we cannot undo history we can offer our repentance and make past experiences the basis for a better future.

We were reminded that religious conflict is not only a fact of the past but that it thrives in our own day. In many countries civil disturbances and persecutions happen in the name of religion. Religious leaders have a responsibility to declare unequivocally that there need be no conflict among people of different faiths, that people of faith can and do live together in co-operation and harmony. Such declarations will not by themselves stop conflict or eliminate persecution. They will, however, remove from these situations any moral or religious sanction. We would go further and suggest that there are times when religious leaders have a responsibility to take immediate steps and intervene in conflicts, whether local, national or inter-national, which are rooted in religious differences.

Relevant to this concern is the need, in our analysis of the world situation, to take into account structures of society which perpetuate poverty and oppression. Religious conflicts themselves have often been rooted in or intensified by social and economic differences. If we truly believe that the spiritual and the material are not separable, but are like two wheels of the one cart, then we need not fear adding other insights to those of theology. To do otherwise runs the risk of failing to take seriously the sufferings of our sisters and brothers, and of offering platitudes instead of solutions.

Within many of our religious communities there has been an upsurge of those whose religious zeal is seen by some as triumphalist and intolerant. Often their religious convictions have been linked with nationalistic sentiments. While we differ with those who claim that theirs is the only way to truth, we wish to be consistent with our own call to openness and dialogue. We feel great concern about some of their activities but we want also to acknowledge that in so far as they too are seeking truth we have the same objective. There is also a significant number of people with a conservative religious viewpoint who are deeply involved in the struggle for peace and social justice.

In the search for peace we know that there are other people engaged who profess no faith, and yet the task is so urgent that we cannot afford to pass them by or work in isolation. The result is a continuing dilemma. On the one hand how can we be true to ourselves unless we can convey to the world our distinctive contribution, which is the spiritual one? On the other hand, how relevant to these people, many of them in government and decision-making positions, are proposals couched in religious language?

Moving forward together

During our discussions as a Commission we heard many encouraging stories of co-operation among religious people. Some of them were small local initiatives, others were much broader in scope, but all offered hope. We are deeply conscious that such stories could be multiplied many-fold at this Conference. A number of suggestions were made for ways in which the momentum can be maintained:

1. We cannot afford to overlook the insights and valuable contributions to the peace movement of children, youth and women. We note that their voices are still not sufficiently heard in our decision-making structures. One contributions to peace and understanding would be to put young people from different nations and different faiths in touch with each other.
2. We were challenged to broaden the dialogue and involvement in the search for peace beyond religious leaders to be inclusive of people from all walks of life.
3. The world is only now becoming re-acquainted with the ancient spiritual wisdom of people from indigenous religious traditions—whether in Africa, the Americas, the Pacific or elsewhere. These traditions contain many insights, for instance regarding the human relationship to the environment, that we ignore to our great detriment.
4. Education was cited as a means of helping our adherents to revise distorted and unfair opinions of other people. Our schools need to cultivate the love of peace and the abhorrence of war. Textbooks should be examined for militarism, racism and any form of prejudice. New resources—both print and audiovisual—should also be prepared which are acceptable to people of all faiths.
5. The inculcation of the acceptance of people of other faiths and the concern for peace should also rate as a high priority within our religious institutions as part of the religious instruction of children, youth and adults.
6. In view of the large number of people who belong to the religions represented here, the Conference has a great potential for shaping peoples' attitudes toward peace and toward each other. The necessity for communicating what has been said and done here was stressed. The leaders of our respective countries should also be informed about this meeting and the work of WCRP.

7. There are many situations of religious conflict around the world where WCRP and its leaders could offer to exercise a mediating role. We recognize that this has implications in terms of budget and staffing priorities but we suggest that it is an idea that should be considered in any re-structuring of WCRP.

Reports of Working Groups

This Commission heard reports from various Working Groups, in one or other of which all of our members had participated. We could not, and did not wish to, cover the same ground that these people had spent almost two days discussing in depth, but we have made recommendations regarding the disposition of proposals which seemed to fall within the mandate of this Commission.

1.a. *How to dismantle ethnic and religious prejudices which act as obstacles to building and changing society*
This working group developed a theme which figures prominently in our report. Education at all levels was felt to be the most effective weapon in fighting prejudice and promoting peace. An appeal was made for all countries to adhere to international conventions that aim at safeguarding human rights and eradicating all forms of discrimination. We wish to commend the recommendations of the report for the attention and implementation, as appropriate, of WCRP and its members.

1.b. *How to combat racial discrimination as it survives in many parts of the world but is still legally imposed by the apartheid system in South Africa*
Members of this Commission wish to affirm, along with the working group, that none of our traditions can be engaged to justify the persecution of people on any grounds, such as that of skin colour! We state in the strongest possible terms that there can be not theological support for the system of apartheid, nor any religious sanction for the denial of fundamental human rights whether in South Africa or anywhere else in the world.

3. *How to spread education for peace and for multi-religious understanding. . .*
The recommendations which were referred to us regarding educational activities correspond very closely to the strong emphasis many of our members placed on this subject, and we wish to commend the proposals contained in the working group report to WCRP and its members for appropriate action.

7.a. *How to improve planning and sharing multi-religious WCRP and other initiatives at national, regional, and local levels. . .*
The proposals submitted to Commission I from this working group are consistent with our earlier statements about the need for education and interaction among people of different faiths, and are commended to WCRP and its members for action, and where possible, implementation.

205

7.b. *How to elaborate particular projects for international WCRP spon-sorship...*
Two parts of this report were singled out by this Commission as coming within our mandate, and are commended to WCRP for action, as appropriate.
(i) that the international effort of WCRP, in co-operation with local WCRP groups, should focus upon particular areas of conflict where religions is, or is believed to be, a factor;
(ii) the organization of an international Youth Camp in 1985 in an area where there have been inter-religious conflicts.
The final note to the report suggests that WCRP be encouraged to work more closely with the Week of Prayer for World Peace. We have been made aware that other similar organizations also merit support.

In order that the proposal referred to above may be examined more fully, it is our request that they be appended to the text of this report.

Candles of hope
The task before us is daunting, but it is vital if life is to continue on this planet. We need the courage to be able to stand alone within our own nations and our own religious communities, we need also the courage to reach out to others in trust and love.
During our deliberations an image was provided to us in a striking way of what we are attempting to do in WCRP. The auditorium was suddenly plunged into darkness because of a power failure. After the first few moments of surprise and confusion flashlights and candles gradually began to be lighted at various places around the room, relieving the darkness and enabling us to proceed. Is this not a graphic picture of what WCRP, its members and friends, are trying to do—light candles of hope in a world overshadowed by evils of many kinds, not least of which are threats to peace and human dignity?

41

Report of Commission II: Human Dignity, Social Justice And Development of the Whole Person*

The members of this Commission have been charged with the important aspects of human right—namely, human dignity, social justice, and full development of the human person.

Each human is, by his or her very being, a unique creation in this universe, and deserves to be treated with equal dignity, regardless of colour, race, religion, nationality or sex. This is a basic requirement in dealing with human beings in whatever capacity. But this dignity can be maintained only if equal socio-economic and political justice are available to all human beings. Social peace can be maintained only if there is justice as its foundation. The third requirement is equal opportunity to human beings for the full development of the potentialities inherent in each individual. Economic development has not alone been found to be adequate, as it does not make for the full blossoming of the personality with which a human being is endowed by God and by nature.

There were three sessions of the Commission in which six papers were presented and discussed. The Consultant-Experts also presented brief statements with the idea of guiding the discussions in the Commission. The papers presented in the Commission dealt with the problems of discrimination, violation of human rights, religious intolerance, etc. in different societies in different parts of the world, and also presented the views of different religions.

The problem of discrimination was raised by a Japanese delegate representing the Burakus, who described the history and various disabili-

---

*This report was received by the closing plenary session of the Assembly and commended to the WCRP network for further study and action.

ties that the Burakumin suffered in Japanese society, especially in the areas of employment, accommodation and marriage. He was supported by the Japanese participants. Because of the recession and consequent unemployment, the Burakus are more adversely affected. It was disclosed that efforts were being made to rectify the situation although the results are rather slow. The Japanese Expert said that religions could not stop or deter the ill-treatment. The discriminatory attitude is in the minds of the religious people. He urged this assembly to institute prompt action with a view to eliminating discrimination against Burakus.

A Muslim delegate from Pakistan referred to the Islamic values embedded in the Qur'an in respect of dignity, respect for humanity, responsibility of individuals, right to freedoms, tolerance, right of protection, freedom of expression, economic rights, justice, love for and obedience to the Divine.

A Hindu delegate from India considered the economic and social injustices being inflicted upon different peoples in different regions. It was pointed out that protectionism in industrialized nations perpetuates the disparity between rich and poor nations as well as rich and poor individuals. He mentioned that Hinduism advocates the renunciation of wealth and that the present-day poverty in India has its roots in the colonial rule.

The representative of Amnesty International mentioned the different forms of torture inflicted upon dissenting peoples, including political prisoners, to destroy human dignity. Although, by now, torture is illegal in many countries, it is yet widely practised in many countries. Torture is inflicted on political dissenters and tolerated by some other authorities. Amnesty International has prepared a programme for prevention of torture as it is a direct violation of human rights.

An American-Indian delegate brought out the issues of racism, prejudice and oppression of his race, and the efforts to eliminate their culture and traditions. He emphasized the persecution of American-Indians with regard to their culture, in spite of legislation for religious tolerance. He specifically mentioned that American-Indian children were put into foster homes so that they would lose their identity and become alien to their own culture.

A delegate from Australia described the history of economic exploitation and suggested a new economic order to safeguard basic natural resources, to develop renewable resources, to promote a radically new world economic system so that the under-developed countries may have a fair share for the purpose of their development.

A Consultant Expert from India referred to the violation of human rights in different countries, especially in respect to the religious and ethnic minorities. He stated that, in spite of constitutional provisions and government policies and programmes in India meant for the emancipation and advancement of deprived and disadvantaged people, the dominating groups are overbearing and resort to tyranny and oppression, especially in the rural areas. Progress has been made in certain fields, but organized resistance by those who want to maintain the status quo has impeded the pace of progress. He suggested that legislation alone has never succeeded in removing prejudice or in bringing about the desired change in the attitudes of people. Religious organizations, and especially organizations like WCRP, if they take interest and address themselves to the problem, can bring about necessary changes so that discrimination can be eradicated.

A Muslim Consultant Expert from Cameroon referred to three points:

(i) How to achieve religious and ideological tolerance as a vital contribution toward a humane society and respect for human rights?

(ii) What to do against the continuous violation of economic and political rights and the increasing number of refugees around the world?

(iii) How can technology and development be humanized in economic and spiritual terms?

He proposed:

(i) to understand the difference between religion and ideology, to recognize that the goal of both is to become fully humane.

(ii) to outline the elements of a value-oriented education.

(iii) to indicate the ways of action to confront the violation of human rights as a human phenomenon.

(iv) to remedy by education, information and the sharing of responsibility.

(v) to realize that humanity and the humanness in humanity and in society are the goals.

All these are to develop consensus and orientation of action of WCRP, as an institution, and of different participants as individuals, in order to influence actions of different institutions, national and international.

A Consultant Expert from Kenya stressed that humanity is colour-blind, and knows no bounds. Those who discriminate against others do so with the claim that some people are more human than others. The basis for social injustice is greed, because certain persons consider themselves as more privileged. This leads to quarrels and fights everywhere.

The questions of discrimination against the American-Indians and the violation of their human rights was again raised. American-Indians are being denied freedom of religion and local authorities in the USA, it was stated, had taken action against some individuals who were taking part in initiation ceremonies and other functions peculiar to their tribes. The fishing-rights of the American-Indians were another problem raised by the American-Indian delegate.

Burakus, a segregated and discriminated group in Japan, and the problem of Koreans in Japan were compared. All Japanese delegates showed sympathy and gave suggestions to accelerate the pace of progress in the area. Leaders of the Suto sect showed keenness to work for the removal of prejudice from the minds of people and to co-operate with other groups to eliminate discrimination.

Hindu and Jain members of the Indian delegation enumerated many privileges and concessions which the government of India has provided for the benefit of the weaker section of society in India. They took objection to the statement that Hinduism is opposed to equality, owing to the caste system. A Hindu delegate from Sri Lanka stated that it was wrong to say that Hinduism did not advocate equality. In his sect, Saivaism, there was perfect equality and no discrimination. Other Hindu delegates asserted that Hinduism was not a religion, but a way of life.

Racial discrimination against blacks in the USA in employment, housing, education and health care, and even deprivation of life, were mentioned. There were several references to apartheid in South Africa. Suggestions were made for the imposition of sanctions and the implementation of UN resolutions, and resolutions and recommendations made in earlier WCRP assemblies. Many delegates from African countries, as well as from non-African countries, expressed dissatisfaction with the powerful Western block, which was not exerting enough pressure on South Africa to end apartheid. They asked WCRP to invite churches from South Africa to join future conferences of WCRP for concerted action against apartheid.

References were made to the conflict between Israel and Lebanon, the question of Palestine and the Iran-Iraq war. Discussing Sudan, some Christians alleged that Shariat law is being applied to non-Muslims, non-Muslims allegedly being awarded severe punishment, e.g., amputation of hands or feet, stoning, etc., as an application of Shariat law. This claim was supported by other non-Muslim participants, but was vehemently denied by a Muslim delegate from Sudan who said that Shariat law did not apply to non-Muslims, but that in the matter of criminal offences they could not have two different sets of laws—one for Muslims and the other for non-Muslims. Other Muslim delegates from Pakistan, Algeria, Indonesia, Lebanon and the UK supported the Muslim delegate from Sudan, asserting that Shariat law *ipso facto* cannot apply to non-Muslims. A Sudanese Muslim delegate asserted that secular laws had failed and therefore the Government was trying Muslim law (Shariat). A delegate suggested that the allegation of the misapplication of Shariat law to non-Muslims should be studied by WCRP.

It was noted that there were world-wide violations of human rights, dignity and social justice, especially in respect to women in almost all countries, but more so in developing countries where some religions have prescribed and perpetuated prejudice and discrimination against them. An Indonesian delegate pointed out that women receive discriminatory treatment in all cultures and societies in the areas of wages, employment, succession, divorce, adoption, sexual exploitation, etc.

Commission members suggested action-oriented policy and programmes. They demanded deletion of words indicating subservience of women to men, and replacing terms such as "man"" by "man and woman", and "mankind" by "humankind," etc. It was suggested that WCRP should speak out against discriminatory treatment meted out to women in all spheres of life, and also undertake education of women so as to make them aware of their rights.

On the subject of torture, one delegate said that religions object to all torture as a means of punishment, and understand it to be a violation of human dignity, no matter who the victim is.

The matter of the influx of refugees from Sudan and other African countries into Kenya, and from South Africa and Namibia into Lesotho was also raised, since they create economic, social and political problems in the host countries.

Education was thought by many delegates to be an effective means to eliminate prejudice and discrimination in the minds of people. A Japanese professor laid emphasis on the fact that education geared for peace and the integration of society, addressed to a multi-religious people, was the only way. The younger generation is very sensitive, and in the interests of peace and justice it is very important to train their minds. The Universal Declaration of Human Rights and other relevant international conventions should be included as part of syllabi. Educators should lay emphasis on mutual respect and human dignity, and impart multi-religious education to young people. Many delegates stressed the importance of education, because it is the only way of influencing the younger generation. Stress was laid on education for the growth of the whole personality and the strengthening of human values in society. Suggestions were made to introduce ethical principles, common to all major religions, so as to have an integrated society—diverse but united.

Co-operation between different religious groups and faiths is necessary, and many delegates stressed the need to establish a forum for the removal of contradictions which have caused misunderstandings, disparities, and numerous anomalies and vices such as untouchability, apartheid and racial discrimination. In certain matters of social discrimination, the eradication of poverty and multi-religious action could achieve results.

In regard to poverty and charity, all religions enjoin the sharing and the importance of charity. Some Commission members pointed out that improperly used gifts can become the weapon of oppressions in the hands of the rich and powerful against the poor and the weak. It is charity only when it is used to strengthen or stimulate the urge to become strong and independent, rather than weak and dependent.

In the first reading of the report, Commission members made several amendments. They also expressed their desire that apartheid and racial and religious intolerance be highlighted, so as to focus attention on problems which affect a large number of people. After careful consideration of the subjects discussed and the suggestions made, the Commission makes the following recommendations:

1. WCRP should invite the religious leaders from South Africa to

have a dialogue with a view of finding ways and means to a peaceful and practical solution to the elimination of apartheid and the establishment of a society free from fear. If no amicable solution, keeping in view the aspirations of the majority, can be found, violence will be the inevitable result since the patience of people is reaching the end of its tether.

2. Considering that:

(a) some delegates are afraid of stating the facts in regard to the violation of human rights,

(b) some participants tend to hide and deny the existence of discrimination and violations of human rights in their respective countries, and,

(c) members form alliances and divisions along religious lines,

it is recommended that ways and means be found to research facts, so that actions may be suggested for avoiding major catastrophes at later stages.

3. If any law is applied to adherents of a religion other than that of the dominant group in any country, in violation of their human rights, a request may be made to the leaders and theologians in the country concerned to reaffirm the protection afforded to minorities, in respect of the United Nations Declaration.

4. The question of refugees in many countries, especially of Africa, is serious. Many escaped to neighbouring countries due to religious or racial persecution and political reasons. This matter needs consideration, in the light of UN instruments. WCRP units should as a body take up their cause in the respective countries. They should also take appropriate actions in cases of refugees to which UN treaties do not apply.

5. In pluralistic societies of various religions, races and ethnic groups, multi-religious, spiritual and ethical education, laying emphasis on morality, should be introduced at all levels. This should be included in the syllabi at all levels.

6. The women's cause calls for special action. The education of women in regard to their rights, and the collection of information regarding discrimination, together with provisions in different religions and traditions, should be undertaken. A special concern is the growing practice of the sexual commercialization of women.

7. Religious communities and leaders should promote introspection and re-interpretation of the principles of their religious scriptures and doctrines, keeping in view the present trends, scientific discoveries, the expansion of knowledge, and the general awareness among people about human rights as embedded in the UN Charter.

42

Report of Commission III: World Peace and Disarmament *

Like all well attended meetings of WCRP IV, this Commission reflected the wide range of nationalities, faiths and cultures of the Assembly. It provided excellent presentations and thoughtful participation from some 50 men, women and youth. Prof. Iisaka of Japan gave a stimulating paper on "The Holistic Approach to Peace and Disarmament". He noted that a whole is greater than the sum of its parts; the sum is only an aggregate. Peace is far more than disarmament. It includes liberation from injustice which diminishes the quality of life. Public and private discussions of peace must be integrated and these include not only concern for disarmament, but also for development and human rights. Holism requires changes for peace, he said, on both attitudinal and structural levels.

Separate sections of this report will deal with those conflict areas which came under scrutiny. But it was evident that both hope and frustration and too often despair, are in-depth reactions to the awesome, complex problems of the world, its nations and peoples. Yet religionists recognize the strong ethical and moral imperatives of their faith which must underline both thought and action, whether of the individual or of his or her group.

The Commission, in its opening days, was given several poignant experiences. In recital of children's reactions in the class room to certain important questions, a speaker noted: In eight classes of 25 student each, only four had a religion; when asked about their belief in God, they stated they did not know what God was; when asked "What do you think about," the unhappy responses were "Hatred, violence, jealousy, war."

A panel of three women from the Middle East was of special merit, and will be covered in greater detail later. The proceedings of the Commission were concerned not only with the sections that will follow, but

---

*This report was adopted by the closing plenary session of the Assembly.

also with the links between regional conflicts and religious conflicts. Furthermore it was understood that while every area of conflict in the world could not be handled in depth at this Assembly, it was deeply hoped that insights gained here may in some measure be applied to other tensions whether in Latin America, Northern Ireland, or elsewhere—instances too numerous to mention fully.

Whether speakers and participants were from Czechoslovakia or Kenya, from India or China, from whatever large or small nation of the globe, the concerns were for solutions to grave problems inherent in seeking peace, world disarmament, overcoming poverty, hunger, drought and other crises. The role of religion, the need for a deepening spirituality, the necessity for all members of a faith to be united if governments and international bodies were to be influenced by their voice, the defining of how WCRP and its regional bodies can effectively work and offer, if possible, creative non-violent assistance in conflict resolution—all these were in the minds of Commission III members. Hard as it is through religion to realize that religion itself at times is part of the problem, nevertheless it is through religion and religionists that radical changes may yet be possible. Meeting in Africa, we were especially sensitive to the problems and crises of its countries and people.

Finally it should be noted that we carefully reviewed, and where possible incorporated into this report, the applicable sections from the Working Groups of the Assembly. We were grateful for the reciprocal process of Commission members and Working Group members often thinking about interrelated subjects.

I. EDUCATING FOR PEACE

A major task for all who are concerned for humanity and its future is to educate for peace. In a number of Working Groups suggestions were made, as were recommendations from Commission III on this subject. They included:

1.   Education for peace should be a part of all educational systems and institutions—from early childhood through graduate school and in adult education. Special curricula of studies in peace education should be developed, whether to be taught separately or integrated into subjects.

2.   Days or special times in each faith should be established for its adherents to pray and possibly fast for peace. This might be especially effective if held simultaneously world-wide during the Week of Prayer for World Peace (the week spanning United Nations Day, which is 24 October).

3.   Peace education should be more than theoretical; it should be linked to action programmes; some could be undertaken by WCRP and some by its chapters, as well as by others.

4.   Educators, scientists, economists and members of other related disciplines might be drawn together as professionals interested in developing criteria and materials for peace studies, which must include

the varied causes of war and the overcoming of threats to peace by non-violent means. Why and how nations arm should be part of their work.

5. The rights of conscientious objectors to war should be respected by all religions and governments.

6. Respect and understanding, not just a superficial tolerance of differences, must be engendered in all secular and religious study.

7. Private study, not just education for peace among students and scholars, should be part of each person's effort to be a responsible citizen. No education for peace, however well conducted, will bear lasting fruit unless it involves education for selflessness and concern for others.

8. Violence on television and its effect on children and adults must be considered as well as the rôle of the press and media in its reporting and at times adding religious identification needlessly to other more neutral identities.

9. All governments, religionists and peoples should recognize and adhere to the principles of the U.N. Charter and its Declaration on the Elimination of All Forms of Intolerance and of Discrimination Based Upon Religion or Belief.

There have been other valuable points offered but these seem the most critical and to this list each one can add his or her own further insights.

II. DISARMAMENT

A. *Introduction*

1. We met aware of the suffering already caused by the arms race, directly in war and indirectly through its cost; the world-wide anxiety there is about nuclear annihilation; the current failure of the nation states to negotiate any meaningful disarmament measures and the variability of our religions in regard to their response to the disarmament issue.

Whilst reaffirming our solidarity concerning the unacceptability of this situation, we have also tried to indicate the basic issues with which WCRP should be concerned in the immediate future. Certain general principles are implicit in this analysis of issues. They include:

(a) The need for spiritual practices to facilitate a disarming love, even of "enemies". This is part of a holistic approach to disarmament.

(b) The need for us to work within our religions so that the beauty of holiness rather than sectarian suspicion, defines our interactions—especially as regards conflict resolution.

(c) The need for WCRP members to be active in their own areas in non-violent peace and anti-militarist movements, for instance campaigns against nuclear weapons and the arms trade, the peace tax campaign, work to prevent experimentation on animals for military purposes, etc.

(d) The need for us to give strong support to the United Nations as it seeks to fulfil its character and as it works to resolve conflicts. We need the UN for a more peaceful world—one in which the institution of war is abolished.

2. The Commission was unequivocal about stating its objective as nuclear and conventional disarmament. There was no procrastination, no dissenting voice.

Our purpose quickly became one of exploring how we now best respond to, as is said, this "crime against humanity", this "sin against God", manifested in the arms race.

We were of one mind with the recent declarations of 36 National Academies of Science, regarding the prevention of nuclear war, and the work of groups like the Parliamentarians for World Order, expressing the extent that our human survival is in jeopardy.

Finally, we were also aware, especially through the contributions of African and Asian members, of how disarmament is necessary for development.

B. SPECIFIC DISARMAMENT ISSUES

Let us turn now to some of the specific disarmament issues. In this section some suggestions will be made regarding priority tasks for regional and national WCRP chapters. Later the priorities we see for WCRP/International will be defined.

1. Comprehensive Test-Ban Treaty

The pursuit of a Comprehensive Test-Ban Treaty (CTB), to prevent all nuclear testing, has recently received fresh impulses, including a petition campaign by other peace organizations.

Given, as Ambassador Olu Adeniji of Nigeria said at the opening of WCRP IV, that there are no outstanding technical issues (including verification) to prevent a CTB, and given that its successful negotiation would prevent new weapon systems from reaching deployment, these fresh impulses must be supported.

WCRP national groups are urged to develop or co-operate with petition campaigns, and to encourage their governments to give greater support to the pursuit of a CTB at the UN and through their diplomatic contact with nuclear weapon states.

WCRP/USA is urged, particularly, to raise the issue in the context of the US presidential election.

2. The Strengthening of the Nuclear Non-Proliferation Treaty at its Review Conference, September, 1985

The Non-Proliferation Treaty (NPT) is in some danger of collapse at its Review Conference in September 1985, largely because nuclear weapon states have not honoured their obligations, under Article 6, to engage in nuclear disarmament. (This being a condition under which non-nuclear weapon states signed the Treaty.)

Given the perceived link between nuclear weapons and political power, the collapse of the NPT would probably lead to an even greater number of nuclear weapon states.

There are, in any case, very few disarmament measures. The NPT is not perfect, but it is much better than nothing!

The NPT Review Conference will also be important in terms of strengthening safeguards, particularly through the International Atomic Energy Agency, to prevent the transfer of weapons-grade materials from civil nuclear installations into nuclear weapons production.

WCRP national groups are urged to work to support the strengthening rather than the collapse of the NPT at the Review Conference.

3. Nuclear Freeze

The pursuit of a Nuclear Freeze, as described in Dr. Jack's address, was considered a continuing priority, particularly at the UN and through WCRP/USA.

4. Outer Space

The importance of preventing the arms race from spreading into Outer Space found expression in a call for a moratorium on proposed testing of anti-satellite missiles.

The importance of this moratorium follows from three facts:

—Negotiations to prevent the militarization of Outer Space are still possible, especially if they are not forced into the same agenda as other negotiations (e.g., the Strategic Arms Reduction Talks, now stalled).

—Once the weapons are tested and manufacture begins, another series of verification problems will arise to block future attempts to demilitarize Outer Space.

—The call for a moratorium on the testing of anti-satellite missiles, a call to protect the "symbolic heavens", was considered worthy of inclusion in the final reports of WCRP IV.

5. Military Research and Development

The evil of large numbers of people with God-given gifts, and access to the most privileged levels of education, utilizing their lives in military weapons research, is a continuing madness. This is all the more evident given the need for research into areas of real human need, and given the effect of subsequent weapons' "testing" in Third World conflicts.

We must pressure governments for reductions in the funding of military research programmes, and work with scientists regarding alternatives.

6. Conventional Disarmament

There were many moving accounts of the effects of conventional war in terms of human suffering . . .

We cannot only be concerned with nuclear disarmament.

WCRP members are urged to avoid investments in companies involved in arms-trading; to urge governments not to respond to requests for arms from nations in conflict-areas, or to use arms-trading as a means of "solving" domestic recessions.

7. Nuclear Free-Zones

Campaigns for a Nuclear-Free Europe, Africa and South America need sustained support.

Given the failures of the UN Committee charged with establishing a Conference for an Indian Ocean as a Zone of Peace, because of super-power stalling, WCRP groups which are in Indian Ocean nations should explore the scope for a conference on an Indian Zone of Peace amongst those nations. This is a recommended regional initiative.

Support for a Nuclear-Free Pacific was requested from:

•WCRP/Europe, regarding an end to French nuclear testing in the Pacific.

•WCRP/USA, regarding weapons testing and the expansion of super-power nuclear war fighting facilities in the Pacific.

Religious institutions are urged to declare themselves symbolically "nuclear-free," and plant a sign to that effect outside their place of worship.

8. Other Suggestions

•Support for a treaty to prohibit the use of nuclear weapons; conventions to abolish chemical and biological weapons; and a No First-Use declaration by nuclear weapons states.

•Assessment of the impact of cultural influences (war toys, video games, TV violence), as making it easier to imagine a destroyed rather than disarmed world, and as reinforcing the idea that violent solutions are necessary, inevitable, even attractive.

•The need for national departments of peace, financed proportionately to existing departments of war.

•Whilst affirming previous efforts, a call for another WCRP delegation to the leadership of nuclear weapon states.

•The need for resumed talks to curb the conventional arms-trade.

•The exploration of non-violent social defence and other alternatives to military power and military alliances, as the "security system."

•The application of non-violent non-co-operation campaigns if the nuclear weapons states continue to block disarmament.

•The need for WCRP to urge nuclear armed states, particularly the USA and the USSR, to hold regular summit meetings among heads of state to discuss disarmament and specific co-operative international development projects.

C. WCRP/International Disarmament Tasks

Given that there are more issues than WCRP/International can effectively handle at once, the priorities defined were two-fold:

1. WCRP/International staff should be assigned to work for the strengthening of the Nuclear Non-Proliferation Treaty in the period up to, and including, the Review Conference in September 1985. This is a specific project of 12 months duration.

2. The WCRP/International Headquarters in New York must be staffed to work for disarmament, by:

•promoting the agenda items of the UN Conference on Disarmament (which includes many of the issues mentioned above).

•affirming the right of conscientious objection, particularly in countries where military service is compulsory.

•feeding up-to-date information back to WCRP groups to facilitate their peace campaigns.

Conclusion

For those without previous experience of WCRP Assemblies, it has been profoundly encouraging to discover how people of every faith agonize over global militarism, yearn for it to be otherwise, and deeply believe that the application of spiritual wisdoms and energies can contribute to the pursuit of nuclear and conventional disarmament.

Footnote

Joint Chinese-Japanese Proposal to Commission III

We, the delegations of both countries who attended the Fourth World Assembly of WCRP, renewed our friendship and came to an agreement that nuclear disarmament is even more urgent than before for the survival of humanity and realization of world peace.

In WCRP III held in Princeton in 1979, we made a joint proposal that the nuclear weapon states should not only refrain from the first use of nuclear weapons, but also make serious efforts for complete disarmament.

To implement this proposal, we request WCRP/International to make a renewed effort to send its delegation to the nuclear weapon states which have not yet been visited.

—Joint Proposal by the delegations of
the People's Republic of China and Japan

III. THE MIDDLE EAST

The role of WCRP is not only to draw on our religious resources in order to work for peace in the long run and in the whole world, but also to address itself to flash-points in various regional areas. We are convinced that the Middle East is a tinder-box and, like many other conflict-areas in the world, could trigger a global confrontation. At the same time it is also a reservoir of religious creativity and the birth place of three great religions which still flourish there.

With Erasmus we affirm: "True religion is peace"—and we cannot have peace unless we leave the conscience unshackled on obscure points on which certainty is impossible. There are clearly deep areas of agreement among us and the solidarity which we have experienced here in our quest for peace is a foundation on which we intend to build and one which we can extend to all the people of the Middle East through the religions we represent.

Narrative

At the WCRP meeting in Princeton in 1979 the need for further dialogue between the parties to the Middle Eastern conflict was stressed. WCRP IV tried to contribute to that dialogue by having a Palestinian Christian, an Israeli Sephardic Jew and a Lebanese Muslim speak to one of the commissions. Each gave a moving appeal for justice, human rights, and peace from her own experience of living; one feeling as a second-class citizen in Israel and the other two under Israeli occupation. All three affirmed the universal humanity of all and the hope that the Divine in each person would be moved by the evidence that religious values can assert themselves under conditions of war. Both the call to repentance and change of course struck a responsive note. Our group asked the three to draft a statement summarizing their common convictions which is appended to this report with our strong endorsement. (See Appendix I to Middle East Section.)

When our discussion in the commission changed to the working group and we began to wrestle more concretely with issues, things changed drastically. Perhaps new persons joined us who had not heard the earlier presentations, but for whatever reason we began to exchange historical interpretations of past events, level charges, and seek to pinpoint blame. Nevertheless, even in this changed atmosphere certain common themes united us.

Common Convictions

1. We were united in our conviction that the Palestinian problem urgently needs to be solved. Some among us believed that because of their love for Israel they share Martin Buber's conviction that the test of "the dream of Zion, is Israel's ability to form ties with the Arabs—ties of co-operation and partnership, with those Arabs who are also struggling for national liberation and spiritual renaissance". (Testimony before the Anglo-American Commission, March 14, 1946.) Others argued on humanitarian grounds and because of their love for the Palestinians and their great concern for a just and lasting peace. And finally there were those who felt that the Palestinians must be allowed their self-determination, because the Israelis in 17 years of occupation are confined to a rôle as occupier which is alien if not contrary to their genius. We must bear in mind however, that the Palestinians' problem was unresolved both during the 17 years of Israeli occupation and in the previous 20 years under Jordanian "adoption".

There was recognition of the right of the Palestinian people's human rights, dignity and self-determination, including their right if they so choose to establish an independent Palestinian state within the West Bank and Gaza Strip.

Such a state cannot, however, be created, unless there is mutual simultaneous recognition between Israel and representatives of the Palestinians. Israel would be recognized as a sovereign state, established by a world body, entitled to secure borders, and the Palestinian representatives would be recognized by the Israelis as a legitimate entity at the negotiating table.

2. In the discussion of the working group some concrete remarks were made:

a) To say that religion is not causing the Middle East war is fine. But we must acknowledge that it is part of the problem, because religious ideology is a driving force in the development of settlements in the West Bank and also in the internal as well as external warfare and harassment going on in other parts of the region, particularly in Lebanon.

b) In the past ten years there has been an enormous cloud of despair among Palestinians who are harshly and inhumanly treated and subjected to dehumanizing statements. On the other hand we must also acknowledge the presence of peace groups among Israelis whose efforts must be recognized and helped.

c) It was stressed that mutual recognition by Israelis and Palestinians and by Arab governments would be to the benefit of both sides and a step towards peace.

d) The whole Middle East situation is undoubtedly very complex because of irreconcilable interests; so much power, greed, nationalistic passion and fears; a victim-psychology has gripped all sides. Let us not rush quickly into offering a solution to the Middle East crisis.

e) We should rather get down to the bedrock of the human reality there: even the most antagonistic groups basically want the same thing, but they seem unable to find means of getting at their common goal. As a multi-religious group, we must be able to feel the fear of each single warring side, or else we stand no chance of understanding. We need to learn to have compassion for everyone in this situation.

f) We cannot but recognize the tragic corrupting effect on both societies of the prolongation of military occupation. We must not overlook either the unspeakable destruction and horror brought about by the use of "conventional" weapons.

3. We isolated certain factors which now work against peace and invite all members of WCRP to minimize their effects where possible:

a) The kind of nationalism which drives people against each other and does not realize that the destiny of each country is tied very intimately to its neighbour, near and far.

b) Terrorism in its entirety: bombing of civilians, and civilian areas, all governmental, organizational and individual terrorist acts must be condemned.

c) Religious zeal which is not balanced by tolerance of those who belong to other religions or cultures.

d) Those distorted portrayals of the media which identify factions only by religious names, rather than their other socio-political names.

e) The deprivation of the right of self-determination and of land, the cutting off of water or diversion thereof, denial of human rights and dignity, arbitrary detention, and collective punishment, all of which is a reality of the Israeli occupation in the West Bank, Gaza Strip, Southern Lebanon; the same suffering is also imposed on people by different powers in many other countries of this region.

f) The disappearance of persons in Lebanon is another violation of human rights.

g) The denial of their identity to the Palestinians wherever they are dispersed in the world.

h) The failure of the Arab governments in carrying out their responsibilities and obligations vis-à-vis Palestinian refugees and residents within their countries for promoting their social, economic and cultural rights.

i) The powers, regional and international: USA, Europe, and USSR have utilized the conflicts in the Middle East as opportunities to wage the East-West conflict; USA support for Israel and USSR support for Syria reinforce intransigent elements in both countries.

j) The use by the great powers of the Middle East as an arms market and weapon testing ground.

k) Massacres of groups and assassinations of individuals which inevitably lead to vengeance and further killings.

Concrete Actions which can be undertaken by WCRP

a) Solidarity should be expressed with every effort to work for peace by the groups in Israel, the West Bank, the Gaza Strip, Lebanon, and all Jews, Christians, Muslims and all other persons of faith and goodwill.

b) Assistance should be given in creating WCRP chapters in the Middle East with priority placed on Israel, the West Bank, Lebanon and Cyprus.

c) The project of creating a WCRP/Middle East should be linked to other chapters in the world which share their concern. Such a linkage already exists between WCRP/Canada and Lebanon.

d) Special attention should be given to correcting distortions which appear in the media and we invite each member of this working group to make a commitment to work towards that end.

e) That we forward the attached proposal for a WCRP commission on Middle East Peace to our Secretary-General for his study and possible implementation. (See Appendix 2 to Middle East Section.)

Other Conflict Situations in the Region

In the urgent interest of the prompt withdrawal of all military forces from Cyprus, we recommend support for the continuation in a positive and constructive spirit of the intercommunal talks on Cyprus, under the auspices of the UN Secretary-General. We pray for a mutually acceptable and lasting peaceful settlement for all the people of Cyprus.

We urgently appeal to the Iraqi and Iranian governments to put an end to the tragic hostilities and resume peaceful negotiations to resolve their differences. We commend all the efforts of governments and inter-national organizations and the UN which have been made to that end.

We note that negotiations have just begun between Pakistan and Afghanistan and we express our hope and prayer that the war in Afghanistan may come to a conclusion and that justice may be restored to that land.

Appendix 1

STATEMENT ON THE MIDDLE EAST

We are adherents of the three monotheistic religious traditions of the Middle East—Judaism, Christianity and Islam. The teaching of our faith leads us to work for justice and peace, on the understanding that no peace can be achieved without justice.

We are aware that the problems of our area are not purely religious, as they are often presented in the media. But we also recognize that the power of religion has been used and misused for political and individual benefit and interest.

Although in the past decades our region has seen an advancement in science and technology, it has also seen a relentless increase in violence. It is time that we learn to listen to one another and try to begin to speak with a common voice, making some common affirmations.

1. We pledge to honour and respect every race, religion, culture, and individual.

2. We recognize the right of each individual to his or her human rights, as described in the UN Charter.

3. We recognize the sovereignty of all countries of the area, including the Jewish state of Israel.

4. We recognize the right of the Palestinian people to self-determination and their right to establish an independent Palestinian state in the West Bank and Gaza Strip.

5. We call for the immediate withdrawal of all foreign military forces from Lebanon and the restoration of the sovereignty of the state.

6. We urge the formation of a WCRP Office in the Middle East, based in a location to be decided by WCRP representatives, bearing in mind the present situation in the region.

7. We encourage WCRP dialogue and programme in the Middle East

(a) to contribute clarity and understanding to the confusion often perpetrated by the media,

(b) to bring young people from the different religious traditions together,

(c) to bring women active in their own communities and religious traditions together, and

(d) to help create a climate of listening and communication conducive to progress toward peace and justice.

8. We believe that peace in the Middle East will create conditions generative of economic, cultural, and spiritual growth and development for all people in the region and will contribute to the stability and peace of the entire world.

Shelley Elkayam
Nahla Haidar
Jean Zaru

Appendix 2

A PROPOSAL FOR A
WCRP COMMISSION
ON MIDDLE EAST PEACE

The question of whether WCRP can play a useful rôle on behalf of peace in an area of local or regional conflict should be explored. We believe that it should be tested in a conflict situation where religious tensions are an integral part of the conflict. With these considerations in mind it is proposed that WCRP create a special Inter-Faith Commission on Peace for the Middle East, confining itself to the Arab-Israeli conflict.

This Commission should consist of fifteen members of whom six should be drawn from the three major religious communities of the area: two Muslims, two Jews, and two Christians. The remaining would be chosen from other regions of the world and include members of other world religions.

The purpose of the Commission should be to hear the divergent claims, perceptions, fears, and hopes of the religious and political parties to the conflict and to record faithfully what is heard. The resulting preliminary report should be transmitted to the officers of WCRP for communication to the religious bodies and the governments of the Middle East (as well as bodies ranging from the United Nations to the Palestine Liberation Organization) with requests for their written reaction. When the assorted responses have been received and studied—and such revisions made as may seem necessary and appropriate, the Commission shall then deliver to the officers of WCRP its amended report and communications. Among the possible recommendations that might accompany the finished report any one or several of the following options could be adopted.

1. Simple transmittal to WCRP officers with no directives as to further publicity or action.
2. Proposals for publishing the report and distributing it to various groups within and beyond WCRP.

3. Proposals for an extensive programme of information and education about the Middle East conflict starting with study of the Commission's report.
4. Arrangements for consultations and conferences with, between and among representatives of the parties to the conflict in order to explore possible actions which might be undertaken to help solve the conflict.
5. The preparation and publication of a statement of moral, ethical and spiritual principles consistent with various religious traditions, that ought to guide the parties in their behaviour so long as the conflict continues, and which should underline efforts to produce an equitable solution.

Special funding would obviously be required to support the work of this proposed Commission. It should begin its work only when the necessary financing has been obtained.

IV. CONCLUSION

The Commission III Report illustrates how the pursuit of peace involves disarmament, development and human rights issues. Our analysis of some of these issues is to be read in the context of a faith in our spiritual and human capacity to rise above current difficulties and create a world in which all people enjoy a life of security and dignity.

I.

Reports of Working Groups

43

Report of Working Group 1A How to Dismantle Ethnic and Religious Prejudices Which Act as Obstacles to Building and Sharing Society?

Existence of the Problem

The concrete instances cited by the numerous speakers left no doubt about the existence of the phenomenon of ethnic and religious prejudices in both the older traditional societies, as well as in the newly emerging states.

The problem expresses itself in a wide variety of ways, not only through individuals but also through organized social institutions, deliberately denying a section of their own brothers and sisters their birthright as human beings, and resulting often in violent reactions.

Analysis of Causes and Conditions

People are ever caught between the conflicting tendencies of selfishness and altruism, concern for themselves and concern for others, security and insecurity for oneself. Wherever there is reconciliation of these opposing emotional conditions, there is peace and harmony. When people are incapable of such harmonious resolution of conflicting needs within themselves, they resort to defence mechanisms of attack, and strengthening and multiplying their camp-followers, to oppose the sources of danger. Discrimination on the grounds of race, religion, caste, class, colour, language, ideological beliefs, etc. is the manifestation of this state of mind. Moreover, when there is a shortage of material resources to share among the members of a society, discrimination spreads itself into social, political and economic areas of human relations.

It is only the religious dimension in people's understanding of their own selves and their relation to others, to the universe, and to their creator, that can harmonize these conflicts at the very root of their being. Although religion in itself is perfect, the masses who struggle to reach that perfection are themselves imperfect persons, and it is not strange to see religion itself being employed to promote self-interests of groups and individuals. It is then that religion becomes a casualty. The group, while admitting the existence of all types of discrimination in social behaviour, conceded that if it were resolved at the religious level, it should cover other areas of prejudice such as ethnicity.

If more people are better grounded on the true understanding of religion, the more they will see beyond, the easier for them to transcend racial, tribal and all other distinctions that divide man from man.

The group expressed the need for concerted action to present the image of religion as something that extols justice, love and peace, and the concept of religious concern with humanity as something that has no boundaries.

In this regard mention was made of the ways in which religion is propagated and observed by institutions themselves tending to be instruments of discrimination.

It should be clarified that WCRP is not attempting to fashion all religions to achieve some kind of uniformity, but WCRP would be happy if it could contribute toward unity among the adherents of different faiths.

Differences based on traditions, cultures, practices, interpretations, rites and rituals are to be appreciated and respected, but fighting based on misunderstandings, misinterpretations of doctrine and the selfish abuse of religion should be eliminated.

The significance of continuing dialogue in this context was demonstrated in the manner in which the Buraku people's problem in Japan came to be rightly understood. In WCRP III a delegate from the same country completely denied the existence of discrimination against the Buraku people, but with continuing study of the problem, the same delegate at WCRP IV frankly admitted the fact of the religionists being in the camp of discriminating agents. This has paved the way to a better recognition of the problem which will eventually lead to a concerted effort toward amelioration of the Buraku people's condition.

Recommendations
Based on the contributions made by several participants of the group, the following recommendations are forwarded to the relevant commission:

Education
1. Prejudices breed in the minds of individuals. They are deep-seated notions built upon the mind's tendency to accept or reject without an examination of facts. Education, at all levels, is considered the most effective weapon in fighting prejudice. Individuals should be helped to

be aware of prejudices lurking in their own consciousness. The working group, while recognizing the difficulties involved in teaching all religions to children at school, recommends that WCRP adopt a policy of encouraging the teaching of the common values contained in all religions, through publication of curricular materials. We suggest that WCRP appoint a committee of inter-religious educators to attend to this task.

2. In the matter of educating adults, WCRP should encourage and assist its friendly organizations in different countries, through the dissemination of WCRP literature, to conduct lectures, seminars and workshops to bring home to appropriate groups the message of peace through religion. The agents of discrimination and victims of discrimination should be encouraged to enter into dialogue to break the barriers of misunderstandings and forge links of friendship through such community activities.

3. WCRP should encourage and assist in the conducting of inter-faith fora at academic levels to help promote inter-faith understanding and to help identify specific problems pertaining to religious, ethnic, social, economic, educational and cultural areas of disabilities and discrimination. In this process each religion may be encouraged to examine its own conscience to see whether, apart from extolling its ideals for peace, it also lives them out in practice.

4. WCRP should have for itself facilities to obtain information on such peace-promoting programmes undertaken by people in various countries, under varying contexts, and disseminate information on such case studies for the benefit of interested organizations.

Political Issues

1. WCRP should urge all countries to adhere to international conventions that aim at safeguarding human rights and eradicating all forms of discrimination.

2. WCRP/International should examine whether the existing international conventions are adequate for the eradication of all forms of discrimination.

3. WCRP should urge appropriate bodies, such as the United Nations Organization, to formulate new international conventions essential for the eradication of discriminatory policies.

4. WCRP should examine the need and feasibility of sending peace missions or conciliatory missions to locations where discrimination is blatant.

44

*Report of Working Group 1B
How to Combat
Racial Discrimination
As It Survives in
Many Parts of the World
But is Still Legally Imposed
by the Apartheid System
In South Africa*

Preamble

Apartheid, a unique system of governmentally enforced racial discrimination, violates the moral and ethical values of all the world's religions. It also offends the conscience of the world community. The United Nations has repeatedly branded apartheid a "crime against humanity". To say that apartheid is the will of God is blasphemy, and WCRP fully supports the judgment of many Christian churches in South Africa and elsewhere, which by word and action have repudiated the claim of the Dutch Reformed Church of South Africa that apartheid is grounded in principles of the Holy Bible.

In addressing ourselves to apartheid, it is necessary to recognize that it is a unique situation in the world since:

1) apartheid is justified legally and legally enforced.
2) religious arguments are used to support the apartheid system.
3) all sense of humanity is denied the Black community.

Apartheid, a crime against conscience, brings about hunger,

poverty, sickness, imprisonment, suffering, death ... indeed an endless list of suffering to the people of South Africa. We, as religious people from many parts of the world, have to make a concerted effort to rid the world of this evil system that violates the fundamental human rights of the majority of the people of South Africa. No religion can remain aloof from the call to end this blasphemy, to put an end to relocation, to homeland rule, and indeed, to the systemic violence in South Africa. Apartheid therefore is a fundamental concern of all in this World Conference on Religion and Peace for human dignity.

Since the policy and ideology of apartheid are so deeply rooted and entrenched, a variety of strategies needs to be employed in order to combat this evil system. We support efforts, confirmed by repeated United Nations resolutions, to isolate South Africa at every level. To the allegation that isolation and sanctions will hurt the poor in South Africa, we acknowledge that most opponents of apartheid in South Africa welcome this strategy, even if it may temporarily hurt the people involved.

Recommendations
We therefore recommend that:

1.   *WCRP/International—*
a)   reiterate its strong condemnation of the South African Government's policy of apartheid;

b)   call on the churches, internationally and in South Africa, to denounce the Biblical argument used by the South African Government, and to reaffirm that apartheid is a heresy, and as such to reject the South African Government's claim that it is a Christian Government. Furthermore, we commend the All African Conference of Churches, the Symposium of Episcopal Conferences of Africa and Madagascar (SECAM), the World Alliance of Reformed Churches, the Lutheran World Federation, the World Council of Churches, and the Vatican for lending support to the dismantling of the apartheid system, and we call on these bodies to continue to do so;

c)   call upon all religions to assist religious and secular organizations that reject apartheid and withdraw support from organizations that perpetuate the system of apartheid;

d)   effectively conscientize the international community about the true situation in South Africa by using statistics and information available from the United Nations, the South African Council of Churches, WCRP/South Africa and other authentic sources;

e)   conscientize the international community as to why it is necessary to isolate South Africa economically, politically and at other appropriate levels;

f)   foster closer co-operation with anti-apartheid groups both in South Africa and internationally;

g)   condemn the support for, and collaboration with, the South African Government by many industrialized countries and their transnational corporations;

h) strongly condemn the United States Government's policy of "constructive engagement" with South Africa;

i) undertake a concerted effort to expose those Governments that continue to trade with the South African Government and to condemn the economic support of the South African policy of apartheid;

j) call for the imposition of mandatory comprehensive economic sanctions and the enforcement of the United Nations arms embargo against South Africa'

k) call for an international boycott of South African products;

l) condemn the South African Government's attempts to destabilize the front-line states by economic and military activities;

m) condemn the militarization and nuclear potential which is used to maintain the racist regime of South Africa;

n) condemn strongly the following recent events:

  i) the refusal of the Government of South Africa to respect the rights of citizens to leave the country, or return, according to United Nations human rights standards, as seen most recently in the refusal of a passport to Mrs Ela Ramgobin;

  ii) the refusal of the South African Government to respect, as indicated in the United Nations, the freedom of speech, as seen most recently in the detaining of three of the founding members of WCRP/South Africa;

  iii) the South African Government's further entrenchment of apartheid in the latest tricameral parliament system as provided for by the latest constitution, and as promoted by the deplorable collaboration of some people in furthering this policy;

  iv) the extending of the Bantustan policy which destroys the unity of South Africa, making Black people foreigners in the land of their birth, seriously impairing their family life through human influx control measures and mass removals, and, deplorably, inducing some people to allow themselves to be co-opted in furthering this policy;

o) call on all the peoples of all the religions in South Africa to unite in working towards a democratic South Africa peopled by citizens equal and free;

p) reaffirm the previous United Nations and WCRP resolutions and declarations on South Africa and Namibia;

q) continue to give testimony against apartheid at the United Nations;

r) call for the release of all political prisoners and lend support to the campaigns for the release of political prisoners in South Africa;

s) call on the people and Government of South Africa to convene a National Convention in which representative leaders can work out a just and equitable constitution;

t) call on the South African Government to implement immediately and without prior conditions the United Nations Security Council Resolution 435 and thus withdraw from Namibia which it now occupies illegally;

u) appoint a standing committee on apartheid in WCRP.

2. WCRP Local Chapters—

a) learn about the situation in South Africa by closer co-operation with WCRP/South Africa and conscientize the people in their areas;

b) show their solidarity with the oppressed people in South Africa;

c) assist the South African chapter of WCRP in whatever creative method they may decide;

d) encourage people in their area to boycott South African goods;

e) undertake to inform politicians in all countries, especially during elections, about the evils of apartheid, and urge voters to demand from those seeking election a clear denunciation of the policy of apartheid;

f) put pressure on the governments in their areas to reject the apartheid system;

g) encourage their governments and other organizations in their areas to lend support to the front-line states.

3. The WCRP "Project Committee"—

a) call for International Days of Fasting and Prayer on 21 March (International Day for the Elimination of Racial Discrimination—Sharpeville Day), 16 June (Soweto Day), and 26 August (Namibia Day);

b) appoint, in co-operation with WCRP/South Africa, a goodwill multi-religious mission to visit South Africa to gain insight about the situation in South Africa, and convey the concerns of WCRP/International;

c) appoint a committee to educate people about Gandhian principles and establish a peace brigade of interested people for a creative non-violence in South Africa;

d) convene an International Youth Conference in 1985 with special provisions for a session on apartheid in South Africa;

e) generate and circulate documents which, in keeping with religious principles, reflect the aspirations of the people for a new South Africa.

Epilogue

Within the moral and social ruins of present South Africa, where the prevailing system is propped up by military might rather than justice, suspicion and fear rather than trust, greed rather than co-operation and sharing, discrimination rather than respect for human dignity, we commit ourselves to a new and peaceful South Africa.

We deeply cherish and support the people of South Africa, and for this very reason we must continue to quarantine the apartheid regime. The policy of apartheid and its perpetrators must become abhorrent to the world community—all in the hope that peace and justice are achieved for South Africa and the world.

45

Report of Working Group 2
How to Overcome Competing,
Destabilizing and Proselytizing
Religions and Ideologies
Which Act as Forces of Disunity
and as Threats to Peace
In Africa and in Other Parts
of the World

Although we admit that people of religion have often failed in their relations with people of other faiths, we believe that all religions have within them the spiritual and theological resources that would enable them to contribute to the reconciliation needed between religions and in society as a whole.

We therefore offer these two resolutions in the hope that they might assist in overcoming competing, destabilizing and proselytizing ideologies and religions.

Resolution I

Recognizing that some members of religious traditions so understand their uniqueness that they desire to win converts,

Noting that these beliefs, if presented in a legitimate way (without aggression, coercion or misuse of economic resources or social services), need not prevent a creative co-existence nor a positive cooperation in religious dialogue or social action,

Believing that the correct behaviour of any group often depends on its sense of identity and security,

We recommend:

1. That the predominant religion in any situation
   a) assure the minority religions of respect and full protection;
   b) refrain from attempts to undermine a minority religion in any way;
   c) guarantee equal rights and opportunities to the followers of such minorities; and
   d) not merely tolerate minorities, but accept them as having an authentic position within the religious search for truth;
2. That the minority religion in any situation accept a reciprocal responsibility to respect the traditions and beliefs of the predominant religion, and therefore refrain from becoming a destabilizing influence;
3. That all religions work with or help establish local WCRP groups in areas of religious conflict to
   i) achieve a closer understanding of the problems involved; and
   ii) be able to plan appropriate action.

Resolution II

Recognizing the dangers when any group, misusing its power and imposing its ideology or religion on others, infringes on their basic human rights,

Realizing that the proponents of religions at times make use of ideologies to promote their beliefs, and, correspondingly, proponents of ideologies use religions to further their ends,

We call upon WCRP/International, having identified such situations and established an order of priority, to:

1. organize inter-faith fact-finding and conciliatory teams and/or encourage members in other countries who belong to the religious traditions involved to investigate situations in which religion, ideology and state are closely or entirely connected and which are the cause of conflict, and
2. promote research into the formulation of universal guidelines on the relationship and mutual involvement of religion and state.

With reference to these two resolutions we record the particular concerns raised by members of our Working Group, which, we accept, reflect their particular experiences, rather than giving a comprehensive list:

—American-Indians in America (see appendix I)
—Asian immigrants abroad
—Christians in Sudan
—Minority religious communities in the United Kingdom
—Tamils in Sri Lanka
—The situation in Central America

Conclusion

We agreed that religious and ideological conflicts often arise due to the unwillingness of individuals or groups to be self-critical, or to undergo a regular systematic self-examination. Accepting that competing, destabilizing and proselytizing ideologies and religions will continue to act as forces of disunity in the world, we request WCRP/International, in collaboration with other relevant agencies, to develop an international code of ethics which would set guidelines to cover all aspects of life.

241

APPENDIX 1

Submitted by the representative of the Indigeneous People of America
"After 492 years of Western European occupation, the Indigenous People of the USA and Canada continue to experience racism, bigotry and oppression. Examples are:
1. The fishing rights struggle of the Pacific North West.
2. Religious freedom, persecution of tribes and the incarcerated.
3. Political prisoners such as Leonard Peltier.
4. Sterilization of Indian women in South Dakota.

In closing, we request that delegates of the Hopi Nation and the American-Indian Elders Council and the International Treaty Council be given a hearing before the United Nations, and would ask WCRP to assist us in the application process."

46

*Report of Working Group 3
How to Spread Education
for Peace and for
Multi-Religious Understanding
(Including Attitudes of Self-Criticism,
The Promotion of Reconciling
Activities, and The Use of
More Effective Methods
of Communication)*

Religious education and education for peace are essentially interrelated. Religious education for peace encourages a dynamic process and an all-embracing (holistic) vision: internal and external aspects, private and collective practice, individual and group participation, the respectful preservation of life for generations to come, spiritual fulfilment and a just and harmonious world order. Thus there is the necessity to re-think education for peace within the framework of each religion, according to the realities, and at a multi-religious level.

Furthermore, ways should be found to urge governments and religious leaders not to restrict freedom of religion, and to allow religious teaching and practice.

We also encourage the promotion, through educational channels, of the understanding of the dangers of drug addiction. We should take into account this and other specific problems, experienced in many countries, where children and young people reject or do not have the benefit of formal education (e.g., drop-outs in all societies).

47

Report of Working Group 4 How to Draw Upon the Particular Contribution of Women In Cultivating Attitudes and Realizing Values for Peace, Especially in Women's Influence upon the Younger Generation

We feel that there is a need to define clearly the term "social justice". We further perceive the lack of balance in the economic order as undermining the values of life within the family, and leading to the disruption of the social order. We would like to repeat the message from the Women's Meeting, namely that development is not simply a matter of economics, but requires an integrated holistic approach—economic, social, spiritual, and, we might add, cultural. Development requires the active participation by all—women and men, youth and adults. As people of faith, we must learn to relate spiritual values practically to social relationships.

We further recommend that Commission II (on Human Dignity, Social Justice, and Development of the Whole Person) consider the fact that abortion should not be used as a method of population control, and that legalized abortion should not be made a condition of aid from wealthy countries.

48

Report of Working Group 5 How to Arrest Actual and Potential Regional Conflicts; Notably in Southern Africa, Latin America, South East Asia, and Western Asia ('Middle East')

The report of this group was incorporated in its entirety in the "Middle East" section of the report of Commission III.

49

*Report of Working Group 6
How to Close the Widening Gap
Between Rich and Poor,
and Promote a Fair Sharing
of National Resources
Within and Between Societies
(Including the Challenge of the
New International Economic Order,
The Safeguarding
of the Environment,
The Transfer of Technology, etc.)
In the Interests
of Reducing 'North-South' Tensions*

Preliminary Remarks

Most of the countries in the "South" have not yet attained the fulfilment of their basic human needs. These are food, shelter, clothing, basic health care, etc. These are essential for human dignity. Among the basic rights are the right to freedom of expression, and that of not being arrested arbitrarily (habeas corpus).

Suggestions Towards a Solution of the Problem

1. Morality and ethic should count in government, economics, international relations, international and national trade, etc. Profit should not be the sole criterion.

Prices of raw materials should be pegged to technology and finished products. We suggest that a new economic order, under the aegis of the UN, pursue the concept of an international barter system, involving foodstuffs and commodities critical for the accelerated development of countries, with differential pricing based on criteria reflecting real needs, the establishment of an international famine reserve and diminishing dependence on foreign capital investment and loans for survival.

2. Personal relations should strive at voluntary simplicity.

3. The "system" should be simplified (e.g., banking, education, technology).

4. The "power" should belong to the people. This can be achieved by bringing them into the decision-making process, and by building economically viable participatory communities. The people should be informed and conscientized by making them aware of their situation. Here communication and the dissemination of information play an important rôle.

5. There exist inter-cultural problems which could be rectified by knowledge, understanding and appreciation of other cultures. Awareness of cultural identity crises is sometimes salutary.

6. Institutional changes, involving structures, seem necessary.

7. There should be free compulsory education.

8. The importance of social, economic and cultural rights and programmes should be stressed.

9. The possibility of an inter-religious code of social ethics should be investigated.

10. There should be a clear understanding of the requirements for development, i.e., development should be people-centred and based on real needs, and the money currently invested in arms should be spent on development.

11. Aid agencies need to develop new attitudes.

12. It should be underlined that we are one world, and thus aid may be an obligation.

50

Report of Working Group 7A
How to Improve Planning
and Sharing Multi-Religious WCRP
and Other Initiatives At National,
Regional, and Local Levels
To Kindle and Express Hopes for the
Peaceful Future of Humanity
—Both Young and Old,
*Both Weak and Strong?**

The discussions in the Working Group recognized that there are many projects that, in an ideal situation, we would want WCRP/International to fulfil. However, we endeavoured to discipline our suggestions according to three criteria:

1. Projects must capture and express the special identity of WCRP,
2. Projects should build on the previous distinctive work of WCRP,
3. Projects should express what are clear multi-faith concerns.

Project One

1. In full co-operation with local WCRP groups and others, it is recommended that the international effort of WCRP should focus upon

---

*Members of this Working Group would have wished to have more time in order that they would be able to present a more "polished" final report. For more information on WCRP future projects, see "WCRP Multi-Religious Projects.

particular areas of conflict where religion is, or is believed to be, a factor in the conflict. This might take many forms. WCRP could, for example, invite representatives of the religions locally concerned to a consultation to explore any areas of common ground between them, to discuss the possibilities of reconciliation and, generally, to try to see how the spiritual growth of religion can become a force for ending the conflict, instead of religion being a factor in its continuation.

It was decided that considerable flexibility of response is required in constituting the teams to engage in the consultations—each situation having a unique character.

2. The Working Group did not try to specify priorities for this work. Priorities, it was believed, would be defined by factors such as:

  i) whether WCRP/International is able to enter the area;
 ii) the extent that national groups are already active in the area;
iii) the availability of WCRP staff, and the scope for an inter-faith group to form at the most propitious time for such a consultation.

3. As part of the same project, two other concerns have relevance:

  i) WCRP should work, at all levels, to prevent the supply of arms to the protagonists.
 ii) the UN Declaration on Religious Freedom should be promoted as forming part of the moral basis for the consultations.

In summary, the distinctive identity of WCRP is most clearly expressed when it is seeking to be a reconciling agent in situations of "religious" conflict. This is what gives these proposed consultations their priority. It is also the basis on which we can credibly respond to other concerns of our multi-faith community.

Project Two

WCRP IV has demonstrated a consensus that peace through disarmament and human rights are considered fundamental spiritual and moral issues to which WCRP must continue to respond—the more so, given the worsening of the global situation and the despondency that many feel about that. The resilience of our faiths, through the centuries, must be expressed in a persistent quest for disarmament and human rights. There are, however, more issues on both than WCRP/International can effectively handle at once. The priorities defined were twofold:

1. WCRP/International staff should be assigned to work for the strengthening of the Nuclear Non-Proliferation Treaty in the period up to, and including, its Review Conference in September 1985. This is a specific project of 12 months' duration.

2. The WCRP/International office in New York should be staffed to work for disarmament and human rights. The central focus of this work should be at the United Nations, although there are complementary aspects of having a New York office involved in these issues.

Aspects of that work of WCRP/International should include:

i) promoting the agenda items of the UN Conference on Disarmament. These include the Comprehensive Test-Ban Treaty, a demilitarized Outer Space, the Nuclear Freeze, a Chemical Weapons Convention;

ii) co-operating with the UN World Disarmament Campaign, and encouraging WCRP national groups to work with this educational programme;

iii) affirming the right of conscientious objection, particularly in those countries where military service is compulsory;

iv) preventing the supply of arms to protagonists;

v) continuing to monitor and contribute to the UN Human Rights Commission, with the informational support of WCRP national groups.

Project Three

The Youth Report and other contributions to WCRP IV have expressed deep concern for refugees. Aside from affirming the rôle of refugee aid agencies, and encouraging nations to increase their refugee intake, what can WCRP/International contribute? There are several possibilities, the feasibility of which needs further exploration. They include:

i) for WCRP/International to organize in 1985, the International Year of Youth, a Youth Camp in an area where there have been inter-religious conflicts,

ii) from the experience of that Camp, for WCRP Youth and other interested members of WCRP, to visit, as an inter-faith group, a refugee camp.

The two-fold purpose of this would be:

i) to be a reconciling agent where religious differences have, in some way, accounted for the refugee situation;

ii) to provide practical assistance to make the living situations in the camps more humane.

Project Four

WCRP/International should encourage its constituency to participate in the Week of Prayer for World Peace (the week spanning United Nations Day which is 24 October).

51

Report of Working Group 7B
How to Elaborate Particular Projects
For International
WCRP Sponsorship
To Symbolize That Religions Can
and Must Work Together For Peace

We endorse the recommendations contained in the report of the WCRP Youth Meeting in totality, and, in addition, make the following recommendations:

1. *Refugees.* This is a world phenomenon which requires the immediate attention of WCRP. We recommend that WCRP undertake exploratory research as regards the aid and assistance provided by various local, national and international organizations, and undertake suitable action in areas not covered by these organizations, e.g., the work of reconciliation, confidence-building, and moral and spiritual support. We also recommend that WCRP accept in principle the offer of the Kenya Youth Committee to establish a multi-religious consulting office in Nairobi.

2. *Peace Education.* WCRP should emphasize the need for both formal and informal value-based moral education for peace.

3. *Mass Media.* WCRP should make creative use of the mass media for the promotion of peace, justice and human dignity, and monitor and discourage their negative use.

4. *Prayer and Fasting.* WCRP may decide to observe one day a year for praying and fasting for world peace. In addition, national chapters might follow the lead of the Japanese in foregoing one meal each month and donating the money saved to a fund for peace and development.

5. *International Exchange Programme.* WCRP may encourage international exchange programmes for better mutual understanding between members of various chapters. Such programmes could be funded through continuous fund-raising at the regional level.

6. *Pen Pal Project.* WCRP may also encourage the Pen Pal Project which is designed to promote better communication between people.

7. *Overseas Students Project.* WCRP chapters may be encouraged to look after the needs of overseas students at the local level.

8. *Model Project.* WCRP/International may set up a model socio-economic project which would be result-oriented and time-bound.

9. *Co-operation with Existing Projects.* Where there are local projects, already initiated by one particular religious group, local WCRP members could co-operate in promoting multi-religious action, for instance in rural or urban slum areas.

10. *Organization.* We encourage the formation of as many local and national WCRP chapters as possible, so that WCRP becomes a world-wide multi-religious movement. We also encourage the formation of WCRP Women's and Youth sections.

J.

REPORTS

52

Report of the Commission on the Future

I. Introduction

1. When the Commission on the Future was appointed it was given a double mandate. The Commission "will study the objectives of WCRP, its three World Assemblies, its national and regional committees, and its past and current programmes." The Commission "will make specific suggestions for the future of the organisation during the Fourth World Assembly—WCRP IV—at Nairobi in August 1984." (Memorandum, WCRP/International, May 6, 1983.)

2. In order to fulfil this double mandate, the Commission on the Future met from February 13 to 17, 1984, at Bossey near Geneva, Switzerland. The eight members of the Commission represented eight nations, four continents, and four religions. They were supported by four additional members of the Nominating Committee of WCRP, and by five ex-officio and staff participants. (See Appendix I.)

The main input for the meeting was a report submitted to the Commission by Prof. François Houtart of the Catholic University of Louvain, a scholar in the sociology of religion, who had been engaged as Research Director to undertake a research study on WCRP. Prof. Houtart's summary of his study has been added to this Report as Appendix II. The text of his full report is being sent to all those who contributed to the survey. Further copies are available from WCRP/International for US$ 5.00 to cover costs.

In addition, the Commission was provided with the results of a questionnaire on "Future Organization and Programmes of WCRP/International" which was answered by some 40 persons engaged in WCRP activities and presented by Dr. John Taylor, Secretary-General of WCRP/International. (See Appendix III.)

---

*– The Commission on the Future met on 13–17 February, 1984, at the Château de Bossey, near Geneva, Switzerland. Its report was sent as background material to all WCRP IV participants.

The following report is the result of discussions and reflections based upon the materials presented to the Commission as well as upon the personal experiences of the participants who have been involved in WCRP activities for a long time, some of them since the Kyoto Assembly in 1970.

3. We gratefully appreciate the work which has been done by Prof. Houtart and by Dr. Taylor in preparing material for our evaluation of some aspects at least of past developments, and for filling some hearts and minds with a sense of urgency; it led us to reflect with renewed vigour and imagination upon the future contribution WCRP can make to promote peace. Drawing upon the positive experiences of our multi-religious and multi-cultural gathering, we came to realize afresh the specific possibilities which WCRP provides.

At the same time, however, we became aware of our inadequacies and shortcomings. It was not only that the material we had before us was necessarily limited and did not cover the full variety of WCRP experiences and aspirations. During our meeting, we often felt ourselves unable to cope with the larger task lying before us. So in the light of our mandate, we have to be circumspect about the conclusions we have reached.

II. Evaluation

1. Research Study of Prof. François Houtart (See Appendix II for Summary)

a. The research made to evaluate the work of WCRP focused on two aspects: the main thrusts of the various world assemblies, especially on their general conclusions, and a survey made about the orientation of WCRP participants based upon a questionnaire. Limits of time and finance did not allow the inclusion of other resource material apart from some reference to regional follow-up activities. Therefore, the research study did not present a complete picture of all the different dimensions and activities of WCRP. Members of the Commission pointed out some of these missing aspects:

—A full evaluation of WCRP conferences cannot be based only upon the final statements and findings which necessarily are of a more general and sometimes repetitive character. There is an underlying commitment to uncompromised engagement for peace which is articulated in personal testimonies, discussions and lectures, and which gave and continues to give WCRP a "prophetic" dimension. This becomes even clearer when the regional and local activities of WCRP groups are taken into account as well.

—A similar observation was made concerning the major issues of WCRP. While the research study stresses respect for life and human dignity as focal points of agreement among all the religions represented in WCRP, the spectrum of concerns WCRP has dealt with seems to be much larger: issues such as unity of humankind, human dignity, questions of environment, conflict resolution, and intercultural communication are still on the agenda.

—WCRP has always been keen to take a holistic approach to peace in a spirit of justice for the poor, and of love and compassion for all. This spirit, undergirding the movement, must not be lost.

b. Yet such limitations do not minimize the great help the Commission gained from the research study and the presence of the Research Director during the meeting. The critical analysis with which we were presented and the conclusions which we were asked to draw from it were challenging and creative catalysts for the work of the Commission. So some of these conclusions and questions should be mentioned:

—In the face of the multiplication of initiatives in the field of disarmament, human rights, and development, what is the specificity of WCRP?

—What kind of specific spiritual approach could be developed?

—Two main lines of thinking seem to be present in WCRP. The first one emphasizes the individual aspect: peace begins in the heart. The other one emphasizes the structural and global aspects of peace and development. It appears difficult to make the synthesis between the two.

—Making the link between the problems related to peace and religion is no doubt the most difficult task. It is made through ethics, but the main questions remain: how can the individual code of ethics be related to the social dimension of human life, and which type of social analysis should be adopted in order to move beyond generalities?

—In the face of the total vision that peace implies in its links with development, disarmament, justice, human rights, and respect for nature, what specific issues should be tackled?

2. Questionnaire of Dr. John Taylor (See Appendix III for Summary)

Dr. John Taylor presented the results of a Questionnaire on Future Organization and Programmes of WCRP/International. Towards the end of 1983 this questionnaire had been sent to some 70 people closely related to WCRP. There were 40 completed questionnaires returned.

Part I of this questionnaire dealt with the organization of WCRP/International. The majority of the respondents preferred to have world assemblies every four or five years. The majority of respondents favoured the establishment of a multi-religious secretariat. The ideas developed in the Commission and shown later in the report give a possible shape for a secretariat.

Part II of the questionnaire dealt with future programmes of WCRP/International. A majority of the respondents favoured making prevention of nuclear war and peace education priorities in WCRP/International programmes.

The Commission on the Future attempted to integrate this material into its discussions. However the full implications of the results of this questionnaire call for greater study in depth than was possible for the Commission in the course of its short deliberations.

III.   Basic Issues

1.   Specific Focus and Character of WCRP

In order to guide the future action of the Conference and in order to relate adequately to other bodies, organizations, and agencies, it is important to express in a clear way what is the specificity of WCRP. A departure point for reflection can be found in the definition of WCRP given by Prof. Houtart as a voluntary association which aims to promote world peace and which is made up of people belonging to world religions. The main elements are all major religions in all sections of the world on all aspects of peace.

From Kyoto onwards the search has been on to enlist "the forms of inner truthfulness of the spirit as having greater power than hate, enmity, and self-interest", "a realisation that might is not right", and "a profound hope that good will finally prevail".

The main tasks are to share among the people of the world a deeper knowledge of the sanctions and traditions which each religion has for world peace and justice; to discover in the approaches and backgrounds to the different religions some common religious principles conducive to the peace of the human community, and to promote a unity and universality of conscience through them; to apply them in a spirit of social responsibility to the obstacles to peace in the areas of human rights, development, environment, disarmament; to create public opinion in favour of using peaceful methods for solving problems and fostering community to seek to bring these methods to bear on local, national, regional and international levels.

The specific focus of WCRP is a living dialogue of religiously committed persons to the issue of peace through the application of spiritual motivation. Religion's integrating force may, not least, be enlisted through silent reflection/meditation/contemplation, so that spiritual resources and energies are associated with the efforts of social scientists and peacemakers in their search to give a new direction to society.

2.   Nuclear Disarmament

Nuclear disarmament has become nowadays a priority not only because of the failure of all negotiations and because of the continued increase of atomic arms production, but because thereby the whole possibility of nuclear holocaust by calculation or miscalculation is ever greater. However, it is only one side of a larger issue: disarmament in general. It is important to recall, as an indication of the magnitude of the issue, the amount of military expenditure involved during the past years: $90 billion in 1962, $182 billion in 1967, $225 billion in 1973, $400 billion in 1979, and $660 billion in 1983; this amounts to an increase of 733% in 20 years in global armament expenditures.

It is proposed that WCRP/International make a statement about the morality of the nuclear arms race, inspired by various existing statements such as that of the US Catholic Bishops, the World Council of Churches (Vancouver, 1983), and those of other religious bodies. It is hoped that WCRP could promote a multi-religious reaction which would promote the universality of these existing documents.

This statement would be cast in a broad, analytical framework and it would offer a global vision. It could include elements such as the following:

a.   WCRP should show how the increase of nuclear armaments in particular, as well as armaments in general, is linked with a global war economy. Economic decisions are increasingly disconnected from any rational defence purposes. Such a war economy is one of the major obstacles to the solution of economic inequalities in the world. It brings all affected economies into a profound contradiction with their primary purpose, that is, the just distribution of resources to all. It is also one of the elements bringing many nations of the world into financial crisis and impelling them to reduce social and cultural investments and expenditures, necessary for the welfare of their people. In all circumstances, the poorest peoples are the first victims, for example in the shattering of their village barter economies by a market economy which all too often increases the profits and power of an increasingly smaller minority.

b.   WCRP must work further to spell out the link between this war economy and the suppression of human rights and dignity. In all countries, (especially but not only where military dictatorships are imposed), the existing economic relations and systems are hampered in their natural growth by increasing military expenditures. It should be a matter for concern, however, that under every political system, informed public opinion is still insufficiently heeded where military decisions are concerned.

c.   WCRP should show the danger of a "war culture" where war appears as inevitable and where even a so-called "limited nuclear war" is presented as a possibility and accepted among some strata of public opinion.

3.   Towards an International Code of Social Ethics

Peace and religion can be brought together through ethics. Religious traditions may give the inspiration for the promotion of ethical values, but, in order to be adequate to the dimension of the present problems of humanity, those ethical values have to answer to certain conditions. There is a consensus of all religious traditions in their respect for life, human dignity, and equality for all persons or peoples of the world.

From Prof. Houtart's research on WCRP, it appears that diverse positions exist on ethical questions. Some ethical positions emphasize the individual dimension. However, in all WCRP assemblies it has been expressed that a social ethical dimension exists and this cannot be reduced to the level of individual ethical dynamics. It appears that the problem of war and peace cannot be tackled adequately by an individual ethic, asking only for the conversion of hearts. Problems of social, economic, and political structures still exist, requiring other types of action and the development of ethical norms, more in keeping with global solidarity. This has been expressed in various conferences, but important tasks still remain:

a. To study the link between the social and the individual ethical dimension, when peace problems are at stake, with all their roots in economic inequalities, political domination, and ethnic divisions.

b. To take account of the fact that social ethics cannot be expressed only in terms of interpersonal relations, which is a major trend among most religions. This can lead toward social solutions advocating co-operation between nations without a serious analysis of the fundamental contradictions existing between national interests. As a matter of fact, society is not an aggregate of individuals, nor only the co-existence of various nations and social strata, but a somewhat logical network of social relations, which are the result of the way people organise their collective existence and survival. Such organization should also be subject to an ethical approach and the higher claims of the human spirit above drives towards selfishness, greed, and lust for power.

4. *Towards a Spirituality of Peace*

It needs to be stressed that spirituality extends beyond ethics and can also expand and empower people's ethical commitments. Through WCRP many people have experienced and come to appreciate the spirituality of religions other than their own and have thereby been sensitized and inspired as well as being helped to deepen their own religious beliefs. The spiritual experiences of many people of all faiths need to be taken into account: the visions, the dreams, the hopes, the sufferings, all of which can nurture a spirituality of peace.

There should be real attempts to understand each other's cultural viewpoints: that involves multi-cultural understanding and dialogue whereby barriers fall away and the sense of being brothers and sisters in the human family is forwarded. There is need for a spirituality based on the recognition of the universal solidarity of humankind—the vision of one humanity. This needs to be brought to life, little by little, until it becomes a reality. The fellowship of shared spirituality and commitment may express itself in ways of joint witness and meditation for world peace.

There should also be encounters of reconciliation. These may be needed in conflict situations, and may, at times, even avert conflict. These efforts may involve struggle, but bearing witness to a struggle is to sustain a sign of hope; and celebrating the struggle or sharing in it is hope realized.

5. Studying and Acting Together for Peace

WCRP has published significant material concerning the various approaches of individual religious traditions to the peace process and also concerning the rôle of the non-governmental organizations in inter-governmental disarmament and arms control negotiations.

WCRP could appoint a multi-religious committee to formulate questions leading to a better understanding of the ethical basis of peace-seeking, and of attitudes towards communities outside one's own faith tradition.

These questions could be addressed to the appropriate religious authority within each faith community for study and reflection and possible action. It would be important that each community should have an opportunity to judge for itself the impact that these cardinal principles have had on behaviour in the past and in the present. It would be important that the questions and answers be shared first within each faith community. Then, we might share our insights in good will and in good faith.

Our peace actions would then be clearly formulated not only on the ethical base of our own religious tradition, but also on an understanding of the ethical base of religions other than our own. Thus, we may be encouraged to act together for peace.

6. Some Aspects of the Functioning of WCRP Conferences and Activities

The term "expert" is nowadays often understood negatively as meaning those operating in some mysterious level divorced entirely from the understanding of "ordinary" people. Properly understood, however, these are men and women able to bring adequate knowledge and analysis, but also experience, to the complex problems of peace and economic justice. Thus they can assist all sections of society to participate more effectively in making peace.

It must always be borne in mind that the real "experts" in any kind of unjust situation, economic and political, are the people who are experiencing and suffering injustice. For example, it is the "non-whites" in South Africa, or the "untouchables" in India, who are the real "experts" in what racial and caste discrimination are all about. Therefore, their voice should be heard loudly and their points of view should always be present.

These considerations should direct the choice of "experts" made by WCRP. Appropriate expertise is not always welcome, but it is necessary and may bring into the picture new ways of raising the questions and of analysing the problems. We are aware that there is no science which is value-free. Science and technology have become expensive commodities and powerful tools in the hands of those individuals, organizations, or nations which possess them. Therefore, those who possess such knowledge (expertise) must operate under the constraints of ethical and experiential considerations, and not the contrary.

Equally essential for the functioning of WCRP is to strive for a fully participatory organization of its regional and international conferences. Efforts must be made to balance all religions and regions. Religious leaders, the laity, men, women, youth, and elders must always be adequately represented. In all these groups there will be people able to take an active part in the deliberations and proceedings of WCRP conferences. The possibility of a consensus has to be preserved, but without losing the prophetic dimension. Specific means must be pursued in the way that the conferences are organized in order to keep this in mind.

Similarly, WCRP conferences must always remain open to the challenges which may come to them from those who speak from non-religious contexts.

IV. Structures

The Commission on the Future assisted by members of the Nominating Committee considered the question of structures of WCRP/International. Taking up results of the questionnaire presented by Dr. John Taylor, the Commission tried to make the structures at the same time representative of the WCRP constituency, and efficient in promoting the goals of WCRP. In the light of these needs, the following structures are suggested.

1. Leadership

a. *Honorary Presidents.* It was proposed to continue the tradition of appointing Honorary Presidents; in this way the experience and continuing guidance of our older leaders and particular individuals could be brought together to the work of WCRP as a world movement.

b. *Presidents and Advisors.* To lay emphasis on the multi-religious and multi-national character of WCRP/International, it was felt that we should choose eight to ten Presidents, to cover the period between one World Assembly and the next, in order to guide the workings of WCRP/International. It was proposed that at every stage of choosing the leaders of the organization, we have to keep in view the multi-religious and multi-national character of WCRP, but that for the sake of better representation, we should not sacrifice aspects of competence, efficiency, and spiritual leadership. Presidents should cover the various regions and the major religions of the world without ignoring the minority religions. If all these could not be covered among the Presidents, this might be achieved by the next level of some 30 "advisors"; they would normally meet only at Assemblies, unless other opportunities arose, and could constitute the original "Board" members of WCRP/International.

The Presidents, who are responsible for the overall policies and principles of WCRP as developed at World Assemblies, should meet immediately after the World Assembly, and then at least once between the two World Assemblies, unless the need for an emergency meeting arises.

c. *Executive Committee.* Each year, or as required, a small Executive Committee, consisting of one President (elected by the Presidents as the Chairperson of the Executive Committee) and three other Presidents, should meet. This Chairperson and Committee should take decisions for the execution of the principles, policies, and work of WCRP/International.

The Executive Committee should have the power to co-opt or invite members of the Council of Advisors or other persons in the WCRP constituencies.

d. *Finance Committee.* The Presidents should also appoint a Finance Committee, the chairperson of which may be designated as Honorary Treasurer; he or she should already be a member of the Executive Committee. The composition of the Finance Committee may be from among the Presidents, the Council of Advisors, or the wider constituencies of WCRP. The Finance Committee may meet at the same time as the Executive Committee or as required.

As the access to and responsibilities for fund-raising normally lie with the local and regional bodies of WCRP, it seems essential that the Finance Committee should be in close contact with those bodies. There has to be a sense of mutual responsibility about how to share the financial resources among local, regional, and international needs and projects.

2. Staffing

The Secretary-General of WCRP/International is to be the chief executive, and the coordinator of the work of WCRP. To help and assist the Secretary-General in the discharge of his or her duties, it was proposed that, subject to the availability of funds, he or she be given one to three active Associate Secretaries-General, each coming from a different continent, viz., Africa, Asia, and the Americas. The distribution of their work is to be left to the Secretary-General. Efficiency is to be the hallmark of the international secretariat.

The work of the Associate Secretaries-General from different religions and continents would be enlisted to serve the four major continental regions where WCRP has developed. If feasible, these individuals could be seconded to the international secretariat in Geneva or New York for a period of three to four months each year. For the rest of the year they could travel to other areas to interpret both the concerns of WCRP/International and also those perspectives that emerge from their own region. This use of professional staff could help promote multi-cultural and multi-faith understanding.

3. Headquarters

It was recommended to shift the headquarters of WCRP/International to Geneva, but it was felt necessary to have a small but efficient office in New York for active liaison with the UN, and its connected agencies. The New York office should be headed by an Associate Secretary-General, and in his/her absence, a reliable liaison officer would be in charge of the New York office.

4. Nominations

Although the Commission did not have enough time to cover all criteria for the leadership and staff of WCRP/International, they agreed to a *provisional* and *partial* list of names of people who should be approached for their agreement to be nominated at the Fourth Assembly. It was clearly understood that more names might come not only from Commission members, but from WCRP national and regional bodies.

V. Future Programmes

The Commission, after having re-evaluated the objectives of WCRP and considered some of the major issues lying before it, turned to formulating possible action programmes. Therefore, some of the aspects dealt with under "Basic Issues" (see III) really emerge again in the following suggestions.

The Commission considers that the programme of WCRP/International has two complementary aspects, one of which is more directly related with the developing and carrying out of substantive programmes, the other with the developing and nurturing of national and regional WCRP groups. These two aspects are closely interrelated.

1. Substantive Programmes

a. *To help to end the nuclear arms race and to elucidate the relationship between the arms race and the continued oppression of the poor.* Our multi-religious presence must bring pressure to bear on halting the arms race in both its nuclear and conventional forms. WCRP should trace out the dynamic links between the arms race, underdevelopment, and the suppression of human rights. Specific aspects of this WCRP programme were set forth by this Commission in "Basic Issues" (III, 2).

b. *To utilize the holistic approach.* The implementation of the universal goals continues to be holistic: study, education, and action for disarmament, development, human rights, conservation, and conflict resolution. Our unique modality of multi-religious dialogue not only affords clearer understanding and acceptance of differences among faith traditions, but may also become a model for clearer understanding and acceptance among nation states with ideological differences.

c. *To educate for peace.* In the light of the resolutions of the Louvain Assembly concerning peace education, WCRP/International should still consider peace education a priority. In view, however, of the breadth and specialized character of the field, it should not attempt to develop or create its own programme for peace education. It should, therefore, foster the sharing of material which seem particularly suitable, be they from an international body, such as UNESCO, or from a national or regional group.

WCRP/International should recommend to national and regional groups that they consider peace education a priority.

264

d. *To promote spiritual reflection and understanding.* In order to develop an awareness of the potential and actual contributions of each world religion to peace, visits to each other's places of worship may be arranged. These can be steps toward mutual trust and understanding, and may, in some cases, lead to opportunities of binding people together in meditative reflection, and in a fellowship of shared spiritual commitment towards ever greater co-operation in the service of the human family.

2. Developing Regional and National Groups

a. *To encourage WCRP regional programmes.* WCRP/International should not, *per se,* determine regional programmes regarding local issues. It should, however, ask local and regional WCRP groups to share with WCRP/International their experiences of successful initiatives in helping to resolve conflicts or promote social justice and in launching worthwhile programmes such as the European "Initiative for Active Hope." The very fact that people of different faiths meet together regularly is in itself a successful peace event.

b. *To continue multi-religious projects.* WCRP/International should continue to undertake multi-religious projects, in the spirit of the Boat People and Khmer projects. We should continue our multi-religious missions to the world's nuclear capitals such as our mission to the government of China.

c. *Relationships with other bodies.* The continued active presence of WCRP/International at UN Headquarters in New York was strongly affirmed. A WCRP/International NGO representative, working with, and responsible to, the Secretary-General, should be named. This person should be available full-time to the UN and should be of sufficient stature and experience for this task. Representation at Geneva and at the headquarters of other UN bodies should be continued and strengthened.

It was recommended that WCRP/International rather than regional committees would be the body that applied for affiliation with other world-wide bodies. Further, the Commission on the Future welcomed the reported proposal that the name of ARCP be changed to WCRP/Asia.

WCRP/International should explore with national or regional WCRP constituencies how to establish links with other religious bodies. This would be an attempt to move from individual to institutional membership. The differing institutional structures of various religious bodies should be taken into account in this matter.

WCRP/International should similarly explore collaboration with secular peace organisations, and encourage its regional bodies to move along similar lines.

3. Further Recommendations for WCRP

a. *Women.* WCRP/International should recognize the rôle that women can play in fostering peace and promote their continued access to WCRP groups and activities as well as encouraging the development of women's groups where necessary.

b. *Youth.* Recognizing the contribution that youth can make to WCRP, we should give special priority to their participation in our work. In view of the International Year of Youth in 1985, the Secretary-General is requested to explore the possibilities of bringing together youth from various parts of the world. (Youth is defined here as 35 years or under.)

c. *Assembly Proceedings.* We further recommend that the proceedings of WCRP IV be published and distributed in various forms and through diverse communications media as soon as possible after the Assembly.

d. *Organisation Manual.* In carrying out the important work of developing and nurturing national and regional WCRP committees, something which WCRP/International considers an integral part of the programme of WCRP, the Secretary-General should give consideration to the development of a manual for local, national, and regional WCRP groups, giving, *inter alia,* guidelines, suggestions for programmes, ways to facilitate inter-religious meetings, access to various communications media, and other relevant information.

Appendix I

LIST OF MEMBERS OF WCRP COMMISSION ON THE FUTURE AND OTHER PARTICIPANTS

Members of Commission on the Future

1. Sr. Marjorie Keenan, WCRP/USA, 777 United Nations Plaza, New York, N.Y. 10017, U.S.A. (Chairperson of Commission on the Future.) (WCRP/USA)
2. Dr. Inamullah Khan, House No. 4, Bahadurabad Road, No. 2, Karachi 0511, Pakistan. (Chairperson of Nominations Committee.) (WCRP/Pakistan)
3. Rev. Michael Mildenberger, Kirchenamt der EKD, Friedrichstr. 2-6, 6000 Frankfurt/Main, Federal Republic of Germany. (WCRP/Europe and Germany)
4. Prof. S. G. Mudgal B.42, A Wing, G.001 Dayanand Co-op Hsg. Socy. Gokuldham, Goregaon (E) Bombay 400063, India
5. Mr. Masuo Nezu, Rissho Kosei-kai, 7-1 Wada 2-chome, Suginami-ku, Tokyo 166, Japan. (WCRP/Japan)
6. Bishop J. Henry Okullu, Diocese of Maseno South, P.O. Box 114, Kisumu D35, Kenya. (WCRP/Africa and Kenya)
7. Bishop Rémi De Roo, #230-1555 McKenzie Avenue, Victoria, B.C V8N1A4, Canada. (WCRP/Canada)
8. Miss Hannah Stanton, 30 Burtons Road, Hampton Hill, Middlesex TW12 1DA, England. (WCRP/Europe and UK-Ireland)

A. Ex-Officio.

9. President of WCRP/International: Archbishop Angelo Fernandes, Archbishop's House, Ashok Place, New Delhi 110 001, India.
10. Research Director: Prof. François Houtart, Centre de Recherches Socio-Religieuses, Université Catholique de Louvain, Place Montesquieu 1, Boîte 21, 1348 Ottignies—Louvain-la-Neuve, Belgium.

B. Additional Members of the Nominating Committee

11. Mrs. Fredelle Brief, 8 Seneca Hill Drive, Willowdale, Ontario M2J W2E, Canada.
12. Metropolitan Filaret of Kiev, Moscow Patriarchate, External Church Relations Dept., 18/2 Ryleyev St., Moscow G-2, 121002, U.S.S.R.
13. Rev. Toshio Miyake, Konko-kyo Church of Izuo, 21-8, 3-chome, Nishi, San-gen-ya, Taisho-ku, Osaka 551, Japan.
14. Mr. Mehervan Singh, 5001 Beach Road No. 07-24, Golden Mile Complex, Singapore 0719, Republic of Singapore.

C. Staff

15. Miss Rénate Belck. (Staff of WCRP/International)
16. Mrs. Reiko Blauenstein, 3D rue de Moillebeau, 1209 Geneva, Switzerland. (Interpreter for Rev. Miyake)
17. Dr. Homer A. Jack, 489 Willow Road, Winnetka, Illinois 60093, U.S.A.
18. Mr. Toshio Kozai. (Interpreter for Rev. Miyake)
19. Dr. John B. Taylor, WCRP/International, 14 chemin Auguste-Vilbert, 1218 Grand-Saconnex, Geneva, Switzerland.
20. Mr. Mstislav Voskressensky. (Interpreter for Metropolitan Filaret)

Regrets

1. Dr. Dana McLean Greeley, First Parish, Concord, Massachusetts 01742, U.S.A.

In Attendance

1. Mrs. Ingeborg Jack.
2. Mrs. Singh.
3. Mrs. Margaret Taylor.

Appendix II

Summary of Report of Research Director, Prof. François Houtart, WCRP Commission on the Future

The research carried out in order to evaluate the work of WCRP centred on two main questions: the main orientations of the various conferences and a survey about the orientations of the participants. Here are the main conclusions.

I. From the Conferences

An analysis of the content of the general statements approved at the various world and regional conferences enables us to make the following remarks.

1. There has been an *extension of the topics* treated under the motto of Religion and Peace. The various dimensions of peace, not only with respect to war preparation and armament, but also with respect to social and economic roots, have been brought to light. The disadvantage, however, has been the dispersion of themes.

2. From one conference to another *different aspects have been accentuated.* This reveals the concerns of the time: development, nuclear armament, human rights, ecological questions, etc. However there has been considerable *repetition,* probably because the main topic remains somewhat the same and it is difficult to say new things in the relatively short period of time between the conferences.

3. *Two main lines of thinking* seem to be present throughout the various conferences. The first one emphasizes the individual aspect of the problems: peace begins in the hearts of men. The other one emphasizes the structural aspects of peace and development. It appears difficult to make the synthesis between the two. In the last conference, at Princeton, the spiritual dimension was emphasized more than at the other meetings.

4. During the Asian conference in Singapore, the idea of the *failure of the Western spiritual currents* to face the present problems of the world was expressed and an appeal was made for more attention to be given to the great Eastern traditions.

5. Making the *link* between the problems related to *Peace* and *Religion* is no doubt the most difficult task. It is made through ethics, but the main questions remain: how individual codes of ethics can be related to the social dimension of human life and which type of social analysis should be adopted in order to move beyond simple generalities.

6. In the texts we have analysed, members of *various religious traditions* have explained the ways in which religion was related to peace in their faiths. Two main ideas are central: the value of and respect for life and the dignity of humanity.

At all the conferences it was clearly stated that the aim of such meetings was not to compare the various religions, nor to come to some kind of syncretism. It was not the intention to use religions as pure means, nor to offer the world solutions which religious groups do not possess. The real aim has always been to mobilize spiritual resources to join forces with the efforts towards international peace and to help an international code of ethics penetrate international relations. The idea is to join with the movement to search for answers, knowing that the challenge facing the religions themselves is "not what to say, but how to be"

The awareness that verbal expressions of such matters were rapidly being exhausted led to the idea that something concrete should be accomplished together (as well as the on-going activities of the secretariat). Two initiatives were taken in South East Asia: a project for the Vietnamese Boat People and humanitarian aid for Kampuchean refugees. Many problems of an organizational, financial, and above all, perhaps, political nature, arose in connection with such projects, even if the intention had been to give a joint expression of concern for actual people. They had the advantage of being an experiment, which made the relevant authorities aware of the needs of refugees.

During the Asian conference in Delhi in 1981 a new concrete initiative was approved: the constitution of a Multi-Religious Mission, which would visit the political leaders of the nuclear powers of the world. A Mission of ten persons was received in China in 1982.

II. From the Survey

1. The Four Main Types of Opinion

Four main orientations about the conception of peace and the rôle of religion in connection with peace (1) have emerged. The first is: *peace*

---

(1) These orientations were found by applying a factor analysis, with the help of the computer, to the answers given by 135 persons representing quite adequately the participants in the various conferences.

through justice and demilitarization. The majority of respondents in all religious groups expressed agreement with this major idea. Some reservations were expressed by about one quarter of the respondents on the subject of total disarmament and the encouragement which should be given to popular movements fighting injustice, in particular national liberation movements but also worker and peasant movements.

A second line of thought which meets with only a very small amount of support can be expressed in the following way: *war is inevitable and peace is the result of order.* Only 6.7% of the respondents agreed with these ideas whereas 32% rejected them. However, a good number were hesitant, particularly about the idea that war is a recurrent state of affairs among human beings. Although in general the respondents are optimistic about the possibility of peace, about one third of them express a certain fatalism and a pessimistic view of humanity.

The third emphasizes *the strength of the religious institution, help to the poor, and military strength.* The main line of thought seems to be clearly related to the central role of religion, and to religious affiliation as a priority. Only 8.1% gave total approval to such a line of thought, but if we include those who gave partial approval, there are 26%, which means a large minority.

The last trend is centred on the individual: *peace through the religion of the individual.* There is an important trend in favour of this opinion model: 18.5% in total agreement and 23.0% in partial agreement, when only 0.7% are in disagreement and 3.0% in partial disagreement.

All this shows the importance of coming together on issues of peace and also the difficulty of establishing common grounds on a matter in which religion can only be linked through ethics. However, there is unanimous belief that because of the situation of humankind today, such efforts must be continued. Among the initiatives to be taken, the following have been proposed:

—action against armament;
—struggle against unjust political, economic and social structures;
—activities in favour of mass education in the field of peace;
—initiatives within the religious sphere to emphasize the spiritual dimension;
—humanitarian and development projects;
—research on causes of conflict and on common religious values.

2. The General Meaning of These Types of Opinion
a) Synthesis

We give in summary some of the main characteristics of the opinions expressed. It is obvious that they reflect the minds of a public deeply—and as it were by definition—interested in the issue of peace. However it is also quite obvious that the majority of respondents are aware of the social dimension of peace and that they are ready to involve themselves—and at some risk—for the cause of peace. A certain elitist vision seems to be associated with the former position, expressing some distance from popular social and political movements, favouring definitely non-violent action, and very much concerned with the question of human rights.

The central position of religion is also something which emerges in the opinions expressed again and again. This could be interpreted as quite normal because of the type of persons questioned: more than half of them are religious leaders or are directly connected with institutions dependent on religious bodies. All of them are believers. It also appears that there is a certain awareness of the status of religion and of religious institutions in society. This may be at the origin of a relatively strong moralizing approach to human realities.

b) Sociological Reflections

On the basis of these orientations we may propose three sociological remarks. The first concerns the religious character of the persons who responded. Being in the main religious leaders, or defining themselves in terms of their religious adhesion, they seem to be inclined to interpret reality from a religious perspective. As a result some of them tend to give fundamental importance to the unity of religious groups as a guarantee of peace or to give the religious leaders priority over the political ones, in issues related to peace.

A more fundamental hypothesis can be put forward: the priority given to a moralizing approach to reality is also dependent on religious adhesion. Such an approach tends to escape analysis or to adopt an implicit analysis, taking into account the immediate visibility of social facts, but not their structural components. As religious belief is related to human behaviour, whether personal or collective, through ethics, i.e., through norms, religious people who want to influence such behaviour tend to look at reality in moralizing terms. the final goal is efficient action. But very often there is little awareness that the religious field does not control reality as a whole. Indeed a social analysis is necessary if we are to perceive the other dimensions, in particular those not directly visible or intentional, such as social relations in the economic field, cultural models, etc. To reduce human reality to individual morality or the ethics of inter-personal relationships, which are directly visible and which can be directly influenced by religious arguments, is to condemn oneself to a partial approach and to illusory solutions.

Similar problems arise when the human social reality is approached from other specific fields: political, educational, military, etc. specialized agents of these fields of human activity or persons who identify themselves with such specific dimensions always tend to look at the whole from their own particular perspective. This is related to the specialization of the tasks and also to the necessary social reproduction of rôles and institutions. It is easy to understand on the other hand that when people are fully engaged in certain types of activity or are even in charge of certain institutions, the way in which they view reality is influenced by their position. Their view of the world tends to be exclusive; their cultural schemes are modelled by the place they occupy in society. Social reproduction, on the other hand, is a natural concern in any institution. This is mainly assured by the continuity of rôles and by what we could call—without any negative meaning—vested interests.

All this is also true in religious groups and religious institutions because these are social processes we find everywhere. In order to relativize the field from which one views human reality and to see it as a complex whole, one needs to distance oneself intellectually and emotionally and also to have moral (or religious) motivation. The first requisite is an awareness of the need for social analysis. Its choice is not a purely neutral matter and it may be influenced by moral or religious motives. Whatever the case, the mediation of a social analysis between religious beliefs and ethics is inevitable.

The second remark concerns the respondents' social origins. None of them is from popular social classes, i.e., workers or peasants; nor are they connected with popular organizations such as trade unions or liberation movements. Hence they come from a relatively elitist type of background. However, this does not necessarily mean that they are unable to distance themselves somewhat from their social background. This is verified by some of the opinions expressed, and such a distancing is clearly related to their religious beliefs or to their place as intellectuals.

A third consideration brings together the first two. On the basis of their reading social reality from a religious point of view and coming from somewhat elitist social backgrounds, one may consider the respondents' political orientations. They are characterized by a search for democracy, with considerable concern for human rights. A minority, which we could estimate at about 10% of the respondents, are in favour of "law and order" and do not hesitate to emphasize the necessity of military strength related also to some strong religious traditions. Another minority of about 20% would be in favour of radical social transformations of the capitalist system, based on the action of popular movements, encouraged or even inspired by religious motives.

The majority position corresponds to the political option of most of the religious leaders in the present political organization of the world. It corresponds to various types of situations: parliamentary democracies, populist régimes, social democracies, all of them accepting a certain adaptation of the capitalist relations of production, with some degree of control to satisfy some of the aspirations of the popular classes. Such systems generally also leave quite a lot of room for the activities of religious bodies, not only in the religious field, but also in cultural and social ones. These reasons seem to underpin the political options of the majority of the respondents.

c) The Impact of the Various Religions

One question remains to be raised: what is the impact of the various religious backgrounds on the opinion patterns? We have said several times in the commentary on the results that religions as such were not the main factors of differentiation between the opinions. However this does not mean that they do not exercise any influence. Of course the number of respondents is not large enough and the religious memberships are too scattered for us to make more than just a few hypotheses.

The emphasis on the individual mind as a factor in peace or war, and on the rôle of religion as a spiritual response to the individual, is more accentuated among the respondents of Asian religion (empirically defined as all religions surveyed except Christianity and Judaism). This corresponds to their great spiritual traditions. It is also in this same group that we find more importance is given to the central character of the religious bodies in society. But it is not a unanimous trend among the respondents.

We must recall that the origins of several of the religions are strongly related to social movements, as is the case with Islam for example, or with some reactions against a specific social pattern, as is the case with Sikhism in the face of the caste system. Moreover the respondents generally belong to some kind of reformed branches of such religions: new Shinto in Japan, Buddhist movements such as Rissho Kosei-kai in the same country, modern Hindu philosophical currents, etc. It means that they have integrated an awareness of the new dimensions of human problems, which could not be faced without new thinking on the part of the great religious traditions.

Nor yet is there any unanimity between Christianity and a social reading of the problems of war and peace, even though the Christian faith was confronted earlier than other religions with the development of a world market economy and with the problems of world wars. Individualist and pietistic trends also exist, generally among religious movements born with the Reformation or as forms of elitist types of spirituality. If the causes are different, the results as regards the approach to peace, war, and justice, are quite similar to the position explained before.

III.   General Conclusions

1.   World Economy and World Wars

In the historical perspective that we have adopted, the international dimensions of the social relations that we experience today are really a new development. Inter-regional trade has of course been developing since ancient times; enormous empires have been built, such as Ashoka's in India, the Mughuls throughout Asia, Axum in East Africa, the Mayas of Central America or the Incas of the South of the continent, Constantine or Charles the Great in Europe, without even mentioning the Arab conquests. But the interrelation between the various peoples of the world has never been as great as it is today, and never before have the problems of economic development or of arms races been so interrelated on a world scale. All this began and developed outside what we could subsume under the single heading: the religious sphere.

Such an evolution is the fruit of the expansion of a new economic logic, based on a market economy and on tremendous technical developments. The mercantile economy has been in existence for a long time and some religions have played an important rôle in working out the code of ethics of such societies: Islam for example and others too, such as Jainism, Calvinism, etc. The world-wide application of this type of economy, through mercantile colonialism first of all and later through the development of industrial societies with their new colonial enterprises and world dependencies, is the fruit of the capitalist system. Historically its centre has been in Europe and in the Western World, but its logic today forms the basis of a world-wide system. What is new here is the fact that its expansion has been based on non-religious values and motives and on a secular code of ethics inspired by liberalism.

2. The Historical Role of Religions in the Orientations of Ethics

The major religions of the world have provided the basis for the ethical orientations and often also for the political orientations of most of the pre-capitalist societies which are not just tribal organizations. For the first time in history religions were no longer playing such a rôle in the new capitalist systems. Religious motivations were still evoked, but more restricted to the field of the interpersonal code of ethics. The expansion of the new economic logic, in Europe and, even more so, in the colonial areas of Africa, Asia, and Latin America, has often provoked religious protests, in the form of movements with some kind of messianic orientation. They were mostly reactions against the penetration of the new social relations of the capitalist system, but with reference to value-systems linked to the past, as has been the case with various caste movements in India, when society was changing from a caste to a class society. We could give similar examples in Islamic, Buddhist, or Christian societies.

In short, we can say that religions were ill-equipped to cope with the new situations. It is very difficult for everyone to understand what is going on and no religion had the intellectual, theological, or institutional tools required to face these problems. This could only come about through the development of a code of ethics, which would consider all aspects of the new realities. The world-wide scale of the economic system has also had repercussions in the form of reactions against inequalities brought about by the logic of capitalism, inequalities between social classes, on the national level, but also on the international one. The reaction was the development of a contradictory logic: the socialist movement. Today this is at the root of the main world antagonisms, even if many complex problems are mixed up with it, and at the root of the threats to peace that the arms race is increasingly generating for the whole of mankind.

Historically speaking, Christianity was faced with this problem before other religions were. For a long time the identification of Christianity with the Western World has made it into a very ambiguous reality. Being continuously caught between the critique of the socio-economic model of the capitalist system and its hidden ideology, the desire to accept modernization and the ambiguities of institutional reproduction, the Christian churches have been caught in many contradictions. The other religions have rather tended merely to receive the shocks caused by the new situation. It is only very recently that some intellectuals and spiritual leaders have begun to re-think the religious traditions taking into account the tremendous scientific and technical development of the world and the unjust social and international relations established at the same time.

3. Relation Between Religion and Peace Through Ethics

On this background, the problem of peace can only be related to religion through ethics, but today this implies an ethic which is not religious in itself. Ethics are a matter of norms for social and international relations, which are not natural products, but which are the result of human undertakings. No one can represent this reality any longer as the direct result of a social order coming from above, which has to be respected because it has been imposed by supernatural beings. Ethical norms have to be worked out according to some criteria. And it is here that the religions are facing difficult problems. The establishing of criteria for a code of ethics is the result of a two-fold approach: one which starts with fundamental values, on which many religions agree, such as respect for life, and dignity of the human person, and a second one which is based on reality itself. And this requires—whether willingly or not, and consciously or not—a certain type of social analysis.

One may give only a simple example: the ethical judgments and norms will be very different if the analysis of society is conducted in terms of a sum of individuals, whose hearts have to be changed in order to transform society, or if it is conducted in structural terms, viewing society as the sum of social relations, in which human beings are of course actors, but in which intentional logics do not always coincide with structural ones.

Because an analysis in structural terms—not necessarily in contradiction to interpersonal ethics—is something relatively new, it has been quite difficult to introduce this perspective in religious traditions, as it has been in many other forms of thinking and philosophies. However, with religions it is more difficult, probably because their potential for action depends on individuals and their personal morality. Religious affiliation seems to be an obstacle getting beyond an interpersonal ethic. It seems that this has been revealed quite clearly in many WCRP texts and also in the survey. Contrary to what could be thought, it is not exclusive to Eastern religions. Not only do we find this characteristic among Western believers and churches, but the contrary is also true: even if Oriental religions are emphasizing individual salvation and the spiritual dimension of human commitment, some believers of these religions are basing a social ethical judgment on a new type of social analysis. However, in the majority of cases, in all religious traditions, we are faced with religions of individual salvation or with a non-analytical social vision.

Here we come up against a second difficulty: the link between religious faith and ethics. Often we find a simple juxtaposition of the two and some of the theoretical attempts to bring them together seem rather artificial, because they do not take into consideration the social and historical conditions in which the religious beliefs have been expressed. In most of the major religious systems, however, some new perspectives are developed.

There is some agreement among all believers on certain major principles: the permanent affirmation of life vs. death, an opposition on which all religions are centred, even if the concrete expressions are very different. Such expressions are linked with the kind of society in which one lives and also the kind of analysis which is made. The value of life is expressed in Hinduism or Jainism, for example, by the radical respect for any living being. In the new theological thinking of Latin America, the existing social and economic structures are qualified as structures of death, because they are at the root of infant mortality, low life-span, many illnesses, illiteracy, and all kinds of oppression. It is of course in the domain of war, armaments and militarization that the problem of life and death becomes the most apparent. Peace is advocated in the name of the value of life and this could be the most obvious common position of all religions.

The dignity of the human person is also another source of agreement. However, it is not always easy to give a concrete interpretation of such a general concept. It is a logical consequence of the first common heritage. Some religious discourses tend to remain in an abstract sphere, using generous but rather useless concepts, forgetting that there is only a dignity of actual human beings in concrete situations.

And it is precisely when we come to these actual situations that contradictions and disagreements tend to appear. According to the WCRP documents and the answers to the survey, it was not so much along religious lines that the lack of agreement occurs. It is rather as regards the social and political analysis of the situations. Such judgments are not only the result of a religious vision. They are always linked to the "place" from which the problem is analysed, not only in the geographical sense, but also in the ideological one. Therefore a good knowledge of this "location" is a necessary spiritual exercise for everyone.

Appendix III

Summary of Replies to
Dr. John Taylor's Questionnaire
on Future Organization and
Programmes of
WCRP/International

40 Replies:

Africa: 2,
Americas: 7,
Australasia (inc. Middle East): 13,
West Europe (inc. Cyprus): 17,
East Europe: 1.
Buddhists and Shintoists: 2,
Christians: 21,
Hindus and Sikhs: 6,
Jews: 2,
Muslims: 7,
Parsees: 2.

I. Organization.

A. World Assemblies.

1. How often should WCRP assemblies be held?
   Every 4–5 years: 30
   More frequently 6
   Less frequently 4
2. How do you rate the utility of world assemblies?
   High 18
   Low 3
   Medium 17

3. How can the financial support for world assemblies and other expenses of WCRP/International be increased and become more diversified (in the past 90% has been given by Japanese Buddhists, West German Catholics, and US Protestants)?

    Religious bodies and charities: 5; peace foundations and national branches: 4; burden for all countries—major responsibility for rich ones: 4; Arab world: 3.

B. *International Secretariat.*

1. What are the major rôles of the international secretariat?
    Prepare world assemblies: 25
    Implement world assemblies: 17
    Establish new branches: 14
    Aid regional and national branches: 18
    Give substantive leadership on issues: 20
    Other: Information and interreligious links: 2
2. Would you like to see an enlarged, multi-religious secretariat (realizing that each new staff member would cost $50,000 a year, including salary and support)?
    Yes: 25
    How many: 1–7
    No: 9
3. How much priority should be given to relationships with various UN agencies, in New York, Geneva, Paris (UNESCO), etc.?
    High: 22
    Low: 3
    Medium: 13
4. Where should the WCRP/International office be located after WCRP IV?
    New York: 8
    Geneva: 23
    or: Rome, London, Istanbul, or "Third Wc ᵗ ' received
    1–2 preferences each.

C. *Regional WCRP Conferences.*

1. What is the prime purpose of WCRP/Europe, ACRP, WCRP/Africa?
    Help establish national chapters?   16
    Sponsor multi-religious projects?   18
    Service national chapters?   10
2. What responsibility should regional conferences assume for WCRP/International financing?
    Some: 36
    None: 4

3. Should regional conferences apply for affiliation to world-wide bodies (e.g., the UN) following the example of WCRP/International?

Yes: 12
No: 28

D. *National Branches.*

1. How effectively do delegates to international assemblies from national or local branches bring their influence to bear upon the international assembly and organisation?

Very effectively: 5
Adequately: 20
Ineffectively: 9

2. How far should the constitutions and structures of national branches be submitted to the international organization for approval?

Always: 16
Optionally: 23

E. *Special Chapters.*

1. Do you think it important to deploy an effort from the international staff for establishing a young people's network or perhaps a series of student chapters in various universities with a pluralist student-body?

Yes: 18
Not a priority: 5
Better left to regional conferences and national branches: 16

2. Some express a need for groups of women from different religious traditions to constitute women's groups for WCRP; would such women's chapters involve international stimulus or co-ordination?

Yes: 12
Not a priority: 7
Better left to regional conferences and national branches: 20

F. *Areas with few or no Links with WCRP*

1. In what priority should initiatives be taken to strengthen or establish groups in areas like the following: (Please indicate order of priority (1, 2, 3, 4).)

The "Middle East": 1
The Pacific: 4
Latin America: 2
Any other area: 3 (Africa, East Europe, India)

2. With what further religious or secular organizations should WCRP seek to establish new relations? Please indicate names or categories.

Muslim groups, World Council of Churches, Carnegie Endowment for Peace

II. *Programmes*

A. *Assemblies/Meetings/Follow-Up*

1. Should more energy be given to strengthening the official or representative attendance at WCRP assemblies and meetings?

Yes: 30
No: 8

2. How many "newcomers", e.g., young people and women, should receive encouragement and, if necessary, subsidy in order to attend an international WCRP assembly or meeting?

10%: 11
50%: 6
30%: 17
over 50%: 2

3. How should the proceedings of WCRP assemblies be published?

Entire proceedings: 5
Pamphlets: 8
Extracts of up to about 60 pages: 22

4. What do you think should be the substantive priorities of WCRP/International for follow-up after WCRP IV? Please indicate order of priority (1, 2, 3, etc.)

Prevention of Nuclear War: 1
Increased Human Rights Everywhere: 3
Elimination of Apartheid: 7
Peace Education: 2
Environment: 8
Economic Development of the Third World: 5
Conventional and Nuclear Disarmament: 4
Resolution of Regional Conflicts: 6
Enhancing the Role of the UN: 9
Other: Many request emphasis on inter-faith dialogue.

B. *Relationships*

1. Should WCRP/International encourage and facilitate bilateral linking of particular regional conferences, national branches, or special chapters to undertake cooperative study or action of common concern?

Yes: 24
No, better left to regional and national branches: 15

2. Should exchange visits or common study programmes or "pressure groups" be organized or co-ordinated between regional conferences, national branches, or special chapters with international sponsorship?

Yes: 26

No, better left to regional and national branches: 12

C. *Projects*

1a. How would you rate the WCRP Boat People Project?

High: 18

Medium: 11

Low: 6

1b. How would you rate the WCRP Khmer Project?

High: 9

Medium: 17

Low: 7

1c. How would you rate the Multi-Religious Disarmament Mission to Beijing?

High: 14

Medium: 11

Low: 9

2. Should WCRP/International sponsor practical multi-religious humanitarian (service) projects:

Several: 13

One or two only: 18

None: 5

3. Should WCRP/International limit itself to fund-raising and perhaps screening of these projects or should it also engage field staff, etc.? Please comment briefly.

Leave most implementation to regional field staff who should be very carefully chosen.

D. *Other Possible Activities/Actions*

1. Of what nature should the multi-religious actions undertaken by WCRP/International be between and within religious bodies? Please indicate an order of preference.

Essentially symbolic: 4

Political: 5

Educational: 3

Humanitarian: 2

2. Should the emphasis of WCRP programmes be between or within particular religions?

Between religions: 19

Within religions: 1

Both: 20

3. Should WCRP programmes be addressed also to people who are apathetic or hostile towards religions?
    Yes: 30
    No: 7

E. Officers, Committee Structures, Etc.
1. What officers are needed for the overall guidance of WCRP/ International?
    No change: 10
    Proposals: Include representation of major organizations wherever this is possible.
2. How far should religious organizations be consulted or perhaps invited to nominate officers or committee members?
    Always: 17
    Sometimes: 1
    Never: 3
3. What committee structures seem appropriate for decision-making and for guiding international staff?
    No change: 12
    Proposals: Representatives are important, BUT body should be small enough to meet and work.

53

Report of the Youth Committee

WCRP Youth wish to affirm the immense value we have found in the two-day youth conference, held at KTTC, Nairobi on 20 and 21 August 1984, prior to WCRP IV.

Our youth conference has covered many issues of concern and generated many ideas of value which are contained herein in a much summarised form as seven recommendations:

    1. We recommend WCRP to:
- i) establish an international youth committee, with constitutional status within WCRP;
- ii) organize an extended WCRP Youth Conference to be held before the next assembly, with the hope that there will be full global participation;
- iii) include a Youth Section in the regular WCRP Newsletter;
- iv) ensure through the standing orders for WCRP Conferences that there be full participation of youth in such conferences;
- v) set up exchange programmes between the different youth chapters of WCRP.

    2. We request WCRP to make work with refugees a priority—we must express tangibly our compassion for the victims of international violence. WCRP Youth given authority by WCRP would seek to work directly with refugees in the camps, as a multi-faith group. WCRP/Kenya is ready to establish a first office in Nairobi to co-ordinate such efforts.

    3. Whilst affirming previous efforts, we request that WCRP convene a meeting of religious leaders as a first step towards a delegation to the leadership of nuclear-weapon States. (The idea being that the world's moral leadership must be more directly applied to the issue of disarmament).

We also request that WCRP maintain and strengthen its permanent office at the UN, to encourage nation-states towards disarmament.

4.   Mindful of the 1985 Year International Year for Youth, we make the following recommendations:

i)   that WCRP Youth organize inter-faith Prayer Meetings for Peace in their various areas;

ii)   that WCRP Youth try to direct the national programmes for IYY especially towards the needs of disadvantaged youth; through media programmes and funding, issues like youth unemployment should be high-lighted;

iii) that WCRP set up an opportunity for dialogue with the UN organizers of IYY prior to 1985; the WCRP delegation to the UN should include representatives from WCRP Youth;

iv)   that Peace Education should be a prominent theme in IYY projects—both projects by WCRP and other projects formed after liaison with national governments and the UN; issues to be covered should include:

a)   the impact of youth cultural influences (war toys, video games, TV);

b)   the scope for and constraints against disarmament measures;

c)   the impact of militarism on the poor;

d)   the extent that development aid reflects the expressed needs of those it is meant for;

e)   establishment of peace education in curricula;

v)   That WCRP organize an inter-faith camp during IYY, ideally in an area where there are inter-faith problems.

5.   Regarding human rights, we recommend:

i)   the formation of a special section of WCRP to monitor human rights violations, receiving information from WCRP members and acting on this information, as is appropriate;

ii)   that WCRP should apply pressure on governments which violate human rights, in co-operation with WCRP members in the countries concerned;

iii) that members of WCRP use every opportunity to express solidarity with other members of the human family who are suffering.

6.   Regarding disarmament—as young people of faith we support general and complete disarmament. Therefore, we resolve that young members of WCRP should continue to support campaigns such as those for

i)   a Comprehensive Test Ban Treaty and Nuclear Freeze;

ii)   the strengthening of the Nuclear Non-Proliferation Treaty at the review Conference in August 1985;

iii) the pursuit of Nuclear-Free Zones, a Chemical Weapons Convention, a Moratorium on the Testing of Anti-Satellite Missiles pending negotiations for a de-militarised outer space.

6.   WCRP should work with groups which seek these goals through non-violent means. Our input should always emphasise the moral issues

involved and should seek to involve as many religious leaders and people as possible in this work.

To this end, we encourage certain specific initiatives:

a) that Regional and National WCRP encourage a Ministry for Peace in each nation. Its work should include developing non-violent social defence as an alternative to military power and military alliances, and more joint projects and programmes to build greater trust and confidence where there is now dangerous mistrust between and within nations;

b) that WCRP campaign for reductions in military spending and a ban on arms trading;

c) that WCRP should plan for Non-violent Non-Cooperation campaigns if the Nuclear-weapon States continue to block disarmament.

7. In putting forth these recommendations, we recognize the need for, and are committed to making sacrifices in terms of time, money and comfort for the sake of the suffering members of the human family.

We would like to thank Badru Kateregga, our Chairman, for his good-humoured, efficient work during these past two days.

54

Report of the
Beyond Nairobi Committee

I.   What is WCRP?

WCRP is a voluntary association which aims to promote world peace and which is made up of religiously committed persons. The main elements are all religions in all sections of the world on all aspects of peace. This brief description points to the specific WCRP approach, different from other organizations and movements committed to the universal task of peace-making. The specific focus of WCRP is an action-oriented fellowship of religious people working for peace through the application of spiritual motivation.

Peace is more tnan the absence of war, just as life is more than physical existence. WCRP takes peace as being a dynamic process involving all aspects of individual and social life. This holistic approach is rooted in a concept of security based on trust rather than on strength and aims at creating conditions which allow all people in all countries to develop their full humanity and live a meaningful life. As peace is for everybody and not just for religious people, WCRP cannot restrict its efforts towards peace, but acts on behalf of and for all people and seeks to communicate also with those who have no religious commitment or who find themselves minorities within their own religious community. WCRP, however, maintains its specificity as a multi-religious body.

There is a deep commitment to the service of peace and human rights in all religious traditions. Through prayer, meditation and conscious religious motivation, we therefore, search to enlist "the forces of inner truthfulness and of the spirit as having greater power than hate, enmity and self-interest," "a realization that might is not right," and "a profound hope that good will prevail finally" (Kyoto Declaration 1970). Such a spirituality of peace includes:

—repentance and a sense of humility as religion so often fails to reconcile and make peace, but instead creates or intensifies conflicts,

—renewal, both personally and institutionally, repudiating selfishness and fostering care for others,

—willingness to deepen and express authentically our own faith and, at the same time, to discover and respect the religious traditions of our fellow humans as having an authentic position within the religious search for truth,

—courage to face conflicts, to struggle for justice, and to take the risk of suffering for peace, seeking always reconciliation, in a spirit of love and justice.

We are motivated by an urgent awareness that religious people are impelled to turn their faith into action. Therefore WCRP is an action-oriented fellowship,

—addressing itself to men and women of all religious traditions in all regions of the world, in particular to the young generation whose future is marred by the destructive powers of selfishness, injustice, and nuclear threat, and urging all of them to participate in our endeavours and experiences,

—sharing among the people of the world a deeper knowledge of the teachings and traditions which each religion has for world peace and justice, offering, together with our human resources, those spiritual and moral principles conducive to peace in order to promote a universality of awareness and conscience among the members of the human community,

—applying such principles in a spirit of social responsibility to the obstacles to peace and human dignity in the areas of human rights, development, environment, and disarmament,

—dealing with conflict situations on a local, regional, and international level, in particular where such situations have a religious dimension, bringing to bear the multi-faith character of WCRP.

While acknowledging that it is the governments and other political bodies, local, national, and international, which primarily have the decision-making power and are responsible for creating conditions conducive to peace, yet we are convinced that WCRP has to make a specific contribution to promoting world peace and justice. We see our contribution as supporting such political, social and other efforts giving to them spiritual motivations and resources, and thus opening ways towards a meaningful life.

II. Programme Areas

Introduction

1. Our purpose is to try to clarify, for the WCRP/International Board and staff, what are considered the major programme areas for the immediate future.

2. Our document endeavours to build on many contributions regarding the shaping of WCRP. These contributions include the Report on the Commission on the Future; the opening speeches

at WCRP IV by our President, Secretary-General and Secretary-General Emeritus, and the work of the Conference, WCRP IV, itself.

3. Our document assumes that the effectiveness of WCRP in the programme areas we shall outline is directly related to the quality and growth of our spiritual life. In particular, deep sustained prayer and meditation will be necessary for WCRP to fulfil its purposes (in which context we recommend Archbishop Fernandes' Prayer for Peace for daily use).

4. Programme areas should satisfy the following criteria:
    —programmes should capture and express the special identity of WCRP;
    —programmes should build on the previous distinctive work of national/regional WCRP committees and of WCRP/International;
    —programmes should reflect what are clear multi-faith concerns;
    —programmes should be responses to urgent needs, consonant with our spiritual and other resources.

5. There are great difficulties in ranking the programme areas in order of importance.
    —An underlying reason for this is that it is impossible to dissect suffering. Where do we turn first when there are forgotten refugees, starving children, people being threatened or killed in religious conflicts? All such suffering requires an urgent response. Who dares to place one need above another?
    —Another reason for the difficulty in ranking programme areas is the tension between promoting organizational growth for future effectiveness, and the need to apply what we have to immediate problems.
    —A final reason is the tension between direct care for those suffering and, on the other side, programmed work for social justice.

    Let us now turn to a discussion of programme areas, recalling that we will refer to, but not detail, the work of the commissions and working groups.

1. Disarmament, Development, and Human Rights

WCRP IV has clearly affirmed that disarmament, development and human rights continue as fundamental moral and spiritual issues for WCRP.

It is, in fact, imperative that WCRP continue to apply the resilience of faith to these areas, given that we meet at a time when:

—the nuclear and conventional arms races are intimidating every life on our planet;

—many are despairing after the failure of peace movements and disarmament negotiations to yet halt this deranged phenomenon;

—the repressed violence of nuclear deterrence is infecting our whole cultural life;

—the poor are oppressed and starved by militarism;

—many are dying violently and without purpose in various regional conflicts; and

—human rights violations, institutional and otherwise, cause unspeakable suffering and diminish us all.

Disarmament

We cannot overstate how the prevention of nuclear annihilation must compel our attention. Everything we do in our lives, every cherished person, is at risk . . .

Commission III has detailed a disarmament agenda, distinguishing particular issues and projects. As regards WCRP/International, Working Group 7B has recommended a two-fold priority for WCRP in the immediate future (regarding the Nuclear Non-Proliferation Treaty Review Conference in 1985, and the work of the WCRP/International New York Headquarters on disarmament and human rights).

A compassionate response to refugees is part of this programme area. They are the victims of international violence. They tangibly manifest the failure of humanity to resolve conflicts according to basic human values.

Working Groups 7A and 7B suggest projects for WCRP refugee work.

Development

In every nation, albeit in varying degrees, militarism diminishes, if not destroys, our ability to meet basic human needs.

Whilst affirming that disarmament is an end in itself—especially regarding the prevention of nuclear annihilation—it is also true that we have to engage in disarmament if we are to have development. It has been, in fact, true for years that the arms race causes the poor to starve. From many parts of the world, WCRP IV has heard how this is even more so today.

WCRP/International must passionately assert how disarmament is needed for the sake of development; especially in its work at the UN in Geneva and New York, where the life-style is not exactly of the poor in the developing countries!

WCRP/International must also, we believe, promote detailed initiatives for development. Commission II and Working Group 6 indicate some such initiatives. Effectiveness regarding such initiatives, as part of a New International Economic Order, will require close liaison between WCRP/International and regional and national committees.

WCRP IV also recognizes that our commitment to development cannot be made dependent on disarmament. The needs are urgent and immediate.

As a final comment, women have evidenced, in Working Group 4 and in the Message from the Women's Conference, that they offer

WCRP a special perspective on disarmament and development. WCRP/International is urged to ensure that women's contributions are incorporated into programme development in this area.

Human Rights

As already noted, it is recommended from Working Group 7B that the WCRP/International offices must continue to build on the previous distinctive work of WCRP on human rights. Particularly in regard to the UN Human Rights Commission, with the informational support of WCRP regional and national committees. Many issues will, of course, require spiritual and programmatic attention.

However, beyond Nairobi, apartheid must continue as a major concern. To be faithful to the experience of WCRP IV in Africa, a special programme, aimed towards the abolition of the apartheid system in South Africa, must be developed in liaison with the South African WCRP Committee.

2. Reconciliation Amidst "Religious" Conflicts

In terms of our criteria for programme areas, disarmament, development, and human rights are expressions of clear multi-faith concerns. They are responses to urgent needs and in each we build on the previous distinctive work of WCRP. They have become an expression of our identity.

There is, however, a particular area in which the distinctive identity and purpose of WCRP must be more clearly expressed: this is in our rôle as a reconciling agent in situations where religion is, or is believed to be, a factor in conflicts. In fact, we must be working in this area in order to give greater credibility to our work for disarmament and development. Working Groups 1A, 2, 3, 5, and 7B all proposed projects for WCRP regional and national committees and WCRP/International in regard to reconciliation amidst "religious" conflicts.

The development of new regional WCRP committees, for example in the Middle East, is a related priority. WCRP/International must take the initiative in forming, as well as strengthening, new local, national and regional committees.

Given that the fighting in such conflicts is largely done by young people, the strengthening of WCRP Youth is a related necessity. The Youth Report urged their equal incorporation into the formal organization of WCRP and its work (and special attention to the International Year of Youth in 1985).

The UN Declaration on Religious Freedom, itself an expression of WCRP's past efforts, should be promoted in and through the work of this programme area.

We reiterate that it is in this area that we can and must illustrate the special identity of WCRP. It is also an area where we look forward to a special contribution from our Secretary-General.

Peace Education

Peace education, at every level, is necessary as a support to the disarmament process and as a means of sustaining peace. Working Group 3 gave this emphasis. We look to the WCRP regional and national committees to continue their work in this area. WCRP is blessed with many committed and gifted peace educators, utilising a holistic approach as defined in the Report of the Commission on the Future. It is important that their insights be made available to WCRP/International in a form that can be applied to programme areas 1 and 2.

Given the fine work occurring elsewhere, including through WCRP members, WCRP/International will not need to develop a Peace Research Institute. In any case, the urgency of needs demand that our style of operation, as noted in the Presidential Address, remains action-oriented. Nevertheless, as Dr. Homer A. Jack said in his address, the New York and Geneva offices keep us in touch with events and possibilities in a way that many non-governmental organizations are not. This information must be conveyed through WCRP/International to regional and national committees in order to facilitate their work for peace. Attention needs to be given to the kind of "newsletter" this requires.

Peace education, broadly conceived, incorporates the need for healthy links with the UN and other organizations. This is not a programme area which should be separately developed. Rather, the links should emerge and be given friendly attention, as relevant to our work for disarmament, development, human rights and the reconciliation of "religious" conflicts.

The fostering of mutual understanding in our multi-cultural societies is also a continuing aspect of peace education. This informal work is best organized at the local level. It is necessary as a preventive measure, so that there is minimal scope for "religious" conflicts. WCRP committees should be urged to create such meeting places for members of their various religious communities.

The International Year of Peace in 1986 should involve WCRP/International and WCRP regional and national committees in special programmes. It is an ideal opportunity for those concerned to educate for peace.

III. Structures

The Beyond Nairobi Committee recommends that the Governing Board compile a manual of structural procedures for WCRP/International, including clear designations of responsibility and accountability. Further, that they adapt WCRP's legal by-laws to these working procedures. To assist the Governing Board in this, we raise the following questions for their consideration:

1. What is the World Assembly?

    —What is the Assembly's rôle in the structure of WCRP?

    —How is it constituted, how are its members defined and nominated?

2. What is the relationship between the Corporation and the World Assembly?

3. What are the responsibilities of the various elected members of the decision-making structures and what are the procedures for elections?

4. What are WCRP's criteria for membership? (Local branches should particularly consider this.)

5. What is the relationship between the Governing Board, the Executive Committee, and the Secretary-General?

6. What is the relationship between regional officers and the Secretary-General?

7. What is the rôle of the International Council? How are its members designated?

8. What are the functions of the Secretary-General?

9. What are the lines of communication between all these bodies?

10. To what extent are practical projects, carried out under the auspices of WCRP, answerable to the Governing Board or the Secretary-General and to what extent are local projects autonomous?

11. How can the structures be modified to allow full participation of youth? (The report of the Preparatory Youth Meeting to WCRP IV recommends WCRP to establish an international youth committee, with constitutional status within WCRP.)

12. How will adequate representation of women be assured in all levels of WCRP structures and in all programmes and activities?

13. What is the relationship of WCRP with other international and local organizations? What criteria should be developed to define these relationships?

14. Could consideration be given to having an editor of publications for WCRP?

15. Can publications in French and other WCRP official languages be envisaged?

16. Is it valid that the number of branches in a region be used as the criteria for representation on the International Council? Will the number of persons on the International Council be increased as the branches increase?

17. Will the yearly meeting of the Governing Board include, among other things:
    a. a review of the performances of the Secretary-General in the light of the established goals of WCRP?
    b. an establishment of objectives for the coming year for the Secretary-General?
    c. receipt of an audit based on standard accounting procedures?

d. progress reports on the activities and development of regional and/or national WCRP committees?

Appended to this report is the structural organization of WCRP/International developed by the Nominating Committee which based its work on the Report of the Commission on the Future.

Concluding Remarks

In his Presidential Address, Archbishop Fernandes said: "In the heart of every person there is a peace movement, a search for harmony as the only real task of life . . . a thirst we must mutually intensify for justice and peace, for living and growing together as brothers and sisters of the human family." It is in this spirit that we commend our suggestions to you regarding the Programme Areas of WCRP Beyond Nairobi. We are excited by our participation in WCRP's work to "usher in a new era in human relations based on truth, freedom, justice and love".

Appointments for Officers, Committee and International Council Members of WCRP/International

(Adopted by the Fourth World Assembly,
Nairobi, Kenya, on August 31, 1984)

(Proposed by Dr. Levy (Canada) and Seconded by Dr. Habibur Rahman
Khan (Pakistan) and Adopted Unanimously)

A. Honorary Presidents
1. Sri R.R. Diwakar (Hindu, India)
2. Dr. Dana McLean Greeley (Christian, U.S.A.)
3. President Nikkyo Niwano (Buddhist, Japan)

B. President Emeritus
Archbishop Angelo Fernandes (Christian, India)

C. Presidents
1. Dr. M. Aram (Hindu, India)
2. Metropolitan Filaret (Christian, U.S.S.R.)
3. Dr. Inamullah Khan (Muslim, Pakistan)
4. Mrs. Norma Levitt (Jewish, U.S.A.)
5. Rev. Toshio Miyake (Shintoist, Japan)
6. Dr. Adamou Ndam Njoya (Muslim, Cameroun)
7. Mme Jacqueline Rougé (Christian, France)

*8. Rector Soedjatmoko (Muslim, Indonesia)
 9. Bishop Desmond Tutu (Christian, South Africa)
 10. Mr. Zhao Puchu (Buddhist, People's Republic of China)

D. Governing Board
    (All the above Presidents are eligible to attend)
 1. Dr. Inamullah Khan, Chairman (Muslim, Pakistan)
 2. WCRP/Japan: Rev. Yasusaburo Tazawa (Shintoist, Japan)
 3. Nominee of WCRP/USA-WCRP/Canada
 4. Nominee of ACRP
 5. Nominee of WCRP/Europe
 6. Nominee of WCRP/Africa
 7. Rev. Toshio Miyake, Chairman of Finance Committee (Shintoist, Japan)
 8. Rev. Jonathan Blake for WCRP IV Youth (Christian, U.K.)
 9. One Youth according to location of meeting.
 10. Secretary to Governing Committee.

E. Executive Committee
 1. Chairman of Governing Board
 2. Chairman of Finance Committee
3–5. Appointed persons (including Youth)
NOTE: The International Council on 1 September, appointed Mme Rougé, Mrs. Levitt, and Rev. Blake.

F. Finance Committee
 1. Rev. Toshio Miyake (Shintoist, Japan)
 2. Prof. Dr. Norbert Klaes (Christian, Federal Republic of Germany)
 3. Rev. Donald Harrington (Christian, U.S.A.)
 4. Plus, if required, Financial Advisors to Executive Committee:
    a) Dr. Landrum Bolling (Christian, U.S.A.)
    b) Mr. Wilbert Forker (Christian (Bahamas/U.K.)
    c) Rev. Motoyuki Naganuma (Buddhist, Japan)
    d) Mr. Tarlok S. Nandhra (Sikh, Kenya)

G. International Council
All the above Presidents and Committee Members, and Presidents/
Secretaries and/or Treasurers or regional and national bodies (indicated

---

*–Dr. Soedjatmoko was unable to accept the nomination.

by " * ") are eligible to attend. Other persons may be consulted or invited with the view to broadening the spectrum, particularly the religious one.

Africa

1. Prof. Musa O. Abdul (Muslim, Nigeria)
2. Bishop Gabriel Ganaka (Christian, Nigeria)
3. Mrs. Joyce Kaddu (Christian, Uganda)
4. Mr. Badru Kateregga (Muslim, Kenya)
5. Rev. Stanley Mogoba (Christian, South Africa)
6. Rev. Englebert Mveng (Christian, Cameroun)
7. Mr. Tarlok S. Nandhra (Sikh, Kenya)
*8. Bishop J. Henry Okullu (Christian, Kenya)
9. Mr. P.S. Saini (Hindu, Kenya)
10. Bishop Peter K. Sarpong (Christian, Ghana)
11. Prof. El-Sayed Al-Taftazani (Muslim, Egypt)

Asia

12. Mrs. Husna Akhtar (Muslim, Bangladesh)
13. Charukeerty Bhattarak Swamiji (Jain, India)
14. Buddhist from Japan.
15. Buddhist from Japan.
16. Chinese.
‡17. Dr. André Chouraqui (Jewish, Israel)
18. Mr. Jack Cohen (Jewish, Israel)
19. Sri Shrivatsa Goswami (Hindu, India)
20. Ven. Veerendra Heggade (Jain, India)
21. Dastoor Monochehr Homji (Zoroastrian, India)
22. Prof. Yoshiaki Iisaka (Christian, Japan)
*23. Priest Kiyotoshi Kawai (Shintoist, Japan)
*24. Dr. Habibur Rahman Khan (Muslim, Pakistan)
*25. Judge Sathitya Lengthaisong (Buddhist, Thailand)
*26. Mr. Harun Lukman (Muslim, Indonesia)
*27. Ven. Visuddhananda Mahathero (Buddhist, Bangladesh)
*28. Dr. S.G. Mudgal (Hindu, India)
*29. Mrs. Gedong Bagoes Oka (Hindu, Indonesia)
30. Mrs. Prabhat Sobha Pandit (Hindu, India)
31. Archbishop Peter Seiichi Shirayanagi (Christian, Japan)
*32. Mr. Mehervan Singh (Sikh, Singapore)

Dr. Chouraqui did not accept the nomination.

33. Rev. Yasusaburo Tazawa (Shintoist, Japan)
34. Dr. Anaruddha Thera (Buddhist, Sri Lanka)
*35. Major-General Sujan Singh Uban (Sikh, India)
36. Mrs. Jean Zaru (Christian, West Bank of Jordan)

Oceania

37. Rev. Philip Huggins (Christian, Australia)

Latin America

38. Rev. Christian Precht (Christian, Chile)

North America

39. Bishop Rémi De Roo (Christian, Canada)
40. Dr. Ms. Diana Eck (Christian, U.S.A.)
41. Dr. Viqar A. Hamdani (Muslim, U.S.A.)
42. Sr. Marjorie Keenan (Christian, U.S.A.)
43. Prof. Jamshed Mavalwala (Zoroastrian, Canada)
44. Bishop Francis Quinn (Christian, U.S.A.)
45. Sr. Layla Raphael (Christian, Canada)
46. Dr. George Rupp (Christian, U.S.A.)
47. Rev. Robert Smylie (Christian, U.S.A.)
48. Mr. Art Solomon (Native Religion, Canada)
49. Dr. Malcolm Sutherland (Christian, U.S.A.)
*50. Rev. Kenryu Tsuji (Buddhist, U.S.A.)
*51. Office Holder of WCRP/Canada (if applicable).

Europe

52. Dr. Smail Balic (Muslim, Austria)
53. Dr. Alexy Bouevsky (Christian, U.S.S.R.)
*54. Dr. P.H.J.M. Camps (Christian, Netherlands)
55. Miss Natalia Dallapiccola (Christian, Italy)
56. Dr. Mrs. Anezka Ebertova (Christian, Czechoslovakia)
57. Rabbi Albert Friedlander (Jewish, U.K.)
*58. Prof. Dr. Norbert Klaes (Christian, Federal Republic of Germany)
59. Mr. Bindu Konnur (Hindu, U.K.)
60. Prof. Harmindar Singh (Sikh, U.K.)
61. Mr. Jerzy Turowicz (Christian, Poland)
*62.. Canon Gordon Wilson (Christian, U.K.)
63. Bishop Anastasios Yannoulatos (Christian, Greece)

64.   Dr. Rifat Yücelten (Muslim, Cyprus)

H.   Secretary-General Emeritus
Dr. Homer A. Jack (Christian, U.S.A.)

I.   Secretary-General
Dr. John B. Taylor (Christian, U.K.)

55

Proposals for WCRP
Multi-Religious Projects

1. Projects for Refugees and Drought Victims in Kenya and Elsewhere in Africa

Purpose: To mobilize the understanding and practical response of the WCRP network and other organizations and individuals of all religious traditions, to help to alleviate the tragedy caused by the increasing phenomenon of political and economic refugees in Africa, not least in Kenya.

Method: WCRP will take expert advice to identify existing or potential projects and will help these to achieve their goal.

Costs: There should be commitments to raise $400,000 (KSh. 6 million) within one year with pledges to receive at least 2/3 of this amount at WCRP IV.

Administration: A Board of Trustees should be appointed by the new Governing board of WCRP/International; a committee of administration, perhaps from some existing agency, should be identified by WCRP/Africa.

2. A Project for Reconciliation in Northern India

Purpose: To bring people of different religions, especially young people, from India, Pakistan, Bangladesh and Sri Lanka together with others from East Africa, East Asia, Europe and the Americas, to work together on a project of humanitarian concern in a particular location and to reflect together on the motivation for and obstacles to for such work.

Method: A small multi-religious team, made up by mainly Indians, working together with the people in a local, probably rural, situation should enlist the help of a wider international group of experts and volunteers, mainly young people, who should devote at least one month to a practical project and then at least one week to reflecting upon their experiences.

Costs: In order to involve local people over one year an amount of $60,000 would be needed; an international youth camp and conference would cost a further $40,000; and it is already included in the budget.

Administration: The WCRP/India committee, in cooperation with ACRP and WCRP/International, should give general oversight to the programme but a local committee of local people of all religions should be given the fullest possible voice in drawing up their priorities and styles of work.

3. The New York Office of WCRP/International

Purpose: To renew the appropriate representation of WCRP concerns at UN Headquarters in New York through official administrative facilities, regular presence of associate secretaries-general, ideally of various religious backgrounds, and possibilities for hospitality to visiting consultants, or WCRP representatives.

Method: As well as a full-time office administrator, two or three part-time associate secretaries-general and/or research consultants should be engaged or their secondment secured from various religious or peace organisations.

Costs: In addition to the $65,000 proposal in the 1985 budget which would cover only one administrator and one half-time associate secretary-general, general resources would be needed to facilitate travel and hospitality for further appointments or seconded staff.

Administration: WCRP/USA would share the facilities of this office and would contribute both financially and managerially to its maintenance and expansion.

4. Further Local Projects

In the follow-up of the Fourth Assembly of WCRP/International all regional and local groups are encouraged to identify inter-religious projects, in peace education, promotion of disarmament (including visits to nuclear capitals), and resolution of conflicts and tension. Proposals or requests for support from other WCRP chapters or conferences should be channelled, where possible and appropriate, through the International Office which has already identified various possible funding sources for such projects.

K.

RELIGIOUS SERVICES

56

The Opening Multi-Religious Service, Kenyatta International Conference Centre

Opening Songs

Greetings and Opening Address

The Honourable Minister of State in the Office of the President, who is our Guest of Honour this morning, all the distinguished guests, both ladies and gentlemen, my dear participants at this Fourth Assembly of World Conference on Religion and Peace, I wish to greet you all in the name of God the Creator, God the Redeemer and God the Sanctifier.

On behalf of the Africa Chapter of the World Conference on Religion and Peace, which it has been my privilege to serve as President, we warmly welcome you to this Assembly. I wish to welcome you, too, to Kenya on behalf of the many religious people and particularly those who are sitting with us in this hall this morning.

The five hundred or so participants are assembled in Nairobi, Africa, for the first time in the life of this religious movement for peace and justice in the world. We are going to be working under the theme 'Religions for Human Dignity and World Peace'. But before we enter into our work for the next several days, we wish to invite the help of the Almighty God the energizer. We will do this in an act of worship led by different religious leaders sitting with me here. Now listen to what God says: "Be still and know that I am God".

Jewish Prayer

Prayer for the President and the
Government of the Republic of Kenya

He who giveth salvation unto Kings and dominion unto Rulers, Whose kingdom is an everlasting kingdom, may He bless Our

President His Excellency Daniel Arap Moi, the Vice-President, and the Government of the Republic of Kenya.
May the Supreme King of Kings in His mercy preserve them in life, guard them and deliver them from all trouble and sorrow. May He put a spirit of wisdom and understanding into their hearts and into the hearts of all their counsellors, so that they may maintain the peace of the Republic, advance the welfare of the Nation, and deal kindly and truly with all Israel. In their days and in ours, may our Heavenly Father spread the Tabernacle of peace over all the dwellers on earth. And let us say AMEN.

Prayer from the Torah
And this is the Law which Moses set before the children of Israel, according to the commandment of the Lord by the hand of Moses. It is a tree of life to them that grasp it, and of them that uphold it every one is rendered happy. Its ways are ways of pleasantness, and all its paths are peace. Length of days is in its right hand: in its left hand are riches and honour. It pleased the Lord, for His righteousness' sake, to magnify the law and to make it honourable.

Blessing of the Priests
Our God and God of our Fathers, bless us with the threefold blessing of the Law written by the hand of Moses Thy servant, which was spoken by Aaron and his sons, the priests, Thy holy people, as it is said,
'The Lord bless thee, and keep thee:
the Lord make His face to shine upon thee,
and be gracious unto thee:
the Lord turn His face unto thee and give thee peace.'

The Talmud says
Rabbi Eleazer said in the name of Rabbi Chanina: The scholars of Torah increase peace throughout the world as it is said, "And all thy children shall be taught of the Lord; and great shall be the peace of thy children (Banayich)." Read not here Banayich, i.e. thy children, but bonayich, i.e. thy builders. Those who have Thy law enjoy a great peace and do not stumble. May peace and prosperity be within Thy palaces. I speak of peace for the sake of my brethren, my friends, and the entire house of the Lord.
The Lord will give strength unto His people and bless them with peace.

Hindu Prayer
O, God!
Lead us to the noble path of Devotion and Grace.

O, Lord!
Thou knoweth all our deeds,

Remove from us all our vices and sins.
We offer in every way our homage and salutation to Thee.

O, Ruler and Supporter of all!
In all these worlds created,
there is none besides Thee who pervades them fully.
Whatever desires we have, we offer them unto Thee.
May they be fulfilled with Thy grace,
May we become the master of Thy love.
May there be Peace, Justice, Truth,
Freedom and Love in this world.

May there be Peace, Peace and Peace!
OM, SHANTI, SHANTI, SHANTI!

Meditation

All over the world, officials and simple people are longing, arguing, crying for peace. Nevertheless, very often one feels that the various proclamations for peace of some of the powerful of the earth are rather masks to cover their own selfish interests.

1. We, all people of faith, have to raise a voice of protest against any kind of this international hypocrisy. We have to emphasize—through creative thinking and action—that peace is not an autonomous entity. It cannot develop alone; it is interrelated with other important values of life. And first of all *with justice*. Peace is a fruit of righteousness and genuine desire for world justice. An unjust, an unright world cannot speak and expect peace.

2. The religious experience points to the heart of the problem, revealing that the real opposite of peace is not war, but *egoism;* personal, communal, national, racial egoism. There is to be found the root of the threat against peace. This should be given more serious attention and effort.

3. The religious experience is confined not only to ethical guidelines; it offers the vision and the spiritual power that continuously overcomes, even destroys egoism; the power of *love*. And speaking as a Christian, I could say the power of the living God who is Love, of Christ who revealed to us the unselfish love, the power of the Spirit who is radiating eternal love in concrete situations, places and times. The God of Love is the God of peace.

4. Authentic religious thinking and life offer an indisputable contribution to the issue of peace that nothing else can replace.

Religious experience speaks about, and aims towards a *perfect peace*, deep, catholic; not conventional, superficial, limited in only some areas. A perfect peace with others, with nature, within ourselves, with God, the Ultimate Reality; a peace embracing everything, everybody, radiating in the whole universe.

307

Sikh Prayer

Almighty God! You are the Master, we pray to You.
The physical body we live in is Your gift to us,
You are our Father and Mother, we are Your children,
Through Your grace and blessings we enjoy many temporal boons.

O God, no one knows Your limits, You are the Highest of all,
The whole universe functions in Your command,
It is Your creation and sustains in Your obedience,
You know all Your Laws of its perpetual motion,
Says Guru Nanak: he shall ever be His sacrifice,
And he who worships and meditates with a true heart,
On the name of Almighty God, finds eternal peace and grace.

Muslim Prayer

O Lord of peace, grant us the wisdom to follow the path of peace as exhibited by our Prophet Muhammad (Peace Be Upon Him) and all other Prophets before him (Peace Be Upon All Of Them).

Almighty God, subdue our inclination to evil and injustice, fill our hearts with justice, truth and peace both individually and severally, internally and externally.

O Benevolent Lord, guide all the men of religion gathered here and beyond and make them the real instrument that will bring together all the peoples of the World in working for the implementation of a lasting international peace in Your name, in order to make our world a better place to live in—a place where man can regain his lost human dignity, equality and universal brotherhood, a world as You wanted it to be!

May God's peace and blessings be upon all of you! Wassalaam.

Catholic Christian Prayer

In the name of the Father, and of the Son, and of the Holy Spirit, Amen.

Reading from the Bible

"Glory be to God in the highest and peace to His people on earth".
(Gospel according to St Luke II, 14)

"But now in Christ Jesus, you that used to be so far apart from us have been brought very close by the blood of Christ. For He is the peace between us and has made the two into one, and has broken down the barriers which used to keep them apart; actually destroying in His own person the hostility caused by the rules and decrees of the Law. This was to create one single humanity in himself, out of the two of them; and by restoring peace through the cross to unite them both in a single body and reconcile them with God in His own person, He killed

the hostility. Later He came to bring the good news of peace: peace to you who were far away, and peace to those who were here at hand."
(Letter of St. Paul to the Ephesians II, 13–17)

Prayers for Peace

"I leave you peace, my peace I give you", Christ tells us.
Peace with the Lord means love to Him and love to our neighbour.
Let us pray.
God our Father, our Creator and Redeemer,
You sent Your Son to make us know Your will,
Your peace means loving You and loving our neighbour.
Your peace means to be one among ourselves.
With humility and clean heart we ask You:
You are the Prince of love and peace,
You, who have gathered us here
And in Your name we are going to discuss religion,
The source of peace in the human society.
We ask you to send out Your Holy Spirit
That our discussions and resolutions may be of great credibility
to all of us,
To the whole humanity and therefore for Your grace and glory on earth.

Lead us from death to life,
  from falsehood to truth.
Lead us from despair to hope,
  from fear to trust.
Lead us from hate to love,
  from war to peace.
Let peace fill our heart, our world, our universe.
And let us go from here in peace. Amen.

Closing Song: Kum Ba Yah

57

The Buddhist Service*

Adoration to the Buddha
I pay homage to the Most Blessed, free of all blemishes, perfectly Enlightened Buddha!

Refugee in the Triple Gem
I take refuge in the Buddha.
I take refuge in the Doctrine.
I take refuge in the Sangha—the Disciples. (3 times)

Contemplation on the Powers of the Buddhas
The Buddha is thus the Most Blessed as He has cleansed Himself of all defilements, and is perfectly Awakened to the Reality of things; endowed with perfect knowledge and conduct; well-gone, knower of the world; without a peer, tamer of the untamed, teacher of gods and men; thus indeed is the Buddha.

Power of the Doctrine
The doctrine proclaimed by the Buddha has the following virtues and powers:
"Well-proclaimed is the dhamma and rightly lived,
bears fruit here and now.
It is timeless;
It is inviting—'Come and see for yourself!'
Once tasted, leads one onwards yielding expected results.
It is a teaching to be personally experienced by the wise."

Virtues of the Noble Disciples
The noble disciples of the Buddha are well on the Right Path.
They are upright in conduct,

---

*—The services appear in alphabetical order and not in the order that they were presented to the Assembly.

followers of the correct and proper course.
They fall into eight gradations in terms of attainment.
Worthy of offerings are they,
worthy of worship,
worthy of adoration,
unique, and
a worthy field for cultivating merit are they.

UDĀNA (The Unborn)

"There is, monks, a sphere wherein there is neither earth, nor water, nor fire, nor air, nor the infinity of space, nor the infinity of consciousness. That is neither this world, nor the world-beyond; where there is no sun and no moon. That state, monks, do I call neither a coming, nor a going, nor a rising up, nor a falling away. Without evolution, without fixity . . .

That is, indeed, the end of the suffering."

"Hard to see is the infinity, hard to see is the Truth. Craving is eliminated by one who knows. He who sees clings not to anything."

"There is, monks, an unborn, a not-become, a not-made, a not-created, a not-conditioned."

"If there were not, monks, this that is unborn, not-become, not-made, not-conditioned, there is not the liberation from what is born, become, made, and conditioned. But since, monks, there is an unborn, a not become, a not-made, an unconditioned, then therefore he who is born, made, created, conditioned, is able to liberate himself."

Divine Abiding in Universal Compassion

"May all beings be happy and secure; may their hearts be wholesome!

Just as a mother would protect her only child at the risk of her own life, even so let me cultivate a boundless heart towards all beings.

Let my thoughts of boundless love pervade the whole world—above—below—and across—without any obstruction, without any hatred, without any enmity.

Whether I stand, walk, sit or lie down, as long as I am awake
May I be full of this mindfulness.

As it is said, this is the highest conduct for man!

A Special Blessing

"May all blessings be with you
May all divine protection be with you
By the power of all the Buddhas
May you enjoy Peace and Happiness!"

"Let there be rain in due season,
So that plentiful harvest there may be!
May all beings of the world be at Peace,
And the rulers reign in righteousness!"

58

The Christian Worship

Hymn

Now thank we all our God
With hearts and hands and voices
Who wondrous things hath done
In whom His world rejoices;
Who from our mothers' arms
Hath blessed us on our way
With countless gifts of love
And still is ours today.

O may this bounteous God
Through all our life be near us,
With ever-joyful hearts
And blessed peace to cheer us,
And keep us in His grace,
And guide us when perplexed,
And free us from all ills
In this world and the next.

All praise and thanks to God
the Father now be given,
The Son, and Him who reigns
With Them in highest heaven,
The one eternal God,
Whom earth and heaven adore;
For thus it was, is now,
And shall be evermore.

A Reading from the Gospel of St. Mark (Chapter II)

"And He came to Jerusalem and He entered the temple and began to drive out those who bought at the temple; and He overturned the tables of the money-changers and the chairs of those who sold pigeons; and he would not allow anyone to carry anything through the temple. And He taught and said to them: "Is it not written 'My house

312

should be called a house of prayer for all the nations"?; but you have made it a den of robbers". And the chief priest and scribes heard it and sought a way to destroy Him, for they feared Him because all the multitude was astonished at His teaching . . ."

Exposition: Dr. Kwesi Dickson

From the very first day of this conference at the Kenyatta Conference Centre the Secretary-General made a comment which has remained with me, particularly as the comment has been echoed again and again in my Commission. He more or less asked the question: "Is religion part of the problem?" This is what has brought to my mind this particular passage about the driving out of those merchant men from the temple.

There are at least four types of person in this account: there are the religious authorities who were in charge of the system, leaders of thought, those who were in charge of the tradition. They obviously were not ready to let go of their authority, they were in charge and they were ready to see the traditions being operated under any circumstances, and so they were not ready to drive out those who were making things difficult in the temple. As we shall presently see, the system must go on and they were there to make sure it went on.

Then there were the worshippers; these people had come with great enthusiasm to the temple, some of them had come from outside Palestine to worship, and they did not mind going on with their worship, going through the formalities. They did not even mind being exploited: there were these other people in the temple selling their wares, overcharging them, giving them the wrong exchange rate, but they did not mind; they wanted to be sure that they went through the motions of worship.

Then there were the non-Jews, who I suspect were present in the temple at that time. We need to remember that those merchant men had their wares in that part of the temple to which only the non-Jews could go; it did not bother them that they may have spread themselves about so much so that there was very little space for these seekers; it did not bother them that these seekers who would probably wonder about all that was going on and wonder whether indeed they were seeing the essence of the faith in which they were interested.

And then lastly there was Jesus himself. He, throughout his life, challenged the religious authorities; He rode rough-shod over their susceptibilities; He did not teach the way they taught, and people acknowledged His authority. But His authority came from God not from man. Traditions were important then; there were moments when He acknowledged tradition; but He believed that everything must be subordinated to love and understanding.

That is the idea that comes into my mind as we contemplate today and the rest of our stay here: Is religion possibly part of the problem? Do

313

we then go with Jesus Himself, Who loved and yet wanted to make sure that religion did not enslave, but freed. Amen.

Prayers for Peace

Lord, make us instruments of Your peace.
Where there is hatred, let us sow love;
Where there is injury, pardon;
Where there is doubt, faith;
Where there is despair, hope;
Where there is darkness, light;
Where there is sadness, joy.

Lord, help us that we may seek
Not so much to be consoled, as to console;
To be understood, as to understand;
To be loved, as to love;
For it is in giving that we receive;
It is in pardoning that we are pardoned;
And it is in dying that we are born to eternal life.
Lord, make us instruments of Your peace.
Amen.

Closing Prayer and Blessing

Our Gracious Father,
We thank Thee for our coming together here in Nairobi
For the Fourth Assembly of WCRP.
You have given abundance of life and love.
Grant that we do live here as the children of God,
And do love one another as brothers and sisters.
We thank Thee for the precious opportunity for us to live together,
Dine together, talk together, and pray together,
Irrespective of our different backgrounds of religion,
Race, colour, culture, nationality, and so forth.
You have made us closer and dearer to each other
Through this life together.
You have taught us to respect each other
Respond to each other
Love each other
And pray for each other.

O God, our Father,
Make us more peace-loving,
Work harder for peace, sacrifice even more for peace.
And make us the humble instruments of Your great love and peace.
Let us be true friends of the poorest of the poor,
Of the weakest of the weak,
So that the works of love may become the works of peace.

O God,
Please guide us through the rest of the conference
So that this conference may come up with complete actions for peace
And services for our fellow men and women
Who are looking for our help.

O Lord, the King of Peace,
Let Thy peace be with all or none,
In the name of our Lord, Jesus Christ.
Amen.

Psalm 23

The Lord is my shepherd; I shall want nothing.
He makes me lie down in green pastures,
and leads me beside the waters of peace;
He renews life within me,
and for His name's sake guides me in the right path.
Even though I walk through a valley dark as death
I fear no evil, for Thou art with me,
Thy staff and Thy crook are my comfort.

Thou spreadest a table for me in the sight of my enemies;
Thou hast richly bathed my head with oil,
and my cup runs over.
Goodness and love unfailing, these will follow me
all the days of my life,
and I shall dwell in the house of the Lord
my whole life long.

59

The Hindu Service

Lead us from unreal to the Real
Lead us from darkness to Light
Lead us from death to Immortality

This is the ultimate Reality,
This Reality remains so in fullness for all times;
Even if fullness is taken out of fullness,
Fullness remains eternal.

This universe is pervaded by the supreme;
This is the clarion call for the entire humanity,
for all beings, that renunciation is the sole path to bring
the blessings of the Lord Almighty who is omniscient and omnipresent.
May our action, for all times, remain pure so that we do not covet
what belongs to others.

Could it be possible to wipe out sorrow and agony
from the face of this earth?
Yes, there is a way;
The moment we perceive in ourselves the image of the rest of the
creation, and when others similarly perceive me in their thoughts
and action, all agony melts away.
How ever can there exist any lust or sorrow when we are all alone!

Let us all live in perfect harmony—
in action, speech and thought.

We bow to you the very embodiment of Truth—
The Creator, the Personification of Supreme Knowledge—
One who provides sanctuary to all,
One who bestows Salvation,
The Omnipresent and the Eternal.

We bow to you alone;
You are the only One who can receive our prayers,
who can create, preserve and destroy;
You are the Crown of one and all.

You are fierce to the most ferocious.

316

You are the One who comforts all beings,
who confers all honour,
the Greatest, the Loftiest of all the Protectors.

I do not crave for power;
neither heaven nor Salvation do I desire;
But I do ardently desire end to the plight of those afflicted
by sorrow and misery.

May all be free and happy;
May all that is good prevail;
and let there be none with sorrow and suffering.

60

The Jain Service

I bow before the worthy ones (Arhat)—the Jinas;
I bow before the perfected beings (Siddha)—those who have
attained Moksha;
I bow before the mendicant leaders—(Sadhu);
I bow before the mendicant preceptors (Upadhyaya);
I bow before all mendicants (Sadhu) in the world.

I always seek sanctuary at the feet of the perfect liberated souls,
those free from the vicious cycle of birth and death,
bereft of the perversities of birth, decay and death,
the supreme souls venerated alike by the Lords of celestial firmaments
as well as of super-humans;
those who are indeed worshipped by denizens of the three worlds.

Let us bow before the Omniscent Vardhamana Mahavira who showers
benevolence on all beings in the three worlds, from whom emanates
the supremely comforting gospel of exemplary conduct and forbearance, and the dispenser of eternal plenitude.

Dharma—the quality of righteousness—is the fount of all-embracing
happiness and beneficence.

The learned glean Dharma all the while. The supreme bliss of salvation is attained solely through Dharma.

I salute the Dharma.

For mortals enmeshed in the coil of life, there exists no friend other
than Dharma.

The basis of Dharma is the quality of kindness.

I always have my heart set on Dharma.

O Dharma, do protect us.

O Lord, seldom do devotees take sanctuary at your feet out of sheer
love. The horrific world of a multitude of afflictions drives them
to you. The scorching summer sun setting aflame the entire globe
compels the afflicted to seek shelter in the comfort of the moon's rays,
in water or shade. So do those bent down by mountains of sorrow
seek shelter at thy feet.

May people everywhere enjoy the blessings of peace; May the rulers and administrators be strong, efficient, law-abiding and righteous; the rains be timely and adequate, all ailments and diseases disappear, no one in the world be even for a moment afflicted with famine or scarcity, with theft, loot, plunder and devastation, or with epidemics and pestilences. May the Lord Jina's wheel of righteousness (Dharmachakra), constantly confer the boon of bliss on all, everywhere.

May the Lord Jina bestow peace on the devoted, the pious, the saints and all the ascetic aspirants, on the land, the nation, the city and the state, the rulers and the people.

Let peace come to the virtuous who follow the dispensation of the Jina. May the ascetics in constant penance with desire to attain salvation be blessed with peace.

May the saints who have attained spiritual eminence by overcoming the bondage of attachments realize peace. And peace be on the seers of tranquil mind.

O Lord Jina, we the representatives of different religions assembled here, pray at thy feet for world peace and happiness to all.

O Lord Jina, you know that all are not for cruelty, but a few, who have forgotten you, are in blissful ignorance. We all pray together to give such of those our awareness of the miseries of war and transform their minds.

O Lord Jina, we hope ardently that our efforts will be fructified by Thy unbounded Grace and mercy to save humanity from disasters.

O Lord Jina, pardon us, by Thy supreme forgiveness, if anything we have done against Thy will, keep on blessing us as ever.

Lord Jina, Thou art the preceptor of Peace Eternal; May the blessings lead humanity away from destructive warfare, blind prejudices, and animosities between brotherly nations.

O Lord, may the world torn today by futile conflict among brothers, see the light of thy guidance leading to world peace. May the world be freed from the horror of armaments and be led by Thy blessings to the path of universal disarmament.

O Lord Jina, may the men and women of all nations be blessed with souls untainted by difference of colours, race or creed and be redeemed from the false skin-deep distinction of black or white. May discriminations and barriers dividing humanity disappear altogether with the eternal light of Thy purifying message.

O Lord, may people everywhere see the wisdom of non-violence, the quality of each soul. May our innate desire for co-operation and co-existence dispel the clouds of misunderstanding and suspicion.

Let our prayer this day, Our Lord, crown the efforts of religion for peace with sure success, whatever be the impediments. O Lord, Jina of infinite bliss and peace, do guide us to universal brotherhood and peace.

OM SHANTI, OM SHANTI, OM SHANTI

61

The Jewish Sabbath Service

Opening Prayer

O come, let us exult before the Lord. Let us shout for joy to the Rock of our salvation. He is our God, our Shepherd, Who leads us into pastures of peace. We are the people of His pasture, united in the quest for peace, longing for the coming of the Sabbath, the universal Sabbath of peace for all humanity. As evening approaches, we yearn for the Sabbath, as the dry land around us yearns for the life-giving rain. We need the visions of peace, we need the knowledge which unites us as one community assembled together in love and friendship. Let not our hearts be hardened as at Meribah, as in the days of Massah in the wilderness. But let us sing a new song unto the Lord; let all the earth sing and bless His name.

Barchu and Sh'ma (The Call to Worship and Proclamation of the One God)

And thou shalt love the Lord thy God with all thine heart, and with all thy soul, and with all thy might. And these words which I command thee this day, shall be upon thine heart: and thou shalt teach them diligently unto thy children, and shalt talk of them when thou sittest in thine house, and when thou walkest by the way, and when thou liest down, and when thou risest up. And thou shalt bind for a sign upon thy hand, and they shall be for frontlets between thine eyes. And thou shalt write them upon the doorposts of thy house, and upon thy gates.

(Deuteronomium 6:5–9)

A Prayer for Rest and Peace

Cause us to lie down in peace, O Lord our God, and to rise up unto life, O our King; and spread over us the tabernacle of Thy peace; direct us properly by Thine own good counsel; save us for Thy name's sake, be Thou a shield about us; remove from us every enemy, pestilence, sword, famine and sorrow. In this time, in this place, we pray particularly for the end of famine and drought, for the beginning of redemption and the renewal of love and comradeship. May all adver-

321

saries of peace—before us, behind us—may they speedily surrender to the vision of peace which fills us with the approach of the Sabbath. May all find shelter beneath the shadow of Thy wings, O Lord; for Thou art our Guardian and our Deliverer. Guard our going out and our coming in for life and for peace from this time forth and for ever more. O Lord, spread over us the tabernacle of Thy peace. Blessed art Thou O Lord, Who spreadest the tabernacle of peace over us and over all Thy people Israel and over Jerusalem.

The Amidall (Standing prayer)

Recited in Hebrew, which includes and ends with a silent, standing meditation.

The Aleynu Prayer

We therefore hope in Thee, O Lord our God, that we may speedily see the glory of Thy might, when Thou wilt remove the abominations from the world, when the world will be perfected under the kingdom of the Almighty, when all the children of flesh will call upon Thy name, and when Thou wilt turn unto Thyself all the wicked of the earth. Let all inhabitants of the world perceive and know that unto Thee every knee must bow, every tongue must swear. Let all bow before Thee and honour Thy name. Reign over them speedily, for ever and ever. For the kingdom is Thine and to all eternity Thou wilt reign in glory; as it is written in Thy Law: the Lord will reign for ever and ever. And it is said: And the Lord shall be king over all the earth; in that day shall the Lord be One, and His name One.

Kaddish

The Sabbath Lights Are Kindled

We praise You, O Lord, for the light of the Sabbath which fills our home and shines out into the world; we praise You for the spirit of peace which enters our hearts; we praise You, O Lord our God, King of the universe, Who has sanctified us by the commandments, and has ordained that we should light the Sabbath candles.

Sanctification of Wine

Blessed art Thou, O Lord our God, King of the universe, Who createst the Fruit of the vine. Blessed art Thou, O Lord our God, King of the universe, Who has sanctified us by Thy commandments and hast taken pleasure in us, and in love and favour hast given us Thy holy Sabbath as an inheritance, a memorial of the creation—that day also being the first of the holy convocations in remembrance of leaving Egypt. Sanctified, chosen, given the holy Sabbath in love, we bless Thee, O Lord, Who hallows the Sabbath.

Closing Blessing

62

The Muslim Service

In The Name of Allah-God, Most Gracious, Most Merciful.
The praise of all, and of everything existent
Pertains alone to Allah, Most Munificent,
Almighty, Merciful and Most Beneficent,
Of the whole existence the only Lord and Creator,
The Perfector of the universe entire,
Ordainer of Divine Justice here and hereafter.
Only Thee, O Almighty Allah, we adore,
And only Thy help we do always implore,
Lead us in the right way, the way of those whom with
Grace Thou protected, enlightened,
Empowered and made victors,
Thou saved and blessed; and never, O Lord, never in the way
Of those upon whom Thou hurled indignation and curse,
Nor of those who malignantly, mercilessly disregard
Thy orders,
Nor the unrighteous way of strays and traitors.

O men, know your Lord, love Him, obey Him,
Sincerely worship Him and perform good and virtuous deeds,
These shall be the dawn of peace...
Know that Lord-Allah is almighty and eternal,
He is the Commander of peace and happiness,
The single Owner of All-Holiness.
The sole Ruler of the whole universe,
Allah is Greater, Higher and Mightier than all,
Without any failure or decline or fall.
The sole Creator,
The Eternal Source of order, peace and progress.

O men, worship and obey your Lord,
Love Him, pray Him, and follow His light, His word;
He created you and made you supreme in the world,
He gave you means to uphold the right and good,
He prepared this world with every means,

For you, of happiness, peace, delight and ease.
All natural powers shall obey and serve you,
The earth, its riches and beauties, shall be yours;
All for your life and joy there you may obtain,
Arts, knowledge, science, wisdom you may gain.
Allah created the heavens with myriads of suns and stars
To light, to guide, to teach, to show His wonders;
To guide, for mankind, to virtue and eternal Bliss;
To endless advancement and perfection real,
Universal, enduring prosperity and lasting peace.
All these are, surely, the right, The Light of the Lord.

O Nations fallen, O peoples in disaster,
Sincerely follow My orders, and do not despair,
You shall rise, you shall conquer, you shall prosper,
Determinedly avoid sin, evil and crime,
Perform good and virtuous deeds, be pure and clean.
Who work for the happiness, peace and progress of Man,
Shall have peace and paradise here and hereafter,
According to the good they do to others.
This life is short, this world is transient,
Do not prefer the fleeting to the permanent;
Leave earthly glories and unclean ambitions,
Avoid unjust desires, and impure passions.
God gave you a share, entrusted you with duties,
High and low, rich and poor, you have opportunities,
And proportionate responsibilities,
Every action, good or bad, every thought or scheme,
Anywhere in the universe, is known to Him;
He shall judge and recompense in full,
Shall reward every good and punish every evil.
And true believers shall be saved and blessed,
In bliss and paradise the highest placed,
Shall win everlasting peace, brightest victories,
Shall be adorned with never-fading glories.
Their enemies shall be baffled and disappointed.

O nations, by Divine Rules, you shall attain
The highest prosperity, peace and perfection;
These Rules, Unalterable and Divine,
Shall be foundations of real peace and civilization.
Believe in God, trust His Prophets,
Bestow upon other of what God grants you;
You shall have Peace everlasting and ever-new.
God commands His Prophets to lead mankind in all time,
To warn men to know and obey their Creator, their Lord Supreme;
To be just and righteous, to be virtuous and pure;
To be clean in body and soul, to strive to rise and to rise higher;

To respect the rights and life and chastity of each one;
To treat with justice and honesty each man and each woman;
To guard the orphan, to help the needy and the destitute;
To endeavour to learn more, to gain more, and to do more good;
To be merciful and temperate, and to fear the Lord.
His peace and justice shall shine forth and enlighten every action,
He shall judge, reward with peace, without exception.
All shall be weighed and recompensed in exact proportion,
All shall have their due with equality and equation.
Love Him, trust Him, worship Him, and never despair,
Believe Him, serve Him, follow Him, He is all believers' Protector.
CONSIDER:
He created man, gave him life, strength, the senses and reason,
Gave him the power of speech, and many means for expression;
Consider all inscribed by milliards of creatures
In the countless world of the limitless universes;
The Holy Books revealed by Supremest Creator
To save humanity from darkness, disaster and error.

CONSIDER:
Ten Commandments and countless Apostles,
And all the Books which GOD has sent to guide peoples
to His sacred religion, to truth, peace and justice,
To save all mankind from ignorance, vice and violence.
CONSIDER:
He is the Source of knowledge, existence, peace and justice,
The Enlightener of every world and space,
The Creator of countless worlds, moons, stars and suns,
The Originator of every good, peace and perfection,
The Guider to the right, to useful invention;
The Guardian of the faithful and the good,
The Chastiser of the unrighteous and wicked;
The Energizer of every motion and movement;
The Preserver of numberless existences;
The Sustainer of myriads of organisms and lives,
He raises and lowers, enriches and deprives.
The high, the low, poor, strong, weak, young, old,
King, slave, free and serf, the ruler and the ruled,
White and black
Are all equal before the justice of God, Allah.
. . .
Let us all trust God, do our best, follow His Word,
His light;
At every step we shall find new strength, new delight,
New energy, new wisdom, new wonders, new light and peace.
There is no end to the good you can do and prepare,
No end to the highest to which you can soar;

In every good cause God shall give you power,
Your will and work shall raise you higher and higher.
O nations, strive with all your might to rise higher;
Believe in God and your deeds shall shine brighter,
Thank God, work hard, be not idle and never despair.
Strive harder and harder to defeat ignorance, vice and violence,
Love God with all your heart, and trust in His promise.
He has sent His Books and Prophets to guide you to truth
To chastity and cleanliness, to justice, health, peace and happiness,
You shall for ever live in delight and peace.
The Light of God shall shine in all true hearts,
The Love of God shall bring peace to you all,
The Word of God shall rule from pole to pole,
Bright angels of God, innocent and pure,
Shall fill with peace and happiness the world's air;
The whole world shall obey the word of God
All men shall be happy, all hearts shall be in peace.
New powers, new force, new inventions,
New feelings, new instruments, new institutions,
Shall bring to all peoples happiness and peace,
All men shall taste equality, peace and justice.
Injustice shall be unknown, tyranny undermined,
War and slaughter, immorality, vice and violence,
Entirely wiped away from every mind in every place.
O Nations, know and obey and remember the orders of
Almighty Creator,
Be kind and good to every man and creature.
Nothing shall remain secret, nothing hidden.
All shall have every peace, delight and pleasure,
All shall have help, brotherhood, peace and unity.
He will lead you to purity and perfection,
He will lead to light, peace, progress and exaltation.
He will be a blessing to all humanity
He will bring peace and prosperity,
To all He will secure justice and equality,
The rights of man, and moral sanctity,
Universal help and generosity,
Universal peace and prosperity.

O peoples and nations, far and near, in every region
Of East and West, North and South by thousands and millions
Shall join the sacred brotherhood of true union of divine origin
Whole peoples and Nations shall taste equality and peace,
All mankind shall find honour, truth, peace and justice.
O Lord, keep us from every sin and crime and error,
Let us return to you clean and chaste and pure.
Keep us from harmful influence of everything

Dead or alive, cold or hot, dry or living;
Keep us from darkness and ignorance,
From idle thoughts, from vice and superstitions;
Guard us from the dark purpose of evil men,
From intrigues of misleading men and women;
Be our Guard, our shield, against all wicked designs
Of those who are cruel, unjust and envious;
Protect us from every harm to our body and soul,
Keep us away from every injustice and evil,
Save us from every enemy, need and trouble;
Give us Heart, O our Lord, to love Thee for ever,
To love Thee, to trust Thee, to serve Thee, and none other,
To live for Thee, to die for Thee, and be with Thee hereafter.
Grant us victory over all intrigues and injustice,
Give us will to withstand all misguidance and malice,
Give us all everlasting happiness and universal peace.

  Let us altogether pray for lasting peace...
Peace for us, and peace for all peoples.

                                                    Amen.

63

The Shintoist Service

I would like to offer a prayer in the Shinto tradition, which is the Japanese ethnic religion. In Japan you find shrines in all villages and towns. We even have a family altar at our home. Every morning we come in front of this altar and pray for the peace of the day, and every evening we come back to express our gratitude for the peaceful day to God and our ancestors.

When Shintoists come to worship, the traditional and classical Eastern music called Danaku is played. Before the prayer the priest must perform Oharai or Purification Ceremony. Let me explain the meaning of this purification ceremony. When we Japanese welcome special guests to our home, we first clean and purify the rooms and the garden, cook delicious food and we are even prepared to play music and to dance; so the Shinto prayer proceeds in the same manner; that is why we have the water purification ceremony before the prayer.

Could you kindly rise and lower your heads, so that through this ceremony the evils and the sins in our minds and bodies will be driven out. Now we ask the deities to descend here for today's prayer. The symbol of the descending deities is the evergreen tree, called Hiromogi, to which the white paper, called Shide, is attached.

The deities in which Shintoists believe are not like the Absolute and Only One God in Christianity, but among the deities there is one who enlightens men, who is the central figure. There are also other deities whose jobs are to take care of the man's life. The souls of the ancestors are also regarded as gods and protect the family. Today we especially ask

---

*The Shinto ritual is performed in front of an evergreen tree, to which white paper is attached: symbol of the descending deities. The service begins with a purification ceremony. Then the priest asks the deities to descend over the place where the assembly is held and prays that they may help and protect its activities. This prayer is followed by the offering of the Holy Breakfast to the deities and a symbolic offering of an evergreen twig taken from the sacred tree. Finally the Norinto prayer is offered.

not only the Japanese deities, but the God protecting the land of Kenya and the spirits of each of your countries to descend here over this place.

Now we proceed to the ceremony, called Tensen, in which we offer the Holy Breakfast to the Deities. We Shintoists offer rice, which is the Japanese staple food, as well as Japanese rice wine, sake; water; and salt; also the food from the seas, the mountain, the river and the field.

Now we offer a Shinto Prayer, called Norinto. Would all of you kindly rise and lower your heads, while Norinto is being performed.

Norinto Prayer

O God. Amaterasu Omikami and the myriad of
Deities of heaven and earth.

Now the fourth World Assembly of WCRP is happening
here in Kenya, a country of natural beauty.

O Deities, please drive out and purify all evils
and sins that we may have.

O You Deities, May our efforts to attain the
holy aim of the Assembly be rewarded.

O God, Please wipe out wars, starvation and
discrimination from our earth.

O You Deities, May the whole world become blessed,
and everyone be happy everywhere.

64

The Sikh Service

Prayer to the One God Who Can Be Realized Through a True Master's Grace

You are the supreme Lord—My prayer is addressed to You;
My soul and body belong to You;
You are my mother and father and I am Your child.
It is through Your kindness that I enjoy many comforts.
No one knows Your total extent;
You are higher than the highest.
The whole creation is linked in Your thread;
Your command runs through the whole universe.
You alone know Your own design.
Nanak—Thy servant is ever a sacrifice unto Thee.

Sikh Formal Congregational Prayer

Firstly remember the almighty God; then dwell upon Guru Nanak, Guru Angad, Guru Amardas and Guru Ramdas For help. Remember Guru Arjan, Hargobind and Harrai. By concentrating on Guru Harkrishnan all pains disappear. By remembrance of Guru Teg Bahadur miraculous powers are attained. O tenth master Guru Gobind Singh protect us everywhere. We do not have words to describe the treasure in our sacred scripture, Guru Granth Sahib, which enshrines the spiritual light of the ten masters.

Mindful of the sacrifices of the four sons of Guru Gobind Singh, His five loved disciples, four redeemed ones and innumerable Men and women martyrs, let us utter "Waheguru".

May your Sikhs be blessed with faith, the Lord's name, and the sacred Bath in Holy Amritsar. Grant us humility, high and noble thinking And protect our honour. . . "Waheguru".

O true master, we are passing through a critical phase of the machine age. Protect us. Grant us wisdom so that remembering You We share our earnings of honest labour with weaker sections. Be steadfast in the Sikh faith and protect the poor and the meek. Let our symbols ever

330

prosper and religion be ever in ascendance,
Let us utter. . . "Waheguru".

Your will has brought many a religious leader from all over the world
For a conference at Nairobi, Africa. We all pray to You to grant peace
and prosperity to our planet. Grant us power so that we can carry the
message of peace to every home. Rid the world of terrible wars and
lead humanity to the path of love In your own light. We have sought
Your help. Be kind to us.

Through the grace of Nanak let our spirits ever remain high, and all
mankind attain bliss.

65

The North American and African Traditional Services
1. From The North American Indigenous Tradition

Offering of the smoke of the Sacred Medicine and statement about how North American indigenous people feel life:

The sacred ways of our people were given to us
by the creator and brought to us by the spirit helpers.
We recognize the creator in his creation
and for that reason everything that has been created is sacred,
the fire and the water and the air that we breathe are sacred,
the plants and the animals, the birds and the fish are sacred;
they were here on the sacred Mother Earth
before there was human life;
they were able to get along very well without us
but we cannot live without them.
So we constantly give thanks that they support our lives.

We look in the sky and we see our Elder Brother Sun
and we give thanks that he is still following
his original instructions;
we know that without him there would be no life on this earth.

We look again in the sky and we see our Grandmother Moon
and the star world
and we know that our Grandmother Moon is still doing her work
to look after all the female life on the earth;
her work is to take care of the fertility of all the female life.

We know that all the medicine to cure human sickness
was put in the plants,
and when we want medicine for our sickness

we have to talk to the plants and given them sacred tobacco
and explain why we have to take their lives
for our healing, or for our food.
If we take the lives of animals or birds or fish
to support our lives
we give thanks to them,
if we travel on water or use water to keep life in our bodies,
we give thanks to the water because it is life,
for nothing can live without it.
We give thanks for the gift of fire because it is sacred;
it was said that when you offer your tobacco to the fire
"I will see your prayers in the smoke."
We give thanks to all of the creation in that way.
It is said that tobacco is one of the sacred elements
that was given to us to pray with,
so this last morning together I burn four sacred elements:
the sacred tobacco, the sage, the cedar and the sacred sweet grass;
these were given to us to pray with.
When we pray this way we say to our people
that we clean ourselves with this sacred smoke,
so that for this short time that we are praying
it is to bring our hearts and minds together as one,
to eliminate all negative thoughts from our hearts and minds
while we pray.

In our way of praying we are more concerned to give thanks
for so much that is given to us
rather than to ask for more,
because everything is given to us freely for our needs;
we pray for our sisters and brothers and our relations
rather than for ourselves,
except to pray for guidance and blessing and protection
so that we can walk in a good way.

This morning I have first washed myself with the smoke
of these sacred things.
Then I offer them to you for a blessing,
then I give thanks to the four Sacred Medicine-Grandfathers,
to our Earth-Mother,
and to the plant life, animal life, bird life and fish life.
I offer the sacred incense to the fire and the water
and to our Elder Brother the Sun
and to our Grandmother-Moon and the sky-world,
and to the thunder People who bring the rain to give life
to all things.
Then I offer the Sacred Smoke to the Spirit-Helpers
and to my Spirit-Helpers
and to the great mystery, the creator of all things.

There are many sacred ceremonies that we have,
like the sun-dance and the sweat-lodge,
and there are many sacred songs that were given
to some of our people by the Spirit-Helpers.

I would like to share with you the story of the Sacred Pipe.
The stone bowl represents all female life in the creation
and the stem that is usually made of wood
represents all male life in the creation;
together they are complete.
When we pray with the Sacred Pipe we offer tobacco
to the four Sacred Medicine-Powers
to the Earth-Mother and to the Spirit-Beings
and we ask them to sit with us and smoke with us;
and we recognize that we need their help and blessing and guidance
to walk in balance.

The story was told that one day
a Spirit-Being came to a village in the form of a human being
and he told the people
that they would be given a new ceremony
to help them in the time ahead;
he explained the ways in which the pipe was to be used
and that it had a lot of power:
it had the power to harm as well as to help,
and when the pipe was used to make a promise
that promise was never to be broken.
That is how all the treaties in North America were made,
and still today none of our people has ever broken a promise
that was made in that way.
The people were told that on a certain day
they were to send out two warriors to a place that was appointed,
two beautiful young men.
They were standing in that place, and off in the distance
they could see something white coming towards them.
When it came close they saw that it was a beautiful young woman
carrying a bundle in her arms.
One of those young men had the wrong kind of thoughts in his mind;
when she came close she turned to the other
and gave him the bundle that she carried.
Then she said to the first one,
"Now you can do what you want."
As he reached out for her, a cloud covered them
and when the cloud went away
all that was left of the young man were his bones on the ground;
the young woman turned and walked away
and off in the distance she turned into a white buffalo calf.
The original Sacred Pipe that was given from the Spirit-World

is still in America today . . .
Today there are many Sacred Pipes
and our people are using them to pray for all the creation,
for the earth and the people,
who are so much in need of healing.

It is clear to us that all of creation
still follows its original instructions,
except the human family,
and that is why we are in so much distress, so out of balance.

I would like to suggest to you that here we have begun to
weave a tapestry of life together;
each of us has brought a thread that is made
from our own understanding, our hope, our dedication,
our faith in God, and our love for our fellow human beings.
As we work here together during these few days
each of us has contrived to weave our own thread
into the fabric of love that we are making here together.
We need to remember that in Nairobi, here in this sacred land,
we have only begun the weaving,
and when we go to our homes we must join with others
who are also weaving their own parts of that fabric of life.
When we have woven them all into one
we can cover the whole world
with a blanket of peace and tranquillity
which derives from love, which is the power of God.

We must perhaps always remember that we are children of God,
no one less important or less precious than another
and that life is given for us to celebrate, not to endure.
And here we have truly celebrated life together
in our prayers, in our laughter, in our work,
and in our many ways of worship to God.
Yes, we have celebrated life together here
in reverence and respect for each other.
We must walk in that way for as long as we walk on this earth.

When the scientists and the technologists
leave off from solving the mysteries of God and of life
and learn instead to have a reverence for His creation,
then we will have arrived.
We need only to know how to walk in peace and tranquillity
in God's creation,
then we will not have to concern ourselves
about hunger and oppression and injustice.
This is not just a dream,
it is a reality that we can make real for all of us
if we have the courage, the determination and the vision
that we have shared here together;

the power to do it has already been given to us,
it is that irresistible, invincible power called love,
which is the essence of God.

My perception of God is that He is the totality and the ecstasy
and the completeness of the two sacred principles that he created,
male and female,
and in all of His creation everything is created in that way.

We must not say or think,
"I am too small, too insignificant, what I do doesn't matter,"
because each of us is vitally important
in this final battle with the power of evil.
My constant prayer to God is to ask
for that great evil power to be diminished and sent away.

Since each of us is a part of the God who created us
then we have a vital interest in changing the world that we live in
so it is vitally important that we do, with our hearts and minds.

I would like to share a story with you:
it is called the prophecy of the seven fires.
It begins when our people lived by the great salt water
(The Atlantic Ocean);
it told about our migration to the west, perhaps over centuries;
it said there would be seven stopping places (called seven fires);
in each of those places we would establish our Sacred Fire,
(The Sacred fire is used only to pray and to make spirit offerings,
our thanksgiving for all life).
Our last stopping place would be beside a great lake
(Lake Superior).
It said also that we would almost lose our sacred ways;
it ends by saying that the people of the Seventh Fire
would be the ones who would retrace their steps
to find the sacred bundles that were left behind.
We have come to see that we are the people who were spoken of,
The People of the Seventh Fire,
and it said that if the Seventh Fire was able
to light the Eighth Fire,
there would be peace on earth for all the creation.

My truth does not invalidate your truth
and your truth does not invalidate mine.

I say to each of you,
"Do not walk in fear but with courage and clear purpose,
because with the power of God, which is already yours,
there is no way else that we can go but win."

Kige manito,
I give thanks for the power and the beauty
and the sacredness of your creation.

336

2. From The African Indigenous Tradition: The Kikuyu Prayer

Elder: O God, You who have put mounts *(while facing in the direction of each mountain respectively)* Kuinyaga, Kianyahi, Kiambiraluru, Kianyandaruwa in their places, do listen to the petitions which we are going to address to You.

Elder: All of you who are gathered here say,
"May God make us love one another."

People: May He make us love one another.

Elder: All of you who have come here say,
"May God bless our children, our sons and daughters."

People: May He bless them abundantly.

Elder: All of you gathered here say,
"May God bring us rain to make crops grow
and grass to sprout for our children and our animals."

People: May He make it fall right away.

Elder: Every one of you standing here say,
"May God protect us all from human and animal diseases."

People: May He protect us from those diseases.

Elder: All of us gathered here, let us say,
"May God bless our land, our President and his ministers, the visitors to our country, especially whose who have been attending this Assembly."

People: May He bestow His blessing upon them.

Elder: All of you say,
"May God grant us all these favours we have implored Him."

People: Thaai, Thathaya Ngayi, thaai
Thaai, Thathaya Ngayi, thaai,
Thaai, Thathaya Ngayi, thaai.

66

The Zoroastrian Service

Three Short Prayers

Ashem Yohu

Righteousness is best of all that is Good
The Radiant Goal it is of life on Earth;
This Light is attained when one lives righteously
For sake of Highest Righteousness alone.

Yatha Ahu Varyo

As the Ruler of the Universe is ABSOLUTE in his Will,
So is the Teacher supreme through his purity.
Whoever does good deeds, as offerings to the Omniscient,
deserves the gift of Benevolent Mind.
Whoever shelters the needy, shall receive authority from the Lord of
Existence.

Yenghe Hatam

Those women and men both do we adore
Whose every act of worship is alive
With Asha, the Eternal Law of Life
Who are in the sight of Ahura Mazda
As best and noblest mortals recognized
These are the truest leaders of Mankind.

Pazend Tandarosti—Benediction

In the name of the Merciful, the Forgiving, and the Compassionate
Lord, we pray.

To lead a long life, Health is an essential element. May the halo of
Righteousness be ever perennial. May the Celestial and the Terrestrial
Yazatsas, the seven Amesha Spentas approach our glorious offerings.
May this, our prayer, and our benedictions be fulfilled. May the relig-
ion of Zarathustra be an eternal source of Joy unto all mortals. O
Lord God Creator of the Universe mayst Thou grant unto the entire
Anjuman and unto all those assembled here in Nairobi, Kenya, to

work for Peace, longest of long life, health and happiness lasting for a thousand years.

May it be so, we pray.

May Thou preserve the leadership of the worthy ones for His sake for many years. May there be thousands and thousands of benedictions. May the Year be auspicious, the day blissful, and this time blessed. May the Spirit of Righteousness pervade all good acts.

Health be unto all
Goodness be unto all
Excellence be unto all

May this be in accord with Thy will, O Ahura Mazda.

67

The Closing Multi-Religious Service, Kenyatta International Conference Centre

Opening Prayer From The Muslim Tradition:
  Dr Adamou Ndam Njoya
God eternal, enlighten my heart for action.
Guide me. Make the ideas discussed in this meeting realities.
Reality is myself.
Reality around me strengthen my heart. Strengthen my mind.
Strengthen my hands to translate these ideas into facts, by my deeds,
  by my words.
Eternal God, You who are fulfilment,
You who have made me follow Your path, You who knew that we
  would be united,
Even when we had no existence, even when there were no creatures
  yet,
You who knew the knowledge we have gained even when we had no
  existence,
You who since the night of times, called me to fellowship,
Eternal God, here we are gathered around Your name,
We, Your creatures, who from all horizons, from all religions, have
  come with the same fervour, with Your name pending on our lips,
  with Your name founded in our souls.
You, Eternal, Eternal God,
Make the ideas discussed in this meeting be spread in the hearts
of all men around us;
Drive away the forces of forgetfulness.
Guide us, so that we may act for You, for You eternal,
For peace to be spread in our world.

O God,
Allah, Allah, Allah.

Acknowledging Our Need For Repentance—
Leader: Rev. Wesley Ariarajah

All: "We acknowledge the painful fact that religion too often has been misused in areas of strife and conflict to intensify division and polarization. Religious people have too often failed to take the lead in speaking to the most important ethical and moral issues of our day, and more importantly, in taking practical steps toward change."

(Nairobi Declaration)

Leader: O God, Whose goodness fills the Earth, and Whose love enfolds all humanity, give us wisdom and understanding so to love You that we may have the power to rise above our limitations to see humankind as one family. Fill our hearts with Your love, that in spite of the various paths we have chosen to reach You, we may join hands to build a human community that seeks peace and pursues it. May the abundance of Your love and the peace that You give fill our hearts, our lives and our universe. Amen.

Moment of Silence

Our Work at Nairobi
The Nairobi Declaration—Leader: Dr. Diana Eck

Leader: The Nairobi Declaration captures the spirit of our work together in WCRP IV. Here at Nairobi, we have renewed our commitment to peace and justice. Let us cite some of the convictions expressed in the words of this Declaration:

"Disarmament has long been a priority for the work of WCRP, and the urgent necessity of working for disarmament today is undiminished."

All: We pledge our determined commitment to disarmament as we continue our work as a Non-Governmental Organization at the United Nations, and as we work to influence our religious communities and our nations.

Leader: "Disarmament means liberation, not only from the arsenals of weapons ready for use, but from the perpetual fear and insecurity which have accompanied our obsession with the instruments of death."

As men and women of religion, we cannot tolerate the priorities of a world in which there are at least three tons of explosives, but not enough food, for every man, woman, and child on earth.

All: We pledge ourselves, through our religious communities and our governments, and through continued WCRP co-operation with the UN radically to reverse these priorities.

341

Leader: "Along with disarmament and development, human rights are an essential part of the total and holistic peace we seek."

All: We reaffirm our commitment to the UN Universal Declaration on Human Rights, and we insist that these rights are the very basis and foundations of a just and humane society . . .

Leader: "Education for peace is more urgent than ever before."

All: As religious men and women, we pledge ourselves to stressing and raising to public consciousness the foundations of peacemaking within our own religious traditions, through education in temples, churches, mosques, synagogues, and homes.

Leader: "We need to understand one another."

All: We need one another in order to see and understand ourselves more clearly. And we need one another in order to undertake together work that will require the resources and energies of people throughout the world.

The spiritual resources of our religious traditions give us strength to dedicate ourselves to the task ahead. We are compelled to turn the faith and hope that sustains us into dynamic action for human dignity and world peace.

Thankfulness For What Has Been Achieved
Reasons to be thankful: Dr. John B. Taylor

We are thankful for what has just been received.
We are thankful for travelling mercies that brought us here safely.
We are thankful for friendships that have been made,
Especially where we never expected those friendships to be forged.
We are thankful for the warmth and welcome of the local people here
And we hope that those friendships will continue.
We are thankful for the ideas that have been brought to us,
New ideas, but also a confirmation of those oldest and most tradi-
    tional, and most precious ideas in our respective religious traditions,
    as we have struggled together for peace with justice.
We are thankful too for the sense of solidarity with those who could
    not be with us,
    Some through sickness, some because they were detained,
    Some because they could not afford to come.
We are thankful for our fellowship here,
And for the wider fellowship with all our human fellows.

Prayer: Rev. Nikkyo Niwano

We take refuge in the Buddha!
May we with all other beings experience the
Great Way and awake to the unsurpassable intention.

We take refuge in the Law!
May we with all other beings enter the sutra-store
And make our wisdom wide as the sea.

We take refuge to the Sangha!
May we with all other beings be free
From all hindrance to lead many people.

We, the members of WCRP, came together at Nairobi, and spent ten days in the same place, talking with each other and studying each other.

Since we are anxious about the contemporary world situation, there were at times complications in the meeting.

However, with the spirit of sincerity and tolerance, we have searched for the direction in which we should go forward in the future.

And now having obtained many excellent results, we can have a closing ceremony.

It may safely be said that this is entirely the grace of God.

Religion teaches us our incapacity. Therefore, we respect the faith of one another, we supplement and support each other.

We work together for the establishment of justice and peace in the world.

We pray God and request Him to lead us to the way, by His merciful hands, where we strive to build up the peaceful world.

NA MU MYO HO REN GEN KYO

Message: Archbishop Angelo Fernandes

My dear sisters and brothers of all religious traditions, my dear friends in the spirit from all the world, whatever happens in life, say "Thank you, Lord, You know best". That is a good recipe to live by. It launches us on a positive course of lighting a candle instead of cursing the darkness. As for the many good things that WCRP has been instrumental in launching in the world, there is reason to be deeply grateful to the Lord, and to continue and let Him use us as He pleases, for His good and gracious purposes. The fellowship of faith, without any syncretism thrown in, is essential for more meaning to be put into life, at all levels, and for bringing closer to conscious realization the oneness of the human family, and the dignity and equality of every human person in the universe.

WCRP has certainly been one remarkable step in that direction. Our assemblies, meetings, actions, and this Assembly, perhaps in a greater degree than heretofore, provide an experience, the like of which is not available at any other forum, the more so that at all stages, whether of planning, organizing, living, praying and working together, it is multi-religious, multi-cultural, and multi-racial. For that reason alone, it must have a future; this is demanded by the existential situation of today's world; it is for all of us to help make that future a bright one.

Inter-cultural and inter-religious understanding of the different sects of mankind must play a bigger rôle in effecting a breakthrough of the present impasse. And peace education on the right lines from the earliest years is an urgent necessity. The call to communion of hearts in order to have a meeting of minds and meaning is a specific gift of faith to the enrichment of human relations based on truth, freedom, justice and love, the four pillars on which a truly human society must rest. As the African Bishop of the fourth century proclaimed long ago, "You have made us for Yourself, O Lord, and our hearts are restless until they rest in Thee". That is the direction along which the continued quest for peace must go.

The exhibition of power, let loose on the world by the economic machine, the might of modern technology, the blatant militarism, and the over-preoccupation with the nation-state, have brought us to a state of helplessness, not to say hopelessness and despair. Is that why there are signs of a return to faith in God, and with it, faith in man, and the first steps towards mutual trust, and the will to use our resources, spiritual, cultural and material, more responsibly? The consensus arrived at in the working group on the Middle East is one beautiful example; the readiness of religionists to make common cause with scientists and parliamentarians on the prevention of nuclear war is another. This certainly demands an effective follow-up, and soon.

The presence and zestful contribution of youth and women towards mankind's inner journey towards peace is perhaps the most significant new factor for the building of the city of man from the standpoint of the city of God; the two are intertwined. The emphasis on meditation and contemplative prayer—"mystics of the world unite"—has become a constantly expressed need. We listened to and emphasized the urgency of the crisis of today's refugees. Thanks in part to our youth, there has been a manifestation of a strong determination to go beyond discussion, resolutions and declarations, toward enlightened action in favour of the poor, hungry and oppressed. We may cite the new Africa Project which is certainly good news for the world.

Hopefully there will be ever-growing numbers who will in a spirit of WCRP solidarity keep with the Prayer for Peace . . . as they prepare for the world-wide multi-religious celebration of hope on UN Day, October 24. More than ever before, even at this service, WCRP has manifested repentance for and sorrow at the tragedies inflicted on our sisters and brothers in the name of religion. Apartheid, rightly stigmatized as a most horrendous and protracted blasphemy, is one area, along with many others, that demands close attention. We must rise above inadequate and stagnant national policies and engage in efforts at reconciliation in inter-religious conflicts; this would be a welcome and daring step for all our faiths and would show our mutual acceptance in fellowship and love.

We certainly have many reasons for thanksgiving, even if we do it in the African style without words. We are certainly impelled towards greater hope; we are undoubtedly challenged to lift the quality and growth of our personal lives to a greater sincerity, integrity, dedication, and even more, to pass continuously from selfishness to service of others, and from loneliness to kinship with all mankind.

Brothers and sisters, we are set on a course which is indeed a glorious adventure as we place our security and future, not in arms and armaments, but in faith in God and the true human full development of people everywhere, our sisters and brothers in all the world. May the Lord bless each and all of us in our WCRP family and those who will be associated with us in the future. May He bestow on us, and especially on those who handle our affairs, more of His wisdom and light. May God draw us closer to Himself and to each other as we journey together towards peace with justice, and experience from this meaningful enterprise the by-products of happiness and joy for ourselves and even more so for the ever greater number of any called by the name of man, woman and child.

Japanese Hymn
Sung by Youth from Japan, China, Kenya and Europe. Hymn of harmony and hope expressing our love to all those who are suffering in various ways and our readiness to help them.

Exchange of Peace—Led by Khatija Suliman

Prayers For Peace—Introduced by Dr. Jamshed Mavalwala:
We have spent a few days together sharing our lives and learning each from another how we work together for peace, peace at the international level, peace within nations, peace within communities, and peace within each of our home countries. The prayers from many religious traditions have touched our minds and hearts. Each one of us prays for peace, each one of us does peace in the actions of our daily lives. We give thanks that we were able to do peace in a small way here and pray that we shall continue to work for peace. Surely it is a small sign to all of us in WCRP that we were granted the opportunity to help the warm and friendly people of Kenya; we were able through the donations of WCRP delegates and the help of local Sikh manufacturers and transporters to purchase a brick-making machine for the Kikuru Women's Cooperative.

As we pray here in Kenya before departing let us keep in our hearts our pledge to continue to work for peace each in his own way, each in her own way. We shall not be only visitors to Kenya, we shall not be only visitors on this planet earth, we have to be friends caring each for the other.

*From the African Traditional Religions—*Mùthuuri Kìnùthia wa Mùgìïa

From the Jewish Tradition—Mrs. Norma Levitt:

Lord, You give meaning to our hopes, to our struggles and our strivings. Without You we are lost, our lives empty. And so when all else fails us, we turn to You! In the stillness of night, when the outer darkness enters the soul; in the press of the crowd, when we walk alone though yearning for companionship; and when in agony we are bystanders to our own confusion, we look to You for hope and peace.

Lord, we do not ask for a life of ease, for happiness without alloy. Instead we ask You to teach us to be uncomplaining and unafraid. In our darkness help us to find Your light, and in our loneliness to discover the many spirits akin to our own. Give us strength to face life with hope and courage, that even from its discords and conflicts we may draw blessing. Make us understand that life calls us not merely to enjoy the richness of the earth, but to exult in heights attained after the toil of climbing.

Let our darkness be dispelled by Your love, that we may rise above fear and failure, our steps sustained by faith.

Lord, You give meaning to our lives; You are our support and our trust.

Grant us peace, Thy most precious gift, O Thou Eternal Source of peace.

*From the Shinto Tradition—*Rev. Toshio Miyake:

Pray to God with all your heart the words "Ikigamikonkodaizin, Tenchikanenokami," that the grace of God will always exist in your mind and heart.

God created all people equal, in God's eyes we are all the same, as we are all members of one family.

Put your faith and trust in God while you are here on earth, and when you die, God will welcome you into eternal life with God in Heaven.

Do not be selfish, but instead, do good for others as a way of thanking God for all the blessings God has bestowed upon you.

In the face of hardship, do not fear or worry. Pray to God for God's blessing and it will be given. God is always with you.

Pray for the happiness and prosperity of the human race and for world peace. Pray not only for yourself, but also for others. Help others whenever they meet difficulty.

Do not be afraid to sacrifice your life in helping others, since God created us to love and help one another. When you do God's will, God always is with you to protect and help you with love and blessings.

*From the Sikh Tradition—*Mr. T.S. Nandhra:

We confess that the whole world is burning today ever more severely in the fire of lust, anger, greed, attachment and ego—we call them in the Holy Sikh Scripture the Five Mortal Sins.

To keep this planet a liveable place, free from human injustices, for ourselves and for our coming generations, we have to rise above personal, national or international prejudices, politics, cultures and religions. We have to do away with factionalism. We have to divert our inner resourcefulness to peaceful gestures of good will.

According to the word of Gurbani, peace comes from within and not from without. Meditation coupled with social service purifies one's inner self. We should look beyond ourselves with no intention for selfish ends.

Our survival very much depends on our attitudes and education. The task before Man for co-existence is very difficult, but not insurmountable:

"O MAN,
THINK OF PEACE,
TALK OF PEACE,
HEAR OF PEACE,
LIVE FOR PEACE."

"Waheguru"

From the Jain Tradition—Charukeerty Bhattarak Swamiji:

(Shanti Shirodhruta Jineshwara Shasananam
Shanti Nilantara Tapobhara Chavitanam
Shanti Kashaya Jaya Srimbhita Vaiblavanam
Shanti Swablava Mahimanamupagathanam)

Let peace come to the virtuous who follow the dispensation of Shanti Jina.

May the ascetics in constant penance in order to attain salvation be blessed with eternal peace.

May the saints who have liberated themselves from the bondage of attachment achieve peace everlasting.

And peace be conferred on the seers of tranquil mind.

May Lord Bahubali Gomateshwara confer peace on the devoted, the pious, the saints, on all ascetic aspirants, the land, the city, the state— all the nations and the entire world.

May the administrators be blessed with devotion to world peace, and with the desire to bring about international amity.

O Lord Jina, we pray that governments everywhere be imbued with a desire to devote their resources to the well-being of the people.

May scientists turn away from the process of making destructive weapons being used for warfare.

May they work for peace among the people and the nations now hostile to each other.

347

O Lord Jina, we fervently pray that all our endeavours throughout the session be crowned with success.

May people everywhere enjoy the blessing of peace for all time!

(Mangham Bhavatne.)

Om Shanti, Om Shanti, Om Shanti!

From the Hindu Tradition—Mrs. Shobha Pandit:

I do not crave for power; neither heaven nor salvation do I desire.

But I do ardently desire an end to the plight of those afflicted by sorrow and misery.

Even before Hinduism emerged as a religion, a sage and seer of Rigveda declared:

(Ekam Sat, Viprah Bahudha Vedanti)

There is but one supreme truth of existence—many call it differently.

(Eko Devah Sarva—Bhootantaramata,

Eko Dharmah Tadarchanam Sarva Karma,

Jeevanmuktih Muktireka Mata Sa,

Nityanananda Batih Sa Para Ya.)

There is but one shining supreme spirit which pervades everything that exists.

There is but one highest goal: to be liberated even while alive,

And there is but one highest condition of human consciousness: to be in ecstatic joy in meditating on the Supreme Spirit.

From the Buddhist Tradition—Ven. Jing Hui

Prayer for peace in Chinese

From the American Indigenous Tradition—Mr. Art Solomon:

Sisters and Brothers of the world community,

I give thanks to be with you

And I wish to share the story of a vision that was given to me some twenty years ago.

Off in the distance beyond the vision of human beings

I could see what was a set of scales

And the greatest powers in this creation,

as the negative and the positive,

evil and good,

the creator and that other one.

And these scales were totally overbalanced to the negative,

And I wondered if some time

The positive would begin to outweigh the negative.

I watched for many years to see what would happen

And I understood

that the time between 1982 and 1984 was very critical for the human family,

But I did not understand the nature of that crisis.

I went to the island of Mauritius,
and when I left there, some time between there
and the Sixth Assembly of the World Council of Churches,
I saw the possibility of the positive beginning to outweigh the negative.

When I participated in the World Council of Churches' Sixth Assembly,
There I saw
that the positive was beginning to grow
with an irresistible power;
and what I've seen here is an addition to that—
a momentum that is beginning to build throughout the world.
I watched the peace people throughout the world
and now I have been fortunate
to be a part of what we're all doing here together,
and what we're doing
is putting together an absolutely irresistible power.
And I listen to someone say,
"I wonder if the momentum will be lost."
And I say "No"—
the momentum will not be lost,
because in this time that we are living in
we face an imperative
that has never been faced before by the human family.

And so I've seen
the scales begin to change,
and as I looked at them
in those years past
I wondered if the positive would sometime outweigh the negative;
and I would like to say
that for each one of us who puts our little bit
on that scale,
on the positive side,
the Creator puts His part—
that's the invincible part of it.
So I'd like to share that with you.
It is good to be with you,
good to be part of the work that we're doing together
throughout the whole world.

Toward the Future—Led by Dr. Homer A. Jack

All: As we return to our homes, and to our churches,
gurdwaras, mosques, synagogues, and temples, we leave a large
part of our heart in Nairobi. We have experienced the African
way, and have seen the African promise.

As we return to our homes all over the world, we pledge to
associate with the poor and the minorities in our own land and

everywhere. We unite to stave off nuclear war as we work holistically for peace.

So be it.

Closing Hymn by a local Nairobi choir

L.

Additional Assembly Materials

68

Messages to the Assembly

Pope John Paul II

... His Holiness Pope John Paul II conveys his greetings to the participants in the Fourth Assembly of the World Conference on Religion and Peace.

The choice of the theme "Religions for Human Dignity and World Peace" affords the opportunity for a positive and productive discussion of the difficult problems and great challenges which confront the human family at this point in its history. Whatever particular question you will treat—social justice, development, peace—you do so within the context of the common conviction that the centre of all these concerns and questions is related to the reality of the human person endowed by the Creator with a unique dignity and the subject of inalienable rights and freedoms. The solutions sought to the major issues of the contemporary world obtain their validity from the way in which they respect and safeguard the image of God in every human being, irrespective of sex, age, race or creed.

It is the Holy Father's fervent prayer that this Assembly will be the occasion for all the participants to reaffirm their commitment to the value of the human person as free and transcendent and that your discussions may lead to the discovery of new ways of fostering co-operation among the members of different religious traditions in the building of a world in which justice and equity for everyone will become the foundation of true peace among individuals and nations.

With my personal good wishes for the success of the Assembly, I am, Yours sincerely in Christ, Cardinal Casaroli, Secretary of State.

Mr. Javier Perez De Cuellar,
Secretary-General of the United Nations

... That there should be bridges of peace universal, linking all mankind in a spirit of truly concerted efforts to advance the welfare of all human beings, is the very thrust of your activities as well as the United Nations'. I welcome your deliberations, as they come at a time which is plagued by general international divisions and crises, as well as stale-mates on many issues facing mankind. The observations, conclusions and recommendations of this Conference concerning the quest for peace will, therefore, be of special interest to the United Nations.

May I take this opportunity to touch on certain very relevant matters, some of which have already been dealt with in your discussions. The first of these is the fortieth anniversary in 1985 of the United Nations. The General Assembly has decided to set up an inter-governmental committee to make plans for a world-wide celebration of the 40th Anniversary of the United Nations and, in this connection, the Secretary-General has appointed Mr. Robert F. Muller as Assistant Secretary-General for the 40th Anniversary.

I believe WCRP would like to be in touch with Mr. Muller regard-ing the best arrangements that can be made for a truly world-wide and meaningful celebration of the occasion—which should be used to make known to the people of the world the aims and efforts of the United Nations for peace, and to gain their support for the Organization's work.

Secondly, the contribution of non-governmental organizations as well as UN Member States, to the International Year of Peace in 1986, will go a long way towards the achievement of world peace. The Inter-national Year of Peace will be formally proclaimed on the 40th Anniver-sary of the UN . . .

The General Assembly has invited Member States, organizations within the UN system, and non-governmental organizations to co-operate with the Secretary-General in planning and implementing a meaningful programme for the Year on a global scale, as one of the most practical ways available towards bringing the world closer to peace . . .

The third matter I would like to refer to and which many speakers at this Conference have already addressed is that of the policies and practices of apartheid in South Africa. The General Assembly has been seized of this matter since 1952, and has since condemned apartheid as "a crime against humanity". The Security Council has reaffirmed that apartheid is a crime against the conscience and dignity of mankind, and virtually all governments have condemned apartheid. [I] have con-sistently condemned apartheid and urged South Africa to abandon it, because it is an inhuman and dangerous policy, which has already led to tragic ethnic conflicts among the people of South Africa . . .

WCRP has already devoted a great deal of time and thought to some of these matters. The international community appreciates this. All practical suggestions leading to effective ways of solving burning or vital international issues are most welcome. Your contributions are, therefore, most important.

(Read by Mr. Kingsley Dube, Director, UN Information Centre for Kenya, Uganda and the Seychelles.)

Dr. Adamou Mahtar M'Bow, Director General of UNESCO

Religion and peace are the two pillars of your organization and of this Fourth Assembly in Nairobi. It is not by chance that these two are linked. All religions have placed peace and justice at the heart of their concerns. Such peace may sometimes be conceived as individual serenity, but in all religions it tends to imply the aspiration to a world in which peace between all men would be achieved. The central core of such peace is some concept of the unity of mankind, and it leads on to the identification, in all religions, of a number of objectives regarded as good.

The concept of justice is one which in most religions is inseparable from peace. Justice between men or, if you wish, the respect or love of one's neighbour, provides the basis on which a new world could come into being. War and injustice, even when adverse conditions seem to make them appear unavoidable, must be regarded as evidence of man's failure in his efforts to transcend his limitations. This has always been true and it is particularly true in our age. For the first time science and technology make it possible to feed the entire world. For the first time illiteracy can be wiped out. For the first time man can communicate at incredible speed across continents and boundaries. Modern research increasingly brings to light similarities between religions, the recurrence of equivalent texts, as well as a long history of reciprocal influence of one religion on another. We now know, for example, of the influence of Buddhism on the emergence of Christian religious orders, the rise of Islam and its relationship with the religious thought of the time. Muslim mysticism influenced Thomas Aquinas. Catholics and Protestants faced similar questions at the time of the Reformation and Counter-Reformation. You are all familiar with a wealth of other examples. We are similarly aware that religions have not always co-operated in peace, divided rather than brought together in the essential dimension that should unite them.

We know of these things, and it is doubly hard for us to discuss peace in a world threatened by war. War today may amount to local conflicts, which nevertheless take thousands of lives and create hundreds of thousands of refugees. It may also constitute the threat of destruction of all mankind in a nuclear and biological holocaust. At a time when peace and justice are in need of the co-operation of everyone, everywhere, we are faced with the increasing use of science and technology for the development of systems of destruction.

In the face of this, your Assembly shares with us at UNESCO the same hope and ultimately the same fate. Differences of faith are not an essential barrier to co-operation across frontiers. A new world could be constructed, in which peace and justice would be the benefits pursued by men. Fear could be overcome and replaced by the diversity and creativity of many cultures.

UNESCO for its part, besides programmes in education, science and culture, all of which serve the ideal of international co-operation, has two major programmes of importance to this assembly. Major Programme XII, "The Elimination of Prejudice, Intolerance, Racism and Apartheid", concerns religion, since it touches on situations in which religion is used to increase intergroup tensions—a situation that I need not emphasize as contrary to the essence of religious aspirations. It will also study areas in which people succeed in co-operating in the awareness of differences of religious conviction.

The second, Major Programme XIII, "Peace, International Co-operation, Human Rights and People's Rights", deals more concretely with peace and human rights. Both of these programmes are central to your deliberations today.

For UNESCO, the concepts of peace and human rights form a whole, since it is only where human rights are guaranteed that peace becomes a possibility and it is only when war no longer threatens that man can lay a genuine foundation for the respect of human rights.

(Read by Mr. M.J. Kinunda, Regional Education Advisor, UNESCO.)

United Nations High Commissioner for Refugees

First, I should like . . . to thank you very sincerely for this opportunity for UNHCR to be associated with the Fourth World Assembly of the world Conference on Religion and Peace.

UNHCR's presence at this conference clearly demonstrates the importance which [I place] on our good relations with you and [I] hope that we may continue to work even closer together in alleviating the suffering of refugees to lead a decent life in peace and dignity. Indeed, this close association is characteristic and at the core of UNHCR's basic policy of working directly with NGOs numbering well over 200 at present world-wide. [I have] often referred to NGOs as the 'conscience of the world'. Collectively as WCRP and as individual agencies present here today, some of you have worked and continue to work in various capacities in the service of refugees.

[We] have followed closely your deliberations and feel very much encouraged by the interest, goodwill and, above all, genuine concern expressed by several delegates and the respected references made to the vexing problem of refugees world-wide particularly in Africa where the largest proportion of refugees is to be found today. From the very inception of this Conference, these references came out very sharply in the President's opening speech as well as in the Secretary-General's report.

It is through conferences of the kind now being held that some of the basic root-causes of the refugee problem can best be tackled, debated, and recommendations for possible solutions presented to appropriate authorities for concrete and concerted action for removal of these root-causes of the problem. The theme and very basis of this present conference in itself presents a very conducive opportunity for such an undertaking and in this task we wish you all the success.

To conclude, I should like to reassure you of UNHCR's close and continuing co-operation in the interest of refugees.

(Read by Mr. Kwame Afriyie, UNHCR Representative for Kenya.)

Chiara Lubich, President, Focolare Movement

If we look around at our world today, we must say that it is marked by tension: tension between East and West, tension between North and South, tension in precise areas of the globe, such as the Middle East, South Africa, Central America ... Terrorism exists in various forms in more than a single nation. There are wars under way, or which have just ended, and others which may break out. There is the possibility of a nuclear disaster. There are social inequalities, racist divisions ... and countless other evils.

And all this is so entirely out of proportion to any possibility of intervening, as individuals, groups or even nations, that it would seem useless to hope at all.

Humanly speaking, this is all true, and we can witness it day after day. And yet, if we are even a little bit sensitive to another way of seeing which is not merely an earthly one, if we let ourselves be guided by the Spirit, who manifests himself through the signs of the times, we must note something else as well: that in spite of all this contrast, in spite of the divisions and discrimination, *the world*—paradoxically—*is tending today towards unity, towards peace.* Let us mention a few symptomatic facts.

Within Christianity, the various Churches, after centuries of strife and indifference, now feel a thrust towards unification. The World Council of Churches, for example, is an evident sign of this trend.

In the Catholic Church there has been the Second Vatican Council, whose documents are permeated by the idea of unity, and, as a result, secretariats have been formed for promoting Christian unity, for relations with other religions and for dialogue with all persons of goodwill.

Among Christians, as among believers of other world religions, spiritual movements have come to life, emphasizing the concept of unity and the community, and often fostering universal fellowship.

This conference itself, which has brought persons of the most varied religions of the world together for these days here in Nairobi, is a sign of this present-day impetus.

There are nations with varying histories, cultures and languages which, in spite of failures and great fatigue, refuse to give up on an ideal of unity and confederation—as in Europe, for example.

Even ideologies which we believers cannot share are proposing global solutions to the great problems of the world in our times.

Many international bodies and organizations, such as the United Nations, also bespeak this tendency towards unity, and it is fostered by the mass means of communication, which bring the entire world into each community and family.

Truly, if we consider humanity from this perspective, we must come to the conclusion that *in the world today there is a real trend towards unity.*

It is a sign of the times, which can give us an insight of a plan God has for present-day humanity.

This intuition, this view of things, tells us that we are not alone in wanting universal brotherhood and therefore peace. For although unity has been God's will since the very creation of the world—always and for all times—it is also His specific wish for this, our twentieth century, as for that which mankind is now attending.

Thus, in working along this line we are in harmony with God's will, and if this is so, His help and grace will not be lacking; also in this immense task to which we have pledged our efforts: unity among religions for the sake of peace.

We all believe in someone or in something which transcends us. We all believe in God, or in a truth, which for us Christians bears a name—Father. He is the foundation of universal brotherhood. We cannot believe in a Father without acting as brothers and sisters towards all human creatures.

With Him we can contribute in an effective way towards universal brotherhood, which also means contributing to a solid peace. Looking to Him we see all persons as potential candidates for this brotherhood, regardless of race of nation, ideology or creed.

My wish is that this conference may bring a new contribution towards peace in the world.

May this peace reign first of all in the hearts of men and women, in their personal relationship with God. Our faith tells us that the human person has been "created in the image and likeness" of God. He or she is God's counterpart, His "you". This is the sublime dignity which God willed and planned for us. Therefore the human person reaches total fulfilment and hence finds peace in a constant relationship of communion with God.

My wish is also that this conference may give impetus towards a decision to act towards every other human being in that manner called love. That each individual—the greatest number possible—may love his neighbour as himself; that this love become service; that this service be expressed concretely in each person "making himself one" with others; in making himself weak with the weak, ignorant with those who lack learning or instruction, suffering with those who suffer, in making himself all things to all men, in order that many may be pulled along into this same current of love. And that God the Father, for this love which binds brothers and sisters together, may somehow feel impelled to come and dwell among men.

Then He will be in the midst of all, also here in Nairobi, in this open dialogue, sustained by the respect and the mutual love among members of differing religions. And He will surely suggest sound proposals and effective initiatives in view of this year's programme, which is centred on human dignity and world peace. Surely He will make us experience, for the religion which elevates us all, that spiritual unity which binds everyone together and which can become more and more the soul of the world, the soul of humanity today.

358

(Read by Natalia Dallapiccola, Focolare representative at WCRP IV.)

69

Closing Remarks

a) Closing Remarks and Thanks to Retiring Secretary-General: Religious Practice and Co-operation

By President Nikkyo Niwano

Thanks to the co-operation of everyone, the Fourth Assembly of WCRP is now coming to an end, and again I wish here to express my sincere gratitude to all concerned.

I wish to recall for a minute January of 1976, when the first assembly of ACRP was held in Singapore. At that time, numerous people had escaped from Vietnam in small boats and reached the shores of the Malay peninsula as well as the port of Singapore. However, as you may well know, Singapore, for territorial reasons, as well as for lack of space, was unable to allow in any of these refugees.

Due to the situation, there was an evermore increasing number of boat people on the high seas. The danger was that many of these people were certain to perish and be swallowed by the sea as the typhoon season was nearing. At that time, the participants in the conference put their efforts together and set up a project of emergency assistance; hence, food and fresh water were delivered to the boat people. The matter, however, could not be settled in any drastic manner.

As a temporary measure, we chartered a large ship and started to evacuate people from boats endangered by the typhoon as well as refugees stranded on rafts. Since funds were needed to charter the ship and supply food and medicines, the officers of ACRP as well as the

---

* President Nikkyo Niwano, a Buddhist from Japan, is an Honorary President of WCRP/International

officers of WCRP who were attending that conference, had been able to gather a substantial amount from contributions made by each participant country for that purpose.

This action proved to be an incentive, as others and the United Nations followed suit by seriously starting to provide concrete help. I am not telling you this to boast about our past actions, but I merely wish to state through this example that I believe that religionists who possess the genuine spirit of altruism and who practise it earnestly are bound to be granted the assistance of God or Buddha.

While the theme of this Fourth WCRP Assembly is "Religion for Human Dignity and World Peace", there still exist far too many places on the globe where human dignity is conspicuously wanting. Through the sub-theme of the Assembly "Religious practice and cooperation", it stems that practice is one of the indispensable elements of religion.

Such practice is extremely important and cannot exist without religious co-operation, and this becomes quite apparent in view of the dangerous situations present around the world.

Although prayer is indispensable to religionists, action must go hand in hand with prayer. Action means action void of political ideology and, instead, backed up by mercy and sincere love. This is why I believe that it is equally important to act in prayer and to pray in action.

On one occasion, the Executive Director of UNICEF, Mr. Grant, told me that in the world every day 40,000 children die from disease and hunger; the present goal of UNICEF is therefore to reduce the number of dying children by half, namely, from 40,000 to 20,000 by the end of this century.

Following this information, my organization, which had been active in the Donate-A-Meal Campaign for many years, through direct appeal to the public, succeeded in raising 300 million yen for UNICEF. From this amount 100 million yen were earmarked for assistance to the children of Africa.

Furthermore, UNICEF has also launched a large-scale movement named "The Children's Revolution", which is aiming at ridding developing countries of disease and hunger, and at making basic education available to everyone.

Another of our responsibilities as religionists is to train the necessary manpower that can contribute to this Children's Revolution. In the framework of the promotion of disarmament, our other task is to try to direct funds attributed to military purposes to the kind of humanitarian assistance I have just mentioned.

In this context, I believe that one of the pre-requisites is that religionists set apart the old concept that religion is solely for the purpose of spiritual revolution and should aim at working for stronger religious co-operation as a matter of primary importance.

It is said in the Buddhist scriptures that the unfortunates are they who suffer from hunger and thirst and who, through no fault of their own, happen to be put in such distressing situation. On the other hand, people who have food and water in abundance and who do not know their good fortune are viewed as deep sinners and as the bearers of a miserable heart.

Is not this Assembly the perfect occasion for us to join efforts and practise the spirit of true love and mercy? It is with this prayer in my heart that I part from you today.

Now I would like to say a few words about our former Secretary-General, Dr. Homer Jack. The contribution that Dr. Jack made during his long term for the World Conference on Religion and Peace has been outstanding. On behalf of all the WCRP people I would like to express our deepest appreciation for his great and remarkable contribution, by presenting him with this token of our gratitude.

We earnestly hope that Dr. Jack will continue to serve WCRP as its Secretary-General Emeritus for many years to come, as all concerned have a lot to benefit and learn from his past experience.

Thank you very much.

b)   Closing Remarks and Thanks To Out-Going President

By Dr. Dana Greeley*

Mr. Secretary-General, President Fernandes, (I am assuming, Mr. Secretary-General, that you are in the chair.) I think that perhaps if you feel that it is proper to do so you might have this body adopt a resolution by acclamation. I also feel honoured to be able to say these few words at this time.

Whereas Archbishop Fernandes has been our President since the formal organization of the World Conference on Religion and Peace in Istanbul in 1969, and whereas he has served us with distinction, devotion and efficiency and worked most conscientiously with the Secretary-General and all of the officers and personnel and has been ever-sensitive to both our spiritual needs, as well as to our commanding concern for world peace, therefore BE IT RESOLVED that we extend to the Archbishop, citizen of India and of the world, prelate of the Roman Catholic church, our deep gratitude and pledge of abiding affection and co-operation and hope for his continuing intimate involvement in our work, that we may benefit for many years to come from his vision, his judgment and his respect for all people.

---

*Dr. Dana Greeley, a Christian from the U.S.A., is an Honorary President of WCRP/International.

c)   Closing Remarks and Welcome to In-Coming Chairman of Governing Board

By Sri R. R. Diwakar*

It is my pleasant duty and privilege to present to this august assembly Dr. Inamullah Khan as the Chairman of the new Governing Board. I would like to say a few words on this occasion because we have gone through four assemblies and we are looking forward to the fifth assembly. These four assemblies have not by themselves contributed towards the peace that we have all been hungering after, but I think the future is going to be brighter because we have now a new structure which can be called a kind of structure in which almost everyone who can contribute something to this whole work will be involved.

While I congratulate the organizers for the success of this particular assembly, I would rather feel the greater amount of responsibility for what is coming in the future. We have yet many hurdles to pass and at this juncture we have a Governing Board, and as Chairman of the Governing Board, Dr. Inamullah Khan, who has a brilliant past, while even now taking on himself the responsibility of the whole Muslim world by being the Secretary-General of the World Muslim Congress. He has been with us for the last three or four years, and I have known him as a very gentle, very friendly, very co-operative gentleman, and I am sure that in his hands the Governing Board and the new structure will function very effectively.

Our inspiration comes from the spirit, and our approach is religious and our purpose is moral. We have to see that humanity today is going in the wrong way because it has not been guided by human morality. I

---

*Sri R.R. Diwakar, a Hindu from India, is an Honorary President of WCRP/ International

364

think we have a good guide now in Dr Inamullah Khan and we should all promise him our full support and co-operation with the best of our efforts.

I am happy that Dr. Taylor is entering his new era in launching the present effort. This will link both intellectually and emotionally with the project that was so well presented to us earlier today, the project for Africa.

d) Closing Remarks of the Secretary-General Of WCRP IV

By Dr. John B. Taylor

Mr. President Emeritus and all of you who have been such an incalculable support to me in these days of WCRP IV and the days before and upon whose help I count for the days to come, I thank you for your generous response and I remind you, if I may, of the three questions which I posed in my report: the question, "Is religion a force for peace?"; the question, "Is WCRP an instrument for peacemaking?"; and the question, "Can this Assembly be a sign of hope?". It would be good to answer, "Yes", "Yes", "Yes", to all those three questions, but it might be complacent.

It might mean that we were forgetting in the excitement of the ending the moments when we have been very self-critical with each other of how religion has sometimes been misused. It might mean that in the excitement of ending we were forgetting how fragile an instrument, how poor financially, how weak in terms of human power, WCRP is. And it might mean that we were also forgetting that our Assembly, for all the joy and all the fellowship, has also had to face a number of moments of real suffering and real agony. So I would like to reply to those questions: Is religion a force of peace? "It can be!" Is WCRP an instrument of peacemaking? "It can be!" Can this Assembly be a sign of hope? "It can be!" but that conditional is not an answer of hesitation or pessimism, it is an answer of hope. It is an answer of conviction.

I believe that in our search for truth, in our allegiance to the ultimate values of life, we can be a force of peace. We can use WCRP internationally, nationally, locally, as a blessing. We can go from this place not only with hopes for ourselves, but carrying hope to others.

It might have seemed logical that, on a day when I have laid bare a budget which had a $50,000 deficit, I should have asked us to end this Assembly with a pledge for ourselves. That, I believe, would have been wrong. WCRP is not a self-serving organization; WCRP has been brought into being and led with distinction and dedication over the years as an instrument for others; we seek peace not only for ourselves, but we seek it for others; we seek justice not only for ourselves, but we seek justice for all our sisters and brothers, young and old, around the world. It would be not fitting, in my mind, to end this Assembly with an appeal to look after our own house, but rather we should end this Assembly as we have already been inspired this morning by our friends from Asia, Africa and America.

We should end by turning to at least one sign of human need and where more obviously than in this continent, where we have been made so welcome? For ten days we have been lodged and fed, many of us being paid for by another organization; we have been looked after, not only in the college, but in so many other ways in these days, and yet all the time we have been haunted by the knowledge of the suffering of so many people, very close to us geographically, a few miles away in shanty-towns or refugee settlements, and a few more hundred miles away, in the vast zones affected by drought.

We have heard that some people have already made very generous pledges to alleviate this human suffering so that we may leave this Assembly with at least a sign of hope, not for ourselves, but for others. This is a sign of hope in that we are commiting ourselves to the needs of the world. Before we come to prayer, before we come to meditate together, sharing the riches of our many traditions, in our closing act of meditation, we feel that we should try at least to practise what we preach. However small the gift, or however large the gift, it should be offered with love and humility for the service of our sisters and brothers; it may just be an amount which we write on a piece of paper; it may even be a prayer, for we can offer a prayer as well as a gift; it may be a pledge of service, of human labour to work with those whose need is greatest. Each in our own way, we should find a way of pledging ourselves to our brothers and sisters in Kenya and beyond.

There are three baskets that have been brought into the hall which have been woven in the north of Kenya, woven in the area where animals are dying, where old people are dying, where babies are dying, where the surviving able-bodied people are struggling to escape and coming into a city like Nairobi, hoping, but failing, to find the streets paved with gold; the need is enormous and whatever we offer will be only a token gesture. But if, by that token gesture, if by a monetary gift that hurts us, if by a pledge of time and talent that taxes us, if by a prayer that exercises us, we can contribute to our brothers and sisters, we shall, I think, be setting the right tone for our commitment to WCRP, to peace, and to justice. Thank you.

M.

WCRP Activity

70

From Princeton To Nairobi
A Four-And-A-Half-Year Report of
The Secretary-General

By Dr. Homer A. Jack

1. Introduction

This is my final report as Secretary-General of WCRP/
International. It is prepared in June 1984, after I have been Secretary-
General-Emeritus for six months.

This report gains perhaps by perspective, but it suffers from being
written 1,000 miles from the WCRP office and most records. However,
our complete WCRP archives are deposited in the Swarthmore College
Peace Collection in Swarthmore, Pennsylvania, USA. This is being pro-
fessionally maintained and is constantly being used by authors and graduate students.

I hope that the future Boards of WCRP/International will endorse
the tradition of depositing all our records at Swarthmore, even now that
the international office is located in Geneva. Also I hope my successors
in the office of Secretary-General will, squirrel-like, collect everything,
throw no records or reports away, and deposit them with the Peace Collection. The WCRP collection is now stored with the archives of many
other international peace organizations and personalities.

2. Implementation of Findings

There is a tradition that the Findings of the world assemblies of
WCRP are not only put into publications, but every attempt is made to
implement them on various levels, especially through the UN.

A. Publications. The Princeton Declaration of WCRP III was
immediately published, in October 1979, with an edition of 10,000
copies. The Findings of WCRP III were published in a 52-page pamphlet in November 1979. The unabridged proceedings of WCRP III were
issued as a 493-page volume under the title, *Religion in the Struggle for*

World Community. This was published by WCRP in 1980 and sold and otherwise distributed around the world.

B. UN Community. The Findings of WCRP III, as with previous assemblies, were especially given in various UN organs over time, chiefly in the substantive fields of disarmament, human rights, and apartheid.

1. Disarmament. WCRP representatives reflected the substantive findings of WCRP III in various disarmament organs: Disarmament Commission, Committee on Disarmament at Geneva, Second Review Conference of the Treaty on the Non-Proliferation of Nuclear Weapons, the First Committee of the General Assembly, and the Second UN Special Session on Disarmament. The roles of WCRP are best reflected in the volume, *Disarm—Or Die: The Second UN Special Session on Disarmament,* by Homer A. Jack.

2. Human Rights. At the 1980 session of the UN Commission on Human Rights, Ms. Amy Young-Anawaty gave testimony taken from the WCRP Khmer Programme. At the Sub-Commission on Prevention of Discrimination and Protection of Minorities, the WCRP Secretary-General gave testimony in August 1980 urging the freedom of Kim-Dae-Jung of the Republic of Korea, the freedom of the American hostages in Iran, and the Khmer people. He also gave oral testimony to the Sub-Commission in September 1982. Mr. Bhagwan Das of India gave testimony before the Sub-Commission in August 1982 on Untouchability on the sub-continent. Also WCRP maintained contact with the Third Committee during each session of the General-Assembly.

3. Apartheid. WCRP made oral statements at hearings or meetings of the Special Committee Against Apartheid. One occasion was in March 1981. Another was at a memorial service in February 1983 honouring the late Canon L. John Collins of the UK.

4. Future of Kampuchea. WCRP played a role before, during, and after the International Conference on Kampuchea held in July 1981.

3. Relationship with the UN

WCRP/International continued its consultative status with the Economic and Social Council (ECOSOC) and with other organs of the UN. In its quadrennial report to ECOSOC for the years 1978–81, WCRP summarized its relationship to the organization in that period under some of the following headings:

A. Oral Statements. Representatives of WCRP made a number of oral statements to ECOSOC-related bodies and to those dealing with apartheid. These are given in Section 2 above.

B. Written Statements. WCRP joined with representatives of other non-governmental organizations (NGOs) in transmitting several written communications to ECOSOC, especially on the pending draft declaration on religious freedom. Two such statements were transmitted in February 1980 (in document E/CN.4/260) and in February (E/CN.4/

NGO/312). In addition, WCRP participated in a written communication in October 1981 to the President of the 36th General Assembly on the same subject.

C. Consultations. The WCRP Secretariat has, on occasion, held consultation with appropriate members of the UN Secretariat, especially during 1980–81 on the WCRP Khmer Programme and in 1981–82 on the Second UN Special Session on Disarmament. Consultations were held at UN Headquarters and in Geneva, Bangkok, and Nairobi.

D. Conferences. WCRP representatives were observers at the International Conference on Kampuchea at UN Headquarters in July 1981 and at many UN organs and sessions listed in Section 2 above.

E. Dissemination of Information. WCRP has tried to distribute interpretative information regularly about the work of the UN in its newsletter, *Religion for Peace,* its books and pamphlets, selective WCRP reports, and in articles written by its Secretary-General.

F. Role of NGOs. WCRP has, with other NGOs, been concerned about maintaining the role of NGOs in the UN system and, selectively, increasing that rôle. This has taken the form of the WCRP Secretary-General's being Chairman of the NGO Committee on Disarmament (at UN Headquarters) and, in that capacity, an *ex officio* member of the Conference of NGOs in Consultative Status with ECOSOC—known as CONGO. When the WCRP Secretary-General retired from his work in the UN community, a reception was held in his honour at UN Headquarters in November 1983, attended by members of the Secretariat, diplomatic community, press, and NGOs. Also when the WCRP Secretary-General received the Niwano Peace Prize, UN Secretary-General, Mr. Javier Perez de Cuellar, wrote, "We at the UN have deeply appreciated Dr. Jack's steadfast commitment to the ideals of the world organization. His selfless dedication to so many of our activities, and in particular the cause of disarmament, has been exemplary and has earned him the widest admiration and gratitude."

4. WCRP Khmer Fund and Programme

This project evolved during and after WCRP III, especially through contacts that Dr. Howard Schomer had with the Khmer People's Liberation Front (KPNLF) and with the problems of refugees from Kampuchea along the border of Thailand. Dr. Schomer visited this border in October 1979. The WCRP Secretary-General and Mrs. Jack were then given the mandate to visit that area beginning in December 1979 and stay there as long as necessary. In the end, they were in Thailand intermittently until August 1980, while Mr. David R. Hawk began work as Director of what became the WCRP Khmer Fund and Programme on May 15, 1980, and this continued for one full year.

On January 23, 1980, representatives from several WCRP national committees gathered in Bangkok and drew the guidelines for the Programme. A meeting of the Governing Committee in Bangkok on June 2–5, 1980, endorsed the purposes and objectives of the Programme. The latter can be summarized as: 1–monitoring relief supplies for the survival of the Khmer people, 2–supervising the humanitarian and political undertakings of UN agencies and voluntary organizations related to Khmer issues, and 3–contributing, as requested, to the rebuilding of the religious and cultural life of the Khmer people.

A total of 26 "WCRP Reports on Kampuchea" were published. All are now out of print, but the list is available and the material can be photocopied.

Among the achievements of the Programme were sensitizing WCRP to Kampuchean problems, issuing of WCRP reports on Kampuchea, helping the KPNLF, and constructing a model for future WCRP multi-religious action-cum-service projects.

Detailed reports of the Programme by the WCRP Secretary-General and by Mr. Hawk were issued in July 1981 when aspects of the Programme terminated. A detailed accounting of the several hundred thousand dollars raised, and spent, for the Programme is also available.

5. Disarmament Mission to Beijing

At a meeting of the Governing Committee at New Delhi in November 1981, it was proposed to send WCRP missions to the heads of State or Government of at least the five known nuclear weapon States: China, France, UK, USA, and USSR. The purpose would be to stress the urgency of world peace and disarmament and the inadmissibility of nuclear war. It was agreed that the income from the Niwano Fund could be used for this purpose. The missions would presumably be scheduled just before the Second UN Special Session on Disarmament in May/June 1982.

Explorations began still in 1981 to schedule the five missions, but in the end only the People's Republic of China appeared willing to receive the group. A ten-person Mission visited Beijing on May 7–11, 1982, for discussions with top officials on peace, disarmament, and the Second UN Special Session. The Mission was composed of representatives of five world religions, members coming from England, India, Japan, Pakistan, Singapore, and the USA. They were hosted by Mr. Zhao Puchu, President of the Buddhist Association of China.

The Mission was warmly received by both Chinese political leaders and heads of the five major religions of China. It was successful in accomplishing its principal objectives: conveying to key Chinese Governmental authorities the concern of WCRP for disarmament and sensitizing Chinese religious leaders to these concerns. The Mission also emphasized, by default, the difficulties of reaching the other four governments on a high level on this issue, at least at that time.

A detailed, 21-page report of this project was issued late in May 1982 as a WCRP Report: "WCRP Multi-Religious Mission on Disarmament to China".

6. Initiative for Active Hope

WCRP/Europe asked the Governing Committee meeting at Bangkok in June 1980 to endorse the proposal for a WCRP project entitled, "Reason for Hope". This concept, originated by Prof. Jean Barrea of Belgium, was approved and WCRP committees and individuals were asked to submit nominations to WCRP/Europe. A committee was established and it solicited nominations and accounced its choices. These often appeared in the periodical, *Religion for Peace*. Over the years the "Signs of Active Hope" included the following: April 1981—The Danish Parliament approved a law allowing foreigners to vote in municipal and departmental elections; May 1981—The World Health Organization adopted an international code regulating the substitutes for mother's milk; June 1981—The European Parliament adopted, with a large majority, a resolution against capital punishment; 1982—A total of 123 pastors and theologians of the white Dutch Reformed Church in South Africa signed a statement condemning apartheid as not being compatible with the Bible; 1982—A woman was elected for the first time head of the Synod of the Reformed Church of Alsace-Lorraine, France; 1982—The Swedish Government continued the appointment of an Ambassador to Non-Governmental Organizations (NGOs); 1982—The "legitimate rights of the Palestinians" were explicitly recognized in speeches by President Reagan and other high US officials, coupled with the adoption by the Arabic Summit of an Arab Peace Plan which included an implicit recognition of Israel; 1982—War toys were condemned by the European Parliament; 1982—The draft pastoral letter of the Roman Catholic bishops of the USA on nuclear war was released; and 1982—The declaration of the South African Council of Churches condemned apartheid.

Individuals and groups were asked to write to commend these positive, hopeful activities.

In September 1982, at the Katholikentag in Düsseldorf, German Federal Republic, WCRP/Europe sponsored a "Tree of Hope", with visitors writing "signs of hope" on cardboard apples and other fruit and attaching them to the tree.

Prof. Barrea, with Mr. G. Thils, published a volume in Paris on the theological basis of hope, entitled, *Une Pastorale de l'Espérance*.

7. *Regional and National Committees*

The relationship of the international office of WCRP to its regional and national committees is often hard to describe. There is a two-way flow of information and guidance. However, the relationship so far has been informal and not legal.

News of the activities of regional and national committees comes to the international office intermittently and is often reflected in brief stories in the newsletter of WCRP/International. An attempt to develop a manual for regional and national committee has not yet been completed, but one is badly needed.

The Secretary-General has made visits or field trips to most of the regional and national committees in this time period. A regional committee covering all of Africa was established with the encouragement of the international office in August 1982. It held an All Africa Assembly in August 1983 as a backdrop to WCRP IV to be held in Africa in 1984. Attempts have not yet been successful to develop national or regional committees in socialist countries, although close informal relationships continue with religious leaders in the Soviet Union, Eastern Europe, and China. Also it has not yet been possible to establish regional committees in West Asia or Latin America.

8. Finances

A.   General Finances

WCRP/International has suffered from a chronic shortage of funds. If it were not for large, steady contributions from WCRP/Japan and WCRP/USA, WCRP/International would long ago have had to cease operation. In recent years, the capital and income of the Niwano Fund have served as a cushion both for needed cash and, when necessary, to absorb the annual deficit caused, not by unauthorized spending, but by unfulfilled pledges or "askings".

The total income, from all sources, for the calendar—and fiscal—years since WCRP III is as follows: 1980, $175,400; 1981, $158,767; 1982, $203,974; and 1983, $211,656. The total for the four-year period is $749,797.

Major expenses, comparatively, are as follows for the fiscal years 1982 and 1983: personnel, $60,719 and $67,169; office, $20,069 and $19,240; and programme, $36,835 and $25,790. With the addition of certain miscellaneous expenses, the total for 1982 was $119,902 and for 1983 was $113,783.

Major income comparatively, for these two years was as follows: WCRP/Europe, $5,000 and $5,000; WCRP/Japan, $40,000 and $40,000; and WCRP/USA, $20,000 and $24,000. Other income included sale of literature, $1,900 and $5,957 and individual memberships, $3,059 and $3,255. The total was $104,614 in 1982 and $87,600 in 1983. Thus the deficits were $15,288 and $26,183 respectively.

In both years there was an extraordinary budget, in 1982 for the Multi-Religious Mission and also the exploratory meetings in Nairobi for WCRP IV. The extraordinary budget for 1983 included the following items: salary and travel of Associate Secretary, $25,376; grant to WCRP/Africa, $13,201; Commission on the Future, $6,200; International Preparatory Committe , $25,741; Salary and travel of Secretary-General of WCRP IV (Dr. Taylor), $13,000; and Geneva office $6,613. The total was $90,191. The income for this special budget came from WCRP/Japan, $29,000; WCRP/Europe, $20,000; and the Adenauer Foundation, $4,052. The total was $63,052. Thus the shortfall for 1983 in this special budget, due entirely to lack of contributions, was $27,139.

The total deficit for 1983 was $53,322, with an adjustment for prepayments due in 1984 bringing the actual deficit to $46,322.

B. The Niwano Fund

In 1979 President Nikkyo Niwano contributed to WCRP/ International the income he received from being awarded the Templeton Prize. This amounted to $166,000. The total sum of the Niwano Fund was invested in New York City, with the income earmarked for special approved WCRP projects.

Over the period through December 31, 1983, a total of $77,062 was accumulated in interest and an additional $25,994 as capital gains (from the sale of acquired stock). This was a total of $103,055.

In this same period, three demands were made on the Fund: the Multi-Religious Mission to Beijing, the costs of the Commission on the Future ($6,200 during 1983), and necessary cash to continue the operation of WCRP/International because of a shortfall of income during 1982 and 1983.

As of December 31, 1983, the total amount in the Niwano Fund was $146,272, with all income from the Fund expended as indicated above. The figure for December 31, 1982 was $189,845. Since $6,200 was spent on the Commission, this meant that $37,373 was borrowed to make up the deficit of WCRP/International for the calendar year 1983.

A detailed accounting is available from the office of WCRP/ International.

9. Administration

WCRP/International is a non-profit organization incorporated in 1971 under the laws of the State of New York, USA. Its brief by-laws are flexible. The chief decision-making body consists of the Members of the Corporation.

A. Members of the Corporation. The by-laws provide for the appointment of more than 100 persons as Members of the Corporation. During the years, additional Members have been appointed, especially as replacements for those who have died. Members met during WCRP III at Princeton in September 1979 and again outside Nairobi in September 1983. Additional members were named at both meetings. The entire list can be found in the records of WCRP/International.

B. Officers. The officers elected at WCRP III Members of the Corporation include the following persons: President, Archbishop Angelo Fernandes (Christian, India); Honorary Presidents, Sri R.R. Diwakar (Hindu, India), Dr. Dana McLean Greely (Christian, USA), President Nikkyo Niwano (Buddhist, Japan); Vice-Presidents, Swami Chidananda (Hindu, India), Metropolitan Filaret (Christian, USSR), Dr. Inamullah Khan (Muslim, Pakistan), Dr. Maria A. Lücker (Christian, Federal Republic of Germany), Rev. Toshio Miyake (Shintoist, Japan), and Mr. Zhao Puchu (Buddhist, People's Republic of China). Dr. Homer A. Jack was re-elected Secretary-General. These officers have consulted with each other often by correspondence and occasionally in person. The latter occasions include Bangkok in June 1980, New Delhi in November 1981, Beijing in May 1982, Nairobi in August 1982, Limuru, Kenya, in September 1983, and Geneva in February 1984.

C. *Board of Directors.* The members of the Board were elected at a meeting of the Members of the Corporation at WCRP III. They include the following persons: Mrs. Sekinot O. Adekola (Muslim, Nigeria), Dr. M. Aram (Hindu, India), Mr. Smail Balic (Muslim, Austria), Dr. Madeleine Barot (Christian, France), Dr. Petrus H.J.M. Camps (Christian, Netherlands), Dr. Viqar A. Hamdani (Muslim, Pakistan and USA), Mr. Anwar Harjono (Muslim, Indonesia), Prof. Yoshiaki Iisaka (Christian, Japan), Judge Sathitya Lengthaisong (Buddhist, Thailand), Prof. Jamshed Mavalwala (Zoroastrian, Canada), Rev. Englebert Mveng (Christian, Cameroun), Mrs. Gedong Bagoes Oka (Hindu, Indonesia), Mrs. Prabhat Sobha Pandit (Hindu, India), Bishop Bernardino Pinera (Christian, Chile), Sri Radhakrishna (Hindu, India), Ven. Havanpola Ratanasara (Buddhist, Sri Lanka and USA), Rev. Yasuyoshi Sakata (Shintoist, Japan), Dr. Howard Schomer (Christian, USA), Prof. Harmindar Singh (Sikh, UK), Rev. Kenryu Tsuji (Buddhist, USA), Mr. Jerzy Turowicz (Christian, Poland), and Dr. Rifat M. Yücelten (Muslim, Cyprus). The Board met at Princeton on September 7, 1979 and authorized, on the recommendation of the Beyond WCRP III Committee, the election of a smaller Governing Committee.

D. *Governing Committee.* The following persons were named to this Committee: Dr. Alexy Bouevsky (Christian, USSR), Sri Swami Chidananda (Hindu, India), Dr. André Chouraqui (Jewish, Israel), Sri R.R. Diwakar (Hindu, India), Archbishop Angelo Fernandes (Christian, India), Metropolitan Filaret (Christian, USSR), Dr. Dana McLean Greeley (Christian, USA), Dr. Viqar A. Hamdani (Muslim, Pakistan and USA), Mr. Veerendra Heggade (Jain, India), Dr. Inamullah Khan (Muslim, Pakistan), Dr. Maria A. Lücker (Christian, Federal Republic of Germany), Rev. Toshio Miyake (Shintoist, Japan), President Nikkyo Niwano (Buddhist, Japan), Mrs. Prabhat Sobha Pandit (Hindu, India), Prof. John Pobee (Christian, Ghana), Rev. Yasuyoshi Sakata (Shintoist, Japan), Major-General S.S. Uban (Hindu, India), Dr. Herman Will (Christian, USA), and Mr. Zhao Puchu (Buddhist, People's Republic of China). This committee met at Bangkok on June 2–5, 1980, and in New Delhi on November 12–13, 1981. Lack of funds prevented further meetings in this period.

E. *Secretary-General.* Dr. Homer A. Jack remained Secretary-General until he submitted his resignation to the officers in September 1983, effective no later than August 23, 1984, and as early as December 31, 1983. His resignation took effect at the earlier date and he was named Secretary-General Emeritus by a meeting of the officers outside Nairobi. Dr. John B. Taylor, a staff member of the World Council of Churches for ten years, was employed as Secretary-General of WCRP IV by the officers in September 1983, effective October 1, 1983. He was further named Acting Secretary-General as of January 1, 1984, and was appointed by the officers Secretary-General effective March 1, 1984.

F. Other Staff Members. Mr. David R. Hawk of the USA was appointed Director of the WCRP Khmer Program from May 1980 to May 1981, with headquarters in Bangkok. Dr. S.K. Chaturvedi of India was appointed Associate Secretary from March 1, 1981 through December of that year. He worked in New Delhi. He had to withdraw from employment because of the illness of his wife. Dr. Norbert Klaes of the Federal Republic of Germany was appointed Associate Secretary from October 1, 1982 until September 30, 1983, and spent much of his time for WCRP in Africa. Miss Renate Belck continued as Office Administrator during this entire period, moving with the international office to Geneva late in January 1984. Several interns were employed at the New York office, especially in the summer period.

G. Tenth Anniversary. Ten years of WCRP activity were observed, especially by WCRP/Japan, in February 1981.

10. Field Trips

The Secretary-General continued to visit many parts of the world, both to pursue substantive business and to confer with WCRP regional and national committee. An outline of his principal field trips follows:

1979, December–Japan, Hong Kong, and Thailand, primarily to explore the Khmer Programme.

1980, January/March–Thailand, Bangladesh, India, Pakistan, Geneva, German Federal Republic, and the UK.

1980, April/June–Japan and Thailand, Khmer Programme.

1980, June–People's Republic of China, as guest of the religious groups there.

1980, July–Japan, to speak at a conference of World Federalists.

1980, August/September–India and Geneva, primarily to attend the Second Review Conference of the Treaty on the Non-Proliferation of Nuclear Weapons.

1981, November–India, for ACRP and WCRP officers meetings.

1982, April–UK to deliver lectures.

1982, May–Japan and China, primarily for the Multi-Religious Mission to Beijing.

1982, August/September–Kenya, primarily for exploratory meetings for WCRP IV, and Geneva.

1982, December–Norway and Sweden, primarily to attend Nobel Peace Prize ceremonies.

1983, April/May–Montreal, Canada, to attend conferences of WCRP/Canada.

1983, May/June–Japan, Singapore, Thailand, India, German Federal Republic, initially to attend a Japanese-American Inter-religious Consultation.

1983, July/August–Vancouver, Canada, to attend the Sixth Assembly of the World Council of Churches.

1983, August/September–Kenya, to attend the All Africa Assembly and International Preparatory Committee for WCRP IV.

1984, February—German Federal Republic and Geneva, to attend a conference of WCRP/Europe and session of the Commission on the Future.

11. Toward WCRP IV

World assemblies of WCRP are held every four or five years. At the conclusion of WCRP III in 1979 hope was expressed that WCRP IV might be held in Africa. At a meeting of the Governing Committee in New Delhi in November 1981, WCRP IV was first discussed. A number of suggestions were made about the venue. Africa and China remained strong choices. It was agreed at least to convene the African alumni of WCRP to explore holding WCRP IV in Africa.

An exploratory WCRP consultation was convened in Nairobi, Kenya, on August 23–27, 1982. After much discussion, it was agreed to recommend that the continent of Africa be the venue for WCRP IV, with Nairobi being the city. It was further recommended that a properly prepared conference could not be held until mid-1984. This proposal was subsequently approved by the officers.

Also at the WCRP consultation, WCRP/Africa was provisionally established and it was agreed to hold an All Africa Assembly at Nairobi in August 1983 to help prepare for WCRP IV in 1984. Dr. Norbert Klaes, Associate Secretary of WCRP/International, was asked to help WCRP/Africa and its Assembly.

The All Africa Assembly was successfully held from August 30 to September 3, 1983, in Nairobi. It officially inaugurated WCRP/Africa. The meetings of International Preparatory Committee for WCRP IV were held September 4–6, 1983, at Limuru, outside Nairobi. Detailed plans were made by the 50 persons present to hold WCRP IV on August 23–31, 1984, in Nairobi. Dr. John B. Taylor, of the UK, was named Secretary-General of WCRP IV. He set up offices in Geneva, Switzerland, beginning October 1, 1983.

12. Commission on the Future

At a meeting of the officers of WCRP in Beijing in May 1982, the Secretary-General first proposed that a Commission on the Future be established to report to WCRP IV on the future organization and programme of WCRP/International. He felt that WCRP/International was at a turning point, since many of its leaders were on the point of retirement. It was agreed in principle to set up such a Commission, with its expenses to be taken from the income of the Niwano Fund.

After some exploration, Prof. François Houtart of the Catholic University of Louvain was appointed Director of Research in the spring of 1983. He developed a long questionnaire which was sent, in August 1983, to a large cross-section of participants of WCRP world assemblies. Almost 150 answers were received. Dr. John B. Taylor developed a second questionnaire on future organization and programme. This was mailed in the autumn of 1983 and elicited 40 replies. In the meantime, eight members of the Commission were elected from several world religions and continents: Sr. Marjorie Keenan (Christian, USA), Dr. Inamullah Khan (Muslim, Pakistan), Rev. Michael Mildenberger (Christian, German Federal Republic), Dr. S.G. Mudgal (Hindu, India), Mr. Masuo Nezu (Buddhist, Japan), Bishop J. Henry Okullu (Christian, Kenya), Bishop Rémi De Roo (Christian, Canada), and Miss Hannah Stanton (Christian, UK). The Commission held one session on February 13–17, 1984, outside Geneva. Sr. Marjorie Keenan was elected Chairperson. Based on answers to the two questionnaires and recommendations of Prof. Houtart, the Commission drew up a detailed report. This 17-page report was made available late in February 1984 for study and action at WCRP IV.

13. Addresses by the Secretary-General

Dr. Jack, as Secretary-General, has been called upon to give both formal and informal addresses in many parts of the world. A brief sample follows.

Beijing, China—Religion group of the National Committee of the Chinese People's Political Consultative Conference. June 1980.

Geneva, Switzerland—NGO Committee on Disarmament. August 1981.

Karachi, Pakistan—WCRP/Pakistan. February 1980.

Lampeter, Wales—General Assembly of Unitarian Churches of the UK, The Essex Hall Lecture. April 1982.

London, England—WCRP/England and World Congress of Faiths. April 1982.

Montreal, Canada—WCRP/Canada. May 1983.

Nairobi, Kenya—WCRP/Africa. August 1983.

New Delhi, India—Gandhi Memorial Lecture, Gandhi Peace Foundation. January 1980.

New York, USA—UN Fellows in Disarmament, October 1979; World Muslim League, April 1981; Disarmament Forum, UN Headquarters, October 1979; DPI Annual Conference, September 1981; Journalists Encounter, UN Headquarters, June 1982; Temple of Understanding, October 1982; Special Committee Against Apartheid, February 1983.

South Orange, N.J., USA—Third Annual Inter-Religious Institute of Seton Hall University. June 1981.

Stockholm, Sweden—Stockholm International Peace Research Institute (SIPRI). December 1982.

Stuttgart, German Federal Republic—WCRP/Europe. February 1984. Tokyo, Japan—Rissho Kosei-kai, May 1982; Eighteenth World Congress of the World Association of World Federalists, July 1980.

Washington, D.C., USA—Subcommittee on Human Rights and International Organizations, Committee on Foreign Affairs, House of Representatives, March 1982; US Department of State, April 1982.

14. Publications*

A. Written by the Secretary-General

1. Books

1. *Religion in the Struggle for World Community,* edited by Homer A. Jack. New York: WCRP. 443 pp. 1980, $6.95 paperback postpaid.
2. *Disarm—Or Die: The Second U.N. Special Session on Disarmament,* by Homer A. Jack. New York: WCRP. 291 pp. 1983. $15.00 hardcover postpaid; $7.95 paperback postpaid.
3. *The Ghandi Reader,* edited by Homer A. Jack. Reprint of the 1956 Indiana University Press edition, with a new introduction. Madras: Samata Books. 1983. 533 pp. 90 rupees.

2. Chapters in Books

1. "Befreiung von der Atomaren Bedrohung," In *Den Frieden Tun,* ed. by Maria A. Lücker. Freiburg: Herber. 1980. 142 pp. pp. 115–20.
2. "NGOs and Disarmament." In *SIPRI Yearbook 1979.* Stockholm: Stockholm International Peace Research Institute. 1979. 698 pp. pp. 666–80.
3. "Forsok till betygsattning i slutkedet Framgangar och missrakningar" and "De ickestatliga organisationerna och nedrustningen." In *Nedrustning Debat 1978–1982.* (Disarmament Under Scrutiny 1978–1982) ed. by Ulrich Herz. Stockholm: Swedish People's Parliament for Disarmament. 1980. 478 pp. pp. 143–47, pp. 305–24. (In Swedish).
4. "The United Nations Special Session: Two Years After" and "Non-Governmental Organizations and Disarmament." In *Armaments, Arms Control and Disarmament,* ed. by Marek Thee. Paris: UNESCO. 1981. 466 pp. pp. 253–57 and pp. 365–69.
5. "Gandhian Unilateralism Revisited." In *Disarmament and Human Survival.* Special issue of *Gandhi Marg.* New Delhi: Gandhi Peace Foundation. May–June 1982. 444 pp. pp. 329–34.
6. "New Perspectives About Disarmament." In *Aiming at New World Order,* ed. by Kikuo Yamoaka. Tokyo: League for World Federalism. 1982. (In Japanese).
7. "Debatten om Fastfrysing i FN." In *FRYS: Om Frysbevegelsen og Atomvapen i Europe,* ed. by Magne Barth. Oslo: Pax Forlag. 1983. 148 pp. pp. 39–43. (In Norwegian).
8. "Beyond Multi-Religious Dialogue." In *Religions and Man.* ed. by Albert Nambiaparambil. Cochin, India: Chavara Cultural Centre. 1983. 157 pp. pp. 45–58.

9. "Non-Governmental Organizations and Disarmament at the United Nations." In *SIPRI Yearbook 1983.* Stockholm: Stockholm International Peace Research Institute. 1983. 681 pp. pp. 645–57.

3. Pamphlets

1. *Citizen's Guide to the Second Special Session.* Supplement to "Disarmament Times." November 1981. 4 pp. Also translated into German and published by WCRP/Europe. 24 pp. 1982.
2. *Lessening the Nuclear Threat: A Defence of Unilateralism.* London: Lindsey Press. 1982. 26 pp. The 1982 Essex Hall Lecture. $2.00.
3. *The Nuclear Weapons Freeze Goes International: The U.N. Breakthrough.* New York. WCRP and the Douglas Inquiry. 24 pp. 1983. $1.00.

4. Articles

1. "Strategies for Disarmament." *Fellowship.* January/February 1980. pp. 12–13.
2. "Food and Politics in Kampuchea." *The Christian Century.* February 6–13, 1980. pp. 127–29.
3. "Report from Kampuchea: The Lucky Ones—and the Unlucky." *UU World.* February 15, 1980. p. 7.
4. "No Reverence for Life in Cambodia/Kampuchea." *The* (Schweitzer) *Courier.* Spring 1980. pp. 3–4.
5. "The Tragedy of Kampuchea." *Fellowship.* May 1980. pp. 12–13.
6. "Disarmament Forum." *Disarmament.* Vol. III, No. 1. May 1980. pp. 7–8.
7. "The UN Special Session: Two Years After." *Arms Control Today.* June 1980.
8. "Bandung Influence Continues Down the Decades." *Toward Freedom.* June 1980.
9. "U.S. Guilt in the Failure of Disarmament Talks." (With William Epstein). Letter to *The New York Times.* September 23, 1980.
10. "Khmer Lexicon." *The Christian Century.* October 1, 1980.
11. "Non-Proliferation Conference–'Litany of Disappointments'." *Sane World.* November 1980. p. 4.
12. "One Peaceful World." *East West Journal.* December 1980. pp. 33–34.
13. "The Khmer—An Endangered People." *The Church Woman.* January 1981. pp. 10, 24.
14. "Albert Schweitzer and A Comprehensive Test-Ban Treaty." *The Courier.* Spring 1981. pp. 3–4.

15. "Religious Liberals Encouraged by Developments in China." *UU World.* March 1, 1981. p. 8.

16. "The Re-emergence of Buddhism in China Today." *Dharma World.* Vol. 8. September 1981. pp. 1, 4.

17. "The Politics and Hopes for the Second Special Session." *Review of International Affairs.* December 5, 1981. pp. 21–22.

18. "Mapping Plans for UN Disarmament Session." *Sane World.* December 1981, pp. 1, 4.

19. "The Second UN Special Session on Disarmament." *Arms Control Today.* Vol. 12, No. 2. February 1982. pp. 4–5.

20. "The New Abolitionism." *Peace Research Review.* Vol. IX, No. 1. March 1982. pp. 25–39.

21. "Politics and Hopes in UN." *Maryknoll.* Vol. 76, No. 4. April 1982. pp. 16–19.

22. "Norman Thomas and the Nuclear Freeze." Letter to *The New York Times.* June 23, 1982.

23. "Both Sides of UN Plaza." *Friends Journal.* July /15, 1982, pp. 14–16.

24. "An Evaluation of the Second U.N. Special Session on Disarmament: Some Lists." *Gandhi Marg.* August 1982. pp. 566–68.

25. "Disarmament or Annihilation?" *Dharma World.* September 1982. pp. 42–45.

26. "Report on the UN Special Session." *Sane World.* October 1982. p. 3.

27. "Non-Governmental Organizations and Public Opinion at SSOD II." *Disarmament.* November 1982.

28. "A Message of Reconciliation." *Engage/Social Action.* December 1982. p. 21.

29. "The Expanding Rôle of NGOs in the UN Disarmament Body." *Development.* (Society for International Development). 1982. No. 1. pp. 62–64.

30. "Report of the Disarmament Working Groups." *The Case for Binding Triad.* New York: Center for War/Peace Studies. 1982. 13 pp. pp. 9–13.

31. ". . . For Disarmament." In *Why Do We Need the U.N.?* Washington: United Methodist Church. 1982. 12 pp. p. 8.

32. "Disarmament Resolutions: Pressure or a Ritual?" *Transnational Perspectives.* Vol. 8, No. 1 1982. pp. 18–20.

33. "Overcoming the Failure of the Second UN Special Session on Disarmament." *Bulletin of Peace Proposals.* Vol. 13, No. 3. pp. 177–87.

34. "A Political Postmortem: The Second UN Special Session."

Review of International Affairs. Vol. XXXIII, No. 780. 1982. pp. 7–9.

35. "Is Bukovsky a Concealed Communist?" *Religion in Communist Dominated Areas.* Vol. XXI, No. 4–5–6. 1982. p. 94.

36. "The Special Session and Beyond." *Spears or Pruning Hooks? The Impact of the Arms Race on Society.* New York: United Nations. 1982. 28 pp. p. 25.

37. "Soviet Friends' Small Voice in Missile Protests." Letter to *The New York Times.* January 30, 1982.

38. "Correcting Isaac." Letter to *The Nation.* January 1–8, 1983. p. 2.

39. "China." Letter to *The New York Times.* Travel Section. February 27, 1983.

40. "Gandhi Revisited." Letter to *UU World.* February 15, 1983, p. 5.

41. "Religion, Peace, and the Second UN Special Session on Disarmament." *Echoes of Peace.* Vol. 2, No. 1. February 1983. pp. 6–9.

42. "East/West, North/South: Opportunities for the World Disarmament Campaign." *Disarmament: A Periodic Review by the United Nations.* Spring 1983. Vol. VI, No. 3. pp. 33–41.

43. "U.S. Record." Letter in *The Christian Century.* May 18, 1983. p. 509.

44. "Religious Persecution as a Violation of Human Rights." In *Religious Persecution as a Violation of Human Rights.* Hearings and Markup. Committee On Foreign Affairs, House of Representatives, Ninety-Seventh Congress. Washington: Government Printing Office. 1983. 948 pp. pp. 104–45.

45. "Prepared Statement of Dr. Homer A. Jack." In *Nomination of Kenneth L. Adelman.* Hearings before the Committee on Foreign Relations, U.S. Senate. 1983. 241 pp. pp. 139–41.

5.   "Disarmament Times"

Dr. Jack was one of the principal writers for "Disarmament Times" ever since 1978 when that newspaper was established by the NGO Committee on Disarmament (at UN Headquarters). The frequency of his articles is as follows: fourteen articles in 1980, fifteen in 1981, thirty-four in 1982, eleven in 1983, and three in the first issue of 1984. The total is 77. An index of these articles may be obtained from the author.

6.   WCRP Disarmament Reports

1. *The Initial Preparation for the Second Session on Disarmament.* January 1981. 14 pp.

2. *Toward A World Disarmament Campaign.* March 1981. 11 pp.

3. *Opening May 11 or 18 and Lasting Up to Five Weeks: The Work of the First Substantive Session of the Preparatory Committee for the Second Special Session on Disarmament.* June 1981. 21 pp.

4. *Disarmament and Children: UNICEF Attempts to "Remain Unpolitical".* June 1981. 14 pp.
5. *Provisional Agenda of the Second Special Session on Disarmament: The Preparatory Committee Continues Its Deliberations.* October 1981. 30 pp.
6. *Mobilizing World Public Opinion for Disarmament: The Future of the World Disarmament Campaign.* February 1982. 11 pp.
7. *Progress Toward a Comprehensive Program of Disarmament.* March 1982. 17 pp.
8. *The Final Meetings of the Preparatory Committee for the Second Special Session on Disarmament.* June 1982. 17 pp.
9. *WCRP Multi-Religious Mission on Disarmament to China.* May 1982. 15 pp.
10. *Oral Statement of the World Conference on Religion and Peace to the Ad Hoc Committee of the Second Special Session.* June 25, 1982. Homer A. Jack. June 1982. 18 pp.
11. *An Evaluation of the Second U.N. Special Session on Disarmament: Some Lists.* July 1982. 2 pp.
12. *Jack v. Haig: How 318 NGOs Were Denied U.S. Visas to Attend the Second U.N. Special Session on Disarmament.* September 1982. 20 pp.
13. *Rationalizing the Role of NGOs in Disarmament in the U.N. System.* September 1982. 15 pp.
14. *Freeze or Burn: The Nuclear Freeze at the Second U.N. Special Session on Disarmament.* October 1982. 18 pp.
15. *The U.N. Launches a World Disarmament Campaign.* January 1983. 15 pp.
16. *Preventing Nuclear War.* January 1983. 20 pp.
17. *Comprehensive Program of Disarmament.* February 1983. 19 pp.

7. WCRP Reports on Kampuchea

A total of 26 reports were published about Kampuchea from material on massacre published in November 1978 to the final report of the WCRP Khmer Fund and Programme in July 1981. This list is available as are photocopies. Of the 26 reports, 17 were written by Dr. Jack.

8. Other WCRP Reports

1. *Some Notes on the Re-emergence Today of the Religions of China.* September 1980. 36 pp.
2. *When is a NGO not a NGO? The Work of the ECOSOC Committee on Non-Governmental Organizations.* April 1981. 23 pp.
3. *The U.N. Declaration for Religious Freedom: The Results of Two Decades of Drafting.* April 1981. 22 pp. Addendum: 5 pp. May 1981.

4. *Quadrennial Report of the World Conference on Religion and Peace: Activities for the Years 1978–81 and Its Consultative Status with the Economic and Social Council of the U.N.* December 31, 1981. 2 pp.
5. *A Sheaf of Lists on the United Nations.* May 1981. 16 pp.
6. *How the U.N. Religious Declaration Was Unanimously Adopted.* January 1982. 23 pp.

B.   By Other Authors

Eight of the WCRP Reports on Kampuchea were written by Mr. David R. Hawk and one by Dr. Howard Schomer. In addition, the testimony was published of Mr. Bhagwan Das on Untouchability on the Subcontinent, presented to the UN Sub-Commission on Prevention of Discrimination and Protection of Minorities in August 1983.

C.   "Religion for Peace"

This periodical was continued during 1979–84, edited by Dr. Jack. The first issue after WCRP III was No. 25 dated January 1980. The last issue for 1983 was No. 36 dated October 1983.

"Religion for Peace" continues to act as a bulletin-board, unfortunately printed only in the English language, for the WCRP movement. It is mailed free of charge to about 2,000 individuals in 50 countries.

15.   Afterword

This report is somewhat truncated by my resignation as Secretary-General of WCRP/International, effective January 1, 1984. In July 1983, I realized that I did not have the physical strength to put together an excellent WCRP IV and managed a rather quick, and successful, transition, with Dr. John B. Taylor assuming duties as Secretary-General of WCRP IV on October 1, 1983 and as Acting Secretary-General of WCRP/International on January 1, 1984 when my resignation became effective.

The transition was relatively smooth, perhaps because it was done relatively quickly, with Dr. Taylor finally appointed as Secretary-General of WCRP/International at a meeting of some officers in Geneva in February 1984. Thus what WCRP/International accomplished from January 1 through August 23, 1984 is in the province of Dr. Taylor. It consisted largely of preparations for WCRP IV.

Finally, several persons active in WCRP, or identified with it, have died since WCRP III. These include at least the following persons: Mr. J.P. Narayan of India in October 1979; Prof. Al-Nowaihi of Egypt in February 1980; Rev. Riri Nakayama of Japan in July 1981; Bishop Samuel of Egypt (with President Sadat) in October 1981; Lord Philip Noel-Baker of the UK in October 1982; Dr. Maria A. Lücker of the German Federal Republic (and long-time Secretary of WCRP/Europe) in November 1983; and Prof. T.M.P. Mahadevan of India in November 1983.

71

Directory of WCRP Committees

International Secretariat
Dr. John B. Taylor, Secretary-General. 14 chemin Auguste-Vilbert, 1218 Grand-Saconnex, Geneva, Switzerland.

International Headquarters
WCRP/International, c/o Mr. William Thompson, 777 United Nations Plaza, New York, N.Y. 10017, USA.

Africa
WCRP/Africa and WCRP/Kenya: c/o Mr. Wilfred Maciel, P.O. Box 72766, Nairobi, Kenya.

WCRP/Cameroon: c/o Dr. Adamou Ndam Njoya, C.P.1638, Yaoundé, Cameroon.

WCRP/Egypt: c/o Dr. El-Sayed Al-Taftazani, 18 Gamal Noah Street, Heliopolis, Cairo, Egypt.

WCRP/Senegal: c/o Mr. Jean Carbonare, P.O. Box 1887, Dakar, Senegal.

WCRP/South Africa: c/o Rev. Gerrie Lubbe, 08 Piet Meyer St., Mindalore, Krugersdorp, Transvaal, 1740 South Africa.

Ghana: Bishop Peter K. Sarpong, P.O. Box 99, Kumasi, Ghana.

Nigeria: Prof. Musa O.A. Abdul, University of Ibadan, Ibadan, Oyo, Nigeria

Americas
WCRP/Canada: 11 Madison Avenue, Toronto, Ontario M5R 2S2, Canada.

WCRP/USA: c/o Secretary-General, 777 United Nations Plaza, New York, N.Y. 10017, USA.

Other Contacts:

Chile: Rev. Christian Precht, Casilla 59, Santiago 1, Chile.

Australasia
Asian Conference on Religion and Peace: c/o Mr. Mehervan Singh, 5001 Beach Road, No. 07–24, Golden Mile Complex, Singapore 0719, Republic of Singapore.

WCRP/Bangladesh: c/o Ven. Visuddhananda Mahathero, Dhammarajika Buddhist Monastery, Atish Dipankar Sarak, Kamalapur, Dacca 14, Bangladesh.

WCRP/India: c/o Major-General Sujan Singh Uban, C-191 Defense Colony, New Delhi 110 024, India.

WCRP/Indonesia: c/o Mr. Lukman Harun, Jalan Sukabumi No. 11, Jakarta 10310, Indonesia.

WCRP/Japan: c/o Priest Kiyotoshi Kawai, Fumon Hall, 2–6 Wada, Suginami-ku, Tokyo 166, Japan.

WCRP/Pakistan: c/o Mr. Habibur Rahman Khan, 240 Garden East, Kashana-i-Hafeez, Karachi 3, Pakistan.

WCRP/Thailand: c/o Judge Sathitya Lengthaisong, Village No. 1, Chitvisut Soi 1, Bangkrang, Muang Nonthaburi, Thailand.

Inter-Religious Organisation, Singapore. c/o Mr. Mehervan Singh, address above.

Other Contacts:

Australia: Rev. Philip Huggins, Olsen Road, Nar Nar Goon North, Victoria 3812, Australia.

People's Republic of China: Mr. Zhao Puchu, The Buddhist Association of China, Beijing, People's Republic of China.

Israel: Miss Shelley Elkayam, Kedoshei Struma 9, Malcha, Manachat, Jerusalem 96901, Israel.

West Bank of Jordan: Mrs. Jean Zaru, P.O. Box 66, Friends Boys' School, Ramallah, via Israel.

Nepal: Mr. Davendraj R. Upadhya. 21/452 Ram Shah Path, Kathmandu, Nepal.

Sri Lanka: Prof. L.G. Hewage, 28 First Lane, Kirillapona, Colombo 5, Sri Lanka.

Europe

European Committee of WCRP: c/o Mr. Günther Gebhardt, Spessartstrasse 8, 8700 Würzburg, Federal Republic of Germany.

WCRP/Belgium: c/o Dr. Mladen Karadjole, 214 Rue Louis Hap, 1040 Brussels, Belgium.

WCRP/France: c/o Mme Jacqueline Rougé, 6 Rue du Vieux Colombier, 75006 Paris, France.

WCRP/Germany: Rev. Hermann Benz, Pfarrei St. Hedwig, Lieschingstrasse 24, 7000 Stuttgart 80, Federal Republic of Germany.

WCRP/Italy: c/o Rev. Giovanni Cereti, Via Traspontina 18, 00193 Roma, Italy.

WCRP/Netherlands: c/o Dr. Henk E. Schouten, u.d. Brandelerkade 22, 2323 GW Leiden, The Netherlands.

WCRP/UK-Ireland: c/o Miss Hannah Stanton, 30 Burtons Road, Hampton Hill, Middlesex TW12 1DA, United Kingdom.

Other Contacts:

Austria: Prof. Dr. Josef Schultes, Schelhammergasse 17, 3420 Kritzendorf, Klostenburg, Austria.

Cyprus: Dr. Rifat Yücelten, P.O. Box 142, Lefkhosa (Nicosia), Cyprus.
Czechoslovakia: Prof. Mrs. Anezka Ebertova, Hviezdoslavova 1, 101 00 Prague, Czechoslovakia.
Greece: Bishop Anastasios Yannoulatos. Dept. of the Study of Religions, Athens University, G. Seferi 1, Neon Psyhicon, Athens, Greece.
USSR: Dr. Alexy Bouevsky, Dept. of External Church Relations, Russian Orthodox Church, 18/2 Ryeleyev St., Moscow G-2, 121002 USSR.

N.

Participants

72

International Preparatory Committee

Buddhists
Mr. Sathira Bandharangshi, Thailand
*Rev. Kenryu T. Tsuji, USA

Christians
Rev. José Chipenda, People's Republic of Angola
Prof. Kwesi A. Dickson, Ghana
Prof. Anezka Ebertova, Czechoslovakia
*Archbishop Angelo Fernandes, India
Bishop Gabriel G. Ganaka, Nigeria
*Dr. Dana McLean Greeley, USA
*Prof. Yoshiaki Iisaka, Japan
Mrs. Joyce Kaddu, Uganda
Mr. John C. Kamau, Kenya
Miss M. Irene Kessy, Tanzania
Mr. Wilfred Maciel, Kenya
Rev. Dominic Musasa, Malawi
*Bishop J. Henry Okullu, Kenya
Msgr. Joseph O.-A. Osei, Ghana
Dr. Wilhelm J. Otte, Federal Republic of Germany
*Archbishop Bernardino Pinera, Chile
Sr. Layla Raphael, Canada
Miss Hannah Stanton, United Kingdom
Dr. Gerald Wanjohi, Kenya

Hindus
Mr. Vijay Arun, Kenya

---

* –Officer or Board Member of WCRP.
# –Member of Nairobi Planning Committee.

*Sri R.R. Diwakar, India
Mrs. Harinder Durga, India
Prof. S.G. Mudgal, India
Mr. P.S. Saini, Kenya

Jews
Mrs. Fredelle Brief, Canada

Muslims
*Dr. Musa O. Abdul, Nigeria
Mr. S.A. Ali, India
Dr. Khairallah Assar, Algeria
Dr. Yusuf A. Eraj, Kenya
Mr. Lukman Harun, Indonesia
Mr. Badru Kateregga, Kenya
*Dr. Inamullah Khan, Pakistan
Mr. Mohammed Koor, Kenya
Dr. Adamou Ndam Njoya, Cameroun
Prof. El Sayed Al-Taftazani, Egypt

Shintoist
*Rev. Toshio Miyaki, Japan

Sikh
Mr. Tarlok S. Nandhra, Kenya

National, Regional, and International Staff
Prof. Dr. Arnulf Camps, Netherlands
Dr. Donald Harrington, USA
Dr. Homer A. Jack, USA
Prof. Dr. Norbert Klaes, Federal Republic of Germany
Mr. T. Koito, Japan
Mr. Hiroyuki Oshima, Japan
Mr. Ryuichiro Oyama, Japan
Mr. Koichi Saito, Japan
Mr. Mehervan Singh, Singapore
Miss Dinah Stephen, Kenya
Dr. John B. Taylor, United Kingdom
Major-General Sujan Singh Uban, India

73

Nairobi Planning Committee

Administration: Mr. Wilfred Maciel
Finance: Mr. Tarlok S. Nandhra
Hospitality: Mr. John C. Kamau
Multi-Religious Services: Bishop J. Henry Okullu
Programme Coordination: Dr. Gerald Wanjohi
Public Relations: Mr. Mohammed Koor
Transport: Mr. P.S. Saini
Women's Coordinator: Mrs. Gertie Wanjohi
Youth Coordinators: Mr. Badru Kateregga and Miss Shobna Obhrai
Staff: Mr. Peter Nsubuga

74

Assembly Leadership

President: Archbishop Angelo Fernandes.
Vice-Presidents: Sri R.R. Diwakar, Dr. Dana McLean Greeley, and President Nikkyo Niwano.
Secretary-General: Dr. John B. Taylor.
Deputy Secretaries-General: Sr. Marjorie Keenan and Prof. Dr. Norbert Klaes.
Chairperson of Youth Committee: Mr. Hans van Willenswaard.
Chairperson of Women's Committee: Dr. Ms. Diana Eck.
Chairperson of Beyond Nairobi Committee: Sr. Marjorie Keenan.
Chairperson of Nominating Committee: Dr. Inamullah Khan.
Commission I: "People of Faith Working Together for Peace." Moderators: Rev. Nikkyo Niwano, Bishop J. Henry Okullu, and Mrs. Gedong Bagoes Oka. Speakers: Sri Goswami, Ven. Visuddhananda Mahathero, Victor Goldbloom and Ven. Jing Hui. Consultant-Experts: Mr. Shin Anzai, Prof. Kwesi Dickson, Anantanand Rambachan, Dr. George Rupp, and Major-General S.S. Uban.
Commission II: "Human Dignity, Social Justice, and Development of the Whole Person." Moderators: Sri R.R. Diwakar, Rev. Toshio Miyake, and Mr. Mehervan Singh. Speakers: Mr. Harold Belmont, Dr. S.K. Chaturvedi, Mr. Ian Fry, Dr. Eric Prokosch, and Mr. Saichiro Uesugi. Consultant-Experts: Mr. Ernest Beyaraaza, Mr. Bhagwan Das, Dr. Adamou Ndam Njoya, and Prof. Kikuo Yamaoka.
Commission III: "World Peace and Disarmament." Moderators: Dr. Dana McLean Greeley, and Mme Jacqueline Rougé. Speakers: Ms. Shelley Elkayam, Ms. Nahla Haidar and Mrs. Jean Zaru (a panel of three women discussing the Middle East), Prof. Yoshiaki Iisaka, Sr. Brahma Kumari Janki, Brahma Kumari Jayanti, Dr. Lubomir Mirejovsky, and Mr. Shen Derong. Consultant-Experts: Dr. Viqar A. Hamdani, Dr. Norbert Klaes, and Sri Radhakrishna.

75

Delegates

(Including Biographies of National Delegates, Commission Moderators, Speakers, and Consultant-Experts)

Mr. Mohammad Aasim. (Muslim) 3288 Farhat Ullah Khan Street, Kucha Pandit, Lal Kuan, Delhi 110 006, India. Assistant Librarian, University of Delhi; preparing M.S. in Political Science. 31 years.

Dr. El-Sayed M. Aboul Wafa Al-Taftazani. (Muslim) 18 Dr. Gamal Noah Street, Almaza, Heliopolis, Cairo, Egypt. Vice-President, Cairo University for Graduate Studies and Research. Formerly Professor of Islamic Philosophy and Dean of the Faculty of Education, Cairo University. Member of the Supreme Council of Islamic Affairs (Cairo) and of the International Council of WCRP. Author of *Fundamentals of Islam, Egypt in Perspective; Man and Cosmos in Islam; Ibn Sabin and His Mystical Philosophy; Muslim Theology; Ibn Aatallah Al-Sakandari and His Sufism;* and *Studies in Islamic Philosophy.* 54 years.

Ambassador Olu Adeniji. (Christian) Officer for Economic Affairs and International Organizations of the Nigerian Ministry of External Affairs, accredited by the Government of Nigeria to the United Nations.

Mrs. Husna Akhtar. (Muslim) 9 Larmini Street, Dhaka, Bangladesh. Teacher. Member of International Council of WCRP. 40 years.

Mr. Shin Anzai. (Christian) Peace Research Institute of WCRP/Japan. 1271 Kasama-cho, Totsuka-ku, Yokohama-shi, Kanagawa 247, Japan.

Mr. Yuji Aoyama. (Buddhist) 7-2-3-701 Minami-kasai, Edokawa-ku, Tokyo 134, Japan. Director, WCRP/Japan; Director, Doctrinal Division of Gedatsu-kai. 50 years.

Dr. M. Aram. (Hindu) Gandhigram Rural Institute, Gandhigram, T.N. 624 302, India. Vice-Chancellor, Gandhigram Rural Institute. Formerly Director, Nagaland Peace Centre; Secretary, Asian Council, World Peace Brigade; Principal, Rural Institute of Higher Education, Coimbatore. Joint President, WCRP/International. 57 years.

Mrs. Minoti Aram. (Hindu) (See address of Dr. Aram above.) President, Gandhigram Lakshmi Mother Sanga. Formerly, Governing Body Member, Nagaland Peace Centre; Member, Madurai Peace Committee and Anti-Dowry Committee. 43 years.

Cardinal Francis Arinze. (Christian) President, Vatican Secretariat for Interreligious Dialogue, Vatican City, 00120, via Italy. Author of *Sacrifice in Igbo Religion; Answering God's Call; The Holy Eucharist: Our Life; Living Our Faith; In Christ, Through Christ and for Christ.* 51 years.

Dr. Khairallah Assar. (Muslim) B.P. 466, Annaba, Algeria. Professor of Social Psychology and Methodology of Social Sciences. Author of *Modern Science: Its Certainties and Mirages; An Attempt to Build Islamic Models for Research in Sociology; Principles of Social Psychology;* and *Introduction to Literature and Psychology.*

Mr. Mohammed Azam. (Muslim) 9 Newport Road, Balsall Heath, Birmingham 12, United Kingdom. Student for M.S.C. at the University of Birmingham. 25 years.

Mrs. Gedong Bagoes Oka. (Hindu) P.B. Sudirman F.S. 2, Denpasar, Bali, Indonesia. Lecturer, Udayana State University; Chairperson, Bali Ganti Sena Foundation. Member, International Council of WCRP. 63 years.

Mr. Harold Belmont. (Traditional Religion) Member, American Indian Traditional Elders' Circle; Consultant on racism, bigotry and oppression to the American Indians, especially in the areas of fishing rights, political prisoners, religious freedom and Hopi prophecies. 112 15th Avenue, Seattle, WA 98122, USA.

Rev. Hermann J. Benz. (Christian) Lieschingstr. 44, 7000 Stuttgart 80, Federal Republic of Germany. Parish priest at St. Hedwig and Professor of Religion. Formerly Director, German Catholic Mission in Paris. 56 years.

Mr. Ernest K.M. Beyaraaza. (Christian) Kenyatta University College, P.O. Box 43844, Nairobi, Kenya. Lecturer in Philosophy.

Mrs. Deepali Bhanot. (Hindu) Block N.I.L.-17/A, Malaviya Nagar, New Delhi 110 017, India. Lecturer in Sanskrit at the University of Delhi; NSS Programme Officer, Village Project. 36 years.

Ven. Pra Bimaladhamma. (Buddhist) Watmahathat, Prachan Street, Bangkok 10200, Thailand. President, Mahachulalongkorn University.

Rev. Jonathan Blake. (Christian) 47 Roebuck Road, Rochester ME1 1UE, England. Priest; Member, Executive Council of WCRP/International. 28 years.

Rev. Giovanni Cereti. (Christian) Via Traspontina 18, 00193 Roma, Italy. Doctor in Law and Theology; Priest; Professor of Oecumenism;

Member, Oecumenical Commission of Diocese of Rome. Chairman, WCRP/Italy. Author of *Commentary on Decree on Ecumenism; Divorce, Remarriage and Penance in the Early Church; Ecumenism: Lessons on Ecumenical Methodology; Christian Churches and Judaism; Love and Communion in the Marriage;* and *New Religious Movements, Sects and Cults.* 51 years.

Charukeerty Bhattarak Swamiji. (Jain) Sri Jain Math, Shravanbelagola, Hassan, Karnataka, India. Head of Jain Math. Member, International Council of WCRP. 35 years.

Dr. S.K. Chaturvedi. (Hindu) C-230 Greater Kailash I, New Delhi 110 048, India. Joint Secretary, Government of India. Former Indian Delegate to UNCTAD, ECAFE, and ESCAP.

Rev. José B. Chipenda. (Christian) P.O. Box 52, Lobito, Angola. Director, Centre for the Study of Theology and Culture; Programme Secretary, WCC/PCR. 55 years.

Miss Pal Khn Chon. (Buddhist) Iri, Chun-Puk, Republic of Korea. Dean, Graduate School of Won Kwang University: Director, International Bureau of Won Buddhism. 55 years.

Dr. André Chouraqui. (Jewish) Ain Rogel 8, Jerusalem. Doctor of Law, Writer, Chairman of Israel Inter-Faith Association. 67 years.

Rev. Mark Cornelis. (Christian) Sluisstraat 75, 3000 Leuven, Belgium. Military Chaplain; Youth Pastor. Formerly Professor of Religion. Author of *Une Réflexion Chrétienne sur la Problématique Actuelle Concernant la Guerre et la Paix.* 53 years.

Ms. Gill Cressey. (Christian) Sparkbrook Ashram Community Service Project, 23/25 Grantham Road, Sparkbrook, Birmingham B11 1LU, England. Works for a joint Christian-Muslim project. 24 years.

Miss Natalia Dallapiccola. (Christian) Via di Frascati 300, 00040 Rocca di Papa, Roma, Italy. Director, Centre for Contacts with Other Religions of the Focolare Movement. Member, International Council of WCRP. 60 years.

Mr. Dao Shuren. (Buddhist) The Chinese Buddhist Association, Beijing, People's Republic of China. 49 years.

Mr. Bhagwan Das. (Buddhist) BC-1/H, D.D.A. Flats, Munirka, New Delhi 110 067, India. Director, Asian Centre for Human Rights.

Dr. Mrs. Yvonne Delk. (Christian) UCC, 105 Madison Avenue, New York, N.Y. 10016, USA. Executive Director, Office for Church and Society, United Church of Christ. 55 years.

Mr. Mijar K. Dharmaraja. (Jain) A-5, DDA Flats, Saket, Malaviya Nagar Ext., New Delhi 110 017, India. Journalist; Broadcaster. 66 years.

Prof. Kwesi Dickson. (Christian) Box 73, University of Ghana, Legon, Accra, Ghana. Director, Institute of African Studies; Professor of Old Testament Studies.

Sri R.R. Diwakar. (Hindu) 233, Sadashiv Nagar, Bangalore 560 080, India. Chairman, Gandhi Peace Foundation; Honorary President, WCRP/International. Former Governor of Bihar, India. Author of *Satyagraha;* and *Mahayogi Sri Aurobindo.* 90 years.

Mr. Timur Djaelani. (Muslim) Jalan Kramat 7, No. 9, Jakarta 10450, Indonesia. Professor of Islamics, State Institute of Islamics. 62 years.

Mrs. Barbara D'Souza. (Christian) 876 Poonamalee High Road, Madras 600 084, India. Secretary. 38 years.

Mrs. Harinder Durga. (Hindu) 706 Sector 7B, Chandigarh, Punjab, India. Senior Executive, Onkarnath Health Centre.

Miss Ranjana Durga. (Hindu) (See address of Mrs. H. Durga above.) Post Graduate Studies in Journalism. 23 years.

Mr. Rabindranath Duttagupta. (Hindu) 24 Larmini Street, Dhaka 3, Bangladesh. Businessman. 61 years.

Dr. Mrs. Doris J. Dyke. (Christian) 41 Dalton Road, Toronto, Ontario M5R 2Y8, Canada. Professor of Theology. 54 years.

Dr. Mrs. Anezka Ebertova. (Christian) Vinohrady, Hviezdoslavova 1, 101 00 Praha 10, CSSR. Professor of Social Ethics; Woman's Desk, Oecumenical Council of Churches in the CSSR. Author of articles on social theology and social ethics. Member, International Council of WCRP. 61 years.

Mr. Bahtiar Effendy. (Muslim) Gang Mess No. 47, Jln. K.H. Mas Mansur, Jakarta Pusat, Indonesia. Serves on editorial staff of an Indonesian Islamic magazine. Author of *Martin Luther, His Works and the Rise of Capitalism; The Concept of Mankind in Islam; Pesantren and Social Change;* and *Muhammad, Man of Allah.* 26 years.

Ms. Shelley Elkayam. (Jewish) Kedoshei Struma 9, Malcha, Manathat, Jerusalem 96901, Israel. Poetess, authoress of a children's book and an article in *Yated,* a Sephardic periodical. Also representing "The East for Peace."

Dr. Yusuf A. Eraj. (Muslim) P.O. Box 43789, Nairobi, Kenya. Medical doctor.

Dr. Ms. Jane Evans. (Jewish) 103 Wood Hollow Lane, New Rochelle, N.Y. 10804, USA. President, Jewish Braille Institute of America; Consultant to National Federation of Temple Sisterhoods and Union of American Hebrew Congregations; Executive Director Emeritus, National Federation of Temple Sisterhoods. 77 years.

Archbishop Angelo I. Fernandes. (Christian) Archbishop's House, Ashok Place, New Delhi 110 001, India. Archbishop of Delhi; Member, CBCI Commission for Justice and Peace; President Emeritus, WRCP/International. Formerly Secretary-General, Catholic Bishops' Conference of India; Member, Synod of Bishops Secretariat and Pontifical Commission for Justice and Peace. Author of *Apostolic Endeavour; Religion, Development and Peace; Religion and the Quality of Life; Religion and a New World Order; Humanization, A Process of Love.* 71 years.

Ms. Theresa J. Flower. (Christian) 31 Pendrith Street, Toronto, Ontario M6G 1R6, Canada. Staff Facilitator, WCRP/Canada; Facilitator, Mosaic (an interfaith movement). 34 years.

Dr. Albert H. Friedlander. (Jewish) Kent House, Rutland Gardens, London SW7, England. Dean, Leo Baeck College; Rabbi, Westminster Synagogue. Member, International Council of WCRP. 57 years.

Mr. Ian R. Fry. (Christian) Lot 39, Emu Road, RSD Sunbury, Victoria, 3429 Australia. Journalist. Former Agricultural Chemical Industry Executive; Communications Officer, Presbyterian Board of Local Mission, Victoria. 49 years.

Rt. Rev. Gabriel G. Ganaka. (Christian) P.O. Box 494, Jos, Nigeria. Bishop of Jos; Vice-President, Catholic Bishops' Conference of Nigeria; Member, International Council of WRCP. 53 years.

Mr. Balwan T.S. Ghanna (Sikh) P.O. Box 30385, Nairobi, Kenya. Teacher. 48 years.

Rev. H. Lamar Gibble. (Christian) Church of the Brethren, 1451 Dundee Avenue, Elgin, IL 60120, USA. Peace and International Affairs Officer, Church of the Brethren; Member, WCC/CCIA; Chairman, NCC/USA Middle East Committee. Former Pastor. Contributed to "Zumutungen des Friedens," edited by Volkmar Deile. 53 years.

Dr. Victor Goldbloom. (Jewish) 49 Front Street East, Toronto, Ontario M5E 1B3, Canada. President, International Council of Christians and Jews.

Shrivatsa Goswami. (Hindu) Gambhira/Radharamana, Vrindiban 281 121, U.P., India. Director, Sri Caitanya Prema Sansthana; Member, International Council of WCRP.

Dr. Dana McLean Greeley. (Christian) 276 Main Street, Concord, MA 01742, USA. Minister; Honorary President, WCRP/International. Formerly President, Unitarian Universalist Association of North America; President, International Association for Religious Freedom. Author of *Toward Larger Living, A Message to Atheists; Personal Recollections;* and *Know These Concordians.* 76 years.

Mrs. Saroj Gupta Pereira. (Hindu) 8450 Sorbonne, Brossard, Quebec J4X 1N3, Canada. Social Worker. 43 years.

Ms. Nahla A. Haidar. (Muslim) c/o UNDRO, Palais des Nations, 1211 Geneva 20, Switzerland. Relief Coordinator Officer, United Nations Development and Relief Organization.

Dr. Viqar A. Hamdani. (Muslim) Apt. 4H, 5 Stuyvesant Oval, New York, N.Y. 10009, USA. Advisor, Muslim World League; UN Representative, World Muslim Congress; Member, International Council of WCRP. Former Ambassador of Pakistan. 73 years.

Mr. Rusydi Hamka. (Muslim) Jalan Kenanga No. 6, Bintaro, Jakarta, Indonesia. Chief Editor, *Panji Masyarakat* (an Indonesian Islamic magazine). 49 years.

Mr. Han Wenzao. (Christian) China Christian Council, Nanjing, People's Republic of China. Associate General Secretary, China Christian Council; Deputy Director, Centre for Religious Studies, Nanjing University. 61 years.

Mr. Wooday Hanumanthappa. (Hindu) 17 Cunningham Road, Bangalore 560 052, India. Businessman. 62 years.

Dr. Serajul Haque. (Muslim) Road No. 27, Dhanmondi R.A., Dhaka, Bangladesh. Professor Emeritus in Islamic Studies, Dhaka University. 79 years.

Mr. Lukman Harun. (Muslim) Jalan Sukabumi No. 11, Jakarta 10310, Indonesia. Member, Central of Muhammadiyah and Indonesian Ulama Council; Secretary-General, WCRP/Indonesia. Member, International Council of WCRP. Formerly, General Chairman, National Committee of the World Assembly of Youth in Indonesia; Member of Parliament; Secretary-General, Indonesian Muslim Party. 50 years.

Dr. Veerendra Heggade. (Jain) Dharmasthala 574 216, Karnataka, India. Chief, Dharmasthala Manjunatha Temple; Member, International Council of WCRP. 37 years.

Prof. L.G. Hewage. (Buddhist) 28 First Lane, Kirillapona, Colombo 5, Sri Lanka. Formerly Professor of Education; Chairman, WFB-UNESCO Committee and Organizing Committee, World Buddhist Peace Foundation; Director, Asian Centre for Religious and Educational Studies and of Middle Path International. Author of *Metta—Loving Kindness; Binesco, A Buddhist Interpretation of the UNESCO Objectives; Essential Educational Psychology; Introduction to Programmed Instruction; Introduction to Visuddhi Magga (Path of Purity) Through the Stupa;* and *Relevance of Cultural Heritage to Development Education.* 71 years.

Mr. Masahiko Horai. (Shintoist) 4-17, Nishitenman, 5-chome, Kita-ku, Osaka 551, Japan. Chief Priest, Horikawa-Ebisu Shrine; Director, Youth Board of WCRP/Japan. 39 years.

Rev. Philip Huggins. (Christian) Olsen Road, Nar Nar Goon North, Victoria, 3812 Australia. University chaplain; Priest; Member, International

Council of WCRP. Formerly Professor in Economics/Sociology; Government Research Officer. Author of *The Child's Imagination: Video Games and Televised Violence; Australia's Uranium: Critical Analysis; A Multi-Faith Gathering for Peace, WCRP IV;* and *The Church and Peace: A Cloudy Vision Evolves.* 35 years.

Mr. Suryo Hutomo. (Confucianist) 20C Batu Ceper St., Jakarta, Indonesia. President, Confucian Council of Indonesia. Author of *States in Order, World in Order;* and *All Men Within the Four Seas are Brothers.*

Prof. Yoshiaki Iisaka. (Christian) 6-47-8 Shimouma, Setagaya-ku, Tokyo 154, Japan. Member, Peace Research Institute of WCRP/Japan; Professor, Gakashuin University; Member, International Council of WCRP. Author of *Christian Political Responsibility; Modern Political Science;* and *Analysis of the Contemporary Society.* 58 years.

Mr. Yo Ishikawa. (Buddhist) 8 Yanagiyama-cho, Shinomiya, Yamanashi-ku, Kyoto 607, Japan. Director, WCRP/Japan; Vice-Director, Ittoen. 54 years.

Miss Dadi Janki. See Fraternal Delegates, under Brahma Kumaris World Spiritual Assembly.

Mr. Jing Hui. (Buddhist) The Chinese Buddhist Association, Beijing, People's Republic of China. Buddhist Master, 51 years.

Mrs. Joyce Kaddu. (Christian) P.O. Box 14123, Kampala, Uganda. Teacher; Principal, Teachers' College; Member, International Council of WCRP. 45 years.

Mr. Boaz K. Kaino. (Christian) P.O. Box 51091, Nairobi, Kenya. Health Officer. 32 years.

Dr. Mladen Karadjole. (Christian) 214, rue Louis Hap, 1040 Brussels, Belgium. Professor of Theology.

Mr. Badru Kateregga. (Muslim) P.O. Box 70394, Nairobi, Kenya. Professor.

Rev. Kiyotoshi Kawai. (Shintoist) c/o Fumon Hall, 2-6 Wada, Suginami-ku, Tokyo 166, Japan. Secretary-General, WCRP/Japan; Chief Priest, Omiyahachiman Shrine; Member, International Council of WCRP. 63 years.

Miss Florence Kawoya. (Christian) P.O. Box 55729, Nairobi, Kenya. Pediatric Nurse. 32 years.

Msgr. Bruce Kent. (Christian) 39 Duncan Terrace, London N.1, England. General Secretary, Campaign for Nuclear Disarmament (U.K.).

Miss Irene Kessy. (Christian) Physiotherapy Dept., P.O. Box 65000, Dar-Es-Salaam, Tanzania. Physiotherapist.

Dr. Habibur Rahman Khan. (Muslim) 240 Garden East, Kashana-i-

Hafeez, Karachi 3, Pakistan. Medical Consultant; Secretary-General, WCRP/Pakistan; Member, International Council of WCRP. Formerly Member, Government Health Study Group; Founder-President, Allarun Iqbal College; Secretary-General, Islamic Medical Association of Pakistan; President, Pakistan Muslim Association. Author of *Islam in Action for Peace; Contributions of Muslims in Science and Medicine; Ideological Defence for Islam; The Qur'an as a Guide to Science and Technology; Islam for Dignity, Social Justice and Development of the Whole Person;* and *Medical Ethics.* 62 years.

Dr. Inamullah Khan. (Muslim) 4, Bahadurabad, Road No. 2, Karachi 0511, Pakistan. Secretary-General, World Muslim Congress; Joint President, WCRP International; Chairman, Executive Committee of WCRP/International.

Dr. Norbert Klaes. (Christian) Estenfelderstr. 94, 8700 Würzburg 4, Federal Republic of Germany; Member, Governing Board of WCRP. Professor of Theology and Comparative Religion.

Mr. Bindurao B. Konnur. (Hindu) 38 Sevington Road, Hendon, London NW4 3RX, England. Worked as Manager of Publicity Dept. of a shipping company; translated Sri Sukta, soon to be published by the Indian Institute of Culture (London); Member, International Council of WCRP. 73 years.

Mr. Mohammed Koor. (Muslim) P.O. Box 46805, Nairobi, Kenya.

Rev. J.N.J. Kritzinger. (Christian) P.O. Box 19354, Pretoria West, 0117 South Africa. University Lecturer in Christian Theology; Member, South African Missiological Society, Association for the Study of Religion (S.A.) and International Association for Mission Studies. Author of "A Critical Study of the Gospel of Barnabas," in *Religion in Southern Africa;* "Islam as Rival of the Gospel in Africa," in *Missionalia;* and "The Artistic Symbolism of the Tamil Household Prayer Lamp," in *Theologia Evangelica.* 34 years.

D. Harshendra Kumar. (Jain) Dharmasthala 574 216, Karnataka, India. Industrialist. 32 years.

Mrs. Hiroko Kurozumi. (Shintoist) 1-15-1-705 Komagome, Taisho-ku, Tokyo 170, Japan. Member, Women's Board of WCRP/Japan. 62 years.

Rev. Patrick R. Lal. (Christian) 59 Mandir Marg, New Delhi 110 001, India. Secretary, Diocese of Delhi. 44 years.

Mrs. Evelyn M. Lebona. (Christian) P.O. Box 922, Maseru, Lesotho. Teacher; Social Worker; National Link, Mother Teresa's Co-Workers; Chairperson, Save the Children (Lesotho). 60 years.

Mr. Byong Joo Lee. (Confucianist) No. 805-2, Sangwangsimmni-dong, Sungdong-ku, Seoul, Republic of Korea. Medical Doctor; President, Religious Leaders Association of Korea; Chief of Board of Directors,

Sungkyungkwan (a Confucianist organization); Member, National Assembly. Author of *Diary of Chukam.* 72 years.

Mr. Jong Myong Lee. (Confucianist) Room 302, Samick Bldg. No. 62-3, Taipyung-ro 1-ka, Chung-ku, Seoul, Republic of Korea. Secretary-General, Religious Leaders' Association of Korea. 61 years.

Mrs. Ok Young Lee. (Buddhist) A-906, Jang Mi Apt., Yoido-Dong, Young Dong Po-ku, Seoul, Republic of Korea. Director, Women's Buddhist Association. 54 years.

Mr. Sathitya Lengthaisong. (Buddhist) Village No. 1, Chitvisut Soi 1, Bangkrang, Muang Nonthaburi, Thailand. Senior Justice, Court of Appeals; Editor; Lecturer; Member, International Council of WCRP. Author of numerous books and articles pertaining to legal matters. 52 years.

Mrs. Norma Levitt. (Jewish) 15 East 64th Street, New York, N.Y. 10021, USA. Honorary President, National Federation of Temple Sisterhoods; Member, Executive Committee, Union of American Hebrew Congregations; Honorary Vice-President, World Union for Progressive Judaism; Officer, US Committee for UNICEF; Joint President and Member of Executive Committee of WCRP/International. Author of numerous liturgical services, hymns, plays, and articles.

Mr. Joseph Y. Levy. (Jewish) Apt. 9, 4522 Girouard, Montreal, Quebec H4A 3E6, Canada. Professor. 40 years.

Lama Lobzang. (Buddhist) C1-33 Pandara Road, New Delhi, India. Buddhist Monk. 53 years.

Rev. Gerrie Lubbe. (Christian) 08 Piet Meyer St., Mindalore, Krugersdorp, Transvaal, 1740 South Africa. Lecturer; Pastor, Reformed Church in Africa (Black); Inter-faith Person, South African Council of Churches; President, WCRP/South Africa. Author of "From Medina to Beirut," in *Theologia Evangelica;* and "Islam in South Africa," in *New Faces of Africa.* 43 years.

Ven. Visuddhananda Mahathero. (Buddhist) Dhammarajika Buddhist Monastery, Atisa Dipankar Sarak, Kamalapur, Dhaka 14, Bangladesh. Buddhist Monk; Member, International Council of WCRP. Author of *Buddhism in Bangladesh;* and *Raktaghara Den.* 76 years.

Dr. Gamal El-Din Mohammed Mahmoud. (Muslim) Al-Nabatat Street, Garden City, Cairo, Egypt. Secretary-General, Supreme Council for Muslim Affairs. 54 years.

Miss Anshu Mann. (Hindu) 82 Thompson Road, New Delhi 110 002, India. Student. 21 years.

Mrs. C.K. Mann. (Hindu) (See address of Miss A. Mann above.) Government Service. 48 years.

Mr. Brijesh Mathur. (Hindu) Officers' Bungalow No. 6, Sector 19-B, Chandigarh, Punjab, India. Member, Sangit Natak Academy (Chandigarh) and Executive Committee, Indian National Theatre; Honorary Secretary, Panchal Lalit Kala Academy. Former member of Indian Council of Cultural Relations. Author of *Peace Marches in Punjab* and *The Healing Touch of Indian Music.* 49 years.

Mrs. Ljiljana Matkovic-Vlasic. (Christian) Vocarska 11, 41000 Zagreb, Yugoslavia. Free-lance writer and translator. Author of *In Search of Closeness* (poems); *Woman and Church; You Didn't Come Down From The Cross (meditations and prayers); Gathered Days;* and *In the Land of the Living.* 46 years.

Prof. Jamshed Mavalwala. (Zoroastrian) 418 St. Clair Avenue East, Toronto, Ontario M4T 1P5, Canada. Professor of Anthropology; Member, International Council of WCRP. 49 years.

Dr. Edward C. May. (Christian) No. 55, 5202 S.E. 30th, Portland, OR 97202, USA. Director, Office of World Community, Lutheran World Ministries (U.S.A. Committee of Lutheran World Federation). Formerly, President, Wheat Ridle Foundation. 65 years.

Rev. Robert McClean. (Christian) UMUNO, 777 U.N. Plaza, New York, N.Y. 10017, U.S.A. Director, Dept. of Peace and World Order, General Board of Church and Society, United Methodist Church. 51 years.

Rev. Toshio Miyake. (Shintoist) Konko-kyo Church of Izuo, 21-8 Nishi 3-chome, San-gen-ya, Taisho-ku, Osaka 551, Japan. Senior Minister, Konko-kyo Church of Izuo; Joint President, WCRP/International. 81 years.

Mr. Mmutlanyane S. Mogoba. (Christian) P.O. Box 2256, Durban, 4000 South Africa. Teacher; Member, International Council of WCRP. 51 years.

Mrs. Punam S. Mohan. (Hindu) E-29 Saket, New Delhi 110 017, India. Teacher; Director, Delhi's I.A.S. Study Circle. Author of such articles as *Religion in Action; Buddhist Teachings and the World Today;* and *Peace Through Religion.*" 30 years.

Mr. Mohamed M. Mohideen. (Muslim) "Shamrock," 312/6 Nawala Road, Nawala, Sri Lanka. Associate Director, Marga Institute (Sri Lanka Centre for Development Studies); Assistant Chief Commissioner, Sri Lanka Scout Association; Chairman, Sri Lanka-South Asia-Canada Partnership. Author of numerous youth-oriented and cultural papers, several of which have been presented over the national broadcasting system; currently writing a book on *Islam to the Non-Muslims.* 56 years.

Mr. Iwane Mori. (Shintoist) 393, Miteari, Gifu-shi, Gifu 500, Japan. Chief Priest, Gifu Gokuku Shrine. 48 years.

Rev. Josphat W. Mugweru. (Christian) P.O. Box 290, Kerugoya, Kenya.

Executive Director and Development Secretary, Christian Community Services, Diocese of Mt. Kenya. 37 years.

Mr. Kodo Nagai. (Buddhist) 531 Asahi, Koshiji-cho, Santo-gun, Niigata 94954, Japan. Soto Zen Sect. 60 years.

Mr. Motoyuki Naganuma. (Buddhist) c/o Rissho Kosei-kai, 2-11-1 Wada, Suginami-ku, Tokyo 166, Japan. Chief Director, Rissho Kosei-kai; Executive Director, WCRP/Japan; Financial Advisor, Executive Committee of WCRP/International. 61 years.

Mr. Masayuki Nakamura. (Buddhist) 4-7-4 Shibakoen, Minato-ku, Tokyo 105, Japan. Japan Buddhist Federation. 42 years.

Mr. Tashi Namgyal. (Buddhist) P.O. McLeod Ganj, Dharmasala 176 219, India. Secretary-General, Tibetan Youth Congress. 32 years.

Mrs. Edna M. Nanayakkara. (Christian) 201/1 Rajagiriya Road, Rajagiriya, Sri Lanka. National Executive Director, Young Women's Christian Association (YWCA). 51 years.

Mr. Tarlok S. Nandhra. (Sikh) P.O. Box 42180, Nairobi, Kenya. Architect.

Rev. Nikkyo Niwano. (Buddhist) Rissho Kosei-kai, 2-11-1 Wada, Suginami-ku, Tokyo 166, Japan. President, Rissho Kosei-kai and WCRP/Japan; Honorary President, WCRP/International. Former President of the International Association for Religious Freedom. Author of *A Buddhist Approach to Peace; Lifetime Beginner; Buddhism for Today; The Richer Life;* and other books and articles on Buddhism. 78 years.

Dr. Adamou Ndam Njoya. (Muslim) B.P. 1638, Yaoundé, Cameroon. Plenipotentiary Minister; Joint President, WCRP/International. Formerly, Minister of Education, Foreign Affairs and Administrative Reform.

Miss Shobna Obhrai. (Hindu) c/o WCRP/Africa, P.O. Box 70394, Nairobi, Kenya. Secretary.

Mr. Koetsu Oi. (Shintoist) 4-12-26, Higashi, Shibuya-ku, Tokyo 150, Japan. Youth Board of WCRP/Japan. 34 years.

Bishop J. Henry Okullu. (Christian) Diocese of Maseno South, P.O. Box 114, Kisumu, Kenya. Bishop; President, WCRP/Africa; Member, International Council of WCRP. 55 years.

Mr. Richard Ondeng. (Christian) c/o WCRP/Africa, P.O. Box 70394, Nairobi, Kenya. Church executive.

Rev. Dr. Joseph O.-A. Osei. (Christian) P.O. Box 9156, Airport, Accra, Ghana. Secretary-General, SECAM (The Symposium of Episcopal Conferences of Africa and Madagascar). 48 years.

Mrs. Prabhat S. Pandit. (Hindu) M-14 Saket, Malviya Nagar Ext., New

Delhi 110 017, India. Involved in Business and Farming; Social Worker; Member, International Council of WCRP. 59 years.

Adv. Narendra D. Pandya. (Hindu) P.O. Box 25086, Ferreirasdorp, Johannesburg, 2048 South Africa. Lawyer; Member, Swami Naryan Fellowship. Author of *Samaj, The History of Transvaal Hindu;* and *The Gujesaki-Speaking Hindus of South Africa.* 46 years.

Mr. Kil Chin Park. (Buddhist) Iri, Chun-Puk, South Korea. President, Won Kwang University. 69 years.

Dr. Syed A. Pasha. (Muslim) 2, Clanricarde Gardens, London W2, England. International Law Consultant; General Secretary, Union of Muslim Organizations of U.K. and Eire. Former Adviser to the Indian Delegation to the United Nations. Author of *Repatriation Problem of Korean Prisoners of War and India's Contribution to its Solution;* and *Concept of Jihad in Islam.* 54 years.

Miss Peng Cui-An. (Christian) Nanjing Theological Seminary, No. 13 Dajian Yin Xiang, Nanjing, People's Republic of China. Seminary Student. 30 years.

Archbishop Bernardino Pinera. (Christian) Los Carreras 450, La Serena, Chile. Archbishop of La Serena; President, Conference of Chilean Bishops. Author of booklets on pastoral subjects and *Chile Hoy;* co-author of *Chile 2000—Macia la Civilizacion del Amor.* 69 years.

Rev. Christian Precht. (Christian) Casilla 59, Santiago 1, Chile. Vicar-General, Santiago's Archbishop; Member, International Council of WCRP.

Mr. Bogoda Premaratne. (Buddhist) 31 Jayansinhe Road, Colombo 6, Sri Lanka. Executive Director, Fulbright Commission, Colombo. Former Commissioner of Examinations, Education Ministry. 63 years.

Rev. Brian Prideaux. (Christian) 600 Jarvis Street, Toronto, Ontario M4Y 2J6, Canada. Priest; Ecumenical Officer, Anglican Church of Canada. Co-author of *Building Bridges, A Study Guide to Anglican-Roman Catholic Dialogue.* 41 years.

Dr. Sun Kwan Pyun. (Christian) P.O. Box 45, West Gate-ku, Seoul, Republic of Korea. Dean of Graduate School, Methodist Theological Seminary; Professor of Philosophical Theology. Author of *The Finality of Christ in the Perspective of Buddhist-Christian Encounter,* and *Studies of Karl Barth's Theology.* 56 years.

Dr. Muhammad Qasim. (Muslim) 1 Basti Hazrat Nizamuddin, New Delhi 110 018, India. Medical Doctor. 38 years.

Most Rev. Francis A. Quinn. (Christian) P.O. Box 1706, Sacramento, CA 95808, USA. Bishop of Sacramento; Member, International Council of WCRP. Formerly, Superintendent of Schools, Editor of newspaper, and

Director of radio and TV, for the Archdiocese of San Francisco. Co-author of *As One Who Serves,* (a document on the priesthood); and *Complete Group Guidance for Catholic High Schools.* (four volumes). 63 years.

Sri Radhakrishna. (Hindu) 221-23 Deen Dayal Upadhyaya Marg, New Delhi 110 002, India. Secretary-General, Gandhi Peace Foundation. 60 years.

Dr. Anantanand Rambachan. (Hindu) c/o Dept. of Religion, St. Olaf College, Northfield, MN 55057, USA. Researcher in Theology and Religious Studies.

Dr. Ravin K. Ramdass. (Hindu) 3 Azalea Street, Greytown, Natal, 3500 South Africa. Medical Intern; Chairman, Hindu Students Association; Honorary President, South African Hindu Youth Movement. Author of *Education—The Essence of Health for All by 2000;* and two articles: *Broad Guidelines to Effective Teaching;* and *Hindus Facing Identity Crisis.* 24 years.

Mrs. Dorothy Ramodibe. (Christian) 901 Tladi Komako St., P.O. Kwa Xuma, 1868 South Africa. Administrative Secretary, Institute for Contextual Theology; Sunday School Teacher; and Member, Housewife League. Formerly with the South African Council of Churches. 42 years.

Sr. Layla Raphaël. (Christian) 2243 Coursol, Montreal, Quebec H3J 1C6, Canada. Lecturer in Philosophy; Member, International Council of WCRP. Former University Pastoral Animator. Author of books and articles on Wittgenstein; Linguistics; and Lebanon. 54 years.

Mr. Norbert Ratsirahonana. (Christian) VB 81 A Ambatoroka, Antananarivo, Madagascar. Magistrate at the Supreme Court; University Lecturer; Member, National Council, Eglise de Jésus à Madagascar. 46 years.

Mme Jacqueline Rougé. (Christian) 6 rue du Vieux Colombier, 75006 Paris, France. Member, Executive Committee, Pax Christi International and French Section; Pax Christi and WCRP representative at UNESCO, UN, and NGO meetings in Paris; Joint President, WCRP/International. 53 years.

Dr. George Rupp. (Christian) President's House, Rice University, P.O. Box 1892, Houston, TX 77251, USA. Dean, Harvard Divinity School; Member, International Council of WCRP.

Mr. P.S. Saini. (Hindu) P.O. Box 44147, Nairobi, Kenya. Ex civil servant.

Rt. Rev. Peter K. Sarpong. (Christian) P.O. Box 99, Kumasi, Ghana. Bishop; President, Ecumenical Association of African Theologians; Bishop in charge of Ecumenical and Interreligious Affairs, National

Catholic Secretariat of Ghana; Member, International Council of WCRP. 51 years.

Mr. Bhupander Sarup. (Hindu) C-6 Kalindi Colony, New Delhi 110 065, India. Accountant. 40 years.

Prof. Arumugam Sathasivam. (Hindu) 11 Sinsapa Road, Wellawatte, Colombo 6, Sri Lanka. Professor and Head of Dept. of Tamil, University of Peradeniya. Author of *Sumerian, A Dravidian Language;* and *Anthology of Ceylon Tamil Poetry.* 58 years.

Dr. Henk E. Schouten. (Christian) u.d. Brandelerkade 22, 2313 GW Leiden, The Netherlands. Minister; Foreign Student Pastor; Secretary, WCRP/Netherlands. Author of *The United Buddhist Church in Viet Nam and the Buddhist Peace Movement,* 1945–1976. 38 years.

Prof. Dr. Josef Schultes. (Christian) Schelhammergasse 17, 3420 Kritzendorf, Klostenburg, Austria. Professor of Biblical Studies, Religious Pedagogical Academy in Vienna. Former Assistant Professor for Moral Theology. Author of brochures on Biblical interpretations and Christian holidays. 38 years.

Mr. Kartar S. Sewak. (Sikh) P.O. Box 42162, Nairobi, Kenya. Engineer. 67 years.

Mr. Shen De-Rong. (Christian) 169 Yuan Ming Yuan Road, Shanghai, People's Republic of China. Church Worker. 62 years.

Prof. Harmindar Singh. (Sikh) 132 Eastcote Avenue, Greenford, Middlesex UB6 ONR, United Kingdom. Retired from Indian Foreign Service; Member, International Council of WCRP. 68 years.

Mr. Mehervan Singh. (Sikh) 5001 Beach Road No. 07-24, Golden Mile Complex, Singapore 0719, Republic of Singapore. Public Accountant; Secretary-General, ACRP (Asian Conference on Religion and Peace); Member, International Council of WCRP. Former Secretary, Inter-Religious Organisation of Singapore. Author of *Sikhism—Its Impact;* and *Sikhism—East and West.* 65 years.

Prof. Vishal Singh. (Hindu) 67 New Campus, Jawaharlal Nehru University, New Delhi 110 067, India. Professor of South-East Asian Studies; Vice-Chairman, Indian Centre for Studies on Indochina; Author. 53 years.

Mr. Sirajuddin Syamsuddin. (Muslim) Jalan Ibnu Sina I/33 Ciputat, Jakarta, Indonesia. Teaching staff of the University of Ushuluddin. 26 years.

Rev. Robert F. Smylie. (Christian) Room 1244, 475 Riverside Drive, New York, N.Y. 10115, USA. Associate for Peace and International Affairs, Presbyterian Church (USA.); Member, International Council of WCRP. Former Navy Chaplain; Visiting Professor at the Ecumenical

Institute (Geneva); and Consultant, World Council of Churches. Editor of "The Soviet Union: Reexamination & Reconciliation," "A Presbyterian Witness on War and Peace: An Historical Interpretation;" and other peace-related articles which have appeared in *Church & Society* and *Journal of Presbyterial History.* 55 years.

Dr. Soedjatmoko. (Muslim) Rector, United Nations University, Toho Seimei Building, 15-1, Shibuya 2-chome, Shibuya-ku, Tokyo 150, Japan. Former Indonesian Ambassador to the United States, Alternate Permanent Representative of Indonesia to the UN and Member of Indonesian Constituent Assembly, Adviser to Indonesian Delegation to the Asian-African Conference, Author of *An Introduction to Indonesian Historiography; The Re-Emergence of Southeast Asia: An Indonesian Perspective; Southeast Asia in World Politics;* (Published jointly as *Southeast Asia Today and Tomorrow); Development and Freedom.* 63 years.

Mr. Art Solomon. (Traditional Religion) R.R. No. 2, Alban, Ontario POM 1AO, Canada. Prison Ministry as a Native Spiritual Leader; Member, International Council of WCRP. 71 years.

Msgr. Nobuo Soma. (Christian) 2-6-37 Aoi-cho, Higashi-ku, Nagoyashi, Aichi 461, Japan. Bishop of Nagoya Diocese. Member, Board of Directors, WCRP/Japan. 68 years.

Mr. Anil Sooklal. (Hindu) 16 Hendale Place, Newlands, Durban, 4051 South Africa. Lecturer in Indian Religions. 27 years.

Mrs. Kanchana Soonsawad. (Buddhist) 79 Soi Wat Yai Srisupan, Intarapitak Road, Bangkok 10600, Thailand. Document Assistant, UNESCO Regional Office for Education in Asia and the Pacific. Formerly Librarian at ESCAP and Ministry of Finance. 44 years.

Miss Hannah Stanton. (Christian) 30 Burtons Road, Hampton Hill, Middlesex TW12 1DA, United Kingdom. Secretary, WCRP/UK-Ireland. Formerly, Mission Worker in South Africa; University Teacher; and Social Worker. Author of *Go Well, Stay Well.* 71 years.

Dr. David M. Stowe. (Christian) 54 Magnolia Avenue, Tenafly, N.J. 07670, USA. Clergyman; Executive, World Ministries, United Church of Christ, USA. Formerly, Missionary Educator in China and Lebanon; Professor of Religion; Executive, Overseas Division, US National Council of Churches; Chief Officer, Overseas Program, United Church of Christ in the U.S.A. Author of *When Faith Meets Faith; Ecumenity and Evangelism; Partners With The Almighty; The Church's Witness in the World;* and articles which have appeared in *The Christian Century, Religion in Life, A.D.,* etc. 65 years.

Mr. Mahomed Suliman. (Muslim) P.O. Box 297, Warmbaths, 0480 South Africa. Businessman; Muslim Educationist. 58 years.

Dr. Malcolm R. Sutherland. (Christian) P.O. Box 217, Harvard, MA

01451, U.S.A. Clergyman; Member, International Council of WCRP. Formerly, Vice-President, International Association for Religious Freedom; Vice-President, International Religion in an Age of Science; President, Dean of Faculty and Professor at Meadville/Lombard Theological School. Author of *Creator of the Dawn; Personal Faith;* and "Tommorrow's Church Today," in *Voices of Liberalism II;* Co-Chairman, Publication Board, ZYGON. 68 years.

Mr. Kinzo Takemura. (Buddhist) c/o Rissho Kosei-kai, 2-11-1 Wada, Suginami-ku, Tokyo 166, Japan. Head, Overseas Mission Service, Rissho Kosei-kai. 57 years.

Mr. Hisakazu Taki. (Buddhist) c/o Gedatsu-kai, 4 Araki-cho, Shinjuku-ku, Tokyo 160, Japan. Chief, Doctrinal Division, Bedatsu-kai. 36 years.

Mr. George B. Telford. (Christian) P.O. Box 144, Blacksburg, VA 24060, USA. Clergyman; Member, Commission on Faith and Order (NCC) and Task Force on Theological Relationships Between Christians and Jews (PC/USA). Formerly Director, Division of Corporate and Social Mission (PC/US); and Vice-President, National Council of Churches. 50 years.

Ven. Anuruddha Thera. (Buddhist) 214, Bauddhaloka Mawatha, Colombo, Sri Lanka. Vice Chancellor, Buddhist and Pali University of Sri Lanka; Member, International Council of WCRP.

Ven. Thich Thien Chau. (Buddhist) Institut Bouddhique Truc Lam, 9 rue de Neuchâtel, 91120 Villebon/Yvette, France. Director, Institut Bouddhique Truc Lam; President, Association des Bouddhistes Vietnamiens en France. Author of numerous works on Buddhism; Co-Author of *Dictionnaire des Philosophies.* 53 years.

Rev. Kenryu T. Tsuji. (Buddhist) P.O. Box 2337, Springfield, VA 22152, USA. Minister, Ekoji Buddhist Temple; President, WCRP/USA; Member, International Council of WCRP. Formerly, Presiding Bishop, Buddhist Churches of America. 65 years.

Rt. Rev. Desmond Tutu. (Christian) Bishop of Johannesburg, P.O. Box 1131, Johannesburg, South Africa. (Nobel Peace Prize, 1984), more than seven Honorary Doctorates. 53 years.

Major-General Sujan Singh Uban, Rtd. (Sikh) C-191 Defence Colony, New Delhi 110 024, India. Secretary-General, WCRP/India; Member, International Council of WCRP. Author of *Gurus of India.* 71 years.

Mr. Devendraj R. Upadhya. (Hindu) 21/452 Ram Shah Path, Kathmandu, Nepal. Member, Population Advisory Committee, Government of Nepal. Formerly, Director, Radio Nepal; Deputy Permanent Representative of Nepal to the UN; Secretary, Ministry of Commerce, Tourism, Industry and Labour; Permanent Representative to ECAFE;

Professor of Jurisprudence. Author of books on Buddhism, Political Philosophy, Democracy and Trade. 57 years.

Mr. Behram R. Vakil. (Zoroastrian) 16 Boscombe Road, Singapore 1543, Republic of Singapore. High Priest; President, Geeta Ashram of Singapore, Bihar School of Yoga of Singapore. Past President and Current Secretary, Inter-Religious Organisation of Singapore. 65 years.

Mr. N. Vasudevan. (Hindu) c/o Gandhi Peace Foundation, 221 Deen Dayal Upadhyaya Marg, New Delhi 110 002, India. Publications Manager, Gandhi Peace Foundation. 40 years.

Mr. Ante Vunic. (Christian) 9 Ankerstraat, 2700 O.VL. St.-Niklaas, Belgium. Manager. 43 years.

Dr. Gerald Wanjohi. (Christian) P.O. Box 30197, Nairobi, Kenya. Professor of Philosophy.

Mrs. Wanjohi. (Christian) c/o Dept. of Philosophy, University of Nairobi, P.O. Box 30197, Nairobi, Kenya.

Canon Gordon Wilson. (Christian) 4 Byron Close, Hampton, Middlesex TW12 1EL, United Kingdom. Chairman, Anglican Pacifist Fellowship; Organising Secretary, Week of Prayer for World Peace; Member, International Council of WCRP. Author of *War and the Christian Witness; Faith and Power, From Ruin to Rebirth;* and *The Changing Christian View of War and Armed Violence.* 65 years.

Dr. Mrs. Erika Wolf. (Christian) Donatusstr. 32, 5300 Bonn 2, Federal Republic of Germany. Former Member of Parliament.

Mrs. Sugi Yamamoto. (Buddhist) 1-14-38 Minamisawa, Higashikurume-shi, Tokyo 203, Japan. Chief Director, All Japan Buddhist Women's Association; Head, Women's Board, WCRP/Japan. 82 years.

Prof. Kikuo Yamaoka. (Christian) 2-28-20 Ichikawa, Ichikawa-shi, Chiba 272, Japan. Peace Research Institute of WCRP/Japan.

Mr. Yin Liang. (Buddhist) The Chinese Buddhist Association, Beijing, People's Republic of China. Buddhist Master. 22 years.

Mr. Mahmood K. Youskine. (Muslim) 25 Frederik Hendriklaan, 2582 BR The Hague, Netherlands. Policy Advisor, Ministry of Foreign Affairs. 57 years.

Prof. Mrs. Maftuchah Yusuf. (Muslim) Darmawangsa IV/1, Kebayoran, Baru, Jakarta Selatan, Indonesia. Dean, Faculty of Language and Arts, Institute of Teachers Education and Pedagogy; Chairperson, National Private School Council and Moslem Women's Congress. Author of *The Moslem Women in Indonesia: Strength and Potentialities; Moslem*

Outlook on a Changing Society; The Role of Women in Development in Indonesia; Population Education for Very Orthodox Religious Groups; and *Religious Education for the Pre-School Child.* 64 years.

Mrs. Jean Zaru. (Christian) P.O. Box 66, Friends Boys' School, Ramallah, via Israel. Teacher; Social Worker; Work with World Council of Churches and World Young Women's Christian Association; Member, International Council of WCRP.

76

Fraternal Delegates

African National Congress (ANC). Mr. Gerald B. Mohlathe, P.O. Box 170, Dar-Es-Salaam, Tanzania. Mrs. Ruth Mompati, P.O. Box 31791, Lusaka, Zambia.

Amnesty International. Mr. Eric Prokosch, 1 Easton Road, London WC1 8DF, United Kingdom.

All Africa Conference of Churches. Rev. Terence Ensor, P.O. Box 44, Victoria, Seychelles.

Baptist World Alliance. Rev. Arthur Kinyanjui, P.O. Box 1645, Nakuru, Kenya. Rev. Samson S.K. Mathangani, 1628 16th Street N.W., Washington, D.C. 20009, USA.

Berlin Conference of European Catholics. Mr. Claus Hebler, Limonenstr. 26, 1000 Berlin 45, Federal Republic of Germany.

Brahma Kumaris World Spiritual Assembly. Miss Dadi Janki, P.O. Box 12349, Nairobi, Kenya. Brahma Kumari Janki, Pandav Bhawan, Mt. Abu, Rajasthan, India. Sr. Vedanti, P.O. Box 12349, Nairobi, Kenya.

Buraku Liberation League. Mr. Tatsuro Konishi, C22-306, 2-7 Shinsen-rihigashimachi, Toyonaka-shi, Osaka 565, Japan. Mr. Ryu Matsumoto, 2-24-1 Maida, Higashi-ku, Fukuoka-shi, Fukuoka, Japan. Mr. Adinobu Tanimoto, 4-4-46 Kitatsumori, Nishinari-ku, Osaka, Japan. Mr. Saichiro Uesugi, 284-2 Futsukaichi, Tsukushino, Fukuoka, Japan.

Buraku Liberation Institute. Mr. Kenzo Tomonaga, 1-6-12 Koboyoshi, Naniwa-ku, Japan.

Christian Peace Conference. Dr. Lubomír Mirejovsky, Jungmannova 9, 11121 Praha, C.S.S.R. Rev. Stanford A. Shauri, P.O. Box 2537, Dar-Es-Salaam, Tanzania.

Christian Students' Council of Kenya. Mr. Edward Etale, P.O. Box 54579, Nairobi, Kenya. Mr. Enock Z. Okonji, at same address.

Confucius Religion Council of Indonesia. Mr. Suryo Hutomo, 20C Batu

Ceper Street, Jakarta, Indonesia.

Ecumenical Institute of Tantur. Dr. William Klassen, P.O. Box 19556, Jerusalem, Israel.

Ecumenical Institute for Theological Studies. Dr. Landrum R. Bolling, 2008 R Street, N.W., Washington, D.C. 20009, USA.

Eglise Episcopale au Rwanda. Bishop Adoniya Sebununguri, B.P. 61, Kigali, Rwanda.

Focolare Movement. Dr. Rémy Beller, P.O. Box 25220, Nairobi, Kenya. Miss Natalia Dallapiccola, Via di Frascati 300, 00040 Rocca di Papa, Roma, Italy.

Franciscan Missionaries of Mary. Sr. Adrienne N'Dombi, B.P. 198 Moungali, Brazzaville, Congo.

Friends World Committee for Consultation. Mr. Isaac Z. Malenge, P.O. Box 41946, Nairobi, Kenya. Mr. Reuben M. Shibutse, P.O. Box 40624, Nairobi, Kenya.

Inter-Faith Academy of Peace. Dr. Landrum R. Bolling. (See Ecumenical Institute for Theological Studies, above.)

International Association for Religious Freedom. Ms. Lucie Meijer, Dreieichenstr. 59, 6000 Frankfurt 70, Federal Republic of Germany.

International Council of Voluntary Agencies. Sri Radhakrishna, 221-23 Deen Dayal Upadhyaya Marg, New Delhi 110002, India.

International Grail Movement. Mrs. Mary G. Busharizi, P.O. Box 74452, Nairobi, Kenya. Miss Imelda Gaurwa, 2 Lembeni Pare, Moshi, Tanzania.

International Movement of Catholic Students (Pax Romana). Rev. S.J.K. Parker-Allotey, P.O. Box 62106, Nairobi, Kenya.

Islamic African Centre. Mr. Ali M. Abd Al-Rahim, P.O. Box 2469, Khartoum, Sudan.

Israel Interfaith Association. Mr. Jack J. Cohen, P.O. Box 7739, Jerusalem 91077, Israel. Dr. André Chouraqui, 8 Ain Roguel, Jerusalem, Israel.

Italian Interfaith Peace Center. Mr. Gianni Novelli, Via Acciaioli 7, 00186 Roma, Italy.

Konrad Adenauer Foundation. Dr. Josef Lütke-Entrup, Valley Road, P.O. Box 43278, Nairobi, Kenya.

Lutheran World Federation. Rev. J. Odhiambo Nyamgero, P.O. Box 21203, Nairobi, Kenya.

Maryknoll Sisters. Sr. Marilyn Norris, P.O. Box 21605, Nairobi, Kenya.

Methodist Church of Southern Africa. Rev. M. Stanley Mogoba, P.O. Box 2256, Durban, 4000 South Africa.

Missionary Sisters of our Lady of Africa. Sr. Leocadie Kana, P.O. Box 82001, Mombasa, Kenya.

Movement for a Better World. Rev. Denis Mayanja, P.O. Box 2886, Kampala, Uganda.

Muslim World League. Sheikh Nasir Al-Aboudi, c/o Muslim World League, Mecca, Saudi Arabia.

National Christian Council of Kenya. Mr. John C. Kamau, P.O. Box 72766, Nairobi, Kenya. Mr. Max Rafransoa, at same address.

National Council of Catholic Women. Mrs. Anastasia Mhango, P.O. Box 37767, Lusaka, Zambia.

National Council of Churches of Christ in the USA. Dr. JoAnne H. Kagiwada, P.O. Box 1986, Indianapolis, IN 46206, U.S.A.

Orthodox Church in East Africa. Bishop Anastasios Yannoulatos, Dept. of the Study of Religions, Athens University, G. Seferi 1, Neon Psyhicon, Athens, Greece.

Pax Christi International. Mme Jacqueline Rougé. (See address under National Delegates).

Quakers (Religious Society of Friends). Mr. Daniel A. Seeger, 15 Rutherford Place, New York, N.Y. 10003, U.S.A.

The Royal Academy for Islamic Civilization Research (Al Albait Foundation). Mr. Abdel Karim Gharaibeh, P.O. Box 950361, Amman, Jordan.

SEDOS (Servicio dei Documenti e Studi). Fr. Richard Woulfe, P.O. Box 40369, Nairobi, Kenya.

South African Bishops' Conference. Mr. Bernard F. Connor, P.O. Box 815, Springs, 1560 South Africa.

Soto Zen Sect. Mr. N. Kuruma, 3-23 Sugamo, Toshima-ku, Tokyo 170, Japan.

Sudan Council of Churches. Mr. Cyer R. Madut, P.O. Box 469, Khartoum, Sudan.

United Nations. Mr. Kingsley D. Dube, P.O. Box 30218, Nairobi, Kenya.

United States Catholic Mission Association. Rev. Simon E. Smith, S.J., P.O. Box 14877, Nairobi, Kenya.

Pontifical Commission for Justice and Peace/Vatican. Rev. Michel R.C.

Schooyans, Voie du Roman Pays 17/101, 1348 Louvain-la-Neuve, Belgium.

World Association of World Federalists. Rev. Gerard G. Grant, S.J.,* 6525 North Sheridan Road, Chicago, IL 60626, USA.

World Congress of Faiths. Mrs. Ivy Gutridge, 7 Greenly Road, Parkfield, Wolverhampton, West Midlands WV46AL, United Kingdom.

World Fellowship of Inter-Religious Councils. Fr. Albert Nambiaparambil, Prior General's House, Cochin 682 011, Kerala, India.

World Muslim Congress. Dr. Rifat Yücelten, P.O. Box 142, Lefkhosa (Nicosia), Cyprus.

Zimbabwe Christian Council. Mr. Edmund M. Chifamba, P.O. Box 3566, Harare, Zimbabwe.

---

*An unfortunate accident in Nairobi prevented Dr. Grant from participating in the Conference after the first day.

77

Fraternal Observers

Association of Intercultural Communication. Dr. Wilhelm Otte, Olpener Str. 950, 5000 Köln, Federal Republic of Germany.

Benedictine Order. Mr. Cornelius Tholens, Begijhof 37I, 1012 WV Amsterdam, Netherlands.

Committee on Christian-Muslim Dialogue. Mr. Mario R. Mapanao, c/o Dept. of Sociology, Faculty Center, Room 3080, University of the Philippines, Diliman, Quezon City, Philippines.

Consolata Missionary Sisters. Sr. Christiana Sestero, P.O. Box 48301, Nairobi, Kenya.

Evangelical Church in Germany. Dr. Klaus Lefringhausen, Adenauerallee 134, 5300 Bonn, Federal Republic of Germany. Mr. Michael Mildenberger, Friedrichstr. 2-6, 6000 Frankfurt, Federal Republic of Germany.

Focolare Movement. Miss Anne Bustarret, P.O. Box 25220, Nairobi, Kenya. Rev. Julian Ricchiardi, at same address.

Gedatsu-kai, Youth Division. Mr. Shoji Kobayashi, 4 Araki-cho, Shinjuku-ku, Tokyo 160, Japan.

International Grail Movement. Miss Ophelia Ablorh, P.O. Box 6061, Accra North, Ghana. Mrs. M.O. Lijadu, P.O. Box 3702, Lagos, Nigeria. Miss E.M. Namaganda, Uganda Social Training School, P.O. Box 14267, Kampala, Uganda.

Istituto Internazionale di Studi Teologici, Ecumenici e Religiosi (ISISTER). Mr. Daniele Mezzana, Via Luca Signorelli 6, 00196 Roma, Italy.

Kosei Publishing Company. Mr. Akitomo Nukaga, 2-6-1 Wada, Suginami-ku, Tokyo 166, Japan.

Myochi-kai Kyodan. Miss Noriko Yokoo, 5-6-12-303 Yokodai, Isogo-ku, Yokohama-shi, Kanagawa 235, Japan.

Nairobi University Catholic Community. Miss Maria Kitiabi, P.O. Box

30350, Nairobi, Kenya.

New Buddhist Movement Daiei-kai. Mr. Toshikazu Ishikura, 142 Omino, Sakai-shi, Osaka 588, Japan.

Other Japanese Religions. Mr. Hiroharu Kimoto, 3-161 Hassamu 1-cho, Nishi-ku, Sapporo 011, Hoddaido, Japan. Mr. Akihiko Sasahara, Kyoto 607, Japan.

Pax Christi. Miss Lidia Sconciaforni, Basento 78, 00198 Roma, Italy.

Presbyterian Church (USA). Rev. Augustin Battle, P.O. Box 21570, Nairobi, Kenya. Ms. Mary Jane Patterson, 110 Maryland Avenue N.E., Washington, D.C. 20002, U.S.A.

Quakers (Religious Society of Friends). Mr. Benaiah M. Musisi, P.O. Box 48832, Nairobi, Kenya.

Rissho Kosei-kai. Mr. Takashi Fuse, Mr. Masuo Nezu and Mrs. Tomoko Otaki, (all three at) 2-11-1 Wada, Suginami-ku, Tokyo 166, Japan.

Rissho Kosei-kai Youth Section. Mr. Takayoshi Kubo and Mr. Keizo Nakayama, (both at) 2-11-1 Wada, Suginami-ku, Tokyo 166, Japan.

Ritsumeikan University. Mr. Tatsuya Suemoto, 874 Myorenjimae-cho, Omiyahigashiiru, Kyoto 602, Japan.

Salesian University. Fr. Tony D'Souza, P.O. Box 62322, Nairobi, Kenya.

Soto Zen Sect. Mr. Soyu Machida, 1170 Shimosaba, Yamaguchi-shi, Yamaguchi, Japan. Mr. Sachio Monma, 1-26-108 Sakonyama-danchi, Asahi-ku, Yokohama-shi 241, Kanagawa, Japan. Mr. Sogen Yugi, 4464 Naruse, Machida-shi, Tokyo 194, Japan.

Shinri-kyo Church of Umiya-Hachiman. Mr. Kaoru Hayashi, 211 Taiko, Oaza, Hiokigawa-machi, Nishimuro-gun, Wakayama 649-25, Japan.

Shofujuku High School. Mr. Osamu Murakami, 37 Takinozawa, Aza, Sotokoji, Oaza, Hiranai-machi, Aomori 039-33, Japan.

Shoroku Shinto Yamatoyama. Mr. Toyohiro Tazawa, 12-13 Takinozawa, Aza, Sotodoji, Aomori 039-33, Japan.

The Templeton Foundation. Mr. Wilbert Forker, Box N 7776, Nassau, Bahamas.

Uganda Muslim Supreme Council. Mr. Isa Lukwago, P.O. Box 1146, Kampala, Uganda.

UNESCO. Mr. Michael J. Kinunda, P.O. Box 30592, Nairobi, Kenya.

UNHCR. Mr. Kwame Afriyie, Nairobi, Kenya.

Vatican Secretariat for Non-Christians. Rev. John M. Shirieda and Rev. Marcello Zago, (both at) Secretariat pro Non Christianis, 00193 Vatican City.

World Council of Churches' Sub-Unit on Dialogue with People of Living Faiths. Rev. S. Wesley Ariarajah, 150 route de Ferney, P.O. Box 66, 1211 Geneva, Switzerland.

WCRP/Japan Youth Board. Mr. Gensho Hozumi, 40 Inukaijizomata, Sogabe-machi, Kameoka-shi, Kyoto 621, Japan. Mr. Nissin Matsushita, 874 Myorenjimae-cho, Omiyahigashiiru, Teranouchi, Kyoto 602, Japan. Mr. Shogo Tazawa, 12-13 Takinozawa, Aza, Sotokoji, Oaza, Hiranai-machi, Aomori, 039-33, Japan.

Youth Christian Students (Africa). Mr. Munhumeso Manenji, P.O. Box 44335, Nairobi, Kenya.

78

Observers / Spouses / Visitors

Mr. Davati Abolfath, Consulate of the Iranian Islamic Republic, Nairobi, Kenya.

Mr. Malcolm C. Alexander, 28 Friars Stile Road, Richmond, Surrey TW10 6NE, United Kingdom.

Mr. Béla Bartók, Köbölkut Str. 10, 1118 Budapest, Hungary.

Mr. Abraham Bardugo, P.O. Box 2237, Jerusalem, Israel.

Mr. Davinder N. Bhanot, Block N.I.L.–17/A, Malavia Nagar, New Delhi 110017, India.

Ms. Ruth Anna Brown, Apt. 922, 500 University Avenue, Honolulu, HI 96826, USA.

Mr. Hüsrev S. Cagin, P.O. Box 755, Nicosia, Cyprus.

M. Jean Carbonare, P.O. Box 1887, Dakar, Senegal.

Don Antonino Cenacchi, Via Roma 7/A, Montekreto, Modena 41025, Italy.

Miss Claudia Colonnello, Via Monte Pertica 11, 00195 Roma, Italy.

Mr. Andrea Declich, Via Santa Maura 61, 00192 Roma, Italy.

Mrs. Willie J. Dell, 2923 Hawthorne Avenue, Richmond, VA 23222, USA.

Mrs. Euis T. Djaelani, Jalan Kramat 7 no. 9, Jakarta 10450, Indonesia.

Mr. Akinori Eijo, 2-8-75 Yakushi-machi, Yamagata-shi, Yamagata 990, Japan.

Mr. Fabian P. Feil, Königsberger Str. 5, 7000 Stuttgart 70, Federal Republic of Germany.

Mrs. F. Maureen Forker, c/o The Templeton Foundation, Box N 7776, Nassau, Bahamas.

Mr. Charles K. Gakori, P.O. Box 1210, Thika, Kenya.

Mrs. Gharaibeh, c/o The Royal Academy for Islamic Civilization Research, P.O. Box 950361, Amman, Jordan.

Mr. Gustav and Mrs. Lorraine Grob-Duclos, World Circle of the Code, 51 Park Drive, London W3, United Kingdom.

Mr. Cleophas M. Haema, State House Road Hostel, P.O. Box 30344, Nairobi, Kenya.

Mrs. Hanumanthappa, 17 Cunningham Road, Bangalore 560052, India.

Sheikh Mohamed Ali Hemedi, P.O. Box 20213, Dar-Es-S Salaam, Tanzania.

Sr. Mary Ingram, P.O. Box 21668, Nairobi, Kenya.

Mr. Boaz K. Kaino, P.O. Box 59248, Nairobi, Kenya.

Rev. Medadi C. Kantinti, P.O. Box 52034, Nairobi, Kenya.

Sr. Fauzia A. Karume, P.O. Box 16388, Nairobi, Kenya.

Mr. Masami Kasuya, c/o Rissho Kosei-kai, 2-11-1 Wada, Suginami-ku, Tokyo 166, Japan.

Mrs. Bahadur Kaur, 5001 Beach Road no. 07-24, Golden Mile Complex, Singapore 0719, Republic of Singapore.

Dr. Nuruzzaman Khan, 500/S Dhanmondi R.A., Road no. 8, Dhaka, Bangladesh.

Sr. Argyro Kontoyorghi, P.O. Box 46119, Nairobi, Kenya.

Mr. Sanjay Kumar Jain, Delhi 110016, India.

Mr. Gottfried Klinkenberg, Grenzweg 3, 8751 Haibach, Federal Republic of Germany.

Mrs. Azzree Lathan, 3017 S.W. Upper Drive, Lake Oswego, OR 97031, USA.

Sheikh M. Mussa Lenana, P.O. Box 75918, Nairobi, Kenya.

Mrs. Maimunah Lukman, Jalan Sukabumi no. 11, Jakarta 10310, Indonesia.

Mrs. Zuhura Lukwago, P.O. Box 1146, Kampala, Uganda.

Miss Christine Maas, Steinhagen 23a, 4630 Bochum 1, Federal Republic of Germany.

Mr. Fabian Makani, P.O. Box 30364, Nairobi, Kenya.

Mr. Susumu Matsumoto, 5-3-11 Senju, Adachi-ku, Tokyo 120, Japan.

Mrs. Winifred E. May, no. 55, 5202 S.E. 30th, Portland, OR 97202, USA.

Mrs. Marilyn McClean, UMUNO, 11th Floor, 777 United Nations Plaza, New York, N.Y. 10017, USA.

Mrs. Maria V. Miyahira, Via Degli Amodei 12, 00163 Roma, Italy.

Mr. Johnson P. Mlambo, Dar-Es-Salaam, Tanzania.

Sr. Aziza Mohammed, P.O. Box 16363, Nairobi, Kenya.

Mr. Kikuvi R. Mulwa, P.O. Box 1020, Kangundo, Machakos, Kenya.

Mr. Yukiteru Murayama, c/o Rissho Kosei-kai, 2-11-1 Wada, Suginami-ku, Tokyo 166, Japan.

Miss Murithi, c/o Mrs. M. Busharizi, P.O. Box 74454, Nairobi, Kenya.

Mr. Yukichi Nakajima, c/o Rissho Kosei-kai, 2-11-1 Wada, Suginami-ku, Tokyo 166, Japan.

Mr. Yuji Namekawa, c/o Higashi-Kanasa Shrine, 3-6-16 Shibuya, Shibuya-ku, Tokyo 150, Japan.

Mr. Titus N. Nthakyo, c/o K.T.T.C., P.O. Box 44600, Nairobi, Kenya.

Dr. Ralph W. Odom, Apt. 922, 500 University Avenue, Honolulu, HI 96826, USA.

Mr. S.J. Omran, Embassy of the Republic of Iraq, P.O. Box 49213, Nairobi, Kenya.

Rev. Sinclair Oubre, Naamsestr. 1000, 3000 Leuven, Belgium.

Mrs. Connie Price-Truman, 849 Holly Avenue, St. Paul, MINN 55104, USA.

Mrs. Tatiana Prokosch, c/o Amnesty International, 1 Easton Street, London WC1X 8DJ, United Kingdom.

Ms. Mary E. Reynolds, Eleuthera, 9 Regis Beeches, Regis Road, Tettenhall, Wolverhampton WV6 8RY, United Kingdom.

Rev. Gustav Rosenstein, Shira Avenue, Box 795, Moshi, Tanzania.

Mr. Holger H. Rothbauer, Mestetter Str. 21, 7000 Stuttgart 80, Federal Republic of Germany.

Mr. Canisius P. Rusagara, P.O. Box 34186, Nairobi, Kenya.

Mrs. Khaisiah Rusydi, Jalan Kenanga 6, Bintaro, Jakarta, Indonesia.

Mr. Onesphore Rwaje, B.P. 61, Kigali, Rwanda.

Mrs. Salome Rwiliriza, P.O. Box 14206, Nairobi, Kenya.

Miss Sabah A. Salim, P.O. Box 18236, Nairobi, Kenya.

Mrs. Helga Schultes, Schelhammergasse 17, 3420 Kritzendorf, Austria.

Mr. Enock Shinachi, P.O. Box 26, Malava, Kenya.

Mr. M.A. Shoaei, Consulate of the Iranian Islamic Republic, P.O. Box 49170, Nairobi, Kenya.

Mr. Jasbir Singh, 5001 Beach Road no. 07-24, Golden Mile Complex, Singapore 0719, Republic of Singapore.

Mr. W.-E. Solomon, P.O. Box MG 100, Highlands, Harare, Zimbabwe.

Rev. Timothy Stanton, P.O. Box 49027, Rosettenville, Johannesburg 2130, South Africa.

Mrs. Virginia W. Stowe, c/o UCBWM, 16th Floor, 475 Riverside Drive, New York, N.Y. 10115, USA.

Mr. Koji Sugihara, 996 Minato, Tanabe-shi, Wakayama 646, Japan.

Mrs. Khatija Suliman, P.O. Box 297, Warmbaths, 0480 South Africa.

Mr. Tsunetaka Tanaka, c/o Hinomoto Jomae Co., 1-19-19 Nishigahara, Kita-ku, Tokyo 114, Japan.

Mr. Tsuyoshi Tanaka, c/o Shinsei-kai, 3-19 Nihsino-machi, Gifu-shi, Gifu 500, Japan.

Mr. Hiroaki Teranishi, 1-33 Ebaraji-cho, Sakai-shi, Osaka 593, Japan.

Mr. Vishwasain, Shri Jain Math, Shravenabelagola 573135, Hassan, Karnataka, India.

Miss Helga Vunic, Ankerstraat 9, 2700 St. Niklaas O.VL, Belgium.

Mr. Stefan Vunic. (See address above.)

Mr. Robert Ward, 555 Short, Sherbrooke, Québec J1H2E6, Canada.

Mr. Masao Yamada, c/o Rissho Kosei-kai, 2-11-1 Wada, Suginami-ku, Tokyo 166, Japan.

Sheikh Mohammed Yasin, P.O. Box 32506, Nairobi, Kenya.

79

International Secretariat/Coopted Staff

Miss Renate Belck, WCRP/International, Administrative Assistant, 777 United Nations Plaza, New York, N.Y. 10017, USA.

M. Leno d'Alessandri, c/o SIORC, 32 rue de Zurich, 1201 Geneva, Switzerland.

Miss Brigitte Dupraz, WCRP/International, Administrative Assistant, 14, ch. Auguste-Vilbert, 1218 Grand-Saconnex, Geneva, Switzerland.

Mr. Shamsher Durga, House no. 706, Sector 7B, Chandigarh, India.

Dr. Diana Eck, Center for the Study of Religion, Harvard University, 61 Kirkland Street, Cambridge, MA 02138, USA.

Mrs. Tomoko Evdokimoff, 46 Ancienne Route, 1218 Grand-Saconnex, Geneva, Switzerland.

M. Robert Faerber, 24 rue du Fossé-Riepberg, 67100 Strasbourg, France.

Mr. Günther Gebhardt, WCRP/Europe, Spessartstrasse 8, 8700 Würzburg, Federal Republic of Germany.

Dr. Homer A. Jack, Secretary-General Emeritus, WCRP/International. 489 Willow Road, Winnetka, IL 60093, USA.

Mrs. Ingeborg Jack, 489 Willow Road, Winnetka, IL 60093, USA.

Sr. Marjorie Keenan, Sisters Sacred Heart of Mary, Via del Mascherino 75, 00193 Rome, Italy.

Prof. Dr. Norbert Klaes, WCRP/Europe, Estenfelderstr. 94, 8700 Würzburg 4, Federal Republic of Germany.

Mr. Peter Nsubuga, c/o WCRP/Africa, P.O. Box 70394, Nairobi, Kenya.

Mr. Hiroyuki Oshima, Under-Secretary-General, WCRP/Japan, 2-6 Wada, Suginami-ku, Tokyo 166, Japan.

Mr. Ryuichiro Oyama, WCRP/Japan, 2-6 Wada Suginami-ku, Tokyo 166, Japan.

Rev. John Radano, Via della Nocetta 63, 00164, Roma, Italy.

Mr. Koichi Saito, WCRP/Japan, 2-6 Wada, Suginami-ku, Tokyo 166, Japan.

Dr. John B. Taylor, Secretary-General, WCRP/International, 14 chemin Auguste-Vilbert, 1218 Grand-Saconnex, Geneva, Switzerland.

Mrs. Margaret Taylor, "L'Echappée," 1264 St. Cergue, Vaud, Switzerland.

Mr. Hans van Willenswaard, Spanjaardstraat 74, 4331 ES Hiddelburg, Netherlands.

80

Japanese Staff/Aides/Volunteers

Mr. Tatsuo Abe, c/o Rissho Kosei-kai, 2-11-1, Wada, Suginami-ku, Tokyo 166, Japan.

Miss Nobue Aiba, c/o Akasaka Grand House, Niwano Peace Foundation, 8-6-17, Akasaka, Minato-ku, Tokyo 107, Japan.

Mr. Nobuo Amma, c/o WCRP/Japan, 2-7, Wada, Suginami-ku, Tokyo 166, Japan.

Mr. Yoshiaki Azuma, c/o Rissho Kosei-kai, 2-11-1, Wada, Suginami-ku, Tokyo 166, Japan.

Mrs. Masae Esaki, 7-8-3, Fukasawa, Setagaya-ku, Tokyo 166, Japan.

Miss Akiko Goto, c/o WCRP/Japan, 2-7, Wada, Suginami-ku, Tokyo 166, Japan.

Mr. Tadao Goto, c/o Rissho Kosei-kai, 2-11-1, Wada, Suginami-ku, Tokyo 166, Japan.

Mr. Yoshitaka Hatakeyama, c/o Rissho Kosei-kai, 2-11-1, Wada, Suginami-ku, Tokyo 166, Japan.

Mr. Yasuo Hideshima, c/o Rissho Kosei-kai, 2-11-1, Wada, Suginami-ku, Tokyo 166, Japan.

Mr. Masayuki Idei, c/o Rissho Kosei-kai, 2-11-1, Wada, Suginami-ku, Tokyo 166, Japan.

Mr. Issei Inoue, 1-26-18, Torikainono, Settsu-shi, Osaka 566, Japan.

Miss Masayo Kawakami, c/o WCRP/Japan, 2-6, Wada, Suginami-ku, Tokyo 166, Japan.

Miss Hiromi Kon, c/o Isonagi, 3-32-2, Isobe, Chiba-shi, Chiba 260, Japan.

Mr. Toshio Kozai, c/o Konko-kyo Church of Izuo, 21-8 Nishi 3-chome, San-gen-ya, Taisho-ku, Osaka 551, Japan.

Mr. Michinori Maruta, c/o Rissho Kosei-kai, 2-11-1, Wada, Suginami-ku, Tokyo 166, Japan.

Mr. Yukio Matsunaga, c/o Rissho Kosei-kai, 2-11-1, Wada, Suginami-ku, Tokyo 166, Japan

Mr. Hikaru Miyasaka, c/o Rissho Kosei-kai, 2-11-1, Wada, Suginami-ku, Tokyo 166, Japan.

Miss Yuko Mizuno, 2956-13, Katsuragi-cho, Kishiwada-shi, Osaka 596, Japan.

Mr. Yoshio Nishida, 1-27-15, Eifuku, Suginami-ku, Tokyo 168, Japan.

Mr. Kazuo Ogura, c/o Japan Travel Bureau, 1-5-13 Nishi-shinbashi, Minato-ku, Tokyo 105, Japan.

Mr. Yoshitada Okubo, c/o Rissho Kosei-kai, 2-11-1, Wada, Suginami-ku, Tokyo 166, Japan.

Mr. Kenji Saito, c/o WCRP/Japan, 2-7, Wada, Suginami-ku, Tokyo 166, Japan.

Mr. Kazuo Shimano, 1-15-10-302 Midorimachi, Tokorozawa, Saitama 359, Japan.

Mr. Masashi Shimura, c/o Rissho Kosei-kai, 2-11-1, Wada, Suginami-ku, Tokyo 166, Japan.

Mr. Keitaro Suzuki, c/o Japan Akasaka Grand House, Niwano Peace Foundation, 8-6-17, Akasaka, Minato-ku, Tokyo 107, Japan.

Mrs. Takae Suzuki, c/o Rissho Kosei-kai, 2-11-1, Wada, Suginami-ku, Tokyo 166, Japan.

Mr. Tatsuo Takise, c/o Rissho Kosei-kai, 2-11-1, Wada, Suginami-ku, Tokyo 166, Japan.

Mr. Motoyuki Tanaka, c/o Rissho Kosei-kai, 2-11-1, Wada, Suginami-ku, Tokyo 166, Japan.

Mr. Akifumi Yamazaki, c/o WCRP/Japan, 2-7, Wada, Suginami-ku, Tokyo 166, Japan.

Miss Junko Yata, c/o Rissho Kosei-kai, 2-11-1, Wada, Suginami-ku, Tokyo 166, Japan.

Mr. Toshiharu Yoneda, c/o Rissho Kosei-kai, 2-11-1, Wada, Suginami-ku, Tokyo 166, Japan.

81

Volunteers

Miss Margaret Amol, Deanery Dev. Office, P.O. Box 161, Siaya, Kenya.

Ms. Sigrid Belck, 9 rue des Vieux Grenadiers, 1205 Geneva, Switzerland.

Mrs. Libby Blake, 47 Roebuck Road, Rochester, ME1 1UE, United Kingdom.

Mr. Gabriele Fabbri, P.O. Box 25220, Nairobi, Kenya.

Mr. Henry Ireri, P.O. Box 25220, Nairobi, Kenya.

Ms. Deborah Kaddu, P.O. Box 14123, Kampala, Uganda.

Miss Ranbir Kaur, 5001 Beach Road #07-24, Golden Mile Complex, Singapore 0719, Republic of Singapore.

Miss Mariana Kinyuy, P.O. Box 25220 Nairobi, Kenya.

Ms. Suzanne Koehli, 3 rue Jean Gutenberg, 1201 Geneva, Switzerland.

Mr. Alberto Lucchi, P.O. Box 25220, Nairobi, Kenya.

Miss Esther Macharia, U.O.N. Chiromo, P.O. Box 30344, Nairobi, Kenya.

Mr. Daniel Maundu, P.O. Box 59, Kathonzweni, Machakos, Kenya.

Ms. Assumpta Ndolo, P.O. Box 60592, Nairobi, Kenya.

Mrs. Betty Nyakiamo, P.O. Box 21314, Nairobi, Kenya.

Mr. Dominick Nyakiamo, P.O. Box 21314, Nairobi, Kenya.

Mr. Darington Omondi, P.O. Box 54579, Nairobi, Kenya.

Mrs. May Pinto, P.O. Box 70394, Nairobi, Kenya.

Miss Michèle Sabatié, P.O. Box 25220, Nairobi, Kenya.

Miss Eleanor Taylor, "L'Echappée," 1264 St-Cergue, Vaud, Switzerland.

Miss Isabella Wachira, P.O. Box 30350, Nairobi, Kenya.

Mr. William Wanjala, P.O. Box 47529, Nairobi, Kenya.

Mr. Michael Weya, P.O. Box 21286, Nairobi, Kenya.

Additional Volunteers from Kenya

Miss Joan Ambrose

Mrs. Chane

Miss Miriam Gacheru

Miss Susan Gathoni

Miss Rhoda N. Gikuma

Mr. Godfrey Gichuki

Mr. Jean-Marie Gitau

Ms. Mary Heta
Ms. Susan Ikamba
Mr. John Ireri
Mr. Bernard Kaigi
Ms. Margaret Kamara
Mr. Joseph Kamau
Ms. Mercy Kamwithu
Ms. Florence Kariuki
Miss Rita Kawira
Mr. Joseph Kirimi
Ms. Gertrude Kirimuttu
Ms. Margaret Kirimuttu
Mr. Patrick Kithinji
Mr. Calisto Kuja
Mrs. Mary Grace Kuruga
Mr. Daniel Lago
Mr. Stephen Lokeyo
Mrs. Madan
Mr. Fabian Makani
Mrs. Theresa Mandricks
Mr. Paul Marete
Mr. Javan Mavisi
Mr. John Mbugua
Ms. Jane Mburu
Mr. Stephen Ndungu Mburu
Mr. Charles Mutuota Muchoki
Mr. Michael Munyi
Ms. Veronica Murithi
Mr. Jaffer Ahmed Musa
Ms. Fernanda Muthoni
Ms. Myriam Muthoni
Ms. Sarah Muthoni
Mr. Marjan Mwanaisha
Ms. Rose Mwangi
Mr. Samuel Mwaniki
Mr. Martin Mwenga
Dr. Wanjiku Mwotia
Ms. Julia Ngahu
Mr. Moses Nganga
Ms. Agnes Njeru
Mr. Moses Njururi
Ms. Patsy Noronha
Ms. Sebastiana Nyaga
Mr. Michael Nyutu
Mr. Omar Suleiman
Mr. Ndolo Urbanus
Mr. Hussein Walaga

431

Mr. Silas Wanda
Mr. Peter Waweru

82

Delegates By Religions

Buddhists

Mr. Yuji Aoyama, Japan
Ven. Pra Bimaladhamma, Thailand
Miss Pal Khn Chon, Republic of Korea
Mr. Dao Shuren, People's Republic of China
Mr. Bhagwan Das, India
Prof. L.G. Hewage, Sri Lanka
Mr. Yo Ishikawa, Japan
Mr. Jing Hui, People's Republic of China
Mr. Sathitya Lengthaisong, Thailand
Lama Lobzang, India
Ven. Visuddhananda Mahathero, Bangladesh
Mr. Kodo Nagai, Japan
Rev. Motoyuki Naganuma, Japan
Mr. Masayuki Nakamura, Japan
Mr. Tashi Namgyal, India
Rev. Nikkyo Niwano, Japan
Mr. Kil Chin Park, Republic of Korea
Mr. Bogoda Premaratne, Sri Lanka
Mrs. Kanchana Soonsawad, Thailand
Mr. Kinzo Takemura, Japan
Mr. Hisakazu Taki, Japan
Ven. Anaruddha Thera, Sri Lanka
Ven. Thich Thien Chau, France
Rev. Kenryu T. Tsuji, U.S.A.
Mrs. Sugi Yamamoto, Japan
Mr. Yin Liang, People's Republic of China

Christians

Mr. Shin Anzai, Japan
Rev. Herman Benz, Federal Republic of Germany
Mr. Ernest Beyaraaza, Kenya
Rev. Jonathan Blake, England

433

Rev. Giovanni Cereti, Italy
Rev. José Chipenda, Angola
Rev. Mark Cornelis, Belgium
Ms. Gill Cressey, England
Miss Natalia Dallapiccola, Italy
Dr. Yvonne Delk, USA
Prof. Kwesi Dickson, Ghana
Mrs. Barbara D'Souza, India
Dr. Doris Dyke, Canada
Prof. Anezka Ebertova, Czechoslovakia
Archbishop Angelo Fernandes, India
Ms. Theresa Flower, Canada
Mr. Ian Fry, Australia
Bishop Gabriel Ganaka, Nigeria
Rev. H. Lamar Gibble, USA
Dr. Dana Greeley, USA
Mr. Han Wenzao, People's Republic of China
Rev. Philip Huggins, Australia
Prof. Yoshiaki Iisaka, Japan
Mrs. Joyce Kaddu, Uganda
Mr. Boaz Kaino, Kenya
Dr. Mladen Karadjole, Belgium
Miss Florence Kawoya, Kenya
Msgr. Bruce Kent, England
Miss Irene Kessy, Tanzania
Prof. Norbert Klaes, Federal Republic of Germany
Rev. J.N.J. Kritzinger, South Africa
Rev. Patrick Lal, India
Mrs. Evelyn Lebona, Lesotho
Rev. Gerrie Lubbe, South Africa
Mr. Wilfred Maciel, Kenya
Mrs. Lliljana Matkovic-Vlasic, Yugoslavia
Dr. Edward May, USA.
Rev. Robert McClean, USA
Mr. Mmutlanyane S. Mogoba, South Africa
Rev. Josphat Mugwerru, Kenya
Mrs. Edna Nanayakkara, Sri Lanka
Bishop J. Henry Okullu, Kenya
Mr. Richard Ondeng, Kenya
Rev. Joseph Osei, Ghana
Miss Peng Cui-An, People's Republic of China
Bishop Bernardino Pinera, Chile
Rev. Christian Precht, Chile
Rev. Brian Prideaux, Canada
Dr. Sun Hwan Pyun, Republic of Korea
Bishop Francis Quinn, USA
Mrs. Dorothy Ramodibe, South Africa

Sr. Layla Raphaël, Canada
Mr. Norbert Ratsirahonana, Madagascar
Mme Jacqueline Rougé, France
Dr. George Rupp, USA
Bishop Peter Sarpong, Ghana
Dr. Henk E. Schouten, Netherlands
Prof. Josef Schultes, Austria
Mr. Shen De-Rong, People's Republic of China
Rev. Robert Smylie, USA
Bishop Nobuo Soma, Japan
Miss Hannah Stanton, England
Dr. David Stowe, USA
Dr. Malcolm Sutherland, USA
Mr. George Telford, USA
Mr. Ante Vunic, Belgium
Prof. Gerald Wanjohi, Kenya
Mrs. Wanjohi, Kenya
Canon Gordon Wilson, England
Dr. Erika Wolf, Federal Republic of Germany
Prof. Kikuo Yamaoka, Japan
Mrs. Jean Zaru, West Bank of Jordan

Confucianists

Mr. Suryo Hutomo, Indonesia
Mr. Byong Joo Lee, Republic of Korea
Mr. Jong Myong Lee, Republic of Korea
Mrs. Ok Young Lee, Republic of Korea

Hindus

Dr. M. Aram, India
Mrs. Minoti Aram, India
Mrs. Gedong Bagoes Oka, Indonesia
Mrs. Deepali Bhanot, India
Dr. S.K. Chaturvedi, India
Sri R.R. Diwakar, India
Mrs. Harinder Durga, India
Miss Ranjana Durga, India
Mr. Rabindranath Duttagupta, Bangladesh
Shrivatsa Goswami, India
Mrs. Saroj Gupta Pereira, Canada
Mr. Wooday Hanumanthappa, India
Mr. Bindarao Konnur, England
Mr. Lachman Madan, India
Miss Anshu Mann, India
Mrs. C.K. Mann, India
Mr. Brijesh Mathur, India
Mrs. Punam S. Mohan, India

435

Miss Shobna Obhrai, Kenya
Mrs. Prabhat Pandit, India
Adv. Narendra Pandya, South Africa
Sri Radhakrishna, India
Dr. Anantanand Rambachan, England
Dr. Ravin Ramdass, South Africa
Mr. P.S. Saini, Kenya
Mr. Bhupander Sarup, India
Prof. Arumugam Sathasivam, Sri Lanka
Prof. Vishal Singh, India
Mr. Anil Sooklal, South Africa
Mr. Davendraj Upadhya, Nepal
Mr. N. Vasudevan, India

Jains

Charukeerty Bhattarak Swamiji, India
Mr. Mijar Dharmaraja, India
Dr. Veerendra Heggade, India
D. Harshendra Kumar, India

Jews

Ms. Shelley Elkayam, Israel
Dr. Jane Evans, USA
Dr. Albert Friedlander, England
Dr. Victor Goldbloom, Canada
Mrs. Norma Levitt, USA
Mr. Joseph Levy, Canada

Muslims

Mr. Mohammad Aasim, India
Dr. El-Sayed Al-Taftazani, Egypt
Mrs. Husna Akhtar, Bangladesh
Dr. Khairallah Assar, Algeria
Mr. Mohammed Azam, England
Mr. Timur Djaelani, Indonesia
Mr. Bahtiar Effendy, Indonesia
Mr. Yusuf Eraj, Kenya
Ms. Nahla Haidar, Lebanon
Dr. Viqar Hamdani, USA
Mr. Rusydi Hamka, Indonesia
Dr. Serajul Haque, Bangladesh
Mr. Lukman Harun, Indonesia
Mr. Badru Kateregga, Kenya
Mr. Habibur R. Khan, Pakistan
Dr. Inamullah Khan, Pakistan
Mr. Mohammed Koor, Kenya
Dr. Gamal Mahmoud, Egypt
Mr. Mohamed Mohideen, Sri Lanka

Dr. Adamou Ndam Njoya, Cameroun
Dr. Syed Pasha, England
Dr. Muhammad Qasim, India
Mr. Mahomed Suliman, South Africa
Mr. Sirajuddin Syamsuddin, Indonesia
Mr. Mahmood Youskine, Netherlands
Prof. Maftuchah Yusuf, Indonesia

Other Japanese Religions
Mr. Saichiro Uesugi, Japan

Shintoists
Mr. Masahiko Horai, Japan
Rev. Kiyotoshi Kawai, Japan
Mrs. Hiroko Kurozumi, Japan
Rev. Toshio Miyake, Japan
Mr. Iwane Mori, Japan
Mr. Koetsu Oi, Japan

Sikhs
Mr. Balwan Ghanna, Kenya
Mr. Tarlok S. Nandhra, Kenya
Mr. Mehervan Singh, Singapore
Major-General Sujan Singh Uban, India

Traditional Religions
Mr. Harold Belmont, USA
Mr. Art Solomon, Canada

Zoroastrians
Prof. Jamshed Mavalwala, Canada
Mr. Behram Vakil, Singapore

83

*Participants By Nations**

Algeria
Dr. Khairallah Assar

Angola
Rev. José Chipenda

Australia
Mr. Ian Fry
Rev. Philip Huggins

Austria
Mrs. Helga Schultes
Prof. Josef Schultes

Bahamas
Mrs. F. Maureen Forker
Mr. Wilbert Forker

Bangladesh
Mrs. Husna Akhtar
Mr. Rabindranath Duttagupta
Dr. Serajul Haque
Dr. Nuruzzaman Khan
Ven. Visuddhananda Mahathero

Belgium
Rev. Mark Cornelis
Dr. Mladen Karadjole
Rev. Sinclair Oubre
Mr. Michel Schooyans
Mr. Ante Vunic
Miss Helga Vunic
Mr. Stefan Vunic

---

*—In most cases participants are listed according to their country of residence.

Cameroun
Dr. Adamou Ndam Njoya

Canada
Dr. Doris Dyke
Ms. Theresa Flower
Dr. Victor Goldbloom
Mrs. Saroj Gupta Pereira
Mr. Joseph Levy
Prof. Jamshed Mavalwala
Rev. Brian Prideaux
Sr. Leyla Raphaël
Mr. Art Solomon
Mr. Robert Ward

Chile
Archbishop Bernardino Pinera
Fr. Christian Precht

People's Republic of China
Mr. Dao Shuren
Mr. Han Wenzao
Mr. Jing Hui
Miss Peng Cui-An
Mr. Shen De-Rong
Mrs. Yi Luo
Mr. Yin Liang

Congo
Sr. Adrienne N'Dombi

Cyprus
Mr. Hüsrev Cagin
Dr. Rifat Yücelten

Czechoslovakia
Dr. Anezka Ebertova
Dr. Lubomír Mirejovsky

Egypt
Dr. El-Sayed Al-Taftazani
Dr. Gamal Mahmoud

France
Dr. Robert Faerber
Mme Jacqueline Rougé
Ven. Thich Thien Chau

Federal Republic of Germany
Rev. Hermann Benz
Mr. Fabian Feil
Mr. Günther Gebhardt
Mr. Claus Hebler
Prof. Norbert Klaes
Mr. Gottfried Klinkenberg
Dr. Klaus Lefringhausen
Miss Christine Maas
Ms. Lucie Meijer
Dr. Michael Mildenberger
Dr. Wilhelm Otte
Mr. Holger Rothbauer
Dr. Erika Wolf

Ghana
Miss Ophelia Ablorh
Prof. Kwesi Dickson
Rev. Joseph Osei

Greece
Bishop Anastasios Yannoulatos

Hungary
Mr. Bela Bartok

India
Mr. Mohammad Aasim
Dr. M. Aram
Mrs. Minoti Aram
Mr. Davinder Bhanot
Mrs. Deepali Bhanot
Charukeerty Bhattarak Swamiji
Dr. S.K. Chaturvedi
Mr. Bhagwan Das
Mr. Mijar Dharmaraja
Sri R.R. Diwakar
Mrs. Barbara D'Souza
Mrs. Harinder Durga
Miss Ranjana Durga
Mr. Shamsher Durga
Archbishop Angelo Fernandes
Sri Goswami
Mr. Wooday Hanumanthappa
Mrs. Hanumanthappa
Dr. Veerendra Heggade
Mr. Sanjay Kumar Jain
Brahma Kumari Janki

440

Dr. Harshendra Kumar
Rev. Patrick Lal
Lama Lobzang
Mr. Lachman Madan
Miss Anshu Mann
Mrs. C.K. Mann
Mr. Brijesh Mathur
Mrs. Punam Mohan
Fr. Albert Nambiaparambil
Mr. Tashi Namgyal
Mrs. Prabhat Pandit
Dr. Muhammad Qasim
Sri Radhakrishna
Mr. Bhupander Sarup
Prof. Vishal Singh
Major-General Sujan S. Uban
Mr. N. Vasudevan
Sr. Vedanti
Mr. Vishwasain

Indonesia
Mrs. Gedong Bagoes Oka
Mr. Timur Djaelani
Mrs. Euis Djaelani
Mr. Bahtiar Effendy
Mr. Rusydi Hamka
Mr. Lukman Harun
Mr. Suryo Hutomo
Mrs. Maimunah Lukman
Mrs. Khaisiah Rusydi
Mrs. Syamsuddin Sirajuddin
Dr. Soedjatmoko
Prof. Maftuchah Yusuf

Iran
Mr. Devati Abolfath
Mr. M.A. Shoaei

Iraq
Mr. S.J. Omran

Israel
Mr. Abraham Bardugo
Dr. André Chouraqui
Mr. Jack Cohen
Ms. Shelley Elkayam
Dr. William Klassen

Italy

Don Antonino Cenacchi
Rev. Giovanni Cereti
Miss Claudia Colonnello
Miss Natalia Dallapiccola
Mr. Andrea Declich
Mr. Daniele Mezzana
Mrs. Maria V. Miyahira
Mr. Gianni Novelli
Miss Lidia Sconciaforni

Japan

Mr. Tatsuo Abe
Miss Nobue Aiba
Mr. Nubuo Amma
Mr. Shin Anzai
Mr. Yuji Aoyama
Mr. Tatsuo Asai
Mr. Yoshiaki Azuma
Mr. Akinori Eijo
Mrs. Masae Esaki
Mr. Takashi Fuse
Miss Akiko Goto
Mr. Tadao Goto
Mr. Yoshitaka Hatakeyama
Mr. Kaoru Hayashi
Mr. Yasuo Hideshima
Mr. Masahiko Horai
Mr. Gansho Hozumi
Mr. Masayuki Idei
Prof. Yoshiaki Iisaka
Mr. Issei Inoue
Mrs. Sachiko Ishida
Mr. Yo Ishikawa
Mr. Toshikazu Ishikuro
Mr. Masami Kasuya
Rev. Kiyotoshi Kawai
Miss Masayo Kawakami
Mr. Hiroharu Kimoto
Mr. Shoji Kobayashi
Miss Emiko Kodama
Miss Hiromi Kon
Mr. Tatsuro Konishi
Mrs. Chika Kosuga
Mr. Toshio Kozai
Mr. Takayoshi Kubo
Mrs. Hiroko Kurozumi

442

Mr. N. Kuruma
Mr. Soyu Machida
Mr. Michinori Maruta
Mr. Ryu Matsumoto
Mr. Susumu Matsumoto
Mr. Yukio Matsunaga
Mr. Nissin Matsushita
Mr. Yoko Matzuoka
Rev. Tokyo Miyake
Mr. Hikaru Miyasaka
Miss Yuko Mizuno
Mr. Sachio Monma
Mr. Iwane Mori
Mr. Osamu Murakami
Mr. Yukiteru Murayama
Mr. Kodo Nagai
Mr. Motoyuki Naganuma
Mr. Yukichi Nakajima
Mr. Masayuki Nakamura
Mr. Keizo Nakayama
Mr. Yuji Namekawa
Mr. Masuo Nezu
Mr. Yoshio Nishida
Rev. Nikkyo Niwano
Mr. Akitomo Nukaga
Mr. Kazuo Ogura
Mr. Koetsu Oi
Mr. Yoshitada Okubo
Mr. Hiroyuki Oshima
Mr. Tomoko Otaki
Mr. Ryuichiro Oyama
Mr. Kenji Saito
Mr. Koichi Saito
Mr. Akihiko Sasahara
Mr. Kazuo Shimano
Mr. Masashi Shimura
Mr. Nobuo Soma
Mr. Tatsuya Suemoto
Mr. Koji Sugihara
Mr. Keitaro Suzuki
Mrs. Takae Suzuki
Mr. Kinzo Takemura
Mr. Hisakazu Taki
Mr. Tatsuo Takise
Mr. Motoyuki Tanaka
Mr. Tsunetaka Tanaka
Mr. Tsuyoshi Tanaka

Mr. Akinobu Tanimoto
Mr. Shogo Tazawa
Mr. Toyohiro Tazawa
Mr. Hiroaki Teranishi
Mr. Kenzo Tomonage
Mr. Saichiro Uesugi
Mr. Masao Yamada
Mrs. Sugi Yamamoto
Prof. Kikuo Yamaoka
Mr. Akifumi Yamazaki
Miss Junko Yata
Mr. Toshiharu Yoneda
Miss Noriko Yokoo
Mr. Sogen Yugi

Jordan

Mr. Abdel K. Gharaibeh
Mrs. Gharaibeh

Jordan (West Bank)

Mrs. Jean Zaru

Kenya

Mr. Kwame Afriyie
Miss Margaret Amol
Rev. Augustin Battle
Dr. Rémy Beller
Mr. Ernest Beyaraaza
Mrs. Mary Busharizi
Miss Anne Bustarret
Rev. Tony D'Souza
Mr. Kingsley Dube
Dr. Yusuf Eraj
Mr. Edward Etale
Mr. Gabriele Fabbri
Mr. Charles Gakori
Mr. Balwan Ghanna
Mr. Cleophas Haema
Sr. Mary Ingram
Mr. Henry Ireri
Miss Dadi Janki
Mr. Boaz Kaino
Mr. John Kamau
Sr. Leocadie Kana
Rev. Medadi Kantinti
Sr. Fauzia Karume
Mr. Badru Kateregga
Miss Florence Kawoya

Miss Mariana Kiniuy
Mr. Michael Kinunda
Miss Maria Kitiabi
Rev. Arthur Kinyanjui
Sr. Argyro Kontoyorghi
Mr. Mohammed Koor
Sheikh M. Mussa Lenana
Mr. Alberto Lucchi
Dr. Josef Lütke-Entrup
Miss Esther Macharia
Mr. Wilfred Maciel
Mr. Fabian Makani
Mr. Isaac Malenge
Mr. Munhumeso Manenji
Mr. Daniel Maundu
Sr. Aziza Mohammed
Rev. Josphat Mugwerru
Mr. Kikuvi Mulwa
Miss Murithi
Mr. Benaiah Musisi
Mr. Tarlok Nandhra
Ms. Assumpta Ndolo
Sr. Marilyn Norris
Mr. Peter Nsubuga
Mr. Titus Nthakyo
Miss Betty Nyakiamo
Mr. Dominick Nyakiamo
Rev. Odhiambo Nyamgero
Miss Shobna Obhrai
Mr. Enock Okonji
Bishop J. Henry Okullu
Mr. Darington Omondi
Mr. Richard Ondeng
Rev. S.J.K. Parker-Allotey
Mrs. May Pinto
Mr. Max Rafransoa
Mr. Canisius Rusagara
Mrs. Salome Rwiliriza
Miss Michèle Sabatié
Miss Sabah Salim
Sr. Christiana Sestero
Mr. Kartar Sewak
Mr. Reuben Shibutse
Mr. Enock Shinachi
Rev. Simon Smith
Sr. Vedanti
Miss Isabella Wachira

Mr. William Wanjala
Mr. Gerald Wanjohi
Mrs. Wanjohi
Mr. Michael Weya
Fr. Richard Woulfe
Sheikh Mohammed Yasin
. . . and additional volunteers listed on pp. 430–432

Republic of Korea
Miss Pal Khn Chon
Mr. Byong Joo Lee
Mr. Jong Myong Lee
Mrs. Ok Young Lee
Mr. Kil Chin Park
Dr. Sun Hwan Pyun

Lebanon
Ms. Nahla Haidar

Lesotho
Mrs. Evelyn Lebona

Madagascar
Mr. Norbert Ratsirahonana

Malaysia
Mrs. Lorraine Grob-Duclos (see United Kingdom)

Nepal
Mr. Davendraj Upadhya

Netherlands
Dr. Henk Schouten
Rev. Cornelius Tholens
Mr. Hans van Willenswaard
Mr. Mahmood K. Youskine

Nigeria
H.E. Mr. Olu Adeniji
Bishop Gabriel Ganaka
Mrs. M.O. Lijadu

Pakistan
Dr. Habibur R. Khan
Dr. Inamullah Khan

Philippines
Mr. Mario Mapanao

446

Rwanda
Mr. Onesphore Rwaje
Bishop Adoniya Sebununguri

Saudi Arabia
Sheikh Nasir Al-Aboudi

Senegal
M. Jean Carbonare

Seychelles
Rev. Terence Ensor

Singapore
Mrs. Bahadur Kaur
Miss Ranbir Kaur
Mr. Jasbir Singh
Mr. Mehervan Singh
Mr. Behram Vakil

South Africa
Mr. Bernard Connor
Rev. J.N.J. Kritzinger
Rev. Gerrie Lubbe
Mr. Mmutlanyane S. Mogoba
Adv. Narendra Pendya
Dr. Ravin Ramdass
Mrs. Dorothy Ramodibe
Mr. Anil Sooklal
Rev. Timothy Stanton
Mrs. Khatija Suliman
Mr. Mahomed Suliman
Bishop Desmond Tutu

Sudan
Mr. Ali Al-Rahim
Mr. Cyer Madut

Sri Lanka
Prof. L.G. Hewage
Mr. Mohamed Mohideen
Mrs. Edna Nanayakkara
Mr. Bogoda Premaratne
Prof. Arumugam Sathasivam
Ven. Anuruddha Thera

Switzerland
Rev. S. Wesley Ariarajah
Miss H. Renate Belck

447

Miss Sigrid Belck
M. Leno d'Alessandri
Miss Brigitte Dupraz
Ms. Tomoko Evdokimoff
Miss Suzanne Koehli
Miss Eleanor Taylor
Dr. John Taylor
Mrs. Margaret Taylor

Tanzania
Miss Imelda Gaurwa
Sheikh Mohamed Hemedi
Miss Irene Kessy
Mr. Johnson Mlambo
Mr. Gerald Mohlathe
Rev. Gustav Rosenstein
Rev. Stanford Shauri

Thailand
Ven. Pra Bimaladdhama
Judge Sathitya Lengthaisong
Mrs. Kanchana Soonsawad

Trinidad and Tobago
Dr. Anantanand Rambachan (see United Kingdom)

Uganda
Ms. Deborah Kaddu
Mrs. Joyce Kaddu
Mr. Isa Lukwago
Mrs. Zuhura Lukwago
Rev. Denis Mayanja
Miss E.M. Namaganda

United Kingdom
Mr. Mohammed Azam
Rev. Jonathan Blake
Mrs. Libby Blake
Ms. Gill Cressey
Dr. Albert Friedlander
Mr. Gustav Grob-Duclos
Mrs. Lorraine Grob-Duclos
Mrs. Ivy Gutridge
Msgr. Bruce Kent
Mr. Bindurao Konnur
Dr. Syed Pasha
Mr. Eric Prokosch
Mrs. Tatiana Prokosch

Dr. Anantanand Rambachan
Ms. Mary Reynolds
Miss Hannah Stanton
Canon Gordon Wilson

U.S.A.

Mr. Harold Belmont
Dr. Landrum Bolling
Mrs. Ruth Anna Brown
Dr. Yvonne Delk
Mrs. Willie Dell
Dr. Diana Eck
Dr. Jane Evans
Dr. H. Lamar Gibble
Rev. Gerald Grant
Dr. Dana McLean Greeley
Dr. Viqar Hamdani
Dr. Homer A. Jack
Mrs. Ingeborg Jack
Dr. JoAnne Kagiwada
Sr. Marjorie Keenan
Mrs. Azzree Lathan
Mrs. Norma Levitt
Dr. Edward May
Mrs. Winifred May
Mrs. Marilyn McClean
Rev. Robert McClean
Dr. Ralph Odom
Ms. Mary Jane Patterson
Mrs. Connie Price-Truman
Bishop Francis Quinn
Rev. John Radano
Dr. George Rupp
Mr. Daniel Seeger
Rev. Robert Smylie
Dr. David Stowe
Mrs. Virginia Stowe
Dr. Malcolm Sutherland
Mr. George Telford
Rev. Kenryu Tsuji

Vatican City

Archbishop (Now Cardinal) Francis Arinze
Rev. John Shirieda
Rev. Marcello Zago

Vietnam

Ven. Hodac Cu Thich Thien Chau (see France)

Yugoslavia

Mrs. Liljana Matkovic-Vlasic

Zambia

Mrs. Anastasia Mhango
Mrs. Ruth Mompati

Zimbabwe

Mr. Edmund Chifamba
Mr. W.-E. Solomon

84

Regrets

a) National

Mr. S.A. Ali, (Muslim).
Indian Institute of Islamic Studies,
Panchkuin Road, New Delhi
110001, India.

Dr. Musa O. Abdul, (Muslim)
University of Ibadan, Ibadan,
Nigeria.

Mrs. Fredelle Brief, (Jewish)
8 Seneca Hill Drive, Willowdale,
Ontario M2J W2E, Canada.

Rev. Wesley Campbell, (Christian)
Division of Social Justice, Uniting
Church Synod of Victoria, 130
Little Collins Street, Melbourne
3000, Australia.

Dr. P.H.J.M. Camps, (Christian)
Ringlaan 214A, 6602 EH Wijchen,
Netherlands.

Ms. Natalia I. Chernyikh, U.S.S.R.
(Christian)

Mr. S.K. De, (Christian)
A-70 South Extention Part II, New
Delhi 110049, India.

Archpriest Gennadiy Jablonsky,
U.S.S.R. (Christian)

Rev. Clement Janda, (Christian)
Sudan Council of Churches, P.O.
Box 469, Khartoum, Sudan.

Mr. Mohamed Kamal, (Muslim)
P.O. Box 2288, Bangkok 10500,
Thailand.

Mrs. A. Hafeez Begum Khan,
(Muslim)
240 Garden East, Kashana-i-
Hafeez, Karachi 3, Pakistan.

Mr. Vladimir S. Kotlyarov,
U.S.S.R. (Christian)

Dr. Nasseh Mirza, (Muslim)
294 Yarra Street, Warrandyte,
Victoria 3113, Australia.

Ms. Zinaida I. Mossova, U.S.S.R.
(Christian)

Prof. S. G. Mudgal
B.42, A Wing, G.001
Dayanand Co-op Hsg. Socy.
Gokuldham, Goregaon (E)
Bombay 400063, India

Rev. Englebert Mveng, (Christian)
P.O. Box 1539, Yaoundé,
Cameroun.

Archbishop T.O. Olufosoye,
(Christian)
P.O. Box 3075, Ibadan, Nigeria.

Jagadguru Basavaraja Pattadarya,
(Jain)
Sri Jagadguru Gurusiddehwar
Bruhanmath, Guledgudd,
Karnataka 587203, India.

Rev. Arthur Preston, (Christian)
3 Milgate Court, Forest Hill,
Victoria 3131, Australia.

Mrs. Agnes K. Shauri, (Christian)

P.O. Box 2537, Dar-Es-Salaam,
Tanzania.

Prof. Harminder Singh, (Sikh)
132 Eastcote Avenue, Greenford,
Middlesex UB 6 ONR, United
Kingdom.

Mr. Pal Srikuruwal, (Sikh)
3/6 Soi Luenrit, Sampeng,
Yawaraj, Bangkok 10100,
Thailand.

Mr. Leonid N. Svitsun, U.S.S.R.
(Christian)

Dr. Cliff Wright, (Christian)
4 Fairy Street, Ivanhoe, Victoria
3079, Australia.

b) Speakers

Mrs. Andriamanjato, (Christian)
Engineer; President, Popular
Council of Antananarivo. Paroisse
Ambohitantely, près Rue Rangita,
Antananarivo, Madagascar.

Dom Helder Camara, (Christian)
Obras de Frei Francisco
Rua Henrique Dias, 208
Igrejia das Fronteiras
Recife - PE, CEP 50000, Brazil

Cardinal Roger Etchegaray, (Christian); President, Pontifical Commission
on Justice and Peace, 00127
Vatican City.

Archbishop Jean Jadot, (Christian)
Past-President, Vatican Secretariat
for Non-Christians, 00127 Vatican
City.

Rev. Ch. Jugder, (Buddhist)
Secretary-General, Asian
Buddhists Conference for Peace,

Gangdantekchenling Monastery,
Ulan Bator, Mongolia.

Prof. Ali Mazrui, (Muslim)
Professor, University of Nairobi,
Nairobi, Kenya.

Ms. Janet McCloud, (Indigenous
Religion)
a.k.a. "Yet-si-Blue," Community
Worker for Native Americans.
1013 Crystal Springs Street, Yelm,
WA 98597, USA.

Chief K.O.K. Onyioha,
(Indigenous Religion)
President, Head, Godian Religion.
4 Macaulay Street, Umuahia,
Nigeria.

Mrs. Ela Ramgobin, (Hindu)
Social Worker; Grand-Daughter
of Mahatma Gandhi. P.O. Box
331, Verulam, 4340 South Africa.

Rabbi Alexander M. Schindler,
(Jewish)
Executive, Union of American
Hebrew Congregations. 838 Fifth
Avenue, New York, N.Y. 10021,
U.S.A.

Mother Theresa, (Christian)
M.C., Missionaries of Charity, 54A
Lower Circular Road, Calcutta 16,
India.

c) Consultant Experts
Dr. Alan Geyer,
Center for Theology and Public
Policy, 4500 Massachusetts Avenue
N.W., Washington, D.C. 20016,
USA.

Rev. J. Bryan Hehir,
United States Catholic
Conference, 1312 Massachusetts

Avenue N.W., Washington, D.C.
20005, USA.

d) *Fraternal Delegates*
All Africa Council of Churches.
Rev. Dansokho, B.P. 847, Dakar,
Senegal.

Christian Peace Conference.
Dr. Karl-Wolfgang Tröger,
Oranienburger Str. 27, 1040 Berlin,
German Democratic Republic.

Council on Religion and
International Affairs. Mr. Robert
J. Myers, 170 East 64th Street,
New York, N.Y. 10021, U.S.A.

Communauté Juive Marocaine.
M. David Amar, 52 Avenue
Hassan II, Casablanca, Morocco.

Identité et Dialogue.
M. André Azoulay, B.P. 657, 75423
Paris Cedex 09, France.

International Fellowship of
Reconciliation. Dr. Hildegard
Goss-Mayr, Schottengasse 3a/1/
58, 1010 Wien, Austria.

Muslim World League.
Dr. Mohamed I. Momoniat, 213
Lenasia, Johannesburg, 1820
South Africa.

Regional Islamic Da'Wah Council
of Southeast Asia and the Pacific.
Mr. Fadlullah C. Wilmot, 5th
Floor, Perkim Bldg., Jalan Ipoh,
Kuala Lumpur, Malaysia.

World Jewish Congress.
M. Jean Halperin, B.P. 191, 1211
Geneva, Switzerland.

e) Fraternal Observers

Belydende Kring of the D.R.C.
Churches. Mr. Peter Moatsche,
P.O. Box 21, Reddingshoop, Brits,
0252 South Africa.

The East for Peace.
Mr. Johannes Büller, Malchei
Hamayim 21, Jerusalem, Israel.

The Episcopal Church in the USA.
Dr. Charles A. Cesaretti, 815
Second Avenue, New York, N.Y.
10017, USA.

Women, Religion and Social
Change Project, Harvard
University. Dr. Ms. Dorothy A.
Austin, 88 Ossipee Road,
Somerville, MA 02144, USA.

Katholischer Akademischer
Ausländer-Dienst. Mr. Costello
Garang Ring and Mr. Josef
Oduho, c/o KAAD, Reuterstr. 39,
5300 Bonn 1, Federal Republic of
Germany.

World Council of Churches.
Mr. Ninan Koshy, P.O. Box 66,
1211 Geneva, Switzerland.

f) Co-opted Staff

Dr. Donald S. Harrington,
Executive Director, WCRP/USA.
Ten Park Avenue, New York, N.Y.
10016, USA.

Prof. François Houtart,
Research Director, Commission on
the Future (of WCRP). Centre
Tricontinental, Av. Sainte
Gertrude 5, 1348 Ottignies—
Louvain-la-Neuve, Belgium.

g) African Committee
Dr. Mrs. Sehmi,
c/o WCRP/Africa, P.O. Box
70394, Nairobi, Kenya. (Sikh)

h) Alumni/WCRP
Corporation Members
Dr. Elmer Ferrer,
8 Maalindog St., U.P. Village,
Diliman, Quezon City,
Philippines.

Mr. Takeyasu Miyamoto,
26-12 4-chome, Arai, Nakano-ku,
Tokyo 165, Japan.

Ven. Havanpola Ratanasara,
c/o Devasumittaramaya,
Iriyawetiya, Kelaniya, Sri Lanka.

Archbishop Timotheos,
c/o 40 East Burton Place, Chicago,
IL 60610, U.S.A.

Dr. Herman Will,
2523 N.W. 193rd Place, Seattle,
WA 98177, USA.

i) Observers/Visitors/Spouses
Rev. Lynn Hodges,
P.O. Box 10154, Berkeley, CA
94709, USA.

Mr. and Mrs. Malik S. Khan,
4281 S.W. 15th Street, Miami, FL
33134, USA.

Mr. Darshan Lal Laroiya,
P.O. Box 502, Maseru, Lesotho
(Southern Africa).

Prof. Ali Merad,
22 Rue Joliot-Curie, 69005 Lyon,
France.

Mrs. Momoniat,
213 Lenasia, Johannesburg, 1820
South Africa.

Miss Francesca Palombi,
Via Achille Papa, 00195 Rome,
Italy.

Mrs. Rhea Schindler,
6 River Lane, Westport, CT 06880,
USA.

Ven. Bhikkhu Suddhananda,
4142 Atisa Dipankar Sarak,
Dhaka, Bangladesh.

85

Comparisons With WCRP I, WCRP II, And WCRP III

Delegates by Religion	WCRP I	WCRP II	WCRP III	WCRP IV
Buddhism	38	22	28	26
Christianity	97	71	89	75
Confucianism	1	2	1	4
Hinduism	23	24	21	31
Jainism	1	2	3	4
Judaism	7	5	7	7
Islam	18	27	31	27
Shintoism	19	7	10	6
Sikhism	3	4	5	4
Zoroastrianism	2	3	1	2
Miscellaneous Religions	10	5	5	3
Totals	219	172	202	189
Fraternal Delegates	9	31	25[a]	112[a b]
Consultant-Experts		38	18	12
Observers/Guests/Visitors	47	66	35	63
Spouses/Aides/Volunteers	7	28	25	69[c]
International Secretariat	162	72	43	20
	444[d]	407[d]	347[e]	465[f]
Delegates by Continents				
Africa	7	15	17	40[f]
Asia	132	81	94	95
Europe	35	42	38	25
Latin America	6	10	8	2
North America	37	22	41	25
Oceania	2	3	3	2
Countries Represented	39	45	47	60[g]

[a] Some of these were both organizational and national delegates.
[b] These include fraternal "delegates" and fraternal "observers."
[c] In addition there were 54 local youth volunteers.
[d] These figures are not comparable, since some participants attended in more than one capacity.
[e] This does not include eleven translators.
[f] An additional 100 or more persons resident in Kenya attended on an occasional basis.
[g] This figure includes all participants (not only delegates as is the case for the figures of WCRP I, WCRP II, and WCRP III).

459

Appendices

86

A Brief Chronology of WCRP

Predecessors

1893—World Parliament of Religion, held at Chicago during the Columbian Exposition.

1924–1939—World Conference for International Peace Through Religion. National conferences were held in Japan and other countries, but World War II broke out before its world conference could be convened.

1945–1950—Religious groups in Japan, partly as a result of the atomic bombing of Hiroshima and Nagasaki, held inter-religious meetings for peace.

Direct Lineage

1962—Religious leaders in the USA dreamed of a "spiritual summit" to prevent atomic confrontation between the USA and the USSR. This was not held, but a modest inter-religious consultation was convened opposite U.N. Headquarters at New York.

1966—National Inter-Religious Conference on Peace held at Washington, D.C., USA, on March 15–17.

1968—International Inter-Religious Symposium on Peace at New Delhi, India, on January 10–14.

1968—Japanese-American Inter-Religious Consultation on Peace at Kyoto, Japan, on January 22.

1969—Interim Advisory Committee for a World Conference on Religion and Peace at Istanbul, Turkey, on February 21–23.

First Assembly of WCRP

1969—International Preparatory Committee for a World Conference on Religion and Peace at Kyoto, Japan, on December 3–5.

1970—First Assembly of the World Conference on Religion and Peace (WCRP I) at Kyoto, on December 16–21.

1972—Inter-Religious Consultation on Japanese-American Relations at Honolulu, Hawaii, USA, in June.

Second Assembly of WCRP

1974—International Preparatory Committee for the Second Assembly of the World Conference on Religion and Peace at Louvain, Belgium, in March.

1974—Second Assembly of the World Conference on Religion and Peace (WCRP II) at Louvain, on August 28–September 3.

1976—First meeting of the Asian Conference on Religion and Peace (ACRP) at Singapore on November 25–30.

1978—First meeting of WCRP/Europe at Rome, Italy.

Third Assembly of WCRP

1978—International Preparatory Committee for the Third Assembly of the World Conference on Religion and Peace at Princeton, New Jersey, U.S.A., on September 1–6.

1979—Executive Committee of the International Preparatory Committee for the Third Assembly of the World Conference on Religion and Peace at Princeton, on February 12–14.

1979—Third Assembly of the World Conference on Religion and Peace (WCRP III) at Princeton, on August 29–September 7.

Fourth Assembly of WCRP

1983—First All-Africa Assembly of WCRP at Nairobi, Kenya, on August 20–30.

1983—International Preparatory Committee for the Fourth Assembly of the World Conference on Religion and Peace at Limuru, Kenya, on September 4–6.

1984—Fourth Assembly of the World Conference on Religion and Peace (WCRP IV) at Limuru, on August 23–31.

87

Bibliography

1. *Materials Produced Relating Direct to WCRP IV.*

a) In English:

Report of the All-Africa Assembly of WCRP. Nairobi 1983.*
Preparatory Workbook for WCRP IV. This contains a large number of texts related to the subjects discussed at WCRP IV, and a list of peace movements. Geneva 1984.*
Unabridged Proceedings of WCRP IV. *

b) In French:

La Déclaration de Nairobi.**

c) In German:

Informationen des Europäischen Sekretariats der WCRP, Nr. 17. This contains the most important documents from WCRP IV. Würzburg 1985.**

2. *A Selection of Post-WCRP IV Articles.*

a) In English:

Let Us Devote our Energies to Peace, by Dr. William Klassen, in *Interfaith Academy of Peace Newsletter.* Fall 1984.

Religion for Human Dignity and World Peace: The Fourth Assembly of the World Conference on Religion and Peace, by Mrs. Norma Levitt. Printed by the World Union for Progressive Judaism. September 1984.

My Impressions of the Peace Conference, by Mrs. Dorothy Ramodibe, in *ICT (Institute for Contextual Theology) News.* September 1984.

---

*—Available from the Geneva International Secretariat of WCRP.
**—Available from the regional or national secretariat.

United for Peace, by Dr. Donald Nicholl, in *The Tablet.* 15 September 1984.

Developing a Global Perspective on Peace, by Mr. Harold Belmont, in *The Seattle Times.* October 13, 1984.

The Nairobi Experience, by Mrs. Ivy Gutridge, in *The Methodist Recorder.* October 25, 1984.

WCRP IV in Nairobi: Taming the Lions, by Dr. Homer A. Jack, in *The Christian Century.* October 31, 1984.

WCRP IV Meets in Nairobi, in *Dharma World* November 1984. in *Peace Studies.* November 1984.

For Human Dignity and World Peace, by Dr. Jane Evans, in *NFTS Leaders Line.* Fall/Winter 1984.

Peace on Earth, by Rev. Giuliano Ricchiardi, in *New City.* January 1985. *Interfaith News.* Spring 1985.

b) In French:

Construire la Paix, in *Le Journal de la Paix.* November 1984.

Le Sens d'un Prix Nobel, in *Le Journal de la Paix.* January 1985.

c) In German:

Schön Deutsch Zurückhaltend. Nairobi International: Religionen Tagen für den Frieden, by Dr. Michael Mildenberger, in *Deutsches Allgemeines Sonntagsblatt.* 23 September, 1984.

Kleine "Super-UNO" der Religionen. IV. Weltkonferenz der Religionen für den Frieden im Zeichen Afrikas, by Mr. Helmut S. Ruppert, in *Die Katholischen Missionen.* November/December 1984.

Die 4. Weltkonferenz der Religionen für den Frieden in Nairobi, by Dr. Wunden. Published by Herder-Korrespondenz. December 1984.

Religionen für Menschenswürde und Weltfrieden. Die Weltkonferenz der Religionen für den Frieden in Nairobi 1984, by Günther Gebhardt. Published by Evangelische Zentralstelle für Weltanschauungsfragen. April 1985.

d) In Italian:

Tutte le Religioni, di Tutto il Mundo, su Tutti gli Aspetti della Pace, by Rev. Giovanni Cereti, in *Il Regno Attualità.* 15 September, 1984.

Uniti nella Fede contro i Mali del Mondo, by Mr. Renzo Giacomelli, in *Famiglia Christiana.* 23 September, 1984.

Conferenza di Nairobi: Lontani nelle Teologie, Uniti per la Pace, by Rev. Giovanni Cereti, in *Rocca.* 1 October, 1984.

A Nairobi le Religioni per la Pace, by Rev. Giuliano Ricchiardi, in *Città Nuova.* 10 October, 1984.

Tutte le Religioni per la Pace Integrale (Text of Nairobi Declaration, Reports of the Beyond Nairobi Committee, Commissions I and

II, and Speeches by Dr. Chouraqui, Msgr. Kent, Rev. Precht, and Bishop Tutu) in *Il Regno Documenti*. 1 November, 1984.

3. Other Literature Relating to WCRP.

a) In English:

Religion and Peace: Papers from the National Inter-Religious Conference on Peace. Indianapolis: Bobbs-Merrill Co. 137 pp. 1966.

World Religions and World Peace: The International Inter-Religious Symposium on Peace. Boston: Beacon Press. 208 pp. 1968.

Religion for Peace: Proceedings of the Kyoto Conference on Religion and Peace. New Delhi: Gandhi Peace Foundation; Bombay: Bharatiya Vidya Bhavan. 391 pp. 1973.

World Religion/World Peace: Proceedings of the Second World Conference on Religion and Peace. New York: WCRP. 200 pp. 1979.*

Peace Through Religion: A Brief Report of the Asian Conference on Religion and Peace. Tokyo: ACRP. 128 pp. 1977.**

Religion in the Struggle for World Community: Unabridged Proceedings of the Third World Conference on Religion and Peace. New York: WCRP. 418 pp. 1980.*

Religions and Peace: Analysis of the Statements and of the Members' Statements of WCRP. Louvain: C.R.S.R., Université Catholique de Louvain. 98 pp. 1984.*

Religion for Peace. Newsletter published by WCRP/International since 1970.*

b) In French:

Report about WCRP I, in *Terre Entière,* May/June 1972.
Une Pastorale de l'Espérance, by Prof. Jean Barrea.
Information brochure on WCRP. (In preparation)**

c) In German:

Religionen, Frieden, Menschenrechte: Dokumentation der Ersten Weltkonferenz der Religionen für den Frieden. Wuppertal: Jugenddienst-Verlag. 115 pp. 1971.**

Den Frieden Tun: Die 3. Weltversammlung der Religionen für den Frieden. Freiburg im Breisgau: Herder-Verlag. 142 pp. 1980.**

Informationen. Newsletter published regularly by WCRP/Europe.

Index

Printed in Switzerland